Encounters & Reflections

ENCOUNTERS & REFLECTIONS

Art in the Historical Present

Arthur C. Danto

Farrar Straus Giroux

New York

Published simultaneously in Canada by Harper & Collins, Toronto
Printed in the United States of America
Designed by Cynthia Krupat
First edition, 1990

Library of Congress Cataloging-in-Publication Data
Danto, Arthur Coleman.
Encounters and reflections : art in the historical present /
Arthur C. Danto.—1st ed.
1. Art, Modern—20th century. I. Title.
N6490.D237 1990   709'.04—dc20   89-23692   CIP

FOR
DAVID CARRIER
LEO LITWAK
ROBERT SOLOMON
AND
(OF COURSE)
BARBARA WESTMAN

Contents

REFLECTIONS

The dogmas of the quiet past are inadequate to the stormy present. The occasion is piled high with difficulty, and we must rise to the occasion. As our case is new, so we must think anew, and act anew. We must disenthrall ourselves . . . Fellow citizens, we cannot escape history.

ABRAHAM LINCOLN,
First Inaugural Address

Encounters & Reflections

Introduction: Artphilohistocritisophory Today

A FEW YEARS AGO I undertook to write an essay on the battle memorial at Gettysburg. Initially I was interested in the transfiguration of that ground into what an admired critic called a work of art. But soon enough I got caught up in the narrative of the battle itself, and especially in its climactic moment when Pickett's division marched, as if executing a complex figure in close-order drill, into the massed mouths of weapons that made such gestures forever irrelevant in war. Pickett's men were conscious of the picture they made in the eyes of bystanders, for whom, as Sappho writes, "some say a cavalry corps, some infantry . . . are the finest sight on earth." They accepted a code of military aesthetics while facing weapons that conformed only to the quantitative codes of slaughter. And this conflict in codes is carried forward in the familiar memorial statuary of the Civil War, in which soldiers stand erect in brass-buttoned tunics and cloth caps while holding weapons for which such a posture and uniform are no protection at all—rifles that would essentially be those used half a century later in the acknowledged mayhem of World War I. Because we are blind to the future, this conflict would have been invisible to those who had such statues set up in towns and villages across the land. But it gives to these affecting figures a tragic dimension beyond the commonplace tragedies of war, death, and memory to which we seek to give some meaning through art.

It occurred to me that these metal infantrymen were cast in much the same mold, and must have been manufactured like iron fencing or grillwork in factories or foundries; and it seemed to me as if an engraving from some manufacturer's catalogue of the era would make a striking illustration for my piece. Friendly and helpful librarians lugged volumes out of little-used stacks, including a particularly imposing one from the Mott Iron Works on Bleecker Street in New York, as solemn as an ecclesiastical tome, bound in heavy boards, opulent in gilt and green. It was filled with engravings of useful and ornamental things, from valves and fittings to hitching posts and garden furniture—and, along with sinks and tubs, urinals in varieties so far beyond what I could have imagined that I instantly realized that today's sanitary vessels have survived a severe evolutionary trial. There were no war memorials, alas, but the name "Mott Iron Works" was teasingly familiar. For a moment there was only the recognition that it had a meaning for me without my being able to say what the meaning was—like that celebrated taste of lime tea and madeleine that sits poised, in Proust's account, at the barrier of active memory without yet breaking through into consciousness. And then of course there was the revelation: it was from this very company, for all I know from the pages of this very catalogue, that Duchamp selected what an unsympathetic reviewer of my book *The Transfiguration of the Commonplace* called "that wretched urinal." And it came home to me with an extraordinary vividness how many years and pages I have devoted to philosophical reflection upon Duchamp's notorious work, *Fountain*, of 1917, rejected (how?) for a supposedly jury-free exhibition and signed "R. Mutt," in witty allusion to Mr. Mott, whom Duchamp obliquely immortalized through this legendary ready-made.

A different critic, one not known for nuanced invective, perceives my preoccupation with Duchamp, and above all with Warhol, as a kind of aesthetic slumming and hence a perversion of critical values, as if, with all the masterpieces of world art to pass my time among, I chose low company instead—pranksters, charlatans, con men, hoaxers— picking sow's ears every time in preference to silk purses. There really would be a kind of aesthetic pathology in swooning over *Fountain* as if it were a work like *The Jewish Bride* or even *Bird in Flight*, or in saying "I'll take *Brillo Box*" when offered a choice between it and one of Cézanne's *compotiers* or some irises of Van Gogh. But taste and aesthetics do not enter the picture. There are, rather, two connected reasons for thinking about these works at all: philosophical methodology and historical urgency. In fact, these together define the tasks of

[*4*

art criticism, not just as I practice it but as anyone must who is sensitive to the discontinuities between the artistic present and the conceptually comfortable past.

Philosophers typically work with examples that may strike outsiders, anxious for philosophy to be grand or edifying, as unacceptably trivial or bland. The great epistemologists generate their accounts of perceptual knowledge by pondering how round pennies can look elliptical; theorists of human action have pursued the question of free will by seeking to draw a line between simple acts like winking and bare bodily movements like blinking. The effort is not altogether different from that in science which looks to the simplest creatures—sea slugs, say—in order to concentrate on the fewest number of neurons consistent with the possibility of the system being modified by learning. The strategy in philosophy, moreover, is to seek the basis for drawing its boundaries by identifying objects on either side of the boundary which have as much in common as possible, in order to focus on what they don't and can't have in common if the boundaries are real. Nothing can be more like waking experience than dream experience, and the difference, crucial in building up our concept of reality, cannot be found in what they may share. Only when we can imagine works of art that outwardly resemble ordinary things like urinals or packing cases can we begin to draw the line between reality and art, which has concerned philosophers from ancient times. If *Fountain* is an artwork, there must be an answer to the question of why the other urinals in Mott's inventory are not, even if the resemblances are perfect. If *Brillo Box* is an artwork and the ordinary Brillo carton not, surely the difference cannot lie in the obvious differences, such as one being made of plywood and the other of corrugated cardboard, not if the differences between reality and art must divide art from reality on a serious philosophical map.

Now, these are questions that could not have been easily gotten to arise with *The Resurrection* of Piero della Francesca or with the Medici Tomb or the cathedral of Beauvais. It is not just that these are too complex, as the human brain is too complex alongside the simple neural network of *aplysia*. It is that when these objects were made, no one could have imagined there would be or could be works like those of Duchamp and Warhol. Indeed, to have asked, in an earlier century—pointing to one of these great works—why something like this was art though another thing that looked just like it was *not*, would have been conceptually impossible. Pretty much anything that looked like Beauvais would have been a work of art if Beauvais was, except, of course, for mirages and illusions and architectural dreamings, where the problems are altogether different. It would have been like asking why something was an elephant when something else, looking just like an elephant, was not. For it must have seemed as though "work of art" was an expression much like "elephant" that we learn to apply on the basis of perceptual criteria. Duchamp's great philosophical achievement was to demonstrate that it is not this kind of expression at all, and that learning to apply it to things involves a far more complex procedure than anyone would have believed necessary. But this could not have been shown until history made it possible: Duchamp would have been impossible when the kind of conceptual imagination required by his gesture was itself historically impossible. When it did become possible, it became plain that the Beautiful and the Sublime did not belong to the essence of art.

I have always had a passion for painting, and from an early age art was something I looked at and thought about and even tried to make. But even after I became a professional philosopher, I did not find art philosophically interesting—nor did I find what philosophers had said about art philosophically interesting either—until the 1960s, in connection with Pop and, to a lesser degree, with Minimalism. I have often written about the great impact upon me of Warhol's exhibition of Brillo boxes in 1964, and I take a wry satisfaction in the fact that through my first philosophical article on art, Warhol's name appeared in the austere pages of *The Journal of Philosophy* late that year, long before he became such a superstar in the culture of glamour and high gossip. But from the perspective of a quarter century's evolution in the art world, I have come to think that the analysis I wrote of the distinction between artworks and what I termed "mere real things" could not have been written at an earlier moment, for it seems to me that in the mid-1960s a deep revolution in the history of art took place—so deep, in fact, that it would not be an exaggeration to say that art, as it had been historically understood, came to an end in that strange and tumultuous decade.

In retrospect, it is possible to argue that there is a far greater continuity between Modernism and the artistic tradition than anyone might have thought in the years when abstraction and Cubism were being hammered out. The Cubists, after all, adhered to the standard Beaux Arts subjects—the nude, the still life, the landscape, the interior—and it was not all that difficult for Picasso, when occasion arose, to extend his discoveries to the execution of historical paintings. The early abstractionists never forsook illusionism or pictorial convention. Cubism took the perception of objects as a paradigm, and merely elaborated on the concept of aspects. But the sixties, in art, was an age of rupture and discontinuity. "Since the era of the New York School of the 1950s," writes James Ackerman, "every generally accepted standard or rule in art has been broken or challenged." And that meant that a great many things thought to belong to the philosophical definition of art proved adventitious and peripheral. *Brillo Box* was part of a total conceptual upheaval. The meaning of "work of art" could no longer be taught by example or understood through precedent. Not only could works of art no longer be told apart from real things. They could not be seen as obviously like things that had always been regarded as works of art.

Ackerman, a distinguished historian of art, sees this, as does his fellow art historian Hans Belting, as a crisis for their discipline: "There will have to be either a discipline for before 1960 and a discipline for after, or a history that has stopped forever a few years ago to be followed by ahistorical happenings." It is certainly a crisis for the philosophy of art, inasmuch as the features through which something can be counted art must be located at a level far more abstract than the philosophical tradition would have dreamed necessary. It is a crisis for art education and for art making, for the immediate question is: What do we teach those who want to become artists in order to assure proficiency? If all the rules and standards are down, what happens to drawing, composition, the materials of the artist, and the like? And finally, of course, it is a crisis for art criticism itself: how does one judge, what are the appropriate responses, where are there standards, how can one evaluate? Small wonder that a lot of criticism simply consists in piling words up in front of art! In any case, for the past twenty-five years there has been a single omnibus problem that I have designated in my title: *artphilohistocritisophory*. It is a historical moment in which art makers, art historians, teachers, philosophers, and critics of art are so interlocked in one another's activities that the making of any artwork whatever—even if it looks absolutely traditional—demands a complex philosophical justification and a critical apparatus it is often up to the artist also to furnish. One cannot raise a question of the role of criticism in abstraction from the entire complex. The right question to ask, I suppose, is: What is the function of artphilohistocritisophory? You cannot separate art from the complex and ask what its function in the society is: you have to take the whole complex and ask about it as a functioning whole.

It is a mark of the present moment that there are no outward criteria any longer of what can be a work of art: a text (any text); a plash of pigment; an assemblage of objects in any number and of any description; a facsimile of the *Mona Lisa*; a shopping bag of soiled aluminum foil no one dares unwrap; a package of Twinkies. But certain projects are, in virtue of the level of abstractness on which the issues must be transacted, excluded from art making and indeed from art criticism. There is no longer any virtue in the quasi-alchemical pursuit of the pure distilled essence of art. Anything, if a work of art, is as much one as a square of uniform black paint. Nor is there any validity in the critical charge that something is not art because it fails to meet some standard of aesthetic purity. Both these asceticisms defined art-world attitudes within the memory of even relatively young persons; and if there is anything to the theory that art is in the avant-garde of culture, there would be every reason to anticipate the revulsion against ideological purity in the political spheres of the world, where the abrupt demand for looseness, détente, democratization, is everywhere being expressed. But insofar as the history of art in the Modern era has been exactly that quasi-alchemical pursuit of the essential defining attributes of art, we have with Postmodernism in fact entered the Posthistorical phase of the history of art. It is a difficult but wonderful time to be alive, nor could anyone, knowing that this would happen, will to have lived at an earlier time.

Hegel, with characteristic profundity, spoke of beautiful art as the Idea given sensuous embodiment. As a start, this gives us the rudiments of a philosophical concept of art, and a first stab at a theory of criticism: the critic must identify the idea embodied in the work and assess the adequacy of its embodiment. "Embodiment" is a difficult concept, and here is not the place to deal with it directly, but it helps to draw a distinction between the expression and the embodiment of an idea. Perhaps every meaningful sentence expresses an idea, true or false, which is its thought or meaning. But language achieves the status of art when our sentences embody the ideas they express, as if displaying what the sentences are about. A picture becomes art when, beyond representing its idea, properties of itself become salient in the work of embodiment. Rembrandt's paintings embody and do not merely show light.

Criticism, as I practice it, consists in finding how the ideas expressed by the works I discuss are embodied in them to the degree that I can discover this. As a philosopher I am struck by the way in which idea and embodiment in art parallels the way in which our minds are embodied in ourselves as persons. But works differ from one another as personalities differ from personalities. There are better and worse ideas given better and worse embodiments in works, and so there are two dimensions of critical evaluation built into the philosophical structure of the artwork. But greatness in works is like greatness in human beings, and though this may no more be a standard against which to measure other work than greatness in human character gives us the moral measure we need for judging one another, critical evaluation is not deeply different from moral evaluation (and I suppose art education might be thought of in the same sorts of terms as moral education). As a further incidental parallel, there are certain works, as certain persons, one likes or dislikes for reasons having nothing much to do with their excellences or failures. Liking, even loving, belongs to the personality of critics but not to the structure of criticism even if inseparable from it. There are painters I know are good and even great whom I cannot like, Poussin and Ingres being two. I also incline to the view that when someone actually likes or loves these artists, he or she must be a very different person from me.

As a final parallel, I might say that while it is an interesting project to develop a philosophy of the person, it hardly would get us very far in dealing with other human beings as we encounter them in the contexts of life. Like persons, works of art are a great deal richer than philosophy can or should want to capture. I hope something of this richness spills over into the critical encounters with art that make up this volume, which collects nearly all of the essays on art that I have published in my column in *The Nation* magazine since the appearance of my first collection under the title *The State of the Art*. The essay on Veronese was commissioned by *Art News*, the essay on Diebenkorn appeared in the *TLS*, but both of these embody, if I may use that term in connection with my own prose, the virtues and values I seek to instill in the *Nation* pieces. There are two catalogue essays, on David Sawin and on Chuta Kimura, which I have appended to the critical essay on these two artists, and these are more confessional and celebratory, as suits that format—and they express the great personal affection I have for the work of these masters. Finally, there are three long speculative pieces that conclude the volume which address concepts of central concern to me in thinking about art institutionally. "Bad Aesthetic Times," a much-revised version of a piece that appeared in the journal *Modern Painters*, was originally delivered as a lecture for the Virginia Museum of Fine Arts in Richmond, Virginia. Both "Masterpiece and the Museum" and "Narratives of the End of Art" were published as essays in *Grand Street*, and each grew out of a lecture, the first one at the Boston Museum of Fine Arts and the second as a Lionel Trilling Lecture at Columbia University. The introductory essay, "Artphilo-histocritisophory Today," inaugurated a series of reflections on criticism in the magazine *Artforum*, where it appeared in the September 1989 issue. I am grateful to all concerned for their initial willingness to publish my work, and for the permission to use the essays here.

I shall always be greatly in debt to Elizabeth Pochoda, literary editor of *The Nation* during most of that period in which these essays appeared. Maria Margaronis contributed to the final clarity of the pieces when she was Betsy's assistant, and since her departure I have benefited enormously from the clarity of vision and literary good sense of Julie Abraham. I feel myself very much the protégé of Ben Sonnenberg, whose great magazine, *Grand Street*, is one of the ornaments of our era. He has not merely been hospitable to my writings: he has changed my life. Had it not been for his encouragement and vital imagination, I would never have sought a life outside the world of professional philosophy, and would never have known how to find it had it occurred to me that it was something I should seek. Ben opened doors for me, as he has for so many, in my case making it possible for me to be part of the life of my times. My gratitude and affection are boundless.

In the end, I was unable to use a delicious and witty title suggested to me by Ben, and must reserve it for another occasion. The actual title emerged from discussions with Rick Moody, as he gave to the contents I handed over to him the shape of a book. I immediately grasped that whatever Rick thought was right really was right, and I am grateful for his good editorial sense, and for his sympathetic support throughout.

I esteem it a great privilege to have worked with Jonathan Galassi, and to have had the endorsement of his superb literary sensibility. It was an inspiration on the part of my remarkable agent, Georges Borchardt, to have brought Jonathan and me together, and I hope the book justifies the confidence both men showed in the writings of which it is made.

New York, 1989   A.C.D.

ENCOUNTERS

David Sawin's Paintings

I SOMEWHERE READ of a bird genetically so endowed that it makes a run for a dark place immediately upon pecking through its egg. The disposition to make that initial desperate run, upon which its survival depends, is transient: it gets just one shot, and if something intervenes— an ethological kibitzer, say—the bird never again follows its instinctual vector and must wander, unfulfilled and confused, until its early demise. I am unable to discuss this example with ornithological detail or certitude, but it has become for me a metaphor of the condition of the artist in our time. Pipping its way through the shell of its art school, the fledgling artist makes its run for New York, and if for some reason it fails in its institutionally programmed drive for survival, it ekes out a wilderness existence in cruel oblivion.

The art historian Thomas Crow, who taught for a time at a West Coast art school, once narrated, with resigned amazement, the amount of art-world knowledge the students there acquire for their New York dash. They know precisely where to go and what to do and are wired up to paint for success. Once here they turn out the standard glamorous paintings or sculptures or performance works the market demands, and even turn up at such shows as the Whitney Biennial, which are devoted to works that are themselves devoted to being included in just such exhibitions. Thus an artist in his mid-twenties, whom I shall not name, having made the run successfully from California to the East Village, and having been shown, to critical excitement, in Europe and Japan as well as here, is just now having his fifth show, this time at an important gallery in SoHo. His works, which are of a transcendental scruffiness, demonstrate how to be successful though vapid, cynical, simple and immense. His are, in effect, the salon paintings of our time. Like salon paintings always, there would be little reason to execute them were it not for the patronage and preferment that come with the format the artist has found.

It is not only the newly hatched MFAs who languish if they do not make the fateful run, though the art world has so evolved that it is they who are expected, wave upon annual wave, to bring the revolution that the economics of the art market requires in order to advance the hoopla of the Historical New and Important. Older artists, in looser art worlds, art worlds in which collector, curator, dealer, even critic and artist, were less interlocked in a common merchandising effort, may even so have missed a critical moment, only to idle in bitter neglect. Lawrence Weschler recently wrote about Harold Shapinsky, who by rights ought to have risen to eminence with his fellow Abstract Expressionists but, since he was elsewhere when it was necessary to be here, was condemned to total obscurity. When, recently, he was rescued in one of the most romantic chapters in the history of recognition, no fewer than thirty major New York dealers saw no reason to look at his slides. (He has yet to have a New York showing despite considerable success in Europe.) Shapinsky is a special case, since he persisted in painting in the original idiom of Abstract Expressionism long past the time when it was historically relevant to do so, and so remains today a kind of magnificent fossil. In this sense he differs from David Sawin, who followed, to similar unrecognition, a path tangential to recent art history, and did not participate in some larger movement, being, in a way, a movement unto himself. Shapinsky faltered because the movement he was part of entered history without him, Sawin because he entered history without being part of a movement.

Both artists would be natural candidates for an award set up earlier this year by the Francis J. Greenburger Foundation, which specifically sought to identify artists whose achievement was inversely proportional to their recognition. Five judges—Robert Motherwell, Thomas Messer and Clement Greenberg included—were to single out one artist each for celebration. The artists received checks, were included in a group show in a prominent midtown gallery and honored at a reception at the Guggenheim Museum, which was written up in the form of a giggle in the Talk of the Town section of *The New Yorker*. The art world was hostile to the project, largely, I believe, because the effort challenged the premises on which the purveying of art is grounded. It was, according to Arnold Glimcher of the Pace Gallery, "a very naïve idea." His claim, which I shall label "Glimcher's Theorem," is that there are no unrecognized artists. The proof went something as follows: "If the work is powerful, it announces itself. It's very hard to conceal something of great quality." Perhaps this is true if the work is shown, but how is it to announce itself from the unvisited studio? It is not as though a holy star appears in the East over Brooklyn, and some trio of art-world magi—Saatchi, Saatchi and Boone—ride forth in adoration. If the Glimchers will not look, how is anyone to see? "As far as young artists that are good," he went on, coming to the point, "the media and the collectors are in the artists' studios when they are still in kindergarten."

"I am really most interested in the young," a woman of great sensibility and some weight in the museum world once murmured, articulating the historical thesis that the viable artist is either already established or a young running bird of the next revolution. But in truth the great artistic revolutions that define the monumental past for the New York art world were made by artists in their middle years who had internalized the dynamics of art history and broken through into regions of expression so unanticipated that the vivid question for them was whether what they had done was even art. They did know that if it was art, then art had to be redefined in a radical way. In those great artists, the historical transformations in art coincided with their own internal growth as artists, and it is always instructive to witness, in retrospect, the relationship between their early explorations and the immense liberations that followed, explosively, as history achieved itself through them. There is no room in the art world today, structured as it is, for that sort of growth. There is no room for the deepening awareness, for the painfully awakened secrets in the soul of a person's art, for the despairs, the heavy sense of one's own limits, for the redeeming moment of breakthrough and transfiguration, in that intimate and mutual communication between artist and work that resembles a long, difficult and rewarding relationship. Today there is only the fret about finding the right gallery, the right collector, getting good reviews, hitting the right formula, making it.

I have seen two classes of unsuccessful artist, each tragic in a different way. The first group takes as authoritative the salon style of the moment as that is transmitted through the art magazines, much as the latest fashions are carried by *Vogue* or *Elle*. Using these patterns, the artists irrelevantly reenact East Village fashions in provincial ateliers. It is impossible to visit art shows in outlying areas without encountering iterations of last season's work, as though they were the ready-to-wear line of a successful designer. If the artist is at all gifted, the ready-to-wear art she or he puts on fits ill and looks makeshift, and the tragedy is a function of the distance between the artistic personality and the sad work hopelessly turned out. The other class—much smaller—is composed of men and women who labor only for the internal reward, and for the appreciation of those few who happen to notice. Their art worlds have a negligible circumference and consist of persons who not only know the artist personally but are likely to know one another as well. Recognition begins when one's work gets known by people one does not know oneself. But inasmuch as Glimcher's theorem pretty much defines the attitude of the official art world today—if you are not known you are not—it is impossible for such recognition to begin. At least this form of tragedy leaves artistic dignity intact. For these artists it is possible to be, paradoxical as this must sound next to Glimcher's logic, at once unknown and marvelous, at once ignored and deep.

David Sawin, an artist I admire without reservation, has been unable to exhibit except obscurely for the past twenty-five years. Neither established nor in kindergarten, his work is officially nonexistent. It is nonetheless work of the purest and most profound order, and I am grateful that it is being shown at the affectingly old-fashioned Waverley Gallery. There are eighteen recent paintings, most of them small—most of them invisibly small by comparison with the large-scale blasts of today's salon pieces. They use the classical format of still life and landscape, but as occasions rather than subjects, for this artist is concerned with transitions and tensions: like Matisse, he is interested not in the objects themselves but in the relationships between them. Like Henry James (if a literary analogue is licit) whose concern was with characters mainly as points of perturbation in a social field, objects, for Sawin, are there for the purpose of making palpable the forces that define a world of paint. In James, one single word can transform the social field cataclysmically, precipitating the tensions it was the mark of his mastery to reveal. For Sawin, a single splash of color has just that effect. It is exceedingly difficult for readers to make the transition from Zap Comix to *The Golden Bowl*. The transition from Whitney Biennial art to Sawin's work is difficult in just that way.

David Sawin's Paintings

The best of his paintings are ambiguous between landscape and still life, and hence between abstraction and representation. But even when these identities are clear, there will be ambiguities of form and space: a certain shape may be a hill, sloped in Euclidean space, or a meadow tipped up in Cubist space. A line may mark a path through one expanse, or the boundary of another. The indeterminacies are not, I think, what the paintings themselves are about, but consequences of how the objects are addressed. The drama of the work is located where objects impinge upon one another's spaces—I have seen paintings of his in which the objects appear to vie for space, and where the pressures they exert on one another simply distort the space into something that cannot be represented in Euclidean terms. Sawin treats boundaries as the locus of tensions so extreme that they induce vibrations all across the visual field. So the objects—apples, dishes, bottles, if still lifes; meadows, trees, suns, if landscapes—are not located in space but create spaces of a kind possible only in paintings: they serve, one might say, as condensations of space, regarded as an almost viscous medium. So the landscapes are not scenes, as it were, that could be painted *en plein air*, the still lifes are not arrangements of objects in the studio. One gets the sense, rather, that a few lines must be set down on the canvas, a few swipes of paint, and then some complex adjustments and transitions are enacted—and a landscape or a still life is what results. And because of the way form requires form, color demands color, the result is a triumph of resolution, even if the apples or trees are somewhat the worse for wear. Their role is simply to serve as a focus for the decisions as to touch and pigment of which the work consists.

These are extremely beautiful paintings, and the beauty is enhanced by the compressions induced by their small sizes. It is as though the scale exerts a pressure on the forms and colors, raising them to a luminosity stained glass might attain if it were capable of being executed with great subtlety, in tones of green and blue and orange that penetrate one another in such a way that the orange would not be that orange without the cool scrub of green, the green not that very green without the blues and whites and ochers that keep it in place. The paint has the variousness and energy of life. The tonalities, the way the paint adheres to the surface, are almost in a tradition of nineteenth-century American landscape—I think of Inness. But it would have to be an Inness who had studied Cézanne and Morandi, and had forsaken, as it was difficult for Inness to do, sentimentality and ulterior feelings. There is, in each of Sawin's paintings, a mood that suffuses it as a whole. But these are not the identifiable moods that partially define the tradition of the sentimental landscape. Sawin draws on so much of modern art—he would be impossible without the strategies and problems modern art made central—but I know of no artist with whom he can be interestingly compared. His is the kind of vision neglect and resolution make possible. He is very much a loner.

I have known David Sawin for many years, and had I not known him personally, there would have been no way to know his art. But those who love painting are so certain to derive pleasure from the sustained contemplation each work demands that I feel justified in devoting this column to his work, even though I have also used the occasion to reflect on the cost not only the artist but those devoted to art are obliged to pay for an art world driven by the terrible engines of promotion, manipulation and exploitation.

—*The Nation*, October 18, 1986

THE HERO OF *Swann's Way* encounters, at a certain moment in that novel, a phrase of music so mysteriously compelling that he was "filled with love for it, as with a new and strange desire," though he at first was unable to learn the name of the composer or the composition to which the phrase belonged. He was, Proust writes, "like a man into whose life a woman he has seen for a moment passing by has brought the image of a new beauty which deepens his own sensibility, although he does not even know her name or whether he will ever see her again." That a musical phrase should beckon in this way, that it should be dense with a promise Proust can find an analogy to only in the most powerful and in a sense absolute erotic attraction, is not something one would count on happening routinely in the course of listening to music. Vinteuil's "little phrase," as author and hero alike refer to it, was a gift, a surprise, and its discontinuity with the ordinary intensities of musical appreciation was sensed by Swann as "the possibility of a sort of rejuvenation"—a great deal to expect from music, even music of the most sublime order. That it nonetheless happens is one of the redeeming enigmas of art, and if it never happened at all, a life with music would lack something profound, as a life into which a corresponding kind of love had never entered would end, however otherwise successful and rewarding, bereft of its fullest dimension.

David Sawin's Paintings

What one might term the "Vinteuil Syndrome" occurs in poetry as well as in music, and on occasion it occurs in painting. It sometimes happens, in visiting an exhibition, that a certain painting signals so powerfully from across a room that whatever one's intentions may have been in attending the show, one must put them aside and yield to the work, of which, as with the woman Proust writes about, one does not know the name, or perhaps who painted it, or what it means or when it was done or even what it shows. The first time I saw one of Robert Motherwell's Spanish Elegies, I was drawn toward it as toward a person of irresistible charisma. Once, in a collection of brilliant drawings by absolute masters, a watercolor by Cézanne summoned me as peremptorily as a great beauty. Not long ago I was stopped in my tracks by a canvas of Winslow Homer, so tiny that one could not make out the subject even from the distance at which it nevertheless was felt so radiant and intense that its power could not be accounted for by any knowledge of what the painting contained. It was in fact of a man and woman holding fishing poles, a rural scene, but the light transfigured it into something numinous. The first time I saw David Sawin's work, I felt myself to be in the presence of something irresistible, like a nimbus, self-contained in its intense illumination, which drew and held me with a force like love.

There are fine painters whose works never transmit this order of charm, and there are others in whom one feels its presence as stifled, like a buried ember. Sawin is a painter who attains it so consistently that it is almost a defining attribute of his work. There can be very few artists of whom this is true. It is true of Cézanne, certainly, as I feel it to be of Motherwell. It never stopped being true of Morandi, and I felt it immediately in the work of Chuta Kimura, whose death last year robbed the world of an artist as great and nearly as unknown to the art world at large as Sawin himself. These are all masters of incandescence, that presence in their work of something as difficult to characterize but as easy to recognize as spirit, which is there independently of the discoveries that have earned some of them places in the history of art. I have for twenty-five years pondered the works of David Sawin, as one would trace again and again the features of someone preternaturally beautiful, in an effort as unsuccessful as it is irresistible to fathom the secret of how mere paint can recompose itself into something that achieves a *visual* effect parallel to that which, in Vinteuil's phrase, Swann experiences as "that long-drawn sonority, stretched like a curtain of sound to veil the mystery of its incubation." One might almost say that that mystery is the subject as it is the substance of Sawin's amazingly consistent work.

For part of the remarkable meaning of these works is due to the fact that whatever the curtain of color, shape and light may be, it is in active interchange with the pigments from which it arises, so that one is never not aware, in one's awareness of these works, of the sheer physical truth of paint and the sheer physical act of painting. It is only that there are countless paintings in which one is aware of these things without anything further happening—without the recomposition into an immaterial image which never denies, as it were, its material origins as paint and the trace of gesture. There after all were theories abroad when Sawin began as an artist that paintings just were paint, or that they were the tangible expression of the act of painting them. These theories penetrated everything being done in New York at that time, as they penetrated his work then and ever since. But whether because he remained within the boundaries of representation—so that his paintings can be classed as still life or landscape—or for reasons that will forever escape our comprehension, his works transcended the formulae that defined New York painting of that era much, I suppose, as the personality of some marvelous individual transcends the material circumstances of his or her physiological reality. I have never seen one of his works at an early stage in the sequence of stages it must go through as he summons it into being, but I feel certain that he cannot touch the canvas with brush and paint without there *already* being the light and life that only deepen and grow more intense as the work achieves completion.

Everything we admire in Sawin's latest work was present already at the beginning, and it sometimes occurs to me that the entire body of work, taken in its temporal dimension, was latent in the inaugural works, giving the works in the aggregate their astonishing consistency, the coherence of a life lived with a deepening sense of its direction and meaning—a deepening wisdom, one might say. There are very few careers, especially in recent times, of which anything like this is true, and it is perhaps the single blessing Sawin may have derived from the neglect his work has suffered that he has been able to mature in this way, and draw out, further and further, the implications of his gift. He is modern in the sense that only in this century would it be possible for work to resist abstraction, for example, and to bear the effect of its resistances. In some way he is unmistakably American, with submerged echoes of Inness and Homer. But there is finally no one with whom he could be confused, no school to which he belongs, and the chemistry of influence is as much a puzzle as that of the materials the works transform into the glow of artistic truths.

The great value of a retrospective exhibition of an artist who has matured from an originary vision he has also never lost is that we see in the later work what we expect to see in the later stages of a life—a sense of nuance, of refinement, a readiness to discern in one set of forms intimations of another and references to still others, as if, finally, everything went back to an underlying unity, however diverse it appears in its surface. In the end it becomes increasingly difficult to say whether we are looking at a still life or a landscape—or even a piece of architecture in a landscape or, even, a figure or group of figures in an interior. The paintings play with the distinctions between genres, and move us from interpretation to interpretation. Possibly the artist himself does not know in setting out what the painting has decided it wants to be, making a few marks, perhaps, that imply three or four objects, hence a still life, in the course of realizing which the work reveals another identity too strong to resist, this time a meadow, or some hills with a flash of blue in the distance—and then, pursuing this newly recommended landscape, the work decides it wants its earlier identity, but now the still life carries within itself the record of having been a landscape which it might yet become. But this nuance and indetermination were present in the earliest works I know, even if the forms were far less uncertain of their truth. Forms, seemingly definite, become absorbed into their own shadows, so that it is difficult to say where shadow ends and form begins and borders become mysteries; where shadows take on a life of their own so that it becomes impossible to identify any single source of illumination or as if each of the objects has its own; and where shapes struggle to occupy the same space, as if space itself were no longer a containing emptiness but the struggles of objects to displace one another. And nothing can be taken for granted, not light or shade or shape or space though the painting we see seems often as calm as a theorem, disregarding the tensions out of which it arose, though they are all perfectly visible.

There is then this increase in subtlety and allusion, of qualified commitment to form and hue and outline together with a readiness to change direction, so that each painting, more and more, becomes a series of probes and retractions in which the will-to-power of the artist is pitched against the will-to-power of his forms, where he offers a furious yellow the opportunity to be a meadow as it offers him the vision of a tree or a house drenched in an impossible sunlight, and artist and painting settle for something which is all three, somehow, and something else besides. I cannot walk into a room where a painting by David Sawin hangs without being drawn to it, as Swann, upon hearing the phrase of Vinteuil, would become transfixed. That phrase, Proust says, "suggested to him a world of inexpressible delights, of whose existence, before hearing it, he had never dreamed, into which he felt that nothing else could initiate him." And something like this is true of Sawin's work, which awakens us, always, to the true forgotten magic of art.

Eric Fischl

WHEN MARTIN HEIDEGGER died, I was disconcerted to learn from the obituaries of that dark and knotted writer that he had been a connoisseur of fine wines. So luxurious and refined a cultivation was hardly to have been expected in one who spoke, with solemn and prophetic urgency, of authenticity and anguish, boredom and nothingness, death, being and abandonment. One would have imagined the table talk of that gnomic thinker to have consisted of Gothic monosyllables—*Sein! Zeit! Nicht! Tot! Raum! Geist!*—expressing gloomy and shattering profundities, rather than the Gallic frivolities with which the *Feinschmecker* strives to articulate the nuanced differences between Lafite '57 and Château Haut-Brion '46. There is a consistency demanded of prophets from which ordinary thinkers are exempt: their lives must cohere with their messages or we lose confidence in their revelations and imperatives. We would be surprised to learn that Craig Claiborne was constructing a system of metaphysics in his private moments, but we would not lose confidence in his recipes. We would not be surprised at all to learn that a ruler of mankind was a foot fetishist, and might see in this fact an even greater reason to fear him. But if we are as lost as Heidegger depicts us, ought we not to be spending all our time in finding ourselves, and not squander it on mastering a lexicon of delicate differences? And if *he* has time for that, how serious can the existential circumstances of the rest of us be, after all?

I know nothing of the life of Eric Fischl, but I was troubled by what I perceived as an inconsistency between an artistic direction his work seemed to be taking at a recent exhibition at the Mary Boone Gallery, and the overall temper of his painting as it appeared in a major show at the Whitney Museum of American Art. Fischl has been seen as a moralist, as a relentless holder of an ethical mirror in which are reflected, as images, our weak and sleazy moral profiles. One is certain that he means us to see ourselves reflected and, through recognizing our defects and shortcomings, to begin to change our lives. More perhaps than with any other painter working today, the viewer has the sense that Fischl's work is about him or her, and that as subjects of these searching and accusatory representations, we are shown in a troubling judgmental light. There, before us, are all our nagging sexual indulgences and banal perversions and mean appetites and shallow spiritual capabilities. One may, to be sure, seek to exempt oneself from the unwavering *j'accuse* that energizes these paintings by thinking that, in contrast with ourselves, the *Lumpenbourgeoisie* primarily depicted in them are too sunk in lowness and self-preoccupation to have eyes for works of art. But then there must be a complicity between the rest of us and this artist as judges of a soiled and sordid human type, the suburban eroticists Fischl depicts with the authority Hogarth claimed in connection with rakes and harlots, the empty couples locked in marriages of inconvenience. To be sure, they are not monsters of the sort that people the canvases of Leon Golub, so the moral distance between them and us is not vast. Even so, whether as judged or as judges, our relationship to them cannot be neutral, nor our relationship to the paintings themselves purely visual or aesthetic. If this is the case, then what, we want to know, is this artist doing experimenting with shaped canvases, as though he were a recent convert to an avant-garde concerned with exploring the formal problems of painting as painting? How are we to make such formal experiment coherent with the transformative project of awakening his viewers to the moral debilitations of their lives?

Philosophers concerned with the logic of moral discourse have been at pains to show that such language cannot merely be descriptive. It is meant to have some effect on its hearers beyond transmitting information. It exhorts, lobbies, prods, recommends, guides. And much the same must be said of images of morality, rare as their use has been in modern art. They express an attitude toward the unpretty scenes they represent, and seek to encourage a parallel attitude in their viewers. The tableaux on display at Mary Boone carry forward, on one level, that stance of condemnation and injunction that visitors to the Whitney found so unsettling. They are not merely pictures but indictments of the normal dissoluteness of ordinary persons in the wasteland of up-scale housing, in patios and backyards, by swimming pools or barbecue pits, on balconies over beaches or on the beaches themselves, in the living rooms where they party or in the bedrooms where they seek to rub or sleep away the itches of indulgence or the desperations of ir-remediable loneliness. So heavy is this atmosphere that even pictures not obviously part of that vision seem to acquire, by contagion, an aura of stigma and disapproval. There is, for example, a painting of a young girl kneeling on a bed, hugging a large black dog, and grinning out, somewhat vacantly, at the viewer. She is a bit like Little Orphan Annie with her sturdy canine consort, wearing only cotton underpants and plastic curlers. A pubescent girl and her doggie: what is wrong with that? The surrounding pictures cause us to think nasty thoughts. Per-haps the curlers are out of place when worn by a girl still young enough for braces, hinting at a precocious carnality. And is the dog perhaps leering? The relationship between girl and dog begins to thicken with ugly innuendo, and suddenly one feels ready to gossip, to speculate, to cluck one's tongue. The innocence of what might have been a snap-shot of a girl and her best friend is dissolved and replaced by a candid photograph of a slightly unsavory scene between a little tart and an unspeakable animal. The eye of the beholder is flooded by the mind of the moralist.

There is an unmistakable parallel between Fischl's manner of brushing paint generously across large areas and that of Bonnard, although, perhaps in keeping with Fischl's attitude toward his subjects, his paint feels somewhat sick and sticky, as though the sap that infuses Bonnard's pigment had been drained away. Bonnard's pigment retains the juicy warmth that infuses his sun-drenched gardens, or the fleshy resilience of unclothed women toweling themselves down in a patch of light by a tub or basin. In a way, Fischl's connection to Bonnard carries an overcharge of sadness, as if the paint, whose application is so similar in gesture and command, had undergone the same degen-eration as the subjects themselves. Fischl's people are Bonnard's people gone to pot, their flesh itself a metaphor for the decay of meaning in their lives. The women have puffy breasts and sagging bellies and empty looks. Their sexes are often splayed. The men have stiff and sullen pricks and toothy stupid grins. They are metamorphoses, into a sad era, of Bonnard's indolent men or women in that world of bourgeois certitude, in endless afternoons on perfect summer days in the South of France. Fischl has transferred them from villas to condominiums, from gardens to suburban terraces, where they wear the vestments of modern leisure—Hawaiian shirts, Bermuda shorts and bikinis rather than summer frocks and leghorn straw hats—and wash pizza down with diet soda rather than partake of perfect cakes set on checkered cloths. They spread themselves out on king-size water beds before television sets they do not bother to look at, or warm things up in kitchens equipped with new microwave ovens and freezers and Touch-Tone telephones. Something has happened to the peace in Bonnard. Something has happened to the domestic comfort celebrated in the painting that culminated in Bonnard. And the change in the paint somehow emblematizes this negative transformation.

Bonnard's people filled their afternoons with lovely, innocent pastimes, with good things to eat and drink, with pets and flowers. Fischl's people transact little spasms in leisure-worlds of the soul gone dry. A boy is shown masturbating in a plastic pool, before a pair of empty chairs of the plastic-webbing-and-aluminum-tubing variety sold at discount stores. Perhaps they have just been vacated by the boy's parents, and he seizes his sex and sways in solitary ecstasy. The implied narrative I have made explicit is not altogether speculation: many of the paintings are like climactic slashes in narrative time. A splash in a pool, in *Christian Retreat*, implies the occupant of the now empty chaise who has left behind cigarettes and suntan lotion with his (or her?) Bible; a grinning dad flashes approbation from the barbecue pit at a boy swallowing flame; a boy reaches into a woman's purse while she—for all we know, his mother—flashes her sex while doing a toenail; a naked girl trips across the dunes carrying a limp slice of pizza and a bottle, just as two youths leer with definite malice; a boozy couple seem about to head off and screw, leaving behind, in the living room, a boy dressed in a Superman shirt and a girl in pink tights. A woman lies beside a station wagon in some kind of fit. She is surrounded by dogs. And a boy seems about to pull her pants off. Distracted by distraction from distraction, as T. S. Eliot put it, the personages in Fischl's world leave us with a sense of something having gone terribly wrong, with no clear notion of what to do or how to recover. Wherever we go there will be more of the same—tacky people splashing about in resorts and Club Meds, in the very waters where, in one painting, refugees flounder in inadequate boats under dark skies.

Eric Fischl

One does not paint such moral landscapes, it seems to me, unless one means to engage the conscience of the viewer, who is, after all, never so distant from those landscapes that he can defer for very long grasping them as metaphors for his own life. One cannot wiggle out of the generalized indictment by insisting that one does not own a swimming pool or a king-size water bed. The visitors to the Whitney exhibition tended to talk about "them," but surely they came to see that "they" are us, and that something in our lives must be modified, some resolution formed. Of course, the paintings may not detonate in the viewer's conscience in quite this way. There is a wonderful painting of a woman sitting naked, out of doors, her face hidden by a mirror in which she is lost in self-contemplation. Between her spread legs, on the ground, a magazine lies open. It shows what looks to me very like a self-portrait of Fischl beside an easel. The picture shows Fischl staring out, looking dark and intense. The woman is paying no attention: Fischl's work is not a mirror for her, since the mirror she holds in her hand reflects the only reality that concerns her. Titled *Vanity*, the painting is clearly about its immediate subject, a woman peering into a glass. But it may also be about the vanity of the artist who has set out to change lives, and has failed.

The moral transformation of the viewer is an ancient and respected goal of art. It surely underlies the phenomenon of catharsis in Aristotle, and it defined the priorities of censorship in Plato's political aesthetics. In Plato's view, there is a complex transitivity between spectator, artwork and artistic subject which entails that we literally become what we see, so that the art of the republic must be central in the formation of its citizenry. The admonitory, cautionary representation of the virtues and the vices animates much of Christian art, and the art of the Counter-Reformation was explicitly intended to co-implicate the viewer in the suffering of displayed martyrs. And throughout the nineteenth century, values were meant to be reinforced by rhetorical representations of goodness and wickedness. Aesthetics, with its curious notions of disinterest and delectation, was very much an eighteenth-century invention, and except for that period, and again with the Impressionists and Cézanne, art has always been part of the arsenal of moral education. Twentieth-century art has been marked by a series of philosophical experiments intended to isolate the essence of art, and the waning of that impulse in very recent years is precisely what has made it possible for a painter like Eric Fischl to assume a different and traditional artistic role, to bring painting back into life, rather than to act, as artists have been doing, within the isolating atmosphere of an art world for the sophisticated theoreticians that compose its population. But this returns me to my question: What is *this* artist doing playing with shaped canvases and compound panels?

In the Whitney exhibition there are pieces composed of double panels—diptychs—but in every instance the result makes artistic sense. The juxtapositions are those we might see in an altarpiece, with the saved on one side and the damned on the other. Two scenes strengthen each other's message, or narrow it, as with the vacationers on the left and the boat people on the right. Or with the woman, alone, opening the door of her condo, witnessed by a dog, while another woman is shown opposite on that same balcony, her bathing suit bottom down around her ankles, staring at the erection of her moronic youthful companion. The two scenes express the horns of some unedifying dilemma. But this is not the way the panels work in the large compositions at the Mary Boone. The scenes splash portentously across multiple panels, without it being clear why they do so. Why is a panel showing a running dog tacked onto a complex panel showing the usual characters at their sterile recreations? It is as though Fischl had decided to become an experimenter, pointing away from life in the direction of art-world theoretics, concerned with questions of shape and surface, of flatness and edge, concerned, at this late date, to define painting rather than to say something disturbing about masturbation, molestation, loneliness, incest, bestiality, lust, sloth, intemperance, vanity, cupidity, selfishness and loss.

You cannot fuse into a coherent concept propositions about painterly reeducation and instructions to better one's moral condition. You cannot form a coherent audience out of those in the shadows of moral perdition and those obsessed with the metaphysics of painting. And without strenuous and largely misdirected interpretative efforts, it is difficult to dispel, for all the power of his imagery and the certainty of his painterly reflexes, the sense that Fischl has lost his way in these new works, with their irrelevant puzzles and inflated allegory.

—*The Nation*, May 31, 1986

Alex Katz

THE PHILOSOPHER Alvin Goldman once invented the following puzzle. Jones (who else?) is driving through a landscape dotted with what he has every reason to believe are barns but in fact are large, flat pieces of plywood shaped and painted to look like barns. There is one real barn among them, and as he passes it Jones believes he is passing a barn, as indeed he is. He had the same belief as he passed the barn facsimiles, and he will have the same belief again as he passes facsimiles to come. On this occasion the belief is true, but would we say that Jones *knows* that he is passing a barn, since his basis for so believing is the same as it would have been had the belief been false?

I felt as if I were wandering through Goldman's epistemological farmland on the fourth floor of the Whitney Museum, much of which is occupied by Alex Katz's cutouts: freestanding flat effigies of members of Katz's family and various friends from the art world: Sanford Schwartz, Rudy Burckhardt, Frank O'Hara. To be sure, it was not the hallucinatory experience visitors would sustain at a show of Duane Hanson's vivid, lifelike figures, got up to look like visitors to the Whitney. Seeing a crowd of Hanson's figures standing before less mischievous paintings and sculptures, one might believe one was not alone in the gallery. Would one *know* one was not alone when in fact one was not alone? Katz's figures are not in the least intended to fool the eye. They are, in the first instance, unmistakably painted. And they are, secondly, not life-size. In fact they stand to their living models in much the same ratio as our mirror images stand to ourselves—namely, as readers of Gombrich know and as anyone can verify by measuring his or her image in the bathroom mirror, half-size. It is well known that the cutouts came from paintings that did not work out for Katz; he simply detached the image from the background and gave it an identity of its own. The relationship of an image on the surface of the painting to its model may be very like the relationship between one's mirror image and oneself, and that may account for the slightly disconcerting feeling one gets from the cutouts, which seem oddly shrunken. It would be quite disconcerting to see a space filled with mirror images were it possible to liberate them from mirrors and stand them on their own. It would be almost surreal, like seeing someone unpack a box of shadows and spread them around the room. The cutout is insistently an image, and its flatness underscores the fact that it is not to be taken for something else.

The cutout is Alex Katz's most distinctive contribution to contemporary art. The cutouts are not paper dolls for sophisticates, though they stand in fashionable corners of the art world, where the Katz cutout has the cachet once carried by the instantly recognizable Calder mobile (which was also not a toy for sophisticates). The cutout so resembles the figure in a painting by Katz that one could will the problem of determining whether a given painting was of a woman or of a cutout of a woman, for the figures in the paintings have a curious flatness. The answer, I think, is that Katz is engaged in making images and that it is a mistake to look at a painting as anything other than a flat surface with some as yet unliberated images taking up part of that surface. The images have to look like something; they would not be images if they did not. But an image is the kind of entity that exhausts its essence by being pure surface. The cutouts are like the two-dimensional beings of a fictional Flatland, who live their lives in Euclidean planes. They enable us to realize that the paintings, too, are meant to be understood as surfaces. "My theory," Katz stated in a recent interview with Grace Glueck, "is if you get the surfaces right, you get everything else right." *My* theory is that whatever else there is in Katz's work is to be defined in terms of surface.

At a certain moment in the history of recent painting, flatness, which one might have supposed could be taken for granted, seemed an almost impossible goal. Its being a goal was connected with the struggle against illusion, in which abstraction was a strategy. The problem with abstraction is that the moment one makes a mark on the canvas, it seems immediately to assume a position in an illusory, pictorial space. Another mark will be seen as behind it or in front of it or even in the same plane with it, but neither of them seems ready to stay on the surface. What is the point of abstraction when pictorial space seems irremediably illusory? If flatness could be achieved, the painter would no longer be engaged in representing reality but in creating it. But what if flatness cannot be achieved? By cutting his figures out of the picture plane and releasing them into our space, where they nevertheless are not sculpture but painting, Katz made their planar essence palpable. Because they are creatures of the surface, they carry their atmosphere with them, like astronauts on the moon. They cannot exist outside the plane, hence the paintings they belong to are absolute surface. Q.E.D.

Let me bring this out in another way. In one of his paintings, Katz shows a painting that is itself a painting by Alex Katz. It is a mark of this artist's style that it is difficult to imagine a painting *in* a painting by him that is not itself a painting *by* him—as though Alex Katz could paint only Alex Katzes. I know of few painters limited in this way by their own vision of art. Eric Fischl, who has a show on the Whitney's second floor, once exhibited a painting of a child in an interior that included an unmistakable work of Andy Warhol's. Like the child, like the furnishings, the Warhol was executed in Fischl's marvelously brushy way. It was a painting of a Warhol by Fischl; still, the painting was Warhol and not Fischl, and one did not believe that Warhol painted in Fischl's marvelously brushy way any more than one believed the child was made of brushstrokes, or of anything save flesh and blood. In *Gersaint's Shop Sign*, Watteau painted the interior of an art gallery. Any square inch of a Watteau has that artist's distinctive touch, whether it shows a woman's face or a portrait of a king's face. Still, the gallery does not look as though it contains only Watteaus, and in fact I do not believe it contains any. Paintings of paintings, accordingly, raise fascinating questions of pictorial perception, but a painting of a painting by Katz would almost certainly look like a painting by Katz of a painting by Katz. This is because the paintings in his paintings belong, as everything else in the paintings belongs, to the surface—as essential flatnesses. The paintings at the Whitney could in many cases be cutouts of paintings. They would demonstrate their flatness in just the way the irregular cutouts do, having their edges coincide with the edges of their subjects.

Alex Katz is a survivor of the art wars that raged in the teapot art world of the 1950s. He is of the generation that took abstraction as a credo and the image as a heresy. A credo is not an option but an imperative, and to resist such an imperative took great courage and great confidence. What strikes me in this retrospective is that Katz is finally one of the most abstract artists of his period, that in a way he solved the problem of abstraction through the use of images, chiefly by taking away from his figures any reality except what pertains to their status as images. If there were an interior space shown by his works it would be an interior occupied by flat things—by cutouts, in effect—as a stage would be an interior space filled by flat pieces of scenery. So figuration in his case is a means to abstract ends. In the earliest paintings shown, there is often a figure, small in relation to the background, that is often just blank paint, as though Katz had not decided what to do with it. It was as if the figure were waiting to be cut out of this blankness, like a paper doll on a page. When they are cut out it becomes perfectly plain that there is no more to them than meets the eye. They are what they seem. They are seemings. There are no hidden depths because there are no depths. The artist has flung back into the teeth of a famous indictment of Plato his own credo: "Appearance be my reality!"

As pure looks, one expects from the cutouts no more emotion than paper dolls themselves have, or masks. There are no moral depths hinted at by painted eyes when we take them as painted eyes. The faces are arrestingly bland. So there is little to do with them except place them in juxtaposition, or paint clothes on their bodies. The same woman (Katz's wife, as we have been told) is shown with a wardrobe as rich as Barbie's—red coats and rain hats, snow bonnets, kerchiefs, cocktail frocks—doing little more than just being there, posed and placed, filling the maximally thin space between the front and back of the surface. It is a world in which the only problems are artistic problems, problems of scale and shape. The portraits of Katz's wife, of which there are said to be over one hundred, reveal nothing about her except her generalized look. They would not, side by side, give us a record of a character, as Rembrandt's self-portraits would. Katz's subjects have been transfigured out of life into art. They are like the golden birds in the Byzantine throne room, lifted out of nature. He is not a representational artist at all.

Katz's failures arise only when he forsakes his abstract humans

Alex Katz

for things not so easily purged of substantiality—a moose, for example, so badly painted that it looks like the Macy's balloon of Bullwinkle folded around itself; or an atrocious gigantic dog (*Sunny*), which I wanted to turn to the wall; or an ill-advised tree. *Swamp Maple, 4:30*, as the painting of that tree is titled, has begun to crackle, though done only in 1968. Crackling paint is a reminder of a reality these images are designed to flee, and an artist who is bent on celebrating surface ought to handle paint with a greater concern for its chemical treacheries. I was unhappy with some very big flowers, simply because they immediately turned into a floral pattern, making the painting look like expensive wallpaper. In wallpaper, the assumption of surface is instantly granted, and the solution is somehow too easy. What, finally, are best are the wonderful large heads: a woman under an umbrella, with flat raindrops falling in the surface, or wearing a winter hat in snow, or a smashing red coat and hat. My sense is that Katz has paid a certain price for his extreme reductions, which have left his images severely limited to themselves. They are like subjects without predicates, simply there, simply shown, take them or leave them. It is an agreeable art, but not a stirring one.

—*The Nation*, May 10, 1986

35]

Vienna 1900

POSTMODERNIST ART is so dense a tissue of references to past art—of quotations, appropriations, emulations, borrowings, transfers and iterations—that the term "eclectic" can no longer have a use in the working vocabulary of the art critic. Not long ago an artistic reputation would wither under the accusation of eclecticism, but the damning use of the term only came into existence with the romantic exaltation of original genius: if we move further back in the history of art, we find the Bolognese painters of the Roman Baroque proud to have their work recognized as eclectic. For the Carracci, eclecticism meant taking the best from various traditions, somewhat in the manner of a legendary sculptor of ancient times who carved a woman of transcendent beauty by copying the brow of one model, the mouth of a second, the breasts of a third and so on. Leonardo himself recommended as a standard artistic method what in time would come to be stigmatized as eclecticism; the term is one whose shifts in force reflect transformations in the conception of the artistic task. There is perhaps not a single term of critical dispraise that could not have been used in a different time to express unqualified commendation. Sir Joshua Reynolds not only enjoined eclecticism upon his students—he regarded artificiality as a mark of the highest genre of painting.

The term "decorative" condenses, today, a whole class of reasons for putting down the work to which it is applied. A young friend possessed of perfect pitch for the dialects of the art world repeated this comment about the exhibition Vienna 1900 at the Museum of Modern

Art, which she had not yet seen: "Schiele is the really serious artist, and Klimt is just decorative, right?" But it is altogether possible that Klimt would have confessed decorativity as the Bolognese did eclecticism, and thought it an achievement rather than a demerit. In 1891 Bonnard declared, "Painting must be above all decorative," insisting that this was precisely the lesson he learned from Gauguin. Decoration was a common determinant of artistic effort in the 1890s, and one of Bonnard's associates, Verkade, memorialized the spirit of the age thus:

No more easel pictures! . . . Painting must not usurp a liberty that isolates it from the other arts. The painter's work begins at that point where the architect considers his finished. Walls, walls to decorate! Down with perspective! The wall must remain a surface, must not be spoiled by a representation of distant horizons. There are no pictures: there is only decoration.

So the art historian Aby Warburg was out of phase with the art of his time when he asked, rhetorically, in 1890: "Why do we speak of the decline of art when it becomes decorative?" Gauguin's, Bonnard's and, I dare say, Klimt's answer would have been: "We don't." Throughout his life, Bonnard eschewed the easel, painting instead on canvases attached to the wall. Klimt's work, at least in the period of his greatness, implies a wall, a relationship to architecture and to design, to costume, furniture, objets d'art, and it fulfills the imperative that painting should not be isolated from the other arts. So it is genuinely illuminating to exhibit his work, as Vienna 1900 does, in the context of architecture and craft, of couture, ornament and design, with which it was in constant inspirational interchange. And comprehending his work as a celebration of decoration helps us in turn to see these surrounding objects, usually regarded as secondary to painting and sculpture, in a fresh and elevating light. But it also helps identify a tension between Klimt and the remaining painters in the show—Schiele, Kokoschka, Gerstl, Schönberg—for there is no sense in which their art can be seen as decorative. So between Klimt's work and theirs, some new definition of the painter's enterprise must have penetrated the artistic consciousness in Vienna, which in turn perhaps explains the overall decline of Klimt when he tried to comply by becoming an easel painter. And it is this new definition that goes some distance in explaining why Schiele seems one of us, while Klimt appears so locked in his era that it takes a wrench of historical imagination to see him as he should be seen.

The Kiss of 1907–8 falls within Klimt's so-called golden phase, and I would head straight for it. A couple, locked in an intense embrace, kneel at the edge of a thickly flowered expanse. Sometimes the Buddha is shown walking on flowers, and this is not the only Oriental motif in the painting, or for that matter in the Viennese attitude and feeling of the time. Prince Metternich once wittily observed that "the Orient begins at the Landstrasse," and indeed the gold-leaf background of *The Kiss* carries the feeling of a Japanese screen—a mobile wall—conveying a metaphysical sense of an infinite and precious void. The flowered expanse ends abruptly, as at the edge of an abyss, and the woman's feet are poised at the boundary of emptiness, promissory of an annihilating ecstasy. A lighter, more brilliant gold forms a kind of mandala not just surrounding but penetrating the empassioned couple, as though they had become coincident with the aura that is emblematic of their union. The woman is sheathed in a golden dress embellished with jeweled forms that echo the flowered expanse, leaving it ambiguous as to whether they are themselves flowers, or whether the expanse is itself an elaborate jewel. Both figures wear flowers in their hair, and the man's robe, also golden, is animated by irregular ascending rectangles in black, and by golden scrolls. I was reminded of a marvelous description by the French critic Eugène Fromentin of a painting by Jan Van Eyck:

When a Van Eyck picture is beautiful . . . it looks like a piece of jewelry of enameled gold, or one of those many-colored materials having a woof of gold. Gold is suggested everywhere, above and beneath. When it does not play on the surface, it appears under the tissue. It is the bond, the basis, the visible or latent primitive element of this pigment rich above all others.

In Van Eyck, according to Fromentin, "the hand is employed only in making manifest the luxury and beauty of materials by the luxury and beauty of the work," and in this, Fromentin goes on to suggest, the Flemish master shows how close painting then was to its sources "in the art of the goldsmith, the engraver and the enameler." Painting was a craft among crafts, as it is once more in Klimt, which then gives rise to the possibility that the objects we see in the surrounding cases, so opulent and masterful—the coffee services and flatware, the inkwells and cruets, the armchair by Kolomon Moser of rare woods and mother-of-pearl, the bowls, decanters and eggcups, and the spectacular vitrine by Carl Otto Czechka in silver, semiprecious stones, enamel and ivory—were perceived as things transfigured onto some higher and more spiritual plane. The transfiguration of commonplace domestic objects into beings so rarefied that only jewelry of the richest sort can give us a metaphor for their essence is perhaps, beyond decorativity, the ultimate meaning of Klimt's art. It must have given artistic substance to the collective attitudes and longings of the aesthetes who patronized Klimt and his fellow craftsmen, almost as if their works were like holy icons, golden presences from another world.

The flesh of beautiful women is often exalted with metaphors from the realm of jewels and flowers—ruby lips, teeth like pearls, eyes that sparkle like diamonds, rosy cheeks—so it is striking that the flesh of Klimt's women contrasts almost morbidly with the surrounding stuffs and stones and metals. It is bloodless and nearly necrotic. Very little of the lovers' skin is shown in *The Kiss*—the woman's face, her shoulder and elbow, her calves and feet, the man's neck—and what we do see is gray-blue and lifeless, touched, as by some mortuary cosmetician, with rouge. This curious dead flesh is common in Klimt's work of this period: his women are almost totally one with the jeweled splendor of their garments, but their flesh is so consistently unhealthy that one wonders if some chemical change may not have afflicted the paint. The other and, for me, more plausible approach to the anomaly is through an interpretive hypothesis: ornament is the state to which his figures aspire, and they are undergoing some kind of sea change that is to turn them, at last, into something beyond life and longing and decay. If this is true, then Klimt's world, the world he objectifies in his art, was exactly congruent with the sentiment expressed by Yeats:

> *Once out of nature I shall never take*
> *My bodily form from any natural thing,*
> *But such a form as Grecian goldsmiths make*
> *Of hammered gold and gold enamelling.*

The enjewelment of the flesh, the escape into the status of gold and emeralds, casts the eroticism of these works in a special light. It is not the robust, randy kind of eroticism one finds in Renoir, where the flesh sings, nor the prurient eroticism of the pornography it sometimes resembles. It is, instead, the eroticism of the mystic, a technique for slipping out of the flesh, where intense pleasure—or pain—is a means rather than a goal. Vienna's was, beyond question, a hedonistic society but, at least for those men and women for whom Klimt was a great artist, it was not so much an abandonment to the flesh that was sought, but an artistic abandonment of the flesh to art through sex. And my sense is that trying to make one's figures as congruent with the surface of the work as possible is connected with this. Consider the way Klimt rearranges the woman's anatomy in *The Kiss*. It is almost Egyptian, in that the profile of the body and the full face seem to occupy the same plane, as though the woman had no thickness. How greatly this differs from the rearrangements of anatomical parts one finds in Picasso's treatment of women, which puts everything sexually relevant on the same side for the lovers' fullest enjoyment. Picasso and Klimt occupy opposing poles in the circle of sexual possibility, chiefly because in Klimt flesh is something to be overcome.

Some of the uncanny flatness of Klimt's figures is also found in those of Egon Schiele, but with a marked difference: if Klimt's men and women have the opaque thinness of gold leaf—of "hammered gold and gold enamelling"—Schiele's men and women instead have the translucent thinness of membranes, as if the life had been pressed out of them, as with flower petals or insect wings or, to cite a horrible example, a dried human skin I once saw pictures of in an article about monastic practices in Tibet. It seems required that Schiele would use watercolor to achieve this translucency, or oil paint thinned down to a kind of glaze; when he uses oils opaquely, as in rendering hills and houses, his work instantly loses its power and immediacy and, if you like, its terror. His figures, in his characteristic works, are all angles and points, as if, once pressed flat, they were arranged on a sheet in some semblance of lifelikeness. They really are, as has been observed, like marionettes, and if that gives some basis for seeing his project as finally like Klimt's—a way of turning persons into things—then the two artists have more in common, are more similarly Viennese, than meets the eye. What is striking is that Schiele's reduced men and women are often arranged in erotic poses of the least ambiguous kind, as if they were illustrations for sex manuals, and it is pretty clear that sex must have meant something different for him than for Klimt. For Schiele there were no implied choruses and violins in the background, no clouds of incense, no metaphysical lacework, no high-flown death and transfiguration to make the couples believe they were engaged in something of the highest spiritual sort. For him, sex was something done on soiled sheets in hard beds: it was draining and addictive, and his dried, emaciated men and women look as though they had fucked themselves, literally, to death. Picasso's gaunt figures from the Blue Period look starved but emotionally healthy; Vienna steamed with the miasmas of neurosis. Schiele is all nerve and feeling, one of the great draftsmen, and the combination of pathology and genius fits the tragedy of his early death, at twenty-eight, in 1918. He did not have a full life, but at the same time it is impossible to imagine what a full life would have been for him.

It is difficult to situate the third of the great painters of Vienna 1900 in this general pattern, though Oskar Kokoschka did fulfill the imperative of transforming persons into objects by having a doll fashioned in the image of his tempestuous mistress, Alma Mahler, which he carried about with him for a time. But I see this more as a matter of excess of love than of a transfigurative attitude toward sex. There is a powerful anecdote in some dialogues with Chikimatsu, the great Japanese master of the puppet drama, of a lady so consumed with love for a distant gentleman that in her desperation she had a wooden effigy of him fashioned "that did not differ in any particle from the man." I imagine this must have been Kokoschka's impulse as well. The stirring portrait (not shown here) of him and Alma, swept up in a whirlwind of love, really does make *The Kiss* look abstract, willed, passionless and, well, decorative. But Kokoschka's work is confessional and autographic, and belongs more to a form of Mittel-Europa expressionism than to Vienna in particular, at least as it is defined by the furniture, the textiles and the objects of stunning design and execution that fit so well with the paintings of Klimt. The galleries hold some wonderful portraits of Viennese personalities by Kokoschka, including a marvelous self-portrait and the famous double portrait of the art historian Hans Tietze and his wife, Erica—but they look somehow out of place amidst the elegance and artifice established by the Klimts and by the furniture and jewels. And this, I suppose, raises the question of the theme of such an exhibition as this. Kokoschka was certainly in Vienna, was part of its life, and his stature certainly mandates his inclusion in a show of artworks from Vienna in this era. Perhaps it would have been possible to surround him with objects that illuminate his work as the products of the Vienna Werkstätte do Klimt's. As it stands, he is only externally related to the dominant tone the show establishes. In some way he belongs more with the intellectuals—whose presence was so much a part of the Paris show of the art of Vienna at Beaubourg two years ago, which covered a longer span of time—than with the refined financiers and their wives and mistresses for whose patronage the craftsmen, the architects, the dressmakers and *bijoutiers*, the *ébénistes* and decorators and Gustav Klimt himself labored. A more coherent exhibition would have left him out.

On the other hand, the dissonances that are set up between Kokoschka and the remainder of what we are shown testifies to the extraordinary coherence the latter achieves. Perhaps it is a coherence attained at the expense of reducing Vienna to a plane of taste and attitude that merely intersects the historical reality, giving us a distorted unanimity when the reality was perhaps more pluralistic and diffuse, and giving us the illusion of perceiving the *Zeitgeist* when we have instead only one of its facets. Perhaps something truer to the reality would, in the end, be less illuminating of Vienna's outstanding artist. It is appropriate that Klimt should himself be treated as a jewel, and given this kind of setting. Kirk Varnedoe is the author of the exhibition, as of the extremely intelligent catalogue that accompanies it, and it is greatly to his credit that he has sought beyond art to its determinants in society. The objects form a community of mutual illuminations and raise, in the aggregate, questions it is certainly beyond an exhibition's capabilities to answer. But just as an aggregate of luminous things, Vienna 1900 is a very exciting show, and one feels it is bound to have some impact on current taste and fashion.

One consequence of the fact that our own *Zeitgeist* is represented by an art that is thoroughly eclectic is that appropriation excludes influence. Some deeper shock than even very fine exhibitions can administer is needed for that sort of change. Art that draws its substance only from art has cut itself off from avenues of patronage that give point and meaning to it. In that respect the exhibition makes a point dramatically relevant to our age.

—*The Nation*, September 27, 1986

Morris Louis

THE EYE IS an extruded part of the brain, absorbing through the thin retinal tissues whatever emits or reflects quanta in the surrounding world, and serving as a way station for the production of neural images that enable us to stop at red lights and avoid meandering cows. Enough of its mechanisms were known in Darwin's time for him to have written, "The thought of the eye made me cold all over." Darwin's thought makes me cold all over when I think of how much remains to be discovered about the visual system we use so casually. For the eye is also a part of the mind, and what we see depends, demonstrably, on what we feel and how we believe. At the philosophical cross-point of mind and brain, the eye is bound to be a contested salient in the border wars of metaphysics, and today there is little consensus on the degree to which the apparatus of cognition penetrates the physiology of sight.

Not long ago there were those who believed the penetration all but total, that our perception of the visible world is so laden with preconceptions that, in science as in common life, there is no sharp line to be drawn between observation and theory. Philosophers, anthropologists, linguists, sociologists of knowledge and social psychologists insisted that perceptual experience is thoroughly relativistic, as though the human organism were completely plastic and the perceived world nothing but a construct we acquire with our language and our culture. Deep incommensurabilities were believed to divide period from period, culture from culture, gender from gender, race from race and language community from language community, with space, shape, color, even size, fluctuating so radically as to raise the question of whether there is a shared world at all.

There is today a palpable retreat from this giddy position. Color discrimination has proved to be remarkably more invariant than anthropologists dared to believe a decade ago. Cognitive science has been coming up with striking evidence in regard to the processing equipment with which we are all wired as part of our genetic endowment, and the modularity of mind has increasingly defined research in studies of human and animal cognition. The mind is modular to the degree that its functioning is impervious, or at least extremely resistant, to belief and feeling. Thus we continue to experience perceptual illusion as perceptual illusion, no matter what we believe or how much we know about how it takes place. Although I agree that the importance of optical fidelity in pictorial representation is a matter of cultural decision, my own view is that linear perspective is modular despite its having been asserted to be a symbolic form by the art historian Erwin Panofsky, and a mere cultural convention by the philosopher Nelson Goodman. It is doubtful that the retreat from relativism will be total, but no one can predict where the lines of modularity finally will be drawn.

I have lately come to wonder whether our perception of works of art may not be a good bit more modular than most aestheticians are prepared to concede. There are extreme views abroad to the effect that a work of art is but the infinite possibility of interpretation—a view strikingly similar to John Stuart Mill's thesis that a physical object is but the permanent possibility of sensation. It was this attitude, that the artwork itself is pure potentiality, that gave rise to the scandalizing boast of a Yale University critic that the critic is finally more creative than the artist. (Because critics too are subject to infinite interpretation, the theory turns against its proponents, who no longer have grounds for complaining that they have been misread.) The psychology of art perception is waiting for its Stone Age to dawn, but even in our prehistorical situation, we can at least begin to raise the question of the degree to which artworks are penetrable by interpretation, especially now that it is clear that the ability to recognize pictorial content is something we share with other primates and even with mere pigeons. A chimpanzee will scream in fear when shown a photograph of the leader of his pack with fangs bared. But the question of perception remains even with abstract paintings, as is evidenced by the almost total irrelevance to our response to the paintings of Morris Louis of the standard critical theories addressed to this artist's work. These theories are typified in the catalogue that accompanies the exhibition of Louis's work at the Museum of Modern Art. The absolute distance between the catalogue by John Elderfield and the exhibition he has curated makes this one of the most important shows of recent years.

The exhibition shows us Louis as he would have wanted to be seen, but also as those who regard him as a major artist believe he ought to be presented—namely, through the paintings alone, without further context. For Louis did everything he could to destroy his own history (just as he almost succeeded in concealing his technique of painting, so that it is now a matter of informed speculation how his characteristic works were executed). The show is minimally chrono- logical, which is almost mandated by the fact that Louis's *oeuvre* falls into a few successive genres—the Veils, the Unfurled Paintings, the Stripes—and if one decides to segregate the works by genre, it would be perverse to scramble them in time. Louis's period of high creativity was tragically brief, from about 1954 until just before his death from cancer in 1962, with a somewhat barren period between 1955 and 1958. An isolated, nearly reclusive and secretive man, he did away with work he did not wish to be known by, so perhaps an exhibition that placed him in context would have been difficult to mount. Still, enough of the disowned work was out of Louis's hands before he rejected it that were there the curatorial desire to mount such a show, it could have been done—relating earlier work to later; the successes to the tentative painterly probings; Louis's work to that of his sometime associates (including Kenneth Noland), his distant peers (Barnett New- man and Jules Olitski) and his acknowledged influences (Robert Moth- erwell and, above all, Helen Frankenthaler). That it was not done in this way can be appreciated in the spirit of piety as respecting the wishes of a dead artist, and as acknowledging his greatness; but even more, I believe, it must be appreciated as a gesture of curatorial will, expressing the belief that history and biography do not pertain to the aesthetic absorption of his work. What, instead of history and biog- raphy, is required is a body of theory, and the theory is laid out in the catalogue. So the exhibition carries a meaning beyond whatever mean- ing is carried by the works themselves. It is eloquent with its omissions and tacit insistences. It is a monument to the aesthetics of Clement Greenberg.

As such, it constitutes an inadvertent crucial experiment in the perception of art. If in the end these paintings resist transformations by theory, the theory fails at its most fortified position and must retreat vanquished. For Louis was the Greenbergian artist par excellence, the one painter who executed the strategies on which Greenberg insisted, who showed, or was believed to show, what, in its purest state, painting was all about and was always all about, despite the contaminations of feeling and content that have dogged the history of art and criticism. The failure of the theory is not Louis's fault. Louis's paintings are extremely beautiful and even powerful. An artist whose responses I respect told me of having come to love Louis's work in consequence of an exhibition she saw at the Fogg Museum in Cambridge years before she knew anything about Clement Greenberg and New York aesthetics. "It was like being in a marvelous garden," she said. Her experience is the valid experience to have with Louis's work. The sculptor Harold Tovish writes that Louis's work is "too pretty" for his tastes. Tovish's is also a valid critical response to Louis. You like him if you like art that is pretty, or art in which prettiness is raised to a monumental power. You dislike him, or find him tepid, if your taste runs to darker things. Neither of these responses takes into consideration what Greenberg, or what those who follow Greenberg, say is important about Louis's works. That, I claim, is because Greenberg played a crucial role in Louis's life as an artist (he seems to have had no other life). Greenberg's view explains why the work exists in the form it does. It does not explain why it matters, or explains it wrongly.

In his celebratory introduction to the catalogue of the 1974 exhibition of Louis at the Hayward Gallery in London, Elderfield wrote, "With Louis . . . fully autonomous abstract painting came into its own for really the first time, and did so in paintings of a quality that matches the level of their innovation." I want to modify the implied arithmetic of this statement. The paintings are measurably greater than their degree of innovation, just because I do not believe they are fully autonomous abstract paintings. Moreover, I do not believe fully autonomous abstractness is an especially important thing for painting to possess, even supposing it is possible. Fully autonomous abstraction, however, was exactly what Greenberg was urging painters to produce, although the great artists of the New York School, whom Greenberg did so much to publicize, showed no overwhelming inclination to accomplish this. Pollock and De Kooning, the acknowledged leaders, were unregenerately figurative, and human meaning kept insinuating itself into their masterpieces as into their casual work. Even painters who were confessedly abstract—Rothko or Newman—were making paintings filled with extra-artistic meaning.

What Greenberg was demanding was a form of painting that sufficed unto itself: painting about its own means; painting, the meaning of which *was* its means: pigment, canvas, stretchers, surface. I can sympathize with Greenberg's thought in the context of its era. Here was an exalted discipline—painting—that had always been in the service of something outside itself: the church; the nation-state; the crown; the revolution; the oppressed class. And now, a terrible war having concluded, Greenberg raised artists to a dignity high enough that art should at last be in its *own* service. Beyond that, self-reflexiveness had become the mark of purity throughout the West: the autonomy of philosophy, of psychology, of literature, were parallel movements in the aggregate enterprise of professionalization which, in my view, continues most particularly to affect the *criticism* of art. Criticism today is practiced as though it too were done on its own behalf and for its own sake, with no ulterior point or bearing. This explains its standard opacity. It is to Greenberg's credit, or discredit, that he brought about more a style of criticism than a style of painting. Louis may represent his entire artistic army, but the troops in his critical division are legion, and they are marching still.

Here is how an influential critic, Michael Fried, appraised Louis in his widely respected pamphlet *Three American Painters*, which was devoted to Noland, Olitski and Stella. Fried, like Greenberg, gave special prominence to the implications of the way Louis applied paint to canvas. It was soaked into raw canvas to produce a stain. Since a stain is something one cannot altogether draw—one can cause a stain only by soaking or spilling—there are no willed boundaries to it. The stain, in consequence, Fried argues, has no tendency to become detached from the ground and so avoids the illusion we sustain when we perceive drawn outlines (a drawn stain would not be a *stain*) or "are made to feel . . . the painter's wrist." The stain, then, identifies the image with "its woven canvas ground, almost as if the image were thrown onto the latter from a slide projector. The actual weave of the canvas shows through everywhere." So there is no illusion: the materials of the art are all there is; the work is, as it were, an achievement of pure opticality, uncontaminated by any tactile values other than those natural to the medium. Moreover, the stain itself is impersonal.

Once the saturated rag or sponge is brought into contact with the cloth, capillary action takes over, and the stain, like water, seeks its own boundaries. So none of the bravura of De Kooning's, or Pollock's, "wrist" is felt: as Fried has it, "painterliness from the Venetians to De Kooning is renounced."

In truth, so far as we can infer from the work, Louis's interventions in directing the flow of color were active and ingenious. He worked with the fluid by folding or pleating the canvas into channels, collaborating with gravity to make the paint conform to a complex intention. He was like some master dyer, whose work belongs to what, if it were craft, we would class as a lost art. But the renunciation Fried asserts is meant to proclaim the autonomy of the painting even from the painter, as though he stood aside in Oriental detachment and enabled the painting to materialize out of nothing. And the almost studied reticence of Louis with regard to personal disclosure may suggest he was an artist who rendered himself transparent in the cause of making the painting fully autonomous. The highest painting is no painting at all, as the highest acting, as readers of Proust will remember, is the absence of acting.

Small wonder Louis was regarded in 1974, when the magnificent British Arts Council exhibition was held, as a very great painter, as among the very greatest painters, as the one who had discovered the *tao* of painting. And small wonder, again, that my fellow critic David Carrier should write me with a certain amazement that "it's hard to think of anyone who was then high and has fallen lower." For in the end the paintings resisted the theory. In the end it is just impossible to see them as impersonal stains, as enhancements of paint and canvas, as "autonomous abstract paintings." It will be small wonder if the art magazines are anything but hostile in reviewing this exhibition of Louis's work. Louis has betrayed the critical establishment. He has faulted the premises of its practice. The decline is not in Louis. It is in a style of critical address misread as a decline in an artist. Louis is as great as ever.

How then are we to look at the works? Really as lush and beautiful, diaphanous and tremulous, washes of color that, like veils, reveal and conceal, affording the possibility of glimpsed mysteries they also refuse to disclose: majestic cascades of color. "Veils" was not Louis's generic title, nor were many of the individual titles his own. But the spontaneousness with which that title adhered to what I regard as his best

[*48*

works is itself evidence that something more than the paintiness of paint is being transacted in these huge spaces. The soft swags and falls of color are, standardly, cropped at the bottom, and the collusion between the sharpness of the cut and the fluidity of paint-fall is as acutely felt as the contact of sword and veil in a legendary demonstration by the Sultan Saladin of the sharpness of his weapon. At their worst the paintings are just pretty, and the experience like walking through racks of negligees at Bendel. But at their best and greatest they evoke experiences like massed flowers or sunsets.

This is just a beginning. It will be a while before we can say what these paintings are, but without our knowing very much at all, this is a greatly enjoyable show. Louis has confronted us with a module in the sphere of art, and the meaning of interpretation must be rethought against his marvelous achievement. That is the importance of the show. The importance of the work lies elsewhere. Wherever it lies, it is work that transcends its materials more than succumbs to them, and yields the kind of pleasure symphonic music affords.

—*The Nation*, November 15, 1986

John Singer Sargent

VISITING THE GALLERIES of Baroque painting at the Metropolitan Museum of Art one afternoon, some friends and I paused before Rubens's portrait of himself with his family, and reminded one another what a remarkable man he was. A painter of stupefying energy and force, he ran a workshop, listened to music as he painted, did the classical scholarship for cycles of paintings that required erudite references, conversed easily in six languages and discharged ambassadorial missions of great delicacy—his second wife, Helen Fourment, was delivered of his last child nine months after his death. One of my companions, the painter David Reed, said, meditatively, that most artists he knows strive to emulate Van Gogh: "Maybe we ought to try to be like Rubens instead."

I thought then of the balm it would bring those artists, uneasy with their intact ears and stubborn sanity, if they were to embrace an alternative model of the artist as cultivated, emotionally secure and at home in the world. Not even the disappearance of acceptably marginal real estate from our centers of art is likely to dissolve the mandatory artistic persona of the romantic misfit and lunatic genius. So if we use Van Gogh and Rubens as taxonomic markers, the few artists who volunteer for inclusion in the latter's class must resist considerable peer pressure and face accusations of shallowness and *embourgeoisement*. John Singer Sargent was among the unabashed Rubenses of art: urbane, polyglot, at home with the milords and millionaires from whose portraits—and those of their families and mistresses—he earned a handsome living; an extrovert, diner-out, clubman, traveler, marvelous musician and intellectual of sorts, unmarked to a singular degree by the darker passions or stronger drives of the acceptable bohemian. His life, with some exceptions, was a succession of successes, and reviewers of a recent biography seem uniformly resentful of a man who made it through life as an artist without much spiritual agony or material want, and who even died, painlessly, in his sleep. Against the psychopathology of the artistic spirit as we expect it to be lived out, Sargent seems to have been too happy to have been deep.

Still, those who hold briefs for the artistic benignity of suffering might ponder the fact that Sargent's one salient episode of serious reversal—the outrage that his great portrait of Madame Pierre Gautreau (*Madame X*) aroused when exhibited in the Paris Salon of 1884— had just the opposite effect on his career. The brilliant society portraits with which he will be eternally associated came after that, when he removed himself from France and set up as a sort of superficial Impressionist in England. Up to that critical moment he was a child of fortune but a very deep painter indeed, and on the basis of what he achieved in the early 1880s he might have gone on to be very great as well. The wonderfully opportune exhibition of the many sides and phases of his teeming achievement at the Whitney Museum of American Art offers us a singular opportunity to test our theories of the uses of adversity.

Sargent was trained, as it were, to be an Old Master. The Old Master style works from halftones backward to darks and forward to lights which, against the somber tonalities of the canvas, acquire a diamantine luminescence. Think, as example, of Rembrandt, in whose paintings a metaphysically brilliant light splits darkness like a sword and at the same time vests forms with such radiance that it is as though they were redeemed by some holy intervention and touched with grace. Each canvas executes a metaphor of redemption from shadow to light— as if the biblical moment when darkness was lifted from the face of the waters were miraculously reenacted in each biblical episode Rembrandt painted—and even secular episodes take on a kind of biblical intensity. The same amazing light defines special forms against the surrounding darknesses in the painting of Velázquez, and it was Velázquez above all whom Sargent, like the other students in the atelier of the fashionable portraitist Carolus-Duran, was encouraged to emulate. "Velázquez, Velázquez, Velázquez," Carolus-Duran said. "Study Velázquez without respite!" Sargent's first great works—I think, in fact, his greatest works—were done in that mood of darkness slashed and split by light that re-creates the inner force of the Spanish master. These were done in the early 1880s, in Venice, and in terms of their bravura and poetry they are among the most compelling paintings I know. One of them, the *Venetian Interior* of 1880 (or 1882, these works being evidently difficult to date with precision), has obsessed me since I first saw it, at the Clark Art Institute in Williamstown, Massachusetts, partly because of its depth and partly because of the disparity in depth between this early masterpiece and that of the familiar florid portraits through which we mainly know him.

The interior of *Venetian Interior*, as in the other paintings from the brief remarkable period, is a wide corridor that recedes sharply to a back wall where, through a doorway or grilled window, an intense outdoor light is revealed. The interior space seems to have a gentle phosphorescence of its own: the mauve and silver halftones give it a certain submarine quality, perhaps referring to the watery essence of the city of canals and lagoons, and the light is seen as through water. Within these dramatic spaces, shawled women sit, working at monotonous tasks such as bead stringing; or stroll, waving fans; or cluster in intimate groups, exchanging gossip. Doors open on either side, and, somewhat mysteriously, the walls are hung with pictures, as if the spaces had the architectural identity of galleries and the social function of waiting places for slender courtesans. In one of these pictures, a woman looks boldly out at the viewer, as if at a reluctant patron. There is throughout a subdued, suffused but unmistakable eroticism. Because the spaces have a light that is quiet in comparison with the enveloping light we see through the apertures, they seem enclaves of shadow in a world of radiance. This gives them their intimacy and their mystery. In a way, the interiors seem near of architectural kin to Velázquez's studio, as we know it from *Las Meninas*, where, as here, an opened door in the back wall allows in an abrupt golden light, as opposed to the white and mineral light with which Sargent invades his cavernous corridors.

These are not, of course, self-portraits in any obvious sense, but Sargent is present through the bravura of his touches. In the Clark's *Venetian Interior* a blade of light crosses the floor with incredible velocity. In the Carnegie Institute's *Venetian Interior* a flat blade of light is laid in a single sweep, while a vertical flash summons the face of a heavy Venetian chest out of the darkness. In the *Venetian Bead Stringers* three horizontal stabs of light constitute openings on the left; six vertical slashes cut a grille into the outer sky. Sargent is inside and outside at once, not part of the reality depicted but present in the depicting, where we are aware of his astonishing brio. The poetry comes from the desire to be inside among the women. In the *Sulphur Match*, from 1882, a tipsy Venetian leans her chair precariously against a wall, having let a goblet crash at her feet, while Sargent lights her dark partner's cigar (or pipe?) with a single flash of blazing white. The girl is unimpressed by this; Sargent is an intruder, hopelessly alien in this world he can only make visible. It is difficult to imagine a more vivid example of artistic—or sexual—alienation.

Sargent had the ambitions of a Jamesian hero: he wanted to be great as well as successful in worldly terms, which, in the economics of the time, required portraying the rich and powerful. And in his great portrait *Madame X*, he came close to achieving some of the erotic profundity of the Venetian interiors and making a fine fee. This time, of course, he and the subject were of the same world, and there is a familiarity, an intimacy, an almost conversational ease, implied in the relationship between the master painter and the great beauty he de-picts. Madame Gautreau, like Sargent an expatriated American, had made it to the top through her wit, her looks and her social strategy. Sargent portrays her as a creature of tense elegance, with a profile as sharp and precise as if carved out of some hard, brittle material: the pink ear conveys the cameo intentions in her outlined features. She wears the crescent-shaped tiara of Diana the huntress; she is a woman of predatory sensuality, whose black velvet décolleté and lifted flounce is her *costume de chasse*. The costume is as witty as her sly nose and brilliant as her gemstones. The painting provoked a scandal when first exhibited in Paris. The reasons are obscure, but rather than culmi-nating the efforts of a decade in a searing success, Sargent created a furor the like of which had not been seen since Manet exhibited his notorious *Olympia*. (I am touched that Sargent, together with Claude Monet, headed a private subscription to purchase Manet's masterpiece for an ungrateful French state: *Olympia* was not shown until 1917, and Sargent kept *Madame X* in his studio until 1905, twenty-one years after the debacle.) As a result, Sargent cut his ties with Paris, where the great promise of the Venetian years might have been fulfilled, and removed himself to England, which has been an artistic backwater at the best of times. There he turned into a rather superficial artist, the maker of dazzling portraits and dubious Impressionist studies. He tried to make contact with some deeper source of artistic meaning when he undertook the mural cycle for the Boston Public Library. But all light has fled from these turgid works; one feels, for all the glamour of his career, that he had made a profound mistake. The subjects of tragedies can also live happily ever after, the tragedy consisting in just that.

Sargent never lost the Velázquez touch, which is there for us to marvel at in the gallery of stunning portraits that is the heart of the show (even if a heart worn on the sleeve). I had the pleasure of Patricia Hills's company in walking through the exhibition on my second visit— Hills organized the show and edited the catalogue to which she also contributed some fine essays—and together we responded to the authority with which Sargent transacted a lavender sash or evoked a bow out of a few curls and dabs of white paint. No one alive today could show the flesh through thin fabric as in his portrait of Lady Agnew's left arm. No one alive today could, as in a scene of Venetian glass blowers, drag a brush across the canvas so that each bristle picks out a separate rod, and we see brushstroke and rod bundle in a single glance. Of Velázquez, Sir Kenneth Clark once wrote:

I would start from as far away as possible, when the illusion was complete, and come gradually nearer, until suddenly what had been a hand, and a ribbon and a piece of velvet dissolved into a fricassee of beautiful brushstrokes. I thought I might learn something if I could catch the moment at which this transformation took place, but it proved to be as elusive as the moment between sleeping and waking.

The elusive moment is that of the boundary between matter and art, perhaps between body and mind. But you can have that experience over and over in the work of Sargent. He really had the divine prerogative of lifting life out of paint with the turn of his amazing wrist, and it is, I think, a lost art. There is no Carolus-Duran any longer to teach us how. Spend some time studying the buckle on the belt of Mrs. I. N. Phelps Stokes, from 1897. And contemplate her white skirt, which falls in heavy folds to the ground. Sargent is said to have painted it over seventeen times, according to Hills.

But there is none of the poetry that left the work after the fiasco with Madame Gautreau's portrait, and that is so palpable a substance in the Venetian interiors that you will want to return to them again and again. Except for the portraits, in the years after 1884 the work seems to me dry and flat. Sargent tried Impressionism, but that is not a country for Old Masters, and I feel he had no internal understanding of what revolutions in touch and vision Impressionism implied. His watercolors have the look of examples of how to do watercolors, and if one did not know them to be by Sargent, one would suppose them resurrected from the annual of some provincial watercolor society. It was a style of depositing wash on paper that others could and did acquire. I find his drawings equally dry, for all the certitude of touch and his perfect draftsmanly control. In none of the work after 1884 do we sense any urgency of feeling or the presence of a soul.

What we sense, only, is the presence of a great arm, a genius wrist, the dazzle of a virtuoso performer executing, as on a violin, a composition written in order to make virtuosity possible—where the piece is finally about the playing of it by the rare talents capable of doing so in public, with confidence and flourish and flash. There are those who think that painting is what painting is all about, and for them Sargent should be the paradigm artist. I am not one who thinks that, but there is enough of what art is about on my view of it to make this exhibition a joy as well as a moral puzzle. If nothing else there is the pleasure of the menagerie, in which his lords and ladies, his flounced amazons, his opulent merchants and silken mistresses, his candy children and austere dowagers glare past us, as exotic specimens, from an upstairs our very downstairs antecedents could barely guess at.

—*The Nation*, December 13, 1986

Van Gogh at St.-Rémy

IT IS DIFFICULT to understand why the Fauves should have evoked so great an outcry at the Salon d'Automne of 1905 when, a quarter of a century earlier, Van Gogh appears to have been accepted with relative equanimity by the admittedly small number who saw his work. He seems to us fully as radical and innovative as Matisse or Derain, but I sometimes wonder whether his deep originality may not have been masked to contemporary perception by the decorative programs of Art Nouveau, which some of his stylistic emphases outwardly resemble. Thus his twisting vegetation, his flower motifs, his planes of intense and saturated color, his auraed suns and haloed stars, his baroque clouds and his single rural figures in flattened landscapes may have seemed of a piece with the commercial posters, the book jackets and magazine illustrations of the time, which must have found their way even to provincial places like Arles and St.-Rémy. Gauguin was cherished by the artists of the 1890s, preeminently. Bonnard, for his decorative virtues, and Van Gogh, too, who was in constant artistic symbiosis with Gauguin and the painters of Pont-Aven, may have been appreciated in just those terms. A good many of the paintings in the magnificent exhibition at the Metropolitan Museum of Art of the work of his final months, from May 1889 in St.-Rémy to July 1890 in Auvers, seem to have a lot in common with *fin de siècle* painting from Scandinavia to Vienna. And even today the presence of the Van Gogh reproductions in countless apartments the world over, testifying to the taste and cultivation of their occupants, is evidence for the decorative dimension of his work. Still, it is far easier to imagine ourselves part of the hooting Parisian crowd in 1905—or among the outraged Englishmen at the first show of Post-Impressionist painting in London in 1910—than to imagine ourselves taking Van Gogh in as a matter of course in 1889 or 1890.

It was only later, when Van Gogh began to be exhibited as a Post-Impressionist in the company of Cézanne and Rouault, Matisse and Picasso, Vlaminck and Derain, that he began to look eccentric, distorted and sufficiently puzzling to be regarded as part of an art-world hoax, an insult to sensibility and as inept as even the Steins and the Cone sisters originally found Matisse to be, or as we find CRASH and DAZE in our own permissive times. But by then theories were available to deflect outrage, insisting that these artists were not failing to create irrelevant illusions but were instead expressing emotions provoked by realities painters up to then had been content merely to copy. And Van Gogh's work soon became encapsulated in the familiar story of his tormented life, so the temptation must have been irresistible to see those mannerisms that are so peculiarly his own as to render his signature redundant—the twined forms, the pigment used unmixed from the tube, the heavy brushmarks, the urgency of figural contours verging on caricature—as symptoms of feelings of great intensity. What may have been invisible to his earliest admirers came to represent, to a later age, the artistic correlatives of the cropped ear, the swallowed kerosene, the chewed paint tubes, the pulled trigger and the tears, cries, shouts, howls—and silences—of a man who crossed the borders of sanity.

Beyond question there are, especially in the very last paintings, signs of severe emotional stress, for one feels in them the sense of a man losing control, almost in the way that someone drugged or drunk might exhibit diminished control in performing tasks quite within his power when sober. I have seen a sheet on which the great brain physiologist Karl Lashley wrote his signature with his right hand, his left hand, his foot, and with a pencil clenched in his teeth, demonstrating that we transfer skills learned with one part of our body to other parts over which we have precarious dominion: the signatures are readable but decreasingly authoritative. In a similar way, I think, skills may be transferred from one mental state to another, so that we can detect the hand of a master even when his reflexes are muted by stress or toxicity. Still, even if the paintings show severe problems of control, they show no problem of intellect or perception, and though Van Gogh was intermittently insane throughout this period, his work can in no sense be classed as art of the insane. There is none of the cognitive disorder, the hallucination and megalomania we find in the final mad letters written by Van Gogh's contemporary and philosophical counterpart, Friedrich Nietzsche, whose handwriting went nearly abstract as he slid into the shadows of total mental collapse.

If anything, some of Van Gogh's most controlled paintings evince his state of mind as patently as those which show a reduced motor security and optical certitude. For painting was the anchor he believed held him back from lunacy, and he often painted motifs with an exquisiteness of observation in order to demonstrate, to himself as much as to his doctors and attendants, that he was in possession of himself, even as a patient in a home for the insane. Consider the first work he did at the asylum of St.-Paul-de-Mausole, in St.-Rémy, a few kilometers west of Arles, which he entered voluntarily. It is a brilliantly observed segment of the asylum garden, an effort simply to render the marvelous forms of a stand of irises, botanically exact in furled blossoms and bladed leaves, with a carpet of marigolds behind them and, in the upper right-hand corner, what look like daisies in chartreuse grass. It is an early summer day, the light is full—there are no cast shadows—and this is a radiantly luminous work. And given what we know of the time and place of its execution, there are a good many things we feel about it that a mere painting of irises and marigolds alone could not elicit. To begin with, it does constitute a sort of proof—like an accused drunk treading a straight line—that the painter is in control of himself. Its beauty perhaps conveys the proposition that even in so unlikely a spot as an insane asylum loveliness can flourish, making the work an allegory for Van Gogh's own situation. So we may think of it as a brave piece of work, even an optimistic piece of work, and we can say, as a matter of psychological possibility, that the painting expresses courage and hope. Still, these assessments carry us no great distance into the painting itself. If painting were merely expression, in the sense of the outward display of internal states, there would be nothing more to say about the painting than this: we would respond to it as we respond in general to shows of bravery and hope—beautiful virtues—in ordinary human behavior.

From the perspective of expression, understood in this way, it is perhaps appropriate that the exhibition should end with the marvelously controlled *Daubigny's Garden*, as it begins with the study of irises, rather than with the frenzied, apocalyptic and perhaps barely controlled *Crows Over the Wheatfield*, which is often supposed to be Van Gogh's last painting. I think the latter is thought of that way because it seems a fit symbol of death, as though the hovering crows were waiting for the painter's body to fall at the point where two roads cross, like an emblem of Christian sacrifice. But it is not clear that there are last paintings as there are last words, or that a last painting should convey the meaning that it is the last painting, as if it were a kind of suicide note. *Daubigny's Garden*, though not as controlled as the irises, is certainly calm by comparison with *Crows Over the Wheatfield*. This is the comfortable precinct of a successful artist, Daubigny, whose wife is standing beside the garden furniture. In the foreground is a rose bed. There was a cat, painted out though visible in an earlier version, and in the upper right a Romanesque steeple rises into "the pale green sky" (Van Gogh's description). It is appropriate that this should be the last painting, as it is appropriate that *The Twilight of the Idols*, a work of supreme philosophical mastery, should be Nietzsche's last book, or that *Between the Acts* should be Virginia Woolf's. It shows all the hard-won control Van Gogh may have felt slipping away: as with Woolf, the thought of another attack, another bout of madness, was too much to bear, and he shot himself as a final rational act. Ending a life with the crows is too narratively pat, too much a matter of making the already myth-ridden life conform to a suitable artistic denouement. The Met's decision to end the show with *Daubigny's Garden* makes more sense, psychologically, though no one actually knows the furious chronology of those final works.

There is another and more pertinent sense of "expression," however, which has very little to do with the artist's feelings as such but which captures a good bit more of what must be the intention of Van Gogh's art and distinguishes it sharply from decoration. This is the sense in which we might say that a sign expresses a meaning or a sentence expresses a thought—not the speaker's thought, as a psychological reality, but the thought that the sentence is understood to express by other speakers of the language. And this notion of expression connects with what one must consider the limits of pictorial representation: the fact that a picture can show only what is visible, when the artist wants to express a thought that goes beyond what the eye can detect. It is a sense of expression that moves painting away from depiction as such, in the direction of language, and that requires the invention of visual devices for expressing what cannot directly be shown.

Consider the flamelike configuration of the iris leaves. I find this merely pictorially correct, just because botanically correct: that is the way iris leaves are and how they must be shown if we are bent upon recording their look. The flambency may be accentuated by Van Gogh's style, which consists in part in drawing the outlines and edges in a deliberate way that reminds one of Art Nouveau flowers or vines in decorative panels: *Irises* could easily have been translated into a cartoon for a piece of Tiffany glass. It is this that makes the painting look more decorative than it really is. There is nothing expressed by the flambency of the leaves, as something must be expressed by the flambency of the cypress trees in *The Starry Night* or in the stunning *Cypresses*, where the curling flames and flickers are willed, as we know from the drawing, and rise irresistibly to the heavens as though this were a burning bush and God's voice spoke directly through it. In Arles, Van Gogh had written, "I want to paint men and women in that something of the eternal that the halo used to symbolize and which we now seek to give by the actual radiance and vibrancy of our colors." The halo is a convention by means of which artists can give visual embodiment to nonvisual qualities, namely holiness or divinity; in Van Gogh's case these numinous attributes were transmitted by radiance and vibrancy instead. This means we must learn to read the meanings in colors, which never are merely just the colors that objects have, but signify moral qualities sensed by Van Gogh in nature and in persons. Clement Greenberg once explained the surfaces of Van Gogh's work as due to his finding what went on in the canvas more interesting than what went on in the world. This is certainly a false description of the world according to Van Gogh, and distorts his artistic intentions by subjecting them to a formalism as irrelevant as so many theoretical explanations of his work.

The sunflower, *tournesol*, was Van Gogh's favorite flower: Dr. Gachet brought a bunch of them to his funeral. His brother Theo wrote that they were, for Vincent, symbolic "of the light of which he dreamt in hearts as well as in paintings." But it must also have been a metaphor for the relationship of the worshipper to God, as if we, by some tropism of faith, were always face to face with divinity as the flower is face to face with the luminous source of its being. The turn toward the sun symbolizes Van Gogh's own voyage south, in quest of redemption, illumination, love and beauty. But Arles was a psychic disaster, a period of sustained frenzy that climaxed in the cropped ear at Christmas 1888; and when Van Gogh transferred himself from Arles to St.-Rémy, the intense metaphoric color had faded from canvases which are cool, as the iris bed is cool in coloration, and the expressive energy of the work is henceforward carried more by form than hue. So the flamboyant character of the cypresses, or of the olive trees, or of the mountains behind St.-Rémy, or of the wheat in *The Reaper*, or of the blue volutes and whorls around the preoccupied head in one of the last self-portraits, conveys a meaning. I do not venture an interpretation but only present this recurrent pattern as expressive of something objective but undepictable, referring past the boundaries of sight.

Sometimes it is ambiguous in which of the two senses a given work is expressive. There are many landscapes in which it is possible that the artist is under harsh duress, but it is also possible that the world itself is being shown as out of control, as though it were seething and churning, and the hills and fields were a thin and fragile membrane under which forces of immense blind power surge and could break through volcanically. And perhaps these paintings are in some degree hallucinatory. I think these ambiguities arise from a curious sense that came to me for the first time in a lifetime of looking at Van Gogh's work, that the actual presence of the artist's body is tangible in each of the paintings, in a complex relationship with the landscape as an extension of himself. Think once more of the irises. The painting feels as though painted from the bottom, following, as it were, the sequential position of the painter's head as he looked first down, then straight ahead, then up. So the world seems to record the upward curve of the artist's glance, from what lies at his feet through to what he sees at a distance when his head is held erect. Over and over, the world curves outward toward the horizon. When he is in control, we have a record of his glances. When he is losing control, the curve seems transferred to the world, fleeing away and up with a furious velocity.

In the greatest paintings here, both feelings are present. In *The Starry Night*, it is as though the painter is standing on some height, looking down at the roofs at his feet, and at the lower part of the cypress at the left. The tree does not look cropped by the canvas, but rather cut off by the limits of his vision. The tree begins its flaming ascent from the artist's lowest glance, and we follow it with him, almost as if we are present there ourselves and seeing through his eyes, as he

follows its ascent into the starry heavens. Here there are two movements, that of his head and eyes, and that of the tree itself, his movement and the movement of the world in perfect balance and harmony.
On the right the treetops roll away like waves to the mountains of the
horizon, with a promised light behind them. In *Irises* the movement is
entirely his, for he is in perfect control. In *Crows Over the Wheatfield*
the movement seems to belong almost entirely to the world, which is
abandoning him. The artist stands in the middle, just where the two
paths touch, one of them curving so sharply toward the horizon that
one wonders he could keep his balance. He looks to the left, then to
the right, and paths are curving away just as swiftly. Those paths barely
contain the seething wheatfields on either side. The tops of the wheat
are like dull angles with blunt sides. There are hundreds of these golden
carets which, toward the top, change color without changing shape,
turning into black, heavy crows flying upward to meet the pounding
black of descending clouds. The world is beyond him: he does not
know which path to follow, or if he can follow one. It is easy to sympathize with those who want this to be his last statement.

This is a crowded exhibition and tickets must be issued in order
to control the seething populace. The paintings are terribly lonely, filled
with the presence of the painter. Occasionally a single figure drives a
plow against the sky, or bends, like a swimmer, against the golden
waves of wheat. In one utterly amazing work we stand with the artist
amid a driving rain. For my own part I find it reassuring to be with
the crowd, pushing along, even if one sometimes feels the urgencies
of Van Gogh's universe transmitted to the crowd itself, as if it were a
field of human wheat. Some communication comes through: people
stumble out in tears. Try to deduce that from the axioms of formalism!

—*The Nation*, January 17, 1987

Oskar Kokoschka

IN MOST OF its occurrences in English, the verb "to draw" refers to one of the most fundamental modes through which we engage the world, the action of pulling—of traction or *ex*traction—and it would be surprising if there were not a similar meaning connoted by its more narrowly artistic use. To draw a sword, to draw a deep breath, to draw a conclusion, or blood, or a stubborn molar, to draw someone out or to draw out one's story—or to draw (and then quarter) a culprit, which meant to pull his intestines out—are all instances of the same primordial intervention, whose simplest examples would be drawing a wagon or perhaps a sledge. And since it is unlikely that the action of drawing a picture is so described because the draftsman pulls the pencil across the paper—or his Cro-Magnon predecessor a lump of charcoal across the stony surface of a cavern—the term must refer to something that takes place *between* the artist and the subject, rather than merely on the surface of an inscribed sheet. If true, this means that an archaeology of the concept might bring to light some very primitive beliefs about artistic power, what one might properly call "drawing power" (or "attraction") that would explain some of the magic associated with art, and some of the reasons that ancient writers found in it something dangerous and fearful.

Consider the word "portrait." Narrower in its reference than the word "picture," in the sense that something can be a picture of a generalized woman or tree or apple without representing any specific woman, tree or apple, a portrait is a picture of a particular individual.

Accordingly, it would seem that a portrait must exemplify the pictorial relationship most completely: it must resemble its subject as closely as possible. But there is a darker ideal carried by the etymology of the term, which means "draw forth" (from the Latin *pro-trahere*), as if through an act of metaphysical extraction, the person were drawn forth onto or "captured by" the paper. It is possible, that is, to imagine a theory of drawing in which the sheet draws the form from the subject as a poultice draws out an infection or a cold compress draws out a fever. It is as if the artist had the singular power of inducing, by magical transport, the essence of an object, its formal reality, to materialize on some alien surface. In such a view, drawing would primitively have been conceived in much the same terms as we conceive photography, as the capturing of emitted images by the transmission of light. Fox Talbot, the inventor of photography as we know it, spoke of photographs as "photogenic drawings," and one of his publications was titled "The Pencil of Nature." But portraiture must have involved an even more mysterious achievement, the drawing forth, as it were, of the inner self or soul, which, in medieval representations of dying, is shown issuing forth from the mortal's mouth, to be caught, like a fish, by waiting demons or angels. Portraiture may then be a kind of anticipatory dying—one puts one's soul literally in the hands of the artist—and this perhaps accounts for the primitive awe of artistic power. Being portrayed—drawn forth—is the exact inverse of being possessed, hosting an alien self. Art and exorcism then are cognate exercises.

The two conceptions of portraiture—that of exact replication and that of mysterious drawing forth—are conveniently illustrated through two marvelous exhibitions of great portraitists, John Singer Sargent at the Whitney Museum and Oskar Kokoschka at the Guggenheim Museum. Sargent's personages are, in Lucy Flint's words, "all face and fashion," shown as they appeared or wanted to appear, as if they had stood before a mirror in which they composed their features, put on their best face, arranged their garments to suit themselves. But Kokoschka's subjects really look as though they had been extracted, quivering, from their shells, like crustaceans, and are shown with a kind of psychological nakedness: exposed and vulnerable, as if deprived, through a ruthless extractive action, of the protecting carapace of manner and convention. It is exactly as if they had given up the ghost, which had paused before passing on to eternal stations, for a memorial mug shot.

[64

Oskar Kokoschka

The two ideals of portraiture correspond to two conceptions, one of them quite archaic, of representation. The first is that a picture is a copy (and the thesis that the artist "draws" the form from the model guarantees the kind of resemblance that holds between footfall and footprint). The second theory holds that the subject is really present in his or her picture, as the saint was believed to be literally in the icon, which was made holy and potent for just the same reasons that a relic was holy and potent. This view of magical re-presentation was widely subscribed to in Byzantine art; it explains why iconoclasm was so powerful a movement in Byzantine theology and politics, and it offers us a theory of the artist as magician rather than as a mechanism for reproducing form, a kind of living camera. It is striking that the three great portraitists of the recent exhibition Vienna 1900 at the Museum of Modern Art—Klimt, Schiele and Kokoschka—perceived themselves as engaged in magical transformations. This is hardly to be wondered at in view of the deep penetration into Austrian consciousness of beliefs and attitudes from the Ottoman Empire, itself in complex symbiosis with Byzantine civilization, which it conquered and absorbed.

In my review of Vienna 1900, I described how Klimt sought to transform men and women into elaborate jewels, exactly in the spirit expressed by Yeats in "Byzantium." Schiele was more sinister: one feels that in his portraits people have been made into specimens, dried and mounted, and displayed on the page like exotic insects or preserved flowers. Kokoschka sought in *his* subjects precisely what he failed to find in the famous elaborate doll he had fabricated to resemble his tempestuous lover, Alma Mahler—a soul. It was precisely as if he had the power of drawing souls out, perhaps to use them, like a fearful doctor, to bring inanimate objects, like dolls, to life. Art in Vienna was something that took place in a world according to *The Tales of Hoffmann*, and belongs to the same flickering sorcerers' atmosphere that we find in *Dracula* or in *Frankenstein*, or in the workshop of the sinister doll maker of *Coppélia*. And Mittel-Europa sensibility, so remote, after all, from the salons of Mayfair or the country estates which provided Sargent with his artistic habitat, inevitably belongs to a consciousness altogether different from anything we can understand if we think of pictures as simulacra of the outward forms of things. When he was a wild young artist, Kokoschka liked to pose with the figures in the waxworks museum of Vienna and suddenly leap out to terrify the visitors impressed with his lifelikeness. The crossing of the boundary between effigy and life defines the mentality that expressed itself in so morbid a prank.

I advert to the presuppositions of this curious mentality in order to make plain that the early portraits by Kokoschka—of "OK," as he jauntily signed them—are, however great, not necessarily more searching or revealing than the portraits of Sargent, but belong instead to a different conception of art altogether. That his portraits are face and fashion is as much a criticism as a description of Sargent's images, but it is not clear that what OK shows us goes more deeply into the individual than what Sargent fails to show. Ludwig Wittgenstein, that renegade Viennese, argued that the human body is the best picture of the human soul, and that nothing is intelligibly interior which lacks an external criterion. So character has to be something that can be seen, and the Sargent style, accordingly, must be deepened rather than abandoned if our intention is to display character. OK's portraits give us less a depiction of subjective states than a kind of reduction to a ghostly essence, and it is far from clear that this is the reality of the person in question. The philosopher Bernard Williams, in a study of ethics, once remarked that there is something deeply fallacious in the view that character emerges through adversity, that the true self shows after being adrift for ten days without food or water. We really are the way we are seen in normal circumstances, whereas OK shows his subjects in situations that seem so extreme, metaphorically at least, that it is impossible to reconstruct what they are supposed to be doing.

Consider, in this light, the celebrated matrimonial portrait of Hans Tietze and Erica Tietze-Conrat, of 1909. The stunned couple is shown from the elbows up in what looks like a smoldering and wasted landscape: it could in fact be hell. Erica's eyes are dazed and unseeing, her face is spectral: she looks as though she has gone through some terrifying trauma. Hans is shown in profile, his gaze inward. Their scorched hands are held as if seeking warmth from some fire. Or they are like the hands of the dumb, transmitting signals we cannot read— but the couple is not looking at hands, or at anything, so the fingers gesticulate emptily or perhaps redundantly, as if their oneness is so total that each knows what the other means without the other having to say it. So perhaps it is a portrait of the marriage bond, and if so then the surrounding embers dramatize the emotional truth that they do not need the world, and that its emptiness, or even destruction, is something to which in the fullness of their presence to one another they are indifferent. There are some cryptic scratches through the paint, a sun, perhaps, which we can see to be radiant even if we cannot see its radiance, behind Hans's shoulder. Behind Erica's is a scratched sort of rainbow. Sun and rain, light and water—these may be marriage symbols. It is a hermetic, powerful work, certainly one of the great double portraits, and OK, then twenty-three, was never to surpass it. Its period was the period of his masterpieces, all portraits of drawn and agitated, painfully sensitive subjects whose nerves seem all on their surfaces, aristocrats and intellectuals painted with the supreme confidence of an artist secure in his genius.

OK, one feels, never struggled with his art, but took his powers more or less for granted. The means were always at hand to do what he wanted or needed to, and there is, accordingly, none of the concern with the reinvention of painting that has been the epic of Modernism. *Two Nudes* (*The Lovers*) of 1913 is marked by a transitory Cubist mannerism, but for the most part there is little reference to other art in his painting, or any self-reference, for that matter. And although, like every artist, OK responded to influences, one feels in every case that the canvas reflects the subject and the subject is seen through the gestures summoning it to the canvas—drawing it forth—so that the paint is the visible history of summonses and incantatory gestures. The astonishing *Self-Portrait*, of 1913, with the long gothic face and the huge luminous eyes, is filled with marvelous energized sweeps of paint—the intense broken halo in blue pigment is something to which I return and return—but the hand that executed all this is not shown: what is shown is the artist's left hand, pointing to his breast, as if saying, "He whom you see did this." But he looks, as all his subjects of the period look, amazed, stretched, transported, as if he had survived some unimaginable trial and had emerged, resurrected as art, just like the metallic figures in Klimt.

OK was the only major artist to survive Vienna 1900—he lived through ninety-four turbulent years—and he became a kind of ghost in his own life, a restless and driven person, traveling endlessly across borders. He became a literal exile during World War II, but there is a sense in which exile was his standard condition, once he had left Vienna, and though his remarkable reflexes and hooked glances never abandoned him altogether, he never again had, in my view, the strange air of Vienna to give authenticity to the possibility of drawing forth, of painting as a black art and a form of magic. In an art world in which painting was picturing, something was lost even if the paintings are often wonderful. They become, more and more as we follow him through the long cycles of his life, signaled by the descending helixes of the Guggenheim Museum, mere responses to the surfaces of the world, addressed across a certain distance. And the deep, enchanted connection between him and his subject weakens and withers away— until at last he is merely a kind of witness, a disembodied painterly consciousness, and the works correspondingly turn thin, almost weak at the end, pale washes and skinny, uncertain lines, portraits in the conventional sense.

—*The Nation*, February 7, 1987

Hans Haacke and
the Industry of Art

THE ARTIST Hans Haacke achieved a qualified martyrdom in an era generally supposed to have been one of total artistic permissiveness, at the hands of an institution hardly calculated to confer such status on an avant-garde artist seeking to press back the limits of art. Those inauspicious circumstances notwithstanding, an exhibition of Haacke's work was canceled, on the grounds of artistic impropriety, six weeks before it was to have opened, in 1971, at the Guggenheim Museum in New York City. It was annulled by Thomas Messer, then as now director of the Guggenheim, who also discharged the curator, Edward Fry, for persisting in championing an art indexed as unsuitable. The work that chiefly offended was devoted to the activities, over a twenty-year period, of a rapacious real estate operation in New York, and its repression demonstrates that even then, in 1971, real estate had replaced sex as the locus of dark practices and charged fantasy. Anything in the sexual line could be treated with artistic impunity (except perhaps as an advertisement in an art magazine), but it is a tribute to the precociousness of art that a desecration was perceived before it was recognized that housing had become sacred. Haacke had found his way to the heart of the future, and Messer intuited that the heart must be shielded. It hardly matters that the controversy was deflected onto the plane of aesthetics. Messer, who would have represented himself as defending the purity of art, was in reality defending the sanctity of an industry that was soon to transform the imagination in ways undreamt of by art. Haacke, who consistently represents himself as bringing to consciousness the fact that art had become commodified, failed to see that art and real estate had begun to replace one another in the general scheme. Artworks indeed have sunk to the level of commodities. Investing in art futures has become the truth of the 1980s. It is real estate that has taken the place art once knew.

The banned work bore the flatly descriptive title *Shapolsky et al. Manhattan Real Estate Holdings, A Real-Time Social System, as of May 1, 1971.* And even though the "as of May 1, 1971" made an unmistakable revolutionary reference to May Day, the piece itself carried out the severely didactic and informational intentions of the title: it looked, when assembled, like a project executed by earnest students in partial fulfillment of a higher degree in urban studies or applied economics or managerial science. The bulk of the work consisted of 142 photographs of as many pieces of property in Harlem and on the Lower East Side of Manhattan, together with 142 "data sheets" giving the actual addresses of the photographed sites, block and lot numbers, lot size, building code, holding title, corporation address, date of acquisition, prior owner, mortgage and assessed tax value, and the like. Two maps, showing the locations in Manhattan of the 142 pieces of property, completed the work, together with six charts collating individual properties and proprietary corporate and individual owners. Those and only those corporations were displayed that included a member of the Shapolsky "clan" or that had relevant dealings with a member of that clan. The research was painstaking, culled from the New York County Clerk's office, and absolute accuracy, while not guaranteed, was aimed at. It really was a "real-time social system," and the Shapolsky Group was singled out for artistic celebration because in 1971 "it represented the largest concentration of real estate under the control of a single group" in New York.

The work has something of the quality of a Leporello from some shady agency, itemizing the acquisitive histories of a Don Giovanni of the Tenements; as with seductions, sheer quantity carries a legendary weight in the action of cataloguing. On aesthetic grounds I am uncertain whether the intensity of the work might not have dissipated in the rarefied Guggenheim spaces. The work would gain, it seems to me, when all 292 components are densely assembled, rather than spread out along the ramps or punctuated by the alcoves with which any exhibition at the Guggenheim must deal. Such considerations cannot be irrelevant to *Shapolsky et al.*: the use of the typewritten format for the data sheets, the use of the kinds of photographs an insurance representative might take, the absolute absence of comment or flourish, let alone of political slogan, convey a rhetoric of objectivity, detachment, bureaucratic fidelity to fact. The work is as if it were destined for the boardroom of Shapolsky and Company, if it had a boardroom. Its dullness is part of its excitement.

In the early 1970s, a number of artists were dealing in "systems theory." Helen and Newton Harrison, for example, showed works at the Ronald Feldman Gallery which detailed the operation of a desert reclamation project. Haacke himself executed a "Rhine Water Purification Plant," in which water from the polluted river was filtered and passed in and out of a tank of goldfish (the Harrisons too employed fish in their project). The characteristic systems-theory work aspired to scientific exactitude and often enlisted scientists as collaborators: what one saw in galleries would be mock-ups, flow charts, overlays on photographs, schematic drawings, diagrams. Any of this could have been shown without comment at the Guggenheim. It was the fact that *Shapolsky et al.* represented the aggregated real estate holdings of a living owner that engendered the resistance and final prohibition on the part of Mr. Messer, whose recorded testimony emits inky clouds of metaphysical reasoning, as if by a philosophical squid, in defense against a perceived predator. The work was "not a self-contained creative object." It suffered from "designating real people." It had "an ulterior motive." The director clearly found himself in the desperate and unaccustomed position of formulating a philosophical theory to keep out of museum precincts a work that might be taken to call into question a corporate presence that, as Haacke was to recognize, *constitutes* the atmosphere of the museum today. Messer's heroic act was to attempt to stifle a form of consciousness that Haacke had not yet understood it was his mission to awaken. It was a dramatic moment in the history of recent art.

It is difficult to know what the reception of the work would have been on the part of the troops of schoolchildren or tourists who visit the landmark museum on Fifth Avenue, but my guess is that the Guggenheim would have stood empty for the show's duration, except by inadvertence. It would be a resolute aesthete indeed who sought in Haacke the pleasures one ordinarily hopes to find at the Guggenheim. And it could hardly have startled the resident visitor, should there have been any, that large-scale slumlords were abroad in the land, or that among the slumlords someone was the largest. Whatever the effect of viewing the work in 1971, it could not be anything like what it is in 1987. The work may be seen in the first major retrospective accorded Hans Haacke in the United States—Hans Haacke: Unfinished Business, at the New Museum of Contemporary Art in SoHo. The show, consisting of eleven pieces, will travel to the Mendel Art Gallery in Saskatoon, Saskatchewan; to the Museum of Contemporary Art in La Jolla, California; to the Lowe Art Museum in Coral Gables, Florida; and to the Everson Museum of Art in Syracuse, New York. But nothing will parallel the experience of viewing it a stone's throw, as it were, from the bulk of the buildings and sites Haacke documented sixteen years ago. It is impossible to see these houses on Eleventh Street or Third Street or Eighth Street as squalid today. Today the East Village is the Scene, and a nondescript apartment on any one of those streets is not to be had for less than 200K—with luck. Look at the price Shapolsky et al. paid! A few grand! Look at the interest rates—6 percent or less! It is a fairyland for the space-starved, and I saw couples looking longingly at buildings rendered delicious by what has happened in the Manhattan housing market in the years since 1971. Shapolsky et al. emerge as visionaries. At a time when the only question facing Harlem is when it is going to fulfill its destiny as a prime residential area, it is difficult to feel the sort of indignation the work was intended to inspire. Its ulterior intentions have been subverted by the times. One thinks of the opportunities missed, the houses to be had for a song. One might almost expect Shapolsky et al. to acquire *Shapolsky et al.* as evidence of its founder's sagacity (I see that of the edition of two, one is unsold), or even, as a corporation, to fund an exhibition of Haacke's once *contestataire* artworks as a gesture of self-celebration.

The ascension of real estate to its present position of cosmic glory may have robbed *Shapolsky et al.* of its original political point, but it helps dramatize a deeper point that has come to be central in Haacke's evolving project. When business products elicit the attitudes appropriate to the appreciation of art, we may better perceive that art itself has increasingly become a business product, and that the museum, while still requiring the ideology of disinterestedness curators insist on, has been subtly transformed into a showroom for classy investments. It cannot be too heavily stressed that the concept of pure spirituality is indispensable to the commodification of artworks. Haacke's *Manet-PROJEKT '74* (not exhibited here) was proposed for an inter-

[72

national exhibition to be held at the Wallraf-Richartz Museum in Cologne, West Germany. Manet's exquisite *Bunch of Asparagus*, painted in 1880, one of the museum's proud possessions, was to be displayed on an easel, surrounded with placards describing its owners in sequence of acquisition until the work was purchased for the museum at the initiative of Hermann Abs, head of its Kuratorium (i.e., "Association of the Friends of the Museum"), in 1968. Abs's placard listed the nineteen boards of directors of which he was a member, and the project was turned down on the ground that Abs's effort here was purely disinterested and that none of the facts listed on the placard, presented with the noncommittal directness of a reference work but thick with innuendo, should be allowed "to throw even the slightest shadow on it." "A museum knows nothing about economic power," the Wallraf-Richartz director wrote in the manner of Thomas Messer: "It does, indeed, however, know something about spiritual power." The final placard catalogued those who raised the purchase price (a steal at $250,000): some eighty-five banks, corporations, business enterprises and commercial institutions. The museum—any museum—clearly knew enough about economic power to round up the funds needed to make a major acquisition. The question is, what was in it for the donors? What makes art good for business?

That art is believed good for business is thematized in a number of Haacke's works, for example *On Social Grease*, from 1975, composed of six plaques, each bearing a relevantly pointed quotation from Douglas Dillon, Nelson Rockefeller, Frank Stanton, David Rockefeller, Richard Nixon and Robert Kingsley (founder and chairman, Arts and Business Council, New York). The quotations on art and business form part of an artwork about art and business, whose collaboration began to take on epidemic dimensions in the 1970s and continues in our own era. It is not a matter of incidental interest that in the same period corporate art collecting began to assume serious proportions. The corporate curator might now invert the Wallraf-Richartz slogan: "The corporation knows nothing about spiritual power. It does indeed, however, know something about economic power." So it needs some specialists in spiritual power, and the division of labor between the brokers of goods and the brokers of spirit henceforward is essential to the protection of investments in art. The museum's spiritual authority is essential if the corporation is to enjoy any of the economic benefits of its investment in culture. Small wonder that museum directors and curators must insist on the purity of their institutions! Small wonder the museum must represent itself as the shrine of "objects of pure creativity"! It could not serve the ends of crassness if it were perceived as crass in its own right. The relationship between museum and big business is our society's version of the symbiosis of church and state in the great era of exploitation in the name of holiness.

At some point it was recognized that the demand for appreciable artworks—in both senses of the term—was seriously exceeding the supply. There are only so many Manets around, only so many Seurats (another of Haacke's works is devoted to the acquisitional history of Seurat's *Les Poseuses* [*Small Version*]). The response to this, in the 1980s, was the effort to augment the supply by according spiritual status to a number of artists on condition that they look important enough for the serious (read: corporate) collector, and from this time forward the Important Look became an urgent component of contemporary aesthetics, usually defined in terms of size and quantity of pigment, used thickly to connote extravagance, or thinly to connote preciousness. It was inevitable that Haacke should devote a work or more to the interventions into the spiritual marketplace of the firm of Saatchi and Saatchi, publicists of world importance, who are also collectors of contemporary artworks tailored precisely to accommodate the new aesthetic-economic demand.

Charles Saatchi, according to Haacke, was "the driving force" behind the establishment of a group known as the Patrons of New Art Committee, which played the same role in relation to the Tate Gallery as the Kuratorium did in relation to the Wallraf-Richartz. The difference was that the Patrons of New Art helped ("helped") the Tate acquire the newly minted hot artists the Saatchis had acquired in depth. In 1982, the Tate exhibited eleven paintings by Julian Schnabel, nine of which were owned by Charles Saatchi and his wife, Doris. The Tate conferred the needed spiritual authority on the artist, whose values (read: prices) were secured and enhanced. Schnabel is now one of the blue chips in the art-industrial complex, others being (for example), a number of Italians who were displayed in the early 1980s at the Guggenheim, to the dismay of everyone who did not realize that a number of collectible painters needed a quick spiritual fix. Haacke's *Taking Stock (unfinished)* of 1983–84 is in the idiom of an official portrait of Margaret Thatcher, whose campaign was handled by Saatchi and Saatchi. Enthroned on a chair embroidered with the figure of Queen Victoria, Thatcher is posed against a bookcase containing bound volumes, each of which bears the name of a client of what is referred to in London as Snatchit and Snatchit, including the Tate Gallery itself. On the top shelf are cracked plates bearing portraits of Charles and Maurice Saatchi, an iconographic reference to the notorious broken crockery that has become the emblem of the early Schnabel. *Taking Stock* is dense with iconographic allusion, so alluding also to the doctoral dissertations to be written on it and to the role of the art-historical establishment in the future preservation of surplus value.

Very few who follow the auction scene can be unaware of the astronomical prices brought down last year by modern paintings. As the market widens, inflation is as inevitable as it is in the economy when money is issued to meet increased demand for credit. And inevitably, as prices rise at the boundaries, they rise proportionately in the center. A better investment than a certified masterwork is difficult to imagine today: Rosenquist's *F-111* has appreciated a hundredfold in just over twenty years (from $22,500 to $2.09 million). It was well beyond the purchasing power of the Whitney, whose director, Thomas Armstrong, dropped his paddle after his bid of $1.1 million was passed. So one hopes the Whitney will have a group of friends who will bring the painting into the museum, in which it by rights belongs. The museums themselves are needed to certify the investments with which the market is made.

Meanwhile, the trickle-down effect is a feature of contemporary life. The combination of cash and spirituality is irresistible, and the proliferation of art galleries in such enclaves as the East Village of New York has been a means to the abrupt gentrification of the area, including the holdings of Shapolsky et al., just around the corner from the New Museum itself, which by its presence there testifies to the transformation. Haacke's work is often crude and heavy-handed. His show is in part supported by the National Endowment for the Arts, the cultural wing of the governmental corporation that has brought you . . . Still, he is on to something. It is as though he misunderstood the Modernist imperative that art should be about art. It is just that what Haacke says about art was not that dimension of art on which Modernism had its eye. Others had their eye on it, however, and as the auctions emphasize, their inheritors are enjoying the benefits of a wise financial decision.

—*The Nation*, February 14, 1987

David Salle

IN THE CRAFT or sullen art of David Salle, I sense a punk and glowering indifference to criticism so total as to constitute, for me, the chief if not the only critical interest of his *oeuvre*. It is not so much that the work is bad as that its badness seems willed even where there is no clear sign that the artist could do better if he wished to. The work appears to situate itself beyond good and evil, hence outside the sphere of critical discourse altogether, so that such snarls as Oh yeah? So what? Says who? Who cares? What difference does it make? Fuck off! are all the response I would anticipate to my questions and objections. It would be like engaging in moral disputation with an adolescent. But then an art this resolutely other and opposed acquires the curious strength of its negations. It is not the negation of erasure, as with Minimalism. Minimalism sought to identify and isolate the bare, essential purity of art—what remains after we have stripped away all the accidents of charm, depth, vividness, narrative and feeling—but it meant the essence to be that which underlies all the painting or sculpture the Minimalist regards as irrelevantly ingratiating or even profound. Minimalism belongs to the same history, complies puritanically with the same imperatives, that have always defined art. Salle's negativity is of an altogether different and more ultimate order. Its nearest counterpart is the Nothingness discussed by Martin Heidegger in *What Is Metaphysics?*, a Nothingness that reveals the totality of Being by standing absolutely outside whatever there is. Salle reveals the boundaries of art by deliberately refusing to allow himself to be included within them. Alongside so complete a displacement of everything that has made art meaningful, Salle's compeer Julian Schnabel seems after all to be one of us. Like someone who has learned to give all the worst answers in a carefully weighted examination, Salle demonstrates a certain spectacular perversion of artistic intelligence: anyone this consistently awful acquires a certain reverse grandeur, like Lucifer. I clearly dislike Salle's work, but I admire someone who reveals the limits of the world in which my likes and dislikes can have some critical justification. There is more than one way for art to be a mirror.

The characteristic Salle confection has five components when fully equipped. There is, first of all, an appropriated image, usually from a work or a fragment of a work that has a locus in the history of art but sometimes a locus just in the stock of banal images of everyday life, a Christmas sticker for example. Then there is a component that looks, though painted, like a photograph in hideous monochrome, often of a nude or seminude woman displayed in a sexually humiliating posture. These two components are juxtaposed on large, or largish, panels and are overlaid, often, with limp and skimpy drawings marked by an utter absence of draftsmanly grace. The drawings look like the casual underpainting for an as yet unexecuted and perhaps abandoned work— as if their complete lack of interest were to be explained with reference to the fact that they are intended to be submerged by the painting to come. They also suggest that the work on top of which they have been superimposed has itself been abandoned, with the intention that the panel is to be recycled. But they have also the air of having been made by a passing vandal, for their vernacular is that of the wall or sidewalk scribble by a youth who is artistically illiterate but possesses enough talent to be able to draw a likeness, say, of Popeye. The fourth component is some object selected from among the objects of the *Lebenswelt*—a chair or table, or in one case a brassiere—attached in some fashion to the panel and giving the work a real third dimension. The final component is the title, which may resemble a scrap of overheard conversation. (*What Is the Reason for Your Visit to Germany?*), or the innocent pretentiousness of an art student's title (*Melancholy*), or a dimly surrealist label (*Muscular Paper or Shower of Courage*).

As a general rule the title will be as irrelevant to the components of the work as they are to one another. The pictorial components are arrayed somewhat in the manner of the elements of a rebus, in which the images have no apparent relationship to one another, but in which the words used to refer to those images form a coherent sentence when pronounced. Freud described such a rebus in *The Interpretation of Dreams*:

A house upon whose roof there is a boat; then a single letter; then a running figure whose head has been omitted. . . . The man is larger than the house, and if the whole thing is meant to represent a landscape, the single letter has no place in it since they do not occur in nature.

Salle's works present themselves as puzzles to be solved, and part of the tension they arouse comes from the viewer's quest for a coherent solution, which the work persists in frustrating. To be sure, there is doubtless an element of free association that explains the choice of concatenated elements, and Salle could perhaps describe to us what it is in his personal psychological history that explains their assembly in a single work—in which case we would relate to the artist somewhat as the therapist does to the patient, through the medium of the latter's interpretation of his dreams. But that would make the artist himself the subject of the otherwise diverse works, and the question is whether this then is all there is to the corpus, a kind of gallery of nightmares. On the other hand, I am not certain that this is the key to the works, which appear, rather, to be external disjunctions of disparate components brought together for the purpose of falling apart—a kind of tease. I expect Salle would be able to explain what compelled him to appropriate a landscape by Hobbema and jam it into the same frame with a monochrome depiction of what looks like a sappy photograph of the youth who was the model for Michelangelo's *David*, together with some stray eyes and sundry other elements, but I cannot imagine those reasons are what the work is about. The work, I think, is about nothing. To appropriate and misapply an image of Kant, the work conveys a sense of purposiveness with no specific purpose.

Sometimes the tease consists in making a meaning seem flatly obvious and at the same time so shallow that one feels obliged to reject it and press on for something deeper. Consider *Black Bra*, of 1983. The title in this case is literal: a black brassiere dangles, like a fetishist's trophy, in front of the panel, suspended from a rod. On the panel is a painting of a bowl of red apples, which is doubtless appropriated from somewhere, it being an art-historical problem to see from where. The bowl is placed on the forehead of a monochrome representation of a cropped female face, consisting of eyes, eyebrows and hairline. There seems to be a visual pun connecting eyes with apples, and apples with breasts, and breasts with bra in a network so silly and pubescent that one is obliged to suppose either that it is to be rejected or that the "meanings" of the less legible works are not worth pursuing. And this has the cumulative effect of erasing the concept of meaning as of not very great moment in Salle's enterprise, and leaving behind, like a detached grin, the empty concept.

There is a famous episode in *A Passage to India* in which E. M. Forster describes the echo that distinguishes the Marabar Caves. The echo invariably consists of the noise "Bou-oum" no matter what may have been the sound that produced it. You may say "I love you" or "God is one" or recite Gödel's theorem or simply fart, and you always get the same monotonous echo. It refuses to discriminate, and by so refusing it reduces all sounds to mere noise. And that is the way it is with Salle's images: they cancel one another's meaning until a certain dull hermeneutical emptiness settles over the whole. Usually it is a bit of luck if you know the source of a given image. I happen to know the provenance of one of them: a once well-known wry self-portrait of the Japanese-American artist Yasuo Kuniyoshi, which Salle uses in the left panel of a sort of diptych, the title of which is *View the Author Through Long Telescopes*. In a painting I saw in Pittsburgh, Salle took an image from Sargent. Thanks to Lisa Phillips's catalogue essay I know that the twinned grotesque faces in *Muscular Paper* come from a depiction of a clubfooted boy of 1652 by Jusepe de Ribera. There is the reproduction of a Giacometti bust in *Fooling with Your Hair*, which also shows some women, their legs spread, positioned like Mantegna's *Dead Christ*. These learned allusions are certain to flatter those who succeed in making the identifications, and to convey the impression that the artist has a certain art-historical learning. No doubt he does; I gather they must teach something at Cal Art other than how to make it in New York. But sometimes the images are of a stupefying banality, like the Santa Claus sticker in *Wild Locusts Ride* or the gruesome duck who looks as though R. Crumb drew a Mr. Hyde counterpart to Donald Duck as Dr. Jekyll. You get the sense that those images are as interesting to the artist as the others. When an artist chooses to appropriate banal images, one no longer is certain why he appropriates deep ones. I knew a man who formed one of the great postwar collections of Chinese art, but I discovered on meeting him that he was interested foremost in collecting and would perhaps have been willing to trade his collection for a really great collection of baseball cards or match-books. This neutralized the sense I might have had that Chinese art meant something to him. So Salle's images appear to provoke a certain standing "Bou-oum" in the hypothesized sensibility of the artist.

Not all the works have the full five components, and some make multiple employments of the same kind of component, but in the end it does not seem greatly to matter, for the works are of an overwhelming sameness, fully equipped or not. Even critics considerably more sym-pathetic to Salle than I, such as Roberta Smith of *The New York Times*, have remarked on a certain sameness in the exhibition currently on the fourth floor of the Whitney Museum of American Art. It is as though the artist has a kind of formula. It is not true, of course, that if you have seen one Salle you have seen them all, for what you would be missing from a single work is its sameness with the other works. With a single work you might seek an interpretation of a kind neutralized when you see the work in bulk. These, after all, are the products of what, updating the famous title of a book by the art historian Alois Riegl (*Spätrömische Kunstindustrie*), I term the Late Western Art In-dustry. And product recognition cannot be insignificant in a corporate world in which the ability to say "Ah, a Salle!" is as much a mark of having made it to the executive dining room as is the knowledge of how to eat asparagus or whether red wine goes with weisswurst. The ghastly palette, the slouchy drawing, the absent design, the churlish provocation of women pulling down their pants or pulling up their tops, are clear identifying marks, like the Mercedes-Benz trigram or the Izod alligator.

So what? Who cares? I do not hold it against an art that conveys such defenses, any more than I care that the artist should insist that he is serious. The art's entire interest for me consists in its rejections. But that does not keep it from being an exceedingly depressing ex-hibition. I was grateful to leave. Be grateful yourself, dear reader, that you are not an Important Collector.

—*The Nation*, March 7, 1987

Klee

"INVISIBLE GOD created the visible world" is a famous paradigm
of the Port Royal Grammar—a cunning example of how even an analysis of relative pronouns was not immune to the insinuation of dogma
in the seventeenth century. It expresses a thought that sprang vividly
to mind when I began to ponder a beautiful aphorism with which Paul
Klee opens a discussion of artistic creation: "Art does not render the
visible but renders visible." Klee had more than a touch of mysticism
in his artistic personality, and my sense is that we ought to seek whatever invisible content it was that he meant to convey by visible means,
much, I suppose; as the authors of Port Royal would have urged us to
see between the lines of the universe to the invisible presence that
accounts for its being and its form. One cannot emphasize too heavily
the degree to which the early masters of Modernism were seized by
spiritualistic preoccupations, and though Klee was scarcely as committed to occult revelation as Kandinsky, he was, after all, with Kandinsky, a member of the Blue Rider group in Munich, as well as his
colleague and neighbor at the Bauhaus. Kandinsky's book *Concerning
the Spiritual in Art* was among the most intensely discussed texts of
the era; and August Macke, another member of the Blue Rider to
whom Klee was particularly devoted, wrote "Only through form do we
sense the secret powers, the 'invisible God.' " Macke was Klee's traveling companion on his momentous trip to Tunisia. It was there that
Klee had an evidently profound experience in connection with color:
"Color has taken hold of me," he wrote. "I know that it has hold of

me forever. That is the significance of this blessed moment. Color and I are one." His friend and biographer, Will Grohmann, described Klee's pictures as a "penetration into the absolute." That is not the epitaph for an ace graphic designer.

It is difficult to perceive Klee's work in terms of a spiritual vocation for much the same reason that it is difficult to perceive Klee's work at all except as a somewhat coarse version of the sort of graphic design to which it gave rise; designs that would not have existed but for Klee's pictographic ingenuity have become the visual commonplaces of the age. We encounter them in children's book illustration, in high-class commercial design, and we see them in artists such as Saul Steinberg and William Steig, whose political and psychological translations of Klee's paradigms, clever as they are, remain but high exemplars of the cartoonist's aspiration: I am doubtful Klee would have made *The New Yorker* though he is the invisible maker behind half of its visible components. It is true, as John Russell recently observed in *The New York Times*, that "the legacy of Klee is everywhere," but his stunning success in defining a major idiom of our age has obscured his original intention and first meaning, making him look pale and derivative when judged against his own progeny: like Shakespeare, he seems full of trite sayings; or like Lord Burlington, whose architectural solutions so suited his times, he looks like a copycat of the style he originated. In any case it takes a wrench of imagination to perceive Klee's work as a powerful expression of a different order of consciousness altogether than that embodied in the work he influenced, whether in commercial or fine art.

Beyond that there is the fact that his paintings and drawings are tiny, scratchy and extremely comical, and so at the antipodes of the portentousness the somber concept of religious art evokes. But if scale, texture and humor partially define the visible face of his work, whatever it was he sought to make visible must have employed those as means, and it might be just as well to begin by thinking of those characteristics as signifiers in their own right, and then to see if we can read what they signify.

Klee's studio at the Bauhaus has often been described. One of its striking features, also present in his apartment in Munich, was the way its surfaces were strewn with small natural objects—shells, dried leaves, insect wings, pebbles, twisted roots—the detritus of the natural world, which might correspond to the detritus of the urban world assembled by Kurt Schwitters, whom it is instructive to see as city mouse to Klee's country mouse. Those scraps and bits of torn, used, discarded and almost invisible paper that Schwitters lovingly resurrected, giving them a second life in his *Merzbilder*, carry the metaphoric charge of the despised and the rejected that pertains to a religious transvaluation. They were literally as well as metaphorically lifted up by Schwitters, and enthroned in collages, where they acquire the almost comic presence of a supremely humble figure given a place among the elect. Klee's mysticism would not have been of that explicitly Christian order which ranks the last as first. What he must have seen in those tiny patterned objects—a pressed leaf, a discarded claw, a mottled stone— would have been a world in miniature, a projection onto its least parts of some vast ordered structure made especially visible there, or especially legible, if we think of the world as a system of what Berkeley called a "Divine Visible Language." "Glory be to God for dappled things" must have exactly expressed his feeling: "For rose-moles all in stipple upon trout that swim; / Fresh-firecoal chestnut-falls; finches' wings." The accidentalities in Klee's work, as when a smudge of ink adhered to a sheet when another sheet was pulled away from it, must be placed in that perspective.

And smallness appears to have belonged to that enterprise. As early as 1902, Klee wrote:

Imagine quite a small formal motif, and attempt a concise rendering of it. . . . That anyhow is a real action, and small reiterated acts will yield more in the end than poetic frenzy without form or arrangement. . . . I'm learning from scratch, I'm beginning to build form as if I knew nothing at all about painting. For I have discovered a tiny, undisputed property.

Small, concise, small, tiny; and "learning from scratch" almost seems a kind of pun on the sorts of marks, tentative and confident, that were to become Klee's artistic persona. And erasing everything one knew about painting, starting over again, sounds once more like the religious personality that has put behind itself the distorting apparatus of civilized life to face the world as if for the first time. In something like this way, I think, scale and style belong to the revelatory content of Klee's work when, in so much of what came to be influenced by his discoveries, it exists merely on the level of a seductive mannerism.

Grohmann records that Klee had a particular affection for snakes, with whom he enjoyed "talking" on his walks in Weimar during the first phase of the Bauhaus. Talking to a snake as if it were human seems to me connected with his wit, which typically consists of disarming frightening or menacing things of whatever makes them savage. The snake often appears in his work as an animated smile or an absurd wiggle, nothing to be scared of. Or he makes objects or personages that connote danger or dark power gently ludicrous. Who can be frightened, for example, by *Mask of Fear*, when one sees that it conceals two men who carry it, like a canvas shield, on tiny legs and funny feet, and notices that the arrow that sticks up out of its head makes it faintly absurd, or that the two lines that form the sides of its nose are like slender stalks that curve down at the top from the weight of the eyes, which look like flowers drawn by a child?

Or consider, under this aspect, the engaging *Twittering Machine*, a picture that again is obscured by familiarity, though for different reasons this time: it is one of the best-known treasures at the Museum of Modern Art. The eponymous machine is an endearingly inadequate contraption, conceived by some misguided inventor for producing twitters as its mechanical output. It fails, though the painting is clamorous with twitters: a quartet of screwy birds are standing on the looping shaft of the machine, like starlings on a telephone wire; and from their beaks come forth exclamation points, parentheses, an inverted question mark and an arrow—the visual equivalence, all punctuation and no words, of avian chatter. But the twittering is not produced by the machine, it just happens as a benign coincidence. The machine is inert. It consists of a crank attached to a drive shaft as thin as a thread, which barely engages with a spindle providently furnished with a flywheel, on the improbable hypothesis that the machine might rotate too fast and need slowing down. But nobody is turning the handle; the machine would in any case break down the moment it was turned, and probably it has been abandoned to the birds who find it a convenient perch. Klee is making some kind of point about the futility of machines, almost humanizing machines as things from which nothing great is to be hoped or feared, and the futility in this case is underscored by the silly project of bringing forth by mechanical means what nature in any case provides in abundance. Or perhaps he is saying it might not be a bad thing if we bent our inventive gifts to the artificial generation of bird songs. *Twittering Machine* is appropriately rickety as a drawing, enhanced by the cherished accident of lifted inked paper, and its colors are suitably innocent—pink and blue.

Klee

The wonderful exhibition of Klee's work at the Museum of Modern Art comes like spring itself after the harsh winter of David Salle and Hans Haacke. It consists of nearly two hundred paintings and watercolors and about a hundred drawings and prints. You are in for a treat, despite the crowds, and I felt that those who visited it when I was there expressed as much, for everyone was smiling. There cannot have been many smile-inducing exhibitions in recent months, but I think in this case the smiles were on the faces because they were on the pictures. Klee signaled the fact that a picture was beginning to be finished by saying "Now it is looking at me." "The objects in a picture look out at us," he said in a deep and famous lecture in Jena in 1924, "serene or severe, tense or relaxed, comforting or forbidding, suffering or smiling." (In his always astonishing work on aesthetics, Hegel wrote: "It is to be asserted of art that it has to convert every shape in all points of its visual surface into an eye, which is the seat of the soul and brings spirit into appearance.") In the spontaneous language of emotions, the smile is an acknowledgment of benign intentions and a sign that one is amused, and amusement itself is typically the substance of the relationship between viewer and work at which Klee aimed. The tiny joke implanted in the work detonates as a piece of agreeable metaphysics—one feels good in the universe—and reinforces a bond of shared values with the artist. Klee does whatever he can to lodge his points: there are the helpful arrows, like ushers for the eye, and of course the marvelous titles, which explain the meanings of the images and complete the joke. Sometimes the title is written twice, just in case we are in danger of missing it. It is inconsistent with so benign an undertaking that the works should be hostile or aggressive, or glowering and mean. One gets the sense of lightness that comes only from being in the company of someone full of surprising observations and witty responses and wonderful information and unforced affection.

In so intimate an art, it would be remarkable if there were not a strong presence of eroticism. There is a self-portrait of 1919 (the show is filled with self-portraits) called *Absorption: a Portrait of an Expressionist*. What one notices, first, is that it cannot have been executed in the usual way, before a mirror, for the eyes are tightly shut—so it is, as it were, a portrait from within, of how the artist feels about his own face. The face is so dense with concentration—so cut off from external perturbation—that it has no ears. Only an erotic fantasy, one feels, could absorb a consciousness so totally, and the truth of this fact is displayed: the closed eyes have the precise form of vulvas, as though he were thinking of stereoptical sex. In an earlier work scribbled almost as a precociously knowing child would have done, a couple is shown in a moment of flirtation. *Cunning Enticement* shows the male figure on the right, wearing the top hat and mustachios of the roué but otherwise naked; he has one leg lifted as a sign of overwhelming sexual desire, while his penis points, like an arrow, out of the picture to the presumed roomful of etchings. The word "liebe" curves out of his mouth. The female, on the left, wears only a touching topknot, and though she smiles demurely, her hands are on her crotch. In *Metaphysical Transplant*, a couple is shown in a posture of distant copulation rendered comical by the intense seriousness of their expressions. The male, whose mouth this time has the vulva form, has a body shaped very like a set of genitals, the end of the penis curved down, like a faucet, out of which some plump drip is being guided, by a circuitous arrow, into the extruded receptor of the female, which has rotated up, like an erection, to receive it. These are all terribly funny pictures, and though one hesitates to offer a pictographic lexicon to the works of Klee, one cannot help but feel that if penises are arrows, then they are kindly organs, indicative rather than penetrating, with the points there for purposes of direction rather than danger.

Klee led an epic life for someone so contemplative. To have been part of the Blue Rider, to have been a fixture at the Bauhaus, to have been singled out for inclusion in the notorious exhibition of degenerate art mounted by the Nazis—these are stages in the heroic itinerary of modern art in this century. He died in his native Bern in 1940 of a rare disease—scleroderma—in which the skin becomes immobilized, like a carapace: it is as close as the infinite possibilities of human pathology allows for matching the metamorphosis into an insect, which played so important a role in Kafka's famous story. Indeed, an essay could be written on the parallels between Klee and Kafka. Anyway, he remained productive nearly to the end, characteristically drawing angels. His alleged last work, unsigned and untitled, is a still life with a drawing—a picture within the picture. The drawing is ambiguous. It shows two angels, or an angel and a non-angel, the latter enfolded in the wings of the former. The two figures seem united by a smile. You might save a bit of energy for that profound and contemplative work before you leave the show.

—*The Nation*, April 4, 1987

Correggio and
the Carracci

SWOONING HAS NOT BEEN the prescribed response to artistic sublimity for a good century and a half, but in the period during which
pilgrims of taste and sensibility flocked to the cities of Italy in pursuit
of the aesthetic swoon, their transports would have been occasioned,
when not by Michelangelo or Raphael, then by one or another product
of the Emilian style of painting—Correggio, say, or Guido Reni. It is
perhaps as difficult to envision a rehabilitation of the swoon as it is to
imagine Reni once again assuming the preeminence accorded him by
the likes of Stendhal and the later Romantics. Modernism begins with
the repudiation of the swoonable together with the swoon, and my own
historical sense identifies its onset with the Pre-Raphaelite movement,
where what was rejected in favor of a certain formal rectitude and dry
clarity was precisely the art of Emilia-Romagna, the center of what we
might term the *Post*-Raphaelite art of Italy in the sixteenth and seventeenth centuries. During those two hundred years, and indeed, in
spirit long afterward, Emilia-Romagna, and especially its cities of
Parma, Ferrara and Bologna, functioned as an immense artistic heart,
pumping a steady, heady stream of painting into the ducal and eccle-
siastic precincts of the peninsula.

The musical equivalent of the Emilian vision in painting, particularly after about 1600, must be grand opera. The operatic spectrum
comprises the most extreme circumstances of the human spirit—death,
desperation, madness, disease, murder, treachery, thwarted passion,
acute loss, pathological jealousy, betrayal, destiny, revenge, the rape

of tenderness and meaning and the dark perversion of political hope—
an existential pathos so near the limits of emotional endurance that
only the most strenuous singing is capable of giving it expression. It
has always been a matter of some curiosity to me that until *Jesus Christ
Superstar* it had not occurred to operatic composers to exploit the vast
reserves of suffering in the mythic histories of Christianity, with its
crucifixions, visions, ascensions, spectacular martyrdoms of lovely
saints and conversions of lovely sinners. Opera's avoidance of what
one would think its natural subject matter is all the more puzzling
when one reflects that this repertoire of agony and redemption constituted the standard substance of Emilian painting throughout the
seventeenth century, when theatricality became an unavoidable strategy for meeting the obligations of meaning imposed on artists by the
conditions of their commissions. Perhaps the idea of holy librettos was
considered blasphemous because opera itself was regarded as a form
of entertainment until Wagner, who indeed crossed the line into operatic piety.

The Age of Correggio and the Carracci: Emilian Painting of the
Sixteenth and Seventeenth Centuries is an immense exhibition of some
two hundred canvases, some of them very large indeed, on view at the
Metropolitan Museum of Art, where it was expected to attract too
sparse and specialized an audience to have received the corporate fund-
ing it so greatly merits—a fact that tells us much about both corporate
support and the standing of Emilian art today. It is true that saints in
ecstatic transport and martyrs writhing over beds of glowing embers
or raptly awaiting dismemberment or beheading, especially when depicted with dramatic vividness and calculated affect, are very little to
the taste of viewers whose standards have been established in the austere galleries of museums of modern art. And even widely traveled
Americans are likely to have given Parma a pass, despite its fabled
hams and cheeses, its violets and *vino lambrusco*, and its dishes of veal
and eggplant parmigiana, for Correggio is no longer starred as worth
a detour on artistic excursions, and Parmigianino is known chiefly
through John Ashbery's famous poem about his self-portrait in a con-
vex mirror (which in any case hangs in Vienna). Perhaps the most
useful thing I can do in this column, if I am to encourage you to cross
the threshold of the gallery, is to sketch enough of the syntax of the
exhibition to enable you to know what you are in for. It is in fact an
enormously rewarding show, even if the paintings are displayed as if,

in a kind of sulk, the Met had decided to look like a provincial museum, simply hanging the works by school and in a roughly chronological order, on the assumption that only the already interested and informed would be likely to visit them.

The period covered falls into two ages, the later one beyond question the age of the Carracci but both of them, in a sense, the age of Correggio. A considerable stretch of the sixteenth century had elapsed before Correggio was discovered by the Carracci and made into a predecessor for the style of Baroque painting they invented, and which tended to dominate Italian art through the seventeenth century. That means that there is an entire aspect of Correggio to which those who were influenced by him in his own time were necessarily blind. It often happens in the history of art that a body of work is filled with latencies that are released for appreciation only through the retroactive illu- mination of a later body of art: think of what Monet's late paintings came to mean in the light of Abstract Expressionism. So the side of Correggio that was visible to his contemporaries is very different from that which was made visible nearly a century later. The style to which Correggio gave rise in his own century, a certain arch and contrived style known as Mannerism, was rejected by the Carracci. Mannerism was the advanced style of Europe in the 1500s, spreading like an international contagion from Italy to France and the Low Countries. Its greatest representative at that time was Correggio's fellow Parmesan and near-contemporary, Parmigianino, whose name would better characterize the earlier period covered by the show.

The first paintings one sees upon entering the exhibition are Cor- reggio's, two works that are at once exceedingly elegant and exceed- ingly emotional: a lamentation over the dead Christ on the left and a martyrdom of four saints on the right. In terms of the violent emo- tionality of the figures portrayed, these works really belong with the Baroque style, inaugurated perhaps seventy-five years after they were executed—"Circa Sixteen Hundred," to use the famous title of a book by Sidney Freedberg. But in terms of their delicacy and elegance, of the jeweler's virtuosity with which these scenes of severe agony are depicted, they belong with the Mannerists (the demonic goldsmith Cellini is the Mannerist artist par excellence).

So the structure of the exhibition is as follows: two ages are opened up in the gallery devoted to Correggio. You will enter the age of Man- nerism proper upon entering the next gallery, dominated by Parmigianino. Then one leaves Parma, makes a kind of detour through Ferrara, where a certain mode of Mannerism was practiced by Dosso Dossi, traverses a gallery given over to Mannerists of varying degrees of achievement, but where, on a distant wall framed by two doors, one sees the magnificent and epochal *Crucifixion with the Virgin and Saints* of 1583, an early masterpiece by the Bolognese genius Annibale Carracci. This work introduces a new age of artistic expression, that of the Carracci, which connects with the side of Correggio you left behind. The remainder of the show belongs to Annibale, his brother Agostino and his cousin Ludovico, as well as those who carried out the Bolognese imperatives. This show is full of marvels, and if you have penetrated this far you evidently have a tolerance for operatic painting and are in for some considerable treats. Chief among these, to my taste, will be the discovery of a great but virtually unknown artist, Bartolomeo Schedoni. At least I had never heard of him before, and that is like never having heard of Caravaggio, whose equal he is.

Mannerist art is insolently artificial, as exaggerated as high fashion. Its figures are as elongated and as improbably slender as models, with opulent, cold eyes, coiffeurs as intricate as cathedrals or wedding cakes, expressions of aggressive vapidity and porcelain complexions. In one scene by Parmigianino, St. Paul has been knocked off his exquisite silver horse, which flourishes a luxurious saddle blanket of albino leopard skin (a symbol of pride, as in Dante?) and reins of pink silk. The saint, half risen, is garbed in the finery of a duke's mistress, like a transvestite Hercules, and is situated in a fantastic landscape ringed by expansive blue mountains. His left hand delicately but vehemently pushes away the insistent luminosity of his vision, as a lady, concerned for her figure, would operatically reject a dish of sherbet. The golden light through which his Redeemer offers St. Paul the opportunity to turn his spaniel eyes upward illuminates a landscape in which, beneath an ornamental city, whippets tear at a fallen cerf, lions drink with dignity from a tiny stream and camels arch their Mannerist necks. (The elongated neck is a benchmark of Mannerism, as in *The Madonna with the Long Neck* by Parmigianino, unfortunately not in New York but well worth the trip to Florence.) The painting expresses the taste of courtiers and projects the preciosity of men and women who had internalized a complex etiquette, an intricate semiotics of costume and speech; who danced solemn pavanes to the music of lutes;

and who were responsive only to an art of pure contrivance. Indeed, one almost feels that the figures in these works are deployed as dancers—the Angel of the Annunciation in the painting by Bedoli hovers with pointed toes before a balletomane Virgin—and they wear the forced expressions of mimes, as if in order to keep true feeling at an aesthetic distance. It was wholly an art for connoisseurs.

It is not difficult to appreciate that Mannerism had finally to cloy, and that the robust Carracci should have made it part of their program to repudiate its premises in favor of a certain visual truth—small wonder Annibale painted butchers! Mannerism was art for art's sake if ever such an art existed, whereas the Carracci were bent on an art that was to serve ordinary human persons for ends more momentous than fragile delectations. Even so, it would be difficult to imagine a work more Mannerist in spirit than Agostino Carracci's *Portrait of a Woman as Judith*, which is said to have been commissioned by the subject's widowed husband. The husband's own head is portrayed as that of Holofernes, grasped firmly by its curls by his domineering wife, who wears a beaded dress without a spot of gore and waves her sword with the authority of a masochist's dream come true. Perhaps he meant only to say her death cut him in two.

Annibale's *Crucifixion with the Virgin and Saints* exactly answers to Freedberg's perfect description of it: "The scene conveys an instant effect of reality: persons who seem utterly ordinary, the nude Christ not excluded, are described to us with means that remarkably suggest the truth of their existence—heavy figures . . . who convince us still more that they reproduce an ordinary truth because they have abjured altogether the effects of artifice." Two things are being transacted at once in this deep work. It displays the emblematic image of Christianity, Christ on the cross, in a mystical relationship with saints who, for the simplest historical reasons, could not have shared a landscape with Jesus, but who are yet depicted with enough weight and reality to make the vision plausible. And at the same time it is making a statement about the art that it repudiates. It is partly self-referential, drawing attention to the way it shows what it does show.

This is not a mere matter of sixteenth-century style wars. The long shadow of the Reformation dramatized artistic activity in Italy with all the vehemence and urgency of late Baroque representations. And Mannerism took on a certain moral dimension in a world where the very existence of images was coming under iconoclastic attack, insisting on its own pure vision in the face of angry objections as an aristocrat might insist on observing the rituals of correctness when, and just because, mobs howled for his death outside the palace windows. That shadow was crossed by another one, cast this time by the Counter-Reformation, as the Church took measures to strengthen its control of the sacraments and the souls of its adherents. Catholicism entered a period of deepened piety, and in the closing sessions of the Council of Trent, in 1563, some fateful decisions were made that were to affect the practice of art in Italy through the century to come. The Carracci discovered how to meet the Tridentine mandate of clear and convincing, decorous and intelligible images that were at the same time to provide an emotional reinforcement to piety. Even Christ was to be shown as he really was: "afflicted, bleeding, spat upon, with his skin torn, wounded, deformed, pale, and unsightly." The visual psychology must have been this: we are caused, emotionally, to identify with the sufferings of saints and the Saviour, so that, vicariously reenacting their ordeal, our oneness with their sacrifice will be confirmed. Annibale's 1583 *Crucifixion* pointed the new way, and passionate agony passionately expressed became the artistic order of the day as the Church, through patronage and pressure, mobilized an army of artistic militants. Rome became the holy city of painted pain.

The willed artifice of Mannerism and the operatic pathos of the Baroque constitute heavy obstacles for modern taste, and since both are present in Correggio, it is to him that we must now return. It is appropriate that the exhibition should begin with him, and at the same time unfortunate that the first work to strike the eye should be the *Martyrdom of Four Saints*, in which both obstacles are present together. Two of the saints, on the verge of brutal demise, await the destiny of their decapitated peers with expressions of foolish rapture. The male saint, done up in monastic habit, exposes an improbable expanse of his delicately hacked neck to the sword being swung by his athletic executioner, who is wearing pretty boots and showing his snappy buttocks. His crony is running a sword through the flanks of the female saint, as dainty as a shepherdess, dressed for death in a kind of *costume du bal*. The severed head is being swung by its halo as a third martyrizer carries it offstage. I could not help but be reminded of Max Ernst's comically blasphemous depiction of the Christ Child being spanked by the Virgin Mother in the presence of shocked personages, and with sufficient vehemence that his halo has been knocked to the floor.

Correggio and the Carracci

My recommendation is that you use Correggio's stunning painting to liberate your historical imagination. Art historians will whisper that Bernini was greatly influenced by the autonomy of the drapery, and that his St. Theresa was doubtless influenced by the collapsed virgin in the companion piece—but pay them no attention. Correggio did not paint to be rediscovered by Bernini, and you must not allow him to be dissolved into a set of influences. There is a certain internal strangeness to the painting that remains once one has worked through the external strangenesses that inevitably separate us from the work of a very different time. It is like the mystery possessed by someone with whom one is perfectly familiar. Surrender yourself to that, if you can, accepting theatricality as a condition rather than an impediment, and you will be ready to proceed to Parmigianino and Bedoli, and then to the Carracci, like distant Alps, and beyond them to the great painters of Emilia: Domenichino, Reni and Guercino.

You will encounter no such problem with Bartolomeo Schedoni, two of whose works, of transcendent greatness, leap out to startle eyes that have had to adjust to alien illuminations and remote feelings. His *The Entombment* and his *Charity* address us with an immediate luminosity and power across historical distances they render irrelevant. Like Vermeer or Georges de La Tour or Caravaggio, painters of light, of the mystery of draped form and gestural clarity, Schedoni is an absolute, one of the great painters of all time, of his period but also of no period. In the presence of this revelation one feels a bit like St. Paul must have, and it requires an effort to work one's way back through the abruptly twilit work of seventeenth-century figures, twisting to obscure purposes in their shadowed spaces.

—*The Nation*, May 2, 1987

The Whitney Biennial, 1987

UPON SEEING Raphael's *St. Cecilia* altarpiece in Bologna in 1525, Antonio Correggio is said to have muttered, *"Anch'io sono pittore"* ("I, too, am a painter"). The phrase has passed into the language, but in Antonio's mouth it must have meant, among other things, that there were artists in Bologna capable of executing altarpieces as well as any of the hot painters of Rome. Much the same resentment is sustained by artists in Tulsa or Sacramento, Atlanta or St. Paul, when passed over in favor of some chic New York artist for a local commission: "We, too, are artists." And it must have been very largely in the spirit of Correggio's remark that Gertrude Vanderbilt Whitney established the Whitney Museum of American Art in a world where the adjective "American" was hardly expected to qualify the nouns of high culture. "American art" would have struck the knowing as affectingly pretentious, much as "American wine" or "American philosophy" had to sound faintly comical to European connoisseurs and illuminati, capable at best of evincing a patronizing curiosity as to what such desperate oxymorons might denote.

Giorgio Vasari suggested that Correggio might have been a better artist had he studied in Rome, little knowing that the style of painting he prefigured was, a century later, to conquer Rome artistically and to sweep the world. A comparably ironic reversal overtook Whitney's patriotic gesture. The gracious Whitney Museum on Eighth Street (today the home of the Studio School) was in effect like Plato's cave, with the works exhibited there the appearances and shadows of European forms. Who, visiting its mild displays of clowns, nudes, compotes of pears, harbors, gardens and fisherfolk—or, later, its Cubist, Surrealist, Expressionist and Modernist representations of regional lore and dignified, if abject, proletarians—would have guessed that America, and above all New York, was to become the absolute creative center of world art? The itinerary of the Spirit through history is filled with switchbacks and flip-flops, but few more acutely dramatic than those through which Correggio became a prophet rather than an eccentric, and Whitney a visionary rather than a mere enthusiast. Without ceasing to be a museum of American art, the Whitney had thrust upon it the artistic destinies of the world.

The Whitney has accordingly sustained stresses its founder could never have envisioned: like Gettysburg in 1863, or Woodstock in 1969, it intersected with forces vast in proportion to an original identity defined in unassuming terms. There is, in consequence, a spirit of coping and improvisation at its institutional core that distinguishes it and makes it finally more humane than its sister museums in New York, none of which has been required to rethink its mission by external cataclysm. The Guggenheim, the Museum of Modern Art and, of course, the Metropolitan project a distant, chill autocracy. But the Whitney is open, uncertain, erratic, innocent, friendly and almost Chaplinesque in its readiness to dust itself off after a critical disaster and resolve to do better the next time round. The 1985 Biennial sought to reconstitute on Madison Avenue the juvenile exaltations of an East Village disco. Howls went up from the critical community as from a chorus of martyrs. No good? O.K.! No problem! In 1987, the East Village having gone the way of knock-knock jokes and atomic beanies, the tone set by the Whitney's sixty-fourth invitational survey is something wholly different—more dignified, more rarefied, presenting the art of the moment as if it had stood the test of time and were being displayed in a wing of antiquities. 1985 distressed me; 1987 depresses me. I immensely admire the spirit of resilience and responsiveness the Whitney possesses as its institutional persona, and on the present occasion I believe it has succeeded in mirroring the times. The problem this year is not with the Whitney but with the world of art. What it shows is what, alas, alas, alas, there is.

New York is not today the absolute creative center of world art. There is no absolute center, the Spirit having moved on to other matters through which to realize its restless essence. What New York is is the absolute capital of contemporary art making, with some 60,000 hopeful art makers enduring its legendary inhospitabilities in the unlikely dream of making it big as artists. In the art world of today, there is no room for *petit-maîtres*: one makes it big or not at all, and each art maker seeks to achieve what I term "curatorial" art—art exactly suited to just such exhibitions as this. These works have no raison d'être other than to impinge upon curatorial consciousness. Moreover, there is really no longer such a thing as American art, save as an external matter of where or by whom a given piece of art is made: instead there is an international style of art making, whose capital is New York. The New York museums are the showcases of this style, even the Met, whose new wing, one feels, exists specifically for the purpose of getting in on the action. Even so, no museum is subject to such intense pressures as the Whitney, as *the* museum of American art transformed into the museum of international art making, as concentrated in America. The curator must pass through SoHo like Dante through Purgatory, where those who live in desire clutch figuratively at the visitor's garments.

But those pressures are but the consequence of the pressures of the times, which come from money—from what the cover of *New York* for April 20 identifies as "The Passion and Frenzy of the Ultimate Rich Man's Sport." Passionate and frenzied arbitragers and developers have lots of money and have come to want to spend it on art, and that, in market terms, must account in some measure for the 60,000 hardly less passionate and frenzied art makers concentrated here. There is an instructive article by Doris Saatchi in the current *Vanity Fair* in which that powerful collector celebrates Jasper Johns as "the heavy hitter and home-run king of his day," on the basis of the figures his paintings bring at auctions. One cannot detect, in Saatchi's discussion, any recognition that those prices may be internally related to artistic qualities in Johns's work, but then there is little doubt that price obscures aesthetics today as the chief item of what used to be called art talk.

Now, at one point the rich needed the curator as artistic adviser, much as the dealer once needed the museum as the final arbiter of artistic excellence. But lately the museum cannot afford the paintings it requires if it is to execute its various cultural functions, for the sums at its disposal are paltry alongside those commanded by the passionate and frenzied collector. There was no more poignant moment of last year's auction scene (overheated, to be sure, by an anticipated change

[96

in the capital-gains tax) than when the Whitney's director, Tom Armstrong, who embodies to perfection the virtues and dilemmas of his museum, dropped his paddle midway through the bidding for Rosenquist's *F-111*. That painting belongs by artistic right to the Whitney. But with the capacity to outbid has come the confidence to judge, as Armstrong writes, candidly and courageously, in his foreword to the catalogue of the 1987 Biennial:

Contemporary art activity now attracts an unprecedented number of wealthy individuals, many of whom begin to consider themselves as institutions as their judgments are reenforced by the actions of the market place. As this happens, their loyalty to established museums, and to the intellectual base they represent, is dissipated.

Without being curators, the collectors think in terms of the criteria of curatorial art.

So the fourth floor of the Whitney, for all its surface tranquillity, is a battlefield. It is not the scene of the style wars of past years, for today pretty much anything goes. Rather, it is where the institution is fighting for its autonomy. This, I think, goes some distance toward explaining the tone of dignified authority the installation achieves, and the further sense of almost tranquil stability. The exhibition is curatorial consciousness giving itself an institutional expression through works of great solidity and sobriety—there are no lavatories splashed over by commissioned graffiti artists this year. But whatever is taking place here really refers to what is taking place between the Whitney and forces so powerful that its survival against them is on the line. Until the passionate and frenzied rich turn to other ultimate sports—private zoos, perhaps, in which rare species are kept in golden cages amid exotic plants—this will be Fortress Whitney, fighting off the gilded hordes.

Of the seventy-two artists represented, fourteen are here as filmmakers and fourteen as video artists, not counting the veteran video artist Nam June Paik, shown here as a sculptor who uses video referentially in two works consisting of old television sets fitted together to form humanoid personages. So nearly half the art makers are working in forms that produce what was defined by Walter Benjamin—though he had different media in mind—as art of mechanical reproduction. I think this is a brilliant counterattack by the Whitney curators against the museum's affluent enemies, for films and video, though hardly "proletarian," as Benjamin imagined mechanical art must be, are the kinds of things that can be made in numbers large enough and distributed widely enough to make collecting them more like collecting stamps than collecting masterworks. Given the mentality of the collector, of course, it is possible to imagine rarities and externally induced scarcities, so that tapes could be auctioned off at fancy prices. But that would not in any sense penetrate the essence of this art, which dissolves the distinction, except commercially, between original and copy.

The inclusion of so much inherently temporal art creates a serious problem for anyone bent on seeing the Biennial in its entirety. Just the film and video would require, by my calculation, about twenty-one hours of viewing time. In fact it is impossible to see it all, as showings are distributed over the entire duration of the exhibition. The Whitney could greatly reinforce its position in the war against the collector by some kind of rental arrangement—many of those who attend the show are likely to have a VCR—or by negotiating a series on PBS to coincide with the exhibition. I have only seen one of the videos, the superb *J. S. Bach* by Juan Downey, but it possesses everything that one once went to artworks for: intelligence, feeling, meaning, truth. So I would arrange my visit, if I were you, to take advantage of one of its screening sessions. The near-absence of these deep qualities from the nontemporal works on display makes one feel that if it is anywhere in the metropolitan area today, the Spirit is more likely to be hanging out at Crazy Eddie's than at Pearl Paints.

I did not respond very positively to the nontemporal works: if I did not know that a certain amount of curatorial painting was being done outside the Whitney's examples, I would infer from the evidence available here that it was a moribund art. One of Julian Schnabel's works, somewhat surprisingly, conveys a memorable feeling. Characteristically immense, it situates a pathetic little banner of some silken material, bearing the legend "VIRTUE," against a vast olive-drab tarpaulin with an inverted "US" in the upper left corner. The juxtaposition of materials and inscriptions gives a rare meaning to the vocabulary of this portentous artist, whose companion piece, *Mimi*, is more typical of his work and more emblematic of the level of painting in the show. This is somewhat unfair: Donald Sultan, Robert Ryman and Neil Jenney are paradigm cases of high-class curatorial art, though nothing the curators chose by these artists stands out against their known work like *Virtue* stands out against Schnabel's. While this year's show is quiet enough to let one appreciate Ryman, it does no service to his work to display it here. The same is true of De Kooning, included *honoris causa*, whose late style demands a serious exhibition.

Louise Bourgeois is here *honoris causa* as well, and three of her sculptures dominate that variety of nontemporal art, most examples of which come across as trivial. Two works by R. M. Fischer strike the eye as soon as one enters the fourth floor. Large and highly polished fabrications in metal, they appear to belong to some unfathomable technology, whose circuits may be represented by some hard-edged, seemingly color-coded paintings in the same gallery by Peter Halley, a very hot artist indeed. But Fischer has trivialized his works by adding pieces of ornamentation that make them look more like contraptions than sculpture and giving them silly titles like *Snap, Crackle, Pop,* so that it is impossible to retain an interest in them save as puzzling failures.

One disastrous curatorial impulse grouped together a number of Bruce Weber's photographs which, whatever their individual merits, do not add up to a single work of art even if given a single title, *Studio Wall.* Weber is a gifted photographer, known for his studies of athletic males, and the aggregated images of enviable bodies with knobby genitals look like a dream-kit for the once promiscuous. In fact, the best nontemporal things in the show are photographs. I admire those by Clegg & Guttmann, which are large-scale, disturbing images depicting, like group portraits from the Dutch Baroque, financiers, music executives and gallery proprietors. But photographs, too, lie on or near the border of mechanical reproduction.

Very little in the nontemporal sector of the show comes up to the level of the jacket of the catalogue so far as artistic intelligence is concerned. It is printed in green Colonial-style lettering, and says: "BIENNIAL 1987." The typography makes an allusion to the bicentennial of the Constitution, which we are celebrating this year, and gives a mocking weight to the ephemerality of the exhibition. This is further enhanced by the circumstance that the lettering is printed against a background that does not so much simulate wood as it simulates a sheet of Formica that simulates wood. Appropriated typography on a simulacrum of a simulacrum—that pretty well wraps it up, precisely as we expect of a cover. That a mere piece of graphic design should embody the very qualities that are supposed to distinguish cur-

99]

atorial art, so much of which is in fact appropriation and simulation, has to call that distinction into question. This is one of the subtleties of the exhibition, as distinct from the works it contains. At the level of wit, the curators have bested art makers and collectors alike.

—*The Nation*, May 16, 1987

Joan Miró

ON JANUARY 24, 1937, the Catalan artist Joan Miró, prevented by civil war from returning to his homeland, set up in the gallery of his Paris dealer, Pierre Loeb, a still life on which he worked every day for a month. The painting was finished in his studio on May 29 of that difficult year. It consists of an apple, into which a lethal, six-tined fork has been stuck; a gin bottle shrouded in torn newspaper, secured with a thong; a heel of bread; and a left shoe, its lace untied. The apple is brown, so perhaps rotten; the bread is dried; the shoe, we learn from the title *Still Life with Old Shoe*, is worn. Each object relates to a heavy shadow, represented by black free-forms of the sort we associate with Miró's vocabulary of shapes—forms that came to be emblems of modern art in the plaques of Hans Arp, in the flat metal pieces on Calder mobiles and in modernesque jewelry and coffee tables, and which have their natural counterparts in deeply lobed leaves or kidneys or human feet. It is possible to read the shadow cast by the gin bottle as a weeping silhouette, but it is also possible to read too much into the painting, wanting it to be deep. The shoe is painted in yellows and greens, reds and bright blues—footwear for a one-legged harlequin. James Thrall Soby compared the work—polemical, memorial, ostensibly lamentational—with Picasso's *Guernica*, to which it was allegedly intended as an artistic response.

"Form for me is never something abstract," Miró once said. "It is always a token of something. . . . For me, form is never an end in itself." So here is a work of political reference and artistic allusion, a work supposed to draw its meaning from the events that elicited it and from other art elicited by those events. But how could one tell, descending the coiled ramp of the Guggenheim Museum, that this is a piece of political art, an exile's meditation on war and loss, a dark poem in a dark time, a counterthrust in the style wars of Paris? It looks like what its title says it is: a still life with a shoe. The shoe is luminous, parti-colored, comical. But the image is otherwise realistic and recognizable, like a good cartoon. That fact sets it off from the works that immediately surround it: Miró had not painted objects realistically and recognizably since 1923, even if his forms were always tokens of real things. But that fact, if it is even relevant, would not be visible in the painting alone, without the context of its peers.

I saw this wonderful exhibition on a sparkling May morning. The Guggenheim must have had its skylight washed of the accumulated Manhattan soot for the occasion, and the brilliant sky was mirrored in the blue pool (itself almost a Miró shape) at the base of the ramp, making the museum's core a well of light. Outside in the park, under the new green, there were runners in bright costumes, vendors, children, dogs. The paintings themselves were gay and playful, and filled with creatures so inventive and good-humored that one had the sense of passing through a display of zoological or botanical or entomological extravagances—whiskered, flittering innocent beings, utterly unsuited to the struggle for existence, goggle-eyed, bearing the blank staring expressions of brilliant fish in tropical waters, or insects in flower-mad gardens, or radiant birds flying among ornamental planets. Where there were humans, they seemed mainly to be carriers of jolly genitalia. *Still Life with Old Shoe* ought to have stood darkly against the ambient gaiety like the Ancient Mariner at the wedding feast. Instead, it looked like part of the carnival, as if the wedding guests had refused to accept the spell of the old loon's tale, had decked the mariner out with silk and ribbons and made him part of the dance. The external knowledge of the circumstances in which the painting was made, however, fought against this spontaneous assimilation, and demanded that one reflect on the fact that one was traversing a total life in art (Miró died in 1983, at the age of ninety). Ought the contradiction between what we know about this painting and the overall sense of hedonistic celebration call the latter into question? After all, that is exactly the contradiction between the meaning of the painting and its surface. Or is this particular painting a failure, Miró not being up to expressing that level of intention?

Joan Miró

It would, I think, be remarkable if each of the paintings in the show held a tension at all like the one I find in *Still Life with Old Shoe*, for then their meanings would be so external to their formal achievement that we would need a dictionary to read the show. A shoe, a bottle, a piece of fruit with a fork in it or a knife, a crust of bread— these compose the pedagogical still life set up in the art academies of that era. For all one knows, Miró's painting is an exercise in nostalgia for the Barcelona art schools of his youth. There is a tradition of mystical still life painting in Spain, where achingly familiar objects are transfigured by an unearthly light against an impenetrable blackness. In 1922 Miró had painted a number of severe still lifes of carbide lamps and grills, kitchen utensils and, in one case, a blade of wheat, displayed like the emblems of martyrdom in uncanny spaces and immersed in a light so absolute that the shadows have been reduced to thin drawn lines. But these, like almost everything he did before 1923, seem to be about art. There is an early still life in the Cubist manner, in which a live rabbit and rooster are juxtaposed with a demijohn and a smoked fish on a sheet of newspaper together with an onion, a pepper and some greens, which may refer to the *bodegón* tradition of Spanish still life painting, or for that matter may refer to Cubism rather than stand solidly in that style of representation. Standing outside a style to which he refers, a stranger and a commentator, detached, a bit derisive, putting bits and pieces of art to his own ends, associated with the Surrealists but never finally one of them, a Parisian but an outsider, Miró seems insufficiently in the world to be making a statement about it rather than a statement about statements or about styles. So *Still Life with Old Shoe* comes as an interruption. Small wonder we would never have known it was a response to the Civil War in Spain if no one told us. Small wonder it fails to communicate the feeling it was intended to convey. Small wonder the surrounding works refuse to allow it to speak of suffering. It is too isolated, like a single serious and direct thing—"By the way, I am dying"—uttered in the monologue of a great comedian.

Consider in this light Miró's climactic masterpiece, *The Farm*, executed over nine months in the three places that defined his life from 1921 to 1922: the parental farm at Montroig, Barcelona and Paris. In those years, indeed as a regular rhythm until the Civil War put a stop to it, Miró moved between Catalonia and Paris, between the tradition in which he sought his identity and the brittle world of Parisian intellect, where he lived among poets and thinkers rather than the cultural patriots of his native province. The two forms of life, one feels, pulled him in two directions, and this tension is embodied in *The Farm*. The painting has the unsettling quality of something observed and at the same time dreamed of or remembered. Hemingway, who owned it, described it perfectly: "It has in it all that you feel about Spain when you are there and all that you feel when you are away and cannot go there." Hemingway went on to say, "No one else has been able to paint these two very opposing things." What is remarkable about the painting is the oppositions it internalizes, just as Miró himself internalized as a matter of personality the circumstances of his shuttled existence. Picasso belonged wherever he was. Miró belonged only where he wasn't: his not being in Paris defined his Spanish reality, and vice versa.

The Farm is energized by two incompatible artistic realities, corresponding to the polarities of Miró's life. It has the obsessive documentation of visual reality that we find in primitive painting: each leaf on the dominating eucalyptus tree is separately painted, each rock in the stony field to the right is given an autonomous space, each blade of grass is given its own identity. The lichen on the cracked façade of the farm building on the left defeats this impulse: you cannot register lichen spore by spore, at least not in the middle distance of a landscape where spores would be negligible specks in proportion to the façade they adhere to—though the particularity of treatment gives an uncanny microscopy to that surface. The barking dog, the rabbit, the snail, the cock, the donkey, the dove, the pail, the watering can, the wagon, the plow, the dozens of farm implements, the farmer's wife, the baby by the wash trough, are each suspended in the shadowless clarity of a metaphysical illumination—it is the kind of light one gets through an optical instrument. The space recedes to distant mountains, but the trees and bushes at the horizon are treated with the same measured detail as the foreground objects, as if perception were indifferent to distance. All this pulls the farthest objects forward to the surface plane, and indeed, when we look carefully, we notice that the plane on which all these objects are arrayed, and which seems to recede, is itself tipped up. There is, for instance, a tiled area, supposed to be lying flat on the ground, which in fact is parallel to the surface. Behind it, again, is a path that seems at once to go back and to rise up, like an abstract flame. It is as though the artist had intermixed, in a single work, the illusory space of traditional landscape with the shallow space of Cubism, so that everything is on the surface and at the same time bears no relation to the surface, which, after all, is not part of the landscape. There is, for example, a trestle table in the middle distance in the form of a letter *A*. If it is a letter, it belongs on the surface, as writing. An *A* in the landscape is dissonant, as if the work were a rebus puzzle. But a table, of course, belongs to the world of a farm. Everything is inside and outside at once. And superimposed on the primitive meticulousness of a picturesque farm are the devices of the most sophisticated painting of the century so far. Part of what brings everything to the surface are the Cubist rhythms, the sense of pattern, of fragmentation, of reduction and abstraction. "No one could look at it," Hemingway wrote, "and not know it had been painted by a great painter." He is right, but no one who knows great painting can look at it without sensing the divided consciousness and the aesthetic indeterminacy of an artist who sank into his art the oppositions of his vision: Catalan and Parisian, traditionalist and Cubist, naïf and cosmopolite.

Of this great painting, Miró later said, "It was the summary of one period of my work, but also the point of departure for what was to follow." And though he could not then have known what precisely was to follow, the fact that it is the largest painting he had undertaken up to that time is an indication that he had chosen to make an important statement through it. Miró was perhaps not as poor at that stage of his life as artistic mythology maintains, but canvas and paint, then as now, were costly items, especially if one had no idea if one's work was going to sell. The size of the canvas plays a part in an affecting vignette left us by Hemingway, who describes how he bore it home as a birthday present for his wife, Hadley, after paying off the last installment of the 5,000 francs it cost: "In the open taxi the wind caught the big canvas as though it were a sail, and we made the taxi driver crawl along."

It is instructive to think of *The Farm* together with *Still Life with Old Shoe*. The latter is a failure, not so much as a painting but as a painting about war, for its subject never penetrates the work save by the external imposition of a symbolic interpretation. "In some sense," Jacques Dupin claims in his catalogue essay, "this unique and fantastic painting stands as Miró's *Guernica*." Dupin curated the show, and he is an enthusiast. But as Miró's *Guernica*, the painting fails. Miró was certainly sickened by the war in Spain, but he was not finally a political person: Art was the substance of his life and hence of his art, which is most genuine and best when, as in *The Farm*, it is about its own processes. The first works we encounter in the show are two drawings from 1917, before Miró had visited Paris for the first time. They are dense with Parisian references and mannerisms even so: the male and female nudes are geometrized, all arcs and angles, evidence that the news of Cubism had arrived in Spain and was deflecting advanced artists from whatever path their training would have set them on if the twentieth century had not happened instead. Miró was still dealing with Cubism in *The Farm*, painted five years later.

Dealing with Cubism, for he felt at once its seductiveness and its dangers. It could not be ignored, but at the same time it almost guaranteed artistic mediocrity, for Paris in the early 1920s was full of second-generation Cubists. Picasso confided to his dealer, Daniel Henry Kahnweiler, that he had become rich by selling his license to paint guitars, alluding to the endless cubed and stretched guitars that formed the motif of the Cubist legions. *The Farm* was a liberation, even if Cubism remained an internal force in its dynamics. "I will smash their guitar," Miró said when he realized he had found another path, visible in *The Farm* only in the light radiating from his later work, which began, abruptly, in 1923. *The Tilled Field* of that year shows us the Miró we know and love. The space has moved so far forward that the ground is nearly vertical. A tree shows an eye amid its leaves, and has grown a hallucinatory ear from its trunk. The farm animals are there, still recognizable, but the hen has taken the form of a grotesquely unbalanced dumbbell, with a globular body and a tiny head. The mare has developed immovably thick legs, as wavy as sine curves, and her tail swishes forward like a calligraphic question mark. The whole painting is like an exultation at having broken through to the style—pictographic, idiomatic, autographic—that was to be his from now on. If he were a poet, we would say he had found his voice.

The art historian Michael Baxandall has introduced an interesting concept in discussing Picasso's portrait of Kahnweiler. There is a system of interchange between advanced artists and their patrons and critics which is analogous to a market, but which involves ideas and refinements instead of money. He gives this system the name *troc*, which means "barter" in French. Picasso was *en troc* with poets like Apollinaire and intellectuals like Kahnweiler, who demanded certain artistic performances from which they and the artist benefited. The great American painters of the 1950s were *en troc* with Harold Rosenberg and Clement Greenberg. *Troc* requires mutual interchange

Joan Miró

rather than unilateral influence, so that present-day artists are not *en troc* with the intellectuals they admire, such as Derrida, who knows little about painting, and Baudrillard, who cares little for it. Miró was intensely *en troc* with the poets and the theorists of Surrealism, with Picabia and Tzara, Breton and Masson, Artaud, Prévert, Desnos and Michel Leiris. My own sense is that his breakthrough owes a lot to this intimacy. He showed with the Surrealists, and took over a great deal of their ideology and a degree of their silliness, but as long as the conversations rang in his head, as long as he was painting for an audience that was instantly responsive and critical, he maintained a minor greatness.

Miró remained in Paris from 1936 to 1941, the year Normandy was bombed, when he settled in Palma de Mallorca, his mother's birthplace. The next year he returned to Barcelona, where he found he could live after all. His work thinned after the war, though his productivity remained, and his influence became immense, especially in New York, where his ideas were absorbed and transcended by Gorky and Pollock and Motherwell. In a way, his truly creative life ended when the *troc* ended. In this regard he bears a resemblance to Chagall, who was a great artist when he was in tension with the ideologues of the School of Paris, but who simply manufactured Chagalls when the tensions eased and commerce took over. One senses that the greatness of Picasso and Matisse in part consists in their being *en troc* with themselves as their own intellectuals. Appropriately, there is proportionately little painting in the Guggenheim show after 1950. In those years Miró's energies mainly went into ceramics and into a kind of terra cotta sculpture. This was an artistic return, of sorts, to Catalonia, and it was a nice way to round off Miró's particular life. The show has the cadences of a marvelous biography. Go on a really sunny day.

—*The Nation*, June 20, 1987

Kimura/Berlinart

THE GREAT HISTORIAN Fernand Braudel disdained what he regarded as the surface events of history as traditionally conceived—treaties, wars, the death of kings, coups d'état, the rise and fall of empires, the flourishing and passing away of schools of art—in favor of life as lived by ordinary men and women at a level where nothing much changed for periods vast in relationship to the agitated chronology of surface history. Historical existence during what he famously termed the *longue durée*—stretches of time so protracted that one could not speak of them as punctuated by historical events—takes place on a level of consciousness so remote from the courts and corridors of power that what happens to the rich and famous at the top is as distant and mythic as the bickering of the gods was to the grunts and bumpkins of ordinary Troy. Far, far beneath the agonies of Hector and Menelaus, life went on as it had and would go on, though the stories of those events would, in time, begin to shape the consciousness of the *longue durée*. Braudel saw himself writing a kind of non-eventival history, a history with respect to which the structures of narrative would be inappropriate. No doubt even in history so construed, there are points of change, when one *longue durée* gives way to another—but even then there may be a still deeper level at which nothing changes at all, and ordinary persons today are in effect strict contemporaries of the Cro-Magnons. If so, our common humanity must be defined in its terms, as must the possibility of transcultural, as well as transtemporal, understanding.

It is striking that surface history has itself begun to take on some of the attributes of life in the *longue durée*, in that cities the world over have begun to look the same, much as their airports do, and international travelers find themselves eating much the same cuisine and sleeping in much the same rooms, wearing the same clothes except on ceremonial occasions, listening to the same music, watching *Dynasty* and diverting themselves with the same video games from meridian to meridian. More to the immediate point, the cultural life of great cities is very little different from place to place, and much the same contemporary paintings are seen in much the same order of museums—paintings and sculptures familiar from public spaces, such as airports or the lobbies of corporate headquarters or, in smaller versions, the reception rooms of commercial hotels. As Pascal might have said had he lived in our times, *Plus on voyage, plus c'est la même chose.*

Beyond question, differentiated forms of life go on between the deepest and the most superficial levels of historical reality, and it would have been from the intermediate levels of historical consciousness that national styles of art arose in earlier times. For those who could not travel, there were engravings of legendary paintings in Italy or Spain. Since the early nineteenth century, there have been museums for artists to visit, sometimes to great transformative effect, as when Picasso found himself in the ethnographic museum of the Palais de Trocadéro. But in those cases, alien forms were adapted to local vision, and whatever Picasso borrowed from Africa or Oceania became the defining features of the School of Paris. Nothing gives a deeper insight into Northern sensibility than Dürer's copies after Mantegna. Hopper's sojourn in Paris fed into a style of painting that was unmistakably and untransportably American. Kimura remains Japanese for all his protracted residence in France and the profound Bonnardism of his vision. Until very recently, it was with art as it is with wine. Whatever the provenance of the vinestock, it was the local circumstances of soil and light that made the final product distinctively German or Italian or French. And connoisseurship consisted in part in the power to make nuanced discriminations of whatever it is in art that corresponds to vintage and the *goût de terroir* of authentic wines.

The fascinating and somewhat scary Berlinart exhibition at the Museum of Modern Art offers an inadvertent glimpse of the slide toward internationalist entropy of art produced in Berlin from 1961, when the wall first went up and President Kennedy became a Berliner, until the present minute. The earliest works in the show, one feels, could not have been painted by anyone except Berliners responding to the immediacy of Berlin, for that city so penetrates their substance that their being from Berlin and by Berliners is a deeply revealing fact about them. The last paintings, though produced in Berlin by whoever was there, could have been painted by an international artist anywhere: at some point Berlin passed from a cultural outpost to one of the art capitals of the world. The curator of the show, Kynaston McShine, has excluded all Germans who did not work in Berlin, and has included any number of non-Germans because they were working there, as high-class *Gastarbeiter*, so to speak. Thus Malcolm Morley, an English artist now resident in New York, is represented by a large painting, *The Day of the Locust*, based upon a minor American classic and essentially about Hollywood. Its being made in Berlin penetrates its substance not at all, and this is characteristic of most of the work done there in the 1980s.

My sense is that the turning point came with the distasteful and portentous *Zeitgeist* exhibition of 1982 at the Martin-Gropius-Bau near the wall, on which Jonathan Borofsky drew one of his Running Men. That show was in effect the equivalent in painting of the Frankfurt Book Fair, and it marked the sudden canonization of an international confraternity of hot artists working in Germany, Italy, England and America, whose origins were irrelevant and whose homes were wherever their commissions or openings happened to take them. The style they exemplified was demonstrated to be absolutely international in the exhibition that inaugurated the newly refurbished Museum of Modern Art in 1984 (also curated by McShine), where works were brought from everywhere to show the latest lines and fashions, but only the labels indicated national identity. Internationalism is made possible today by the demand for traveling exhibitions, which means that the same works circulate from capital to capital on every continent. But most importantly, I believe, it is facilitated by the excellent color reproductions in the art magazines which carry monthly news to the most distant provinces. Laplanders and Fijians, Patagonians and Watusis are able to see Schnabel, Salle, Chia and Cucchi, Basilitz and Kiefer, in fact or in effigy, and hence the models to be followed as a condition of entry into the circuits of contemporary art making and showing.

The Berlin art before *Zeitgeist* was very immediate and utterly of its place. K. H. Hödicke's somber study of the War Ministry, with its ranks of gray columns, each a single brushload of pigment, and its heavy shadows, darker gray against dirty canvas, is a political postcard bearing the message: "Having a terrible time, be glad you are not here." Bernd Zimmer's *Berlin* of 1978 shows a sinister green automobile, with weeping yellow headlights, proceeding into black paint against sick store windows. Rainer Fetting paints buildings like black broken teeth against a green cloud, with the horizon punctuated by what must be ruins. These are authentic images that convey the feeling of an unholy city bearing the terrible burden of unspeakable devastation. Helmut Middendorf's late *Airplane Dream* shows its subject like a flying cross over a burning city. But international art refers to traditions it stands outside, and tends to be about art, not about whatever the images and styles it appropriates were themselves a response to. So it tends to disappear into its own reflections on itself. Berlin was the city where Hegel gave his final series of lectures on the fine arts in 1828–29, saying, famously, that art had come to an end. This coming to an end meant not so much stopping as turning away from life and toward itself, thus standing outside whatever gave art meaning and becoming an art that exists just to be art. I find Hegel's dire forecast profoundly confirmed by Berlinart, which could just as well have been titled Worldart Incidentally Manufactured in Berlin.

Chuta Kimura's paintings, which are among my great enthusiasms, could not on the other hand have been painted by anyone but a Japanese working in France. These facts penetrate the work in the sense in which comparable facts are external to international paintings. It is an internal fact about Kimura's work that he saw the paintings of Bonnard in Japan and perceived France through that artist's perception of it. This was in 1941, and the experience defined the vision of a distant landscape that became a permanent passion, almost in the sense of imprinting that we find in animal psychology. Kimura wanted nothing more than to be there, amidst the mimosa and bougainvillea, the purples and oranges and vegetal greens, the unforgiving blues of meridional skies and the baked browns of spare hills. The colors of his paintings are French colors, and the spaces are those of Bonnard, where the landscape seems to lie vertically before the viewer, as if rising up to engulf him.

When, in the early 1950s, Kimura was able to consummate the

desire, to see with his eyes the intoxicating aridity and the luxuriance of Provence, it was, one feels, as someone visually obsessed, and he stayed in France from then on. Yet it is characteristic of his complex relationship with the landscape that he remained, one might say, absolutely Japanese, to the point of never learning to speak French, so that he lives surrounded by a bubble of silence. This has enabled him to retain the freshness of perception of a distant yearner who knew the reality first through pictures: he lives in France as one might, impossibly, participate in events one first read about in books. He addresses the landscape finally with the manual energy available only to someone who carries in his reflexes styles of swordsmanship and calligraphy that are archetypally Japanese. It is a fusion of two modalities of perception and gesture that coexist in a state of tension and even of conflict. You can subtract neither the Frenchness of the one nor the Japaneseness of the other from the canvases in which they strive together and against one another. Even his signature, the Japanese name written in Latin characters, carries this double energy: looking at his work I trace and retrace the letters hypnotically, as if watching the movements of one who is altogether familiar and yet remains a mystery, and from whom one cannot lift one's eyes.

Because of its gestural aggressiveness, because of the physicality of pigment as Kimura uses it, his work will inevitably be seen as Abstract Expressionist in inspiration. But it is neither Abstract nor Expressionist. If anything, his work is Impressionist, and he sees himself as being in the same line as Monet. The paintings answer to the stimulus of definite places, corners of gardens or parks, streets, farms, houses and chairs or bicycles and cascades of vegetation or rows of trees and shadows and clouds that must have been there when he made his notations. But the response is not passive and retinal, as Impressionism was obliged to be, insisting as it did on visual exactitudes and using theories of color and optical physiology to underwrite its effects. The duality of Realism or Expressionism almost defines the options available to a Western painter, who must either show what is there, like a camera, or express his feelings about what is there. But Kimura, I believe, does neither, and it is his ability to occupy a third position, not intermediate between these but alternative to them, that may be referred to his Japanese roots. It is as though he wanted the landscape to *express itself*, wants there to come to the surface what does not necessarily meet the eye: a force, a stirring, a shifting and a wildness,

[*112*

a spirit one has to provoke by some counterenergy on the artist's part. It is as though the landscape were some sleeping dragon disguised as hills and meadows, as some peaceful place, but which, with enough prodding, reveals its true power, dissolving into something that writhes and whips and flashes before it subsides back into colors and shapes, leaving the memory of something untamed.

Landscapes like Kimura's reveal, it seems to me, the visualistic premises of Western art, which support the conclusion that nature is something to be seen, that our relationship to it is external, the stance of responders or witnesses rather than of participants or beings engaged with it. It suddenly occurred to me that he is carrying forward a tradition of Japanese art whose most familiar example is *The Great Wave of Hokusai*—is there a single Western work that really shows nature seething with the dwarfing force of that wave?—or perhaps the magnificent screen of irises by Korin, which visitors to the Metropolitan Museum know so well and which now forms the climax of the latter's newly installed Japanese wing. Those irises stand like green blades, dominated by the gardener's and finally the artist's countervailing will. Will: perhaps that ultimately accounts for the difference between the way the non-German artists are "in" Berlin and the way Kimura is "in" France. It is as though we were dealing with different prepositions altogether.

—*The Nation*, July 4/11, 1987

PASCAL FAMOUSLY complained that painting is a frivolous art, for it attaches us to the images of things that themselves would not greatly engage us. Elsewhere, he speaks of eloquence as a kind of painting: it paints our thoughts, transforming them "into pictures rather than portraits." A portrait, for Pascal, would evidently be an image so transparent that it yields the visual equivalent of some scene or thing or person as these would be presented to the senses without the mediations of art. A portrait would be an image we *see through* to the reality it shows. There is, of course, an ideal of verbal transparency as well, where words exhaust their function in disclosing meaning, without calling attention to themselves. So poetry, too, would be a "frivolous" art if it attaches us to the verbal representations of things that themselves would not otherwise engage us.

Pascal seems to have thought of painting as a kind of added coloration, like lip rouge or eye shadow, heightening, or accenting, or prettifying. Still, it is striking that he should have seen painting as an art that attaches us to *images*. For there is, after all, a kind of art which causes us to be attached to the objects it shows by presenting them in some enhanced way. Such an art gives us a picture it also causes us to believe is a portrait, to continue with Pascal's vocabulary. I speak of showing something in a *flattering* light, for example, where the artist endeavors to show the subject as more beautiful or commanding than it really is. Needless to say, this art must not draw attention to the fact that it does this—it must give us the sense that it is "transparent"—or it could not have its intended effect. It would instead display the fact that it was manipulative, causing us to have feelings toward the subject we would not have without benefit of the representation. This art, whose verbal analogue is rhetoric, is a form of pictorial lie. And it is surprising that Pascal condemns painting not for mendacity but for frivolity.

But the whole great mystery of painting has to do with the way it attaches us to images—to the showing of things rather than the things shown. Poetry intrudes itself between the reader and whatever it may be about, attaching us to phrases and cadences which echo and reecho in the mind, and which we repeat for the sheer pleasure of feeling the words on the tongue, irrespective even of meaning or truth. And the paintings we love draw us to them again and again, even if what they are of might leave us cold or indifferent. I cannot see too often the scalloped edge of one of Cézanne's *compotiers*, though the original would have for me only the interest that Cézanne happened to paint it. I trace and retrace the tremulous division between two bottles by Morandi, as if it held some momentous meaning, though it is inconceivable that a bottle against a bottle would move me to anything except a speculation about how Morandi would realize it in paint. I would like someday to make a pilgrimage to Clos St.-Pierre, but only because the marvelous landscapes drawn out of it by Kimura so enchant my vision that I cannot look at them too frequently, and cannot take my eyes off them when I see them. Whatever puritanical disapproval it was that Pascal intended to express, he identified the bewitchment of which great art is capable. One sometimes wonders if Pygmalion after all found happiness with the woman into whom his statue was transformed. He may really have been in love with the image, and wrongly believed it was the object that aroused him—"an image he did grave," Ovid writes, "Of such proportion, shape, and grace as nature never gave / Nor can to any woman give."

The ideal of pictorial transparency, which defined ancient theories of mimetic art, insisted that a representation was to have only the aesthetic properties the thing it showed possessed, and to have no further aesthetic properties of its own: a beautiful painting of a woman would have to be a painting of a beautiful woman. Recent theories, which dismiss the possibility of an innocent eye along with insisting that the strategies of pictorial representation have a history, have maintained that realism in any case is a matter of convention. These might encourage us to be dismissive of Pascal's conception of a nonfrivolous, or transparent, pictorial art. Nevertheless, the ideal of transparency remains so central a component in our experience of art, especially today, that we would find ourselves as indignant as Pascal were anyone discovered meddling with it. I refer to the fact that the bulk of our experience with works of art comes from reproductions—from art books and art magazines and slides (in fact, explicitly called "transparencies"). I know art historians who teach in universities so unfortunately located that their students never actually see real paintings or sculptures, and certainly never the ones they study, which are as remote for them as the Forms of Platonic philosophy are, whose appearances are all they know in the cave of the art-history lecture hall. Malraux speaks of these secondary images as composing a *musée imaginaire*, but whatever the exactitude of this famous theory, there is no question that the reproduction is an image that never attaches us to itself, but only to the object—the painting or statue in question. Obviously, certain properties fail to come through, such as site and scale, and perhaps just as obviously, photographic reproduction is not as transparent as we might care to believe. The degree to which our experience of art is permeated by artifacts of photographic technology is an unexplored topic in the psychology of aesthetic perception. Nevertheless, an extraordinary amount of aesthetic information must come through.

My initial encounter with Kimura was through some reproductions, just as Kimura's first encounters with Western art came through the pictures in the art books he pored over. These reproductions, in my case certainly and in Kimura's case dramatically, attached us to the objects they revealed with something like the power of love. So powerfully was Kimura drawn to the works he saw in those images that he was compelled to undertake the journey of his life, to the country—France—that they depicted, as if he felt he must himself confront the landscape of France if he was to paint the way his models— Bonnard, Renoir, Cézanne—themselves painted. Kimura was so possessed by France that nearly his entire lifetime passed, as in a fairy story, without his ever returning to his native land. I often wonder what the reproductions were that he saw, years before he saw so much as a single piece of French art as such, which summoned him to make his extraordinary transit. It is a tribute to the power of images that they can connect us to realities this way, even when they appear in a culture whose pictorial traditions are greatly different from those to which the reproductions belong. I would be surprised, for example, if the photogravures that he may have seen were anything like the one that so excited me when I first saw it, on the cover of the catalogue of his exhibition at the Phillips Gallery in Washington, D.C., in 1985.

That catalogue was left on my desk by my colleague Professor Hidé Ishiguro, who had invited me to meet this painter. She herself had never met him, but someone she knew long before, when they were students together in Japan, was coming through New York with Kimura and his wife. This was Aki Nanjo, who had become so entranced with Kimura's art that he appeared to be devoting his life to its promotion and celebration. Hidé has a vast network of friends, and is constantly hospitable to passers-through. This was but one further occasion for her to demonstrate her gift for gracious hospitality. She knew that I had a long interest in Japanese art, and she had read with enthusiasm a piece in which I memorialized Shiko Munakata, who had been a friend and an inspiration. I cannot pretend that I was especially looking forward to this new artist, whom I had been told spoke neither English nor French (and I speak not a word of Japanese). It was characteristically thoughtful of Hidé to leave the catalogue for me to see, so that I at least should know what sort of conversation to make. (In truth, one can communicate profoundly without a common language: I had the sense that Munakata and I had a perfect understanding even if our idiom was composed of gestures, pointings and grunts.)

What no one could have counted on was that from that reproduction alone, without even having to open the book and see the other work reproduced there, I should know, immediately and absolutely, that Kimura was among the great artists of the world. The painting shown was evidently a landscape. But no actual landscape could have held my attention as passionately and strongly as this extraordinary image did. Whatever Kimura proved to be as a human being, he had made images so dense with a ferocious beauty that merely to remember them infects me with joy. I had, I realize, grown disenchanted with beauty. I had thought too long of painting in terms of the philosophical questions it raises, as if art were a dislocated form of philosophy itself. Kimura brought back to life for me the irreducible and unanalyzable powers of painting in its highest vocation.

The discovery of a new painter is like the discovery of a new world. One element in the excitement I felt upon seeing that cover image was the promise of a sort of visual brilliance Gauguin might have supposed would fill his eyes when he stepped off the boat at Tahiti, a new land of intense colors and sensuous forms and sharp sensations, vivid against the grays of the Paris he had left behind. Kimura burst upon my consciousness the way he did upon that of so many Americans, when the last thing anyone expected was a new artist of this magnitude of achievement. I am one who lives close to the art world, and had the sense that I knew everyone there was to know who was making art, as we say. One felt, indeed, that one knew not only who was painting what but all the possibilities there were, as if the art world were structured by a finite array—Abstraction, Expressionism, Minimalism and the like. There was the constant fact of young artists seeking to break in, constituting a noisy fringe to the art world—but here was a mature artist who had touched greatness, with hardly anyone in America, so far as I knew, at all aware of his existence. I turned the pages of the catalogue in growing amazement, hardly daring to believe that the promise of the cover illustration was renewed and extended by the marvelous sequence of paintings and drawings that had made up an exhibition that I bitterly regretted not having known about.

My first encounter with Kimura's work came, however, at the time of his first New York showing, at the Ruth Siegel Gallery. Entering that space really was like setting foot in a bright new world, and one painting seemed especially appropriate as a metaphor for the experience. It was of a garden gate, and it was in fact the most recent painting to have been completed before this show. Kimura was very excited by it, and he was anxious to share the excitement he evidently felt in painting it, and we realized then, my wife and I, that Kimura must himself have felt at every moment that sense of exploring a new world—

that it was not merely the extraordinary fact of a new pictorial world for us, but also one for him, at every moment, and that a further component in the visual intensity of the work was the artist's own adventure in bringing it to life. Kimura transmitted to the viewer his own constant amazement and surprise, as if, for him, at each moment, painting was an absolute unforeseenness. The intensity of his pleasure came from working within a world in which nothing could be taken for granted, so that he must have set himself to paint with a sense of total anticipation. It was the work of a happy sensibility, and of an artist for whom everything outside his life as a painter must have been muted, distant, secondary. In truth, one felt in the work the radiance of a religious joy, next to which the ordinary pleasures of even a happy life have barely any weight. Kimura's relationship to his art must have been close to that ecstatic engagement with a radiant reality one reads about occasionally in the literature of mysticism.

I now have before me, beside my typewriter, the image to which I originally responded with such intensity, and I think I can begin to fathom the reason why, just as Pascal said, it is the image and not the object to which it refers which engages the viewer. It is obviously of a landscape, I suppose at or near Clos St.-Pierre, but the elements of the landscape are reduced by Kimura to certain notations, as if for him they were but occasions for the painting, and exhausted their interest in that. What looks like a road, reduced to an irregular blue line, wanders up from the left-hand corner of the painting and then turns parallel to the bottom edge. The same blue is used for the shadow of a tree which bends over the road. The tree itself, with no botanical identity, is scrubbed in with a smudge of yellow green. And in the distance three notational trees in blue hover like tadpoles above the road. The blue road seems at once to recede into the illusory distance of the picture, and to remain on the surface, as if the work were surface and depth at once, illusion and abstraction together. To the right is an intense green field which verges on a patch of pure cadmium yellow, I suppose sunlight. There is a veil of creamy white scrubbed down over much of the surface, a scrim, at once opaque and translucent, like a yellow mist. In the upper right the paint forms what could be a cloud or could be the sun. Peeking around the edge of the scrim are the intense pure colors the scrim mutes—patches of vermilion and magenta, doubtless referring to flora. But the most astonishing feature of the entire work is a sort of loop, drawn with such looseness and authority that it takes the breath away, cropped by the top edge of the canvas. It is the visual daring of this incredible curve in Prussian blue, almost like a calligraphic notation on the surface of the canvas but which could also be the sun, a cloud, or something more mysterious, to which I return again and again. It condenses so much power, inspiration and aesthetic risk that I believe, intuitively, that Kimura felt, once he laid it down, that nothing more should be expected of this painting. A work which makes a gesture of that sort possible is a masterpiece. An art that makes a masterpiece of that kind possible can only spring from the deepest sources of creative adventure.

I have the feeling that Kimura painted in order that some moment like that should suddenly flash upon the surface of the canvas, like a revelation, and that when it happened, he was through with the work. At the time of his second New York show, on Greene Street (see p. 113 above), I wrote:

It is as though the landscape were some sleeping dragon disguised as hills and meadows, as some peaceful place, but which, with enough prodding, reveals its true power, dissolving into something that writhes and whips and flashes before it subsides back into colors and shapes, leaving the memory of something untamed.

I think this was right and wrong. It describes exactly the feeling Kimura's canvases convey, but it mislocates the object and, in a sense, the antagonist. Kimura was not struggling against a landscape but against its image, which he wanted in some way to reveal *its own* power. Kimura attaches us, precisely as Pascal said, to the image rather than to the reality to which it corresponds. His are not pictures of a world which reveals its power in a blinding moment of illumination. It is the pictures themselves that are caused to reveal their power by an act of gestural magic all his own.

—*Contemporanea*, November, 1989

Cindy Sherman

THOUGH THE WORKS of Cindy Sherman must be classed as photographs, and depend for their effect in part on the fact that they are photographs, photography is not her medium. It is, rather, a means to her artistic ends. Her medium is herself. But that is not to say that she is her own subject, for the photographs are of her only in the reduced sense in which Delacroix's *Liberty Storming the Barricades* is of the model who posed for Liberty. The knowledge that they are of Cindy Sherman penetrates our experience and appreciation of these works, but she herself is not what the works are about. They are about whatever she, as her own medium of representation, has transformed her face, her body, her costume and her surroundings to show. She uses herself to achieve an illusion, and the chief contribution photography makes is through its connotations as documentary. The standard photographic situation, however flaunted by artists, is that of a picture which represents its cause by looking like it. The premise of photography is that it is a pictorial record, its image steeped in the visual reality that occasioned it. In Sherman's art, this premise is exploited to enhance the illusion at which it aims.

The illusion in any given picture is importantly limited by the knowledge, these days widely shared, that whatever they may be about, all her pictures are of her. Sherman's face must by now be the second most widely known face in the art world, despite its happy indistinction. She is surpassed in familiarity only by Warhol. Her intentions nevertheless differ from Warhol's almost completely. Warhol meant his own face to be among the images that define our cultural reality, of a piece and on a plane with the Campbell's soup label, the Brillo carton, the *Mona Lisa* and of course the faces of Liz, Elvis, Jackie and Marilyn. Like Washington and Lincoln—or Nixon—but not Fillmore, Polk or Harding, these are the shared icons of contemporary American culture, and it is something of a miracle of publicity and promotion that an Andy is as instantly recognized as a Raggedy Ann by the otherwise artistically illiterate. Sherman, because her impulses are those of an actress and not the ambitions of a star, aspires to be known for her roles rather than her personality. She is aided in her anonymity by the circumstance of being a *femme moyenne sensuelle*, with a standard decent figure and a not unattractive face, but subject to cosmetic modifications that are the right of Western women: lipstick, eye shadow, hair coloring and of course the semiotics of feminine dress. Even so, the knowledge that we are seeing her, whatever the final content of the picture, limits the degree that we can enter the illusion, however compelling. We know, in brief, that we are looking at art and not a transcription through photography of the real world.

This limit is linked, internally and I would say paradoxically, with another one, which goes in the opposite direction. If all you were to see were a single work of Sherman's, you would have no way of knowing that photography in her case was not a means but an end—no way of knowing that it was not just an arty kind of photograph, a bit big for its subject, perhaps. The subject might, for instance, be just a nice healthy-looking girl, Sherman herself being minimally displaced to represent someone's girlfriend, sporty and cheerful, smiling brightly. Told that it *is* Cindy Sherman and *by* Cindy Sherman, one would spontaneously class it as a self-portrait and wonder, dimly, why it was included in the show. The fact that its being by her does not entail that she took the picture, and that it is of her does not mean that it is a portrait, are invisible relevant facts about such a picture. It is only when one has come to see more and more of her work that one recognizes that the two salient facts—that it is a photograph and that it is of her always—must be transcended if we are to understand any work of hers. She is the medium through which the subject is made visible. And it—photography—is the medium that makes the illusion palpable. So the works gain when seen as part of a project, as referring to one another in a way underscored by the fact that each of them is titled *Untitled* and given a number. Because it is the total project, one of the most arresting artistic achievements of this decade, that is the least artistic unit of her work, only the large one-person exhibition is a suitable format for coming to terms with it. I have always felt that showing two or three of her works in, say, the Whitney Biennial is deeply unsatisfactory and misleading. By being photographs, they are falsely contrasted with the paintings and falsely bracketed with the other photographs. Since any given picture draws a measure of its energy and meaning from the evolving project, the wonderful exhibition of more than eighty of her works on the second floor of the Whitney Museum of American Art affords a spectacular experience of inspired imagination and visual daring and moral depth. Before addressing some of the imagery in detail, however, I want to dwell on the paradox that gives a tension to the total project and a special conceptual vibrancy to the individual works.

The paradox is that the wider knowledge of her *oeuvre* greatly enriches the artistic experience of each of its components, but it at the same time severely inhibits the degree that we can fully enter the illusion to which each work aspires: one knows, finally, that it is just Cindy Sherman, gotten up to be X or Y or Z, so that what we see is Cindy Sherman *as*. It is as though one aim must be paid for at the cost of sacrificing the other: the illusion works best in those who misperceive the work. And this may be a heavy price if I am right in classifying Sherman as basically a performance artist. The art of the performance artist undertakes the transformation of the viewer through the transformation of the artist. Now, we can be transformed only if the illusion is achieved, which means that we are subject to transformation only if we stop seeing the artist as (just) the artist. My own view is that Sherman in her best work overcomes the paradox, or even that she uses the paradox to achieve her effects—among the rare successes, if I am right, of the genre of performance art in its modern form.

Performance art is sometimes said to be located on a map of the arts somewhere between painting and theater, but in my view it is located between theater and whatever dark ritual it was out of which theater evolved and against which it was a defense. There are famous theories, according to which Greek tragedy developed from Dionysiac ritual, where the hero/priest interacted with the celebrant/chorus in such a way that at, and as, the climax of the ritual, the distance between them would be orgiastically blanked out, bringing them together into a single body. Theater was predicated on a kind of moral distance it was the purpose of the original ritual to overcome, but the memory of the hope and danger of the earlier practice remained to energize theatrical performance until it degenerated into mere entertainment. Performance art is a response to the separation of artist and community, and is atavistic in seeking to achieve a way of erasing the boundary between art and life. The artist, as if having stepped out of her own images, bodily enters the same space as the audience, and her performance (the best performance artists are for some reason women) is transacted in the hope that something transfigurative and even sublime will take place, raising her and her audience to a higher plane. Its aim is to obliterate the metaphysical distances that separate self from self, and sharing the same physical space seems already to be halfway there. In performance, then, art is restored to its position of magic and danger, though in fact very few artists are quite up to this stunning ambition, and in actual practice, most performance art is ephemeral, sheepish, self-conscious, thin, foolish, scruffy and awful. I once coined the word "disturbation" to describe the ideal moment of performance art. Like its obvious rhyme in English, where mere fantasies culminate in real spasms, disturbatory art seeks real transformations through charged images. And the performer herself is the means of inducing aesthetic climax. It requires great courage.

Cindy Sherman has taken this process one step further: she has reentered the pictures the performance artist has stepped out of, and done so in such a way as to infuse her images with the promise and threats of the performance artist's real presence. Photography, with its connotations of showing reality, is a marvelous enhancement of disturbation in her case. Indeed, I know philosophers who insist that photography is not a representational art at all, and that in seeing a photograph we see the reality present in the picture rather than a representation of it. (The issue is not whether they are right, but that the condition of photography enables them to hold such a view in the first place.) Sherman's genius consists in the discovery that one can be disturbatory through photography (which is related to but not the same thing as being disturbing through photographing disturbing things). There are images of her to which I return obsessively, again and again, as to a peremptory fantasy. My sense is that this is true of all her admirers. She has found a way of penetrating the consciousness of her viewers, and in this way obliterating the insulating distances between her self and our selves.

Sherman's work falls into two main groups: "stills," which are black and white, and done mainly from 1977 to 1980; and "color photographs," which she has done ever since, and which have been growing larger and larger. For reasons not altogether aesthetic, I admire the stills more, at least at my present level of understanding her work. In them she is, as it were, Cindy Starlet as The Girl—the female lead in any nondescript grade B film. The Girl, in Barbie doll garments, waiting, watching, wary, is caught at a moment of suspense and implied narrativity, with just enough by way of props—a suitcase, a letter, an empty glass—to identify the nature of her dilemma. The still *di*stills. It implies the drama it condenses more than the movement it arrests. It was after all the function of the still—in the era before there was film criticism or before people read it and decided on that basis whether to take a film in or let it pass—to provoke, tempt, attract. Under the marquee, on either side of the ticket booth, beneath the lurid poster showing the fragile thing cowering as the shadows near, two or three stills were pinned as come-ons, as mute barker's teases, calculated to cause the coins to be laid down, the passerby to enter the darkness, for the pleasure of seeing sheer fluttering femininity threatened, rescued and redeemed for and through romance. The Arts & Leisure section of *The New York Times* prints stills to much the same purpose.

The Girl is always shown alone, blond sometimes and sometimes brunette, sometimes a working girl, sometimes a wife, pretty in her apron, threatened in her kitchen—and sometimes she is shown mooning with a letter in her hand or someone's bland photograph on her dressing table, under the mirror in which we see her tender back and the reflection of the space into which she stares, with a man's jacket slung on an empty chair, and a drained glass. Feminine to the essence, soft, vulnerable, fragility her middle name, good, still Daddy's brave girl, cutely independent, determined despite the threats and obstacles, a little heroine, The Girl in the Still condenses the myths that defined life's expectations in Middle American fantasy and have since migrated to the paperback romance. The myths retain to this day an undeniable disturbatory power. In an essay from 1984, printed with the catalogue for the show, Peter Schjeldahl writes ("as a male") of these images as "triggering" (masculine) urges to ravish and/or to protect. Lisa Phillips (as a female) asserts that Sherman's women "have a dignity with which we can identify to acknowledge 'our common terror of degradation and disorientation.' " The stills are in no sense pornographic—but they are what we may call "pornographic functions," variables for which we substitute the values of our own dark sexual fears and yearnings. As concept and execution, it is a brilliant achievement.

Since 1980, perhaps in consequence of growing older and hence no longer easily typecast as The Girl despite the extreme plasticity of her features, but more likely because of a certain restlessness in the face of having found a formula, Sherman has left behind the still in favor of large images and more indeterminate, less culturally anchored mythologies. She achieved celebrity through a series in which she lies or squats within the horizontal cell of the centerfold in a kind of Piranesi darkness. These images are less artificial than those that drew on the easy vocabulary of movies, or they are of an order of artifice that belongs to Baroque painting. The Woman could be having visions or be about to receive stigmata or she could be mad. Her gestures, the deployment of limb and body, are operatic and extreme, even if the garments remain often American, 1980s. And she presents herself more directly to the viewer, no longer mediated through Cindy Starlet on location, playing to the camera; she no longer wears the atmosphere of cinematic cliché as a costume to protect her and us. So the myths are more concrete and, so to speak, more possible: these could be real women in real situations. If there is illusion it is no longer the illusion of an illusion, although reality itself has become more fantastic and terrifying. At the same time, these later images—vertical, even square— have become more intertextually implicated in webworks of art-historical allusion. In number 155, she has changed her body for that of Hans Bellmer's creepy Doll, whose buttocks are thrust into our face, the cleft between them painted sadist red. In one we see her terrified face reflected, beyond a puddle of vomit and next to strewn pastries, in a pair of sunglasses, like a bulimic *menina*. In number 167, fragments of her stick up through the loam that has been hastily thrown over her hacked body—her lips here, her teeth there, fingers somewhere else—with only her image intact, reflected in the mirror of her makeup case as if it had survived the dismemberment (unless she is reflected as she bends over her victim).

In these later pictures, the transformations and displacements are more daring and more grotesque. Flesh is added, subtracted or rearranged. It is shown eaten by disease, rot and dissolution. Sherman becomes an animal, real or mythological, an urchin, an idiot, several kinds of victim, an idol, a harridan, a corpse, a skeleton, a monster.

Limbs are swollen and distended, eyes are about to burst, organs are pocked and reddened, blood fills the cavity of the mouth. In one case she has disappeared, or else she is distributed, as gobbets of flesh, in an immense dish, all wurst and ketchup—a stew for a suburban cannibal. Unless, since I thought I read one of the items as the glans of a penis, she is serving up the flesh of . . . who knows? a lover, a husband, just someone she entrapped?—the pretty young wife in frilled housedress having turned into something ferocious, vengeful, terrible. This degree of savage femaleness has not been seen in art since the Bacchae, and it is for this reason that I question whether my preference for the stills is purely aesthetic. In any case one is grateful for the knowledge that the color photographs are contrived iterations still of her, Cindy Sherman, for the illusions have become unendurably powerful.

It is a very unsettling show. When I left, I saw Sherman, like a figural aftereffect, absolutely everywhere—in the jeans ads on the back of buses, on the television screens in video shops, on the front pages of tabloids, in the ads of *The New Yorker* I glimpsed Calvin Tomkins reading on the number 4 bus headed uptown and in the mannequins in Madison Avenue storefronts. I recommend that you decompress before hitting the street. There are all your reassuring old favorites from the Whitney's permanent collection on the third floor, and the museum has considerately installed an exhibition of Red Grooms on the fourth.

—*The Nation*, August 15/22, 1987

Red Grooms

HOBBES, in his quirky lexicon of feelings, defines laughter as "sudden glory"—a thought so pungent and abrupt as nearly to illustrate itself. Sudden glory is made objective and palpable in the assembled work of Red Grooms, and it is this quality to which one immediately responds as the elevator opens onto the fourth floor of the Whitney Museum of American Art, given over entirely to this artist's singular *clownerie*. And since in the precincts of high art the generosity of the clown, bent on the sudden instillation of glory in his viewers, is so rare a virtue, it is worth dilating for a moment on the moral psychology of the artistic goof, a role Grooms has chosen as a way to mediate between audience and reality.

It is not simply that as a clown he is concerned with causing pleasure—a motive so tepid that aestheticians have at times been able to characterize the whole of art in its slack unhelpful terms. It is a pleasure of a specific kind, involving an accommodation to a reality possessed of a certain power or even awesomeness—like Manhattan, or like art itself, conceived of in the nearly sacred terms sometimes accorded it. When the reality falls short of this, and the distances between viewer and reality are correspondingly less vast, clowning degenerates into buffoonery. Grooms occupies a critical space that borders on the latter, or even includes it at times, and the work then takes on the unredeemed slapstick vulgarity of the joke shop. Every form of artistic expression has its peculiar form of failure, the abyss that artistry has to risk as the price of triumph. The mere mess, for example, is the obverse of the spontaneous glory that is Pollock's high achievement. Sheer grotesqueness is the risk one runs in courting distortion. Pallidness is the dark side of purity. Bombast is the shadow cast by exaltation. Incomprehensibility is the penalty the parodist pays in choosing too obscure a subject. The silly is the downside of the sly. Grooms's motives are of such transparent goodness that one loves him even when he falters or flops. For we are always conscious that it is our own well-being that drives him.

Puritanism was sufficiently rife in Hobbes's world that laughter was under suspicion, and his own misanthropy was deep enough that he used the occasion of a discussion on laughter to expose once again the smallness of the human soul. Sudden glory, he tells us, is among other things caused in people "by the apprehension of some deformed thing in another, whereof they suddenly applaud themselves." He goes on to say (excluding himself through the pronoun), "It is incident most to them, that are conscious of fewest abilities in themselves; who are forced to keep themselves in their own favor, by observing the imperfections of other men." It follows that the propensity to laughter weakens with an increase in self-confidence, and a society secure in its complacency would be as little in need of clowns as one of moral purity would stand in need of a redeemer. But then the need for laughter must be an index of our insecurity, and there is a kind of parallel, embodied in the literary character of the fool, between the clown and the savior. Both lower themselves, both take upon themselves the burden of a sacrifice, in order that others should be lifted up. It is neither here nor there that the sacrificer should himself be fulfilled through this supererogatory act.

The art of the clown differs from that of the caricaturist, in that the latter seizes on certain defects, and uses them in order to lower the subject through ridicule. It is for this reason that cartooning has a natural and obvious political location, and is a kind of weapon for bringing down the high and mighty. The clown, by contrast, underlines the same imperfections as a way of raising the audience in its own esteem. The lesson of the caricature is that the subject is no better than we are, bringing him down to our level. The effect of the clown is to show that we are as good as the subject, thus raising us to his level. There is something mean about the caricaturist and something proportionately generous about the clown—but it has also always been easier in politics to bring down the privileged than to raise the general standard. In any case, when the distance between the audience and the subject is perceived as vast, and the shrinking of that distance is sensed as abrupt, sudden glory is phenomenologically exact as a representation of the resulting change in moral focus. Grooms, as an artist, has a theatrical identity just because his aim is the transformation of his viewers rather than the production of an interesting visual object. To treat him as though he were the latter kind of artist, someone for whom visual delectation was primary, is altogether to misrepresent his virtues and his fallings-off. At its best, his work engages us internally and morally, but even at its worst the intentions have the goodness only possessed by the moral will.

Stylistically, and perhaps temperamentally, the work and the will are connected. Grooms is incapable of biting caricature, even when his aims are political and his feelings enraged, as in his 1967 construction *Patriot's Parade*, which shows Lyndon Johnson, a skull painted inside the crown of his doffed Stetson, stomping down some demonstrators with his ornamental cowboy boots, while a demure Miss Napalm stands by and patriots wave the red, white and blue. One of them treads on a redheaded girl who holds aloft a wooden daffodil. For all its guns-versus-flowers indignation, part of the sentimentality of its era, the work remains merely comical—and it could not have looked very different in the 1960s when the protest that engendered it was acute. This is because Grooms early adopted, and never (unless recently) relinquished, the broad exaggerations of the comic strip, and specifically that order of representation the comic artist uses to show that violent feeling and violent action are taking place, deploying a system of visual signs, in themselves often funny, to attain communication. Think of how shock and surprise would be represented in that vocabulary: a man would be shown with his eyes literally popping out of his head like Ping-Pong balls, his tongue lolling out, gobs and not just drops of sweat emitted by his contorted brow, as a light bulb flashes in a thought balloon over him and an involuntary "ULP!" escapes from his Adam's apple. The comic-strip body is infinitely elastic and graphically immortal—its limbs can twist like rubber hoses, it can land KERPLUNK on its head, but no damage is ever final. The Katzenjammer Kids may blow Der Captain and Der Inspector sky-high in a shower of stars and smoke—BLAM-M-M-M!—but they will get walloped in the last frame by the blackened and indestructible figures of authority. One cannot help reading little balloons over the heads of

Grooms's demonstrators—"OUCH!" "HEY!" "@&#!"—and Little Miss Napalm looks about as threatening as the girl in corkscrew curls who embodies the otherness of gender for Dennis the Menace. Grooms's whole style, addressed precisely to the muting and transformation of threat in order to make the threatening world more humane and tractable, is precisely antithetical to the transmission of political outrage. Sometimes comedy is just the wrong way to address a subject one wants to do something about, which explains, I think, the failure of Chaplin in seeking to turn Hitler into the Little Tramp in jackboots.

But the stylistic boundaries that so inhibit Grooms's in any case infrequent transports of political criticism serve him magnificently in the far more characteristic healing interventions of the clown. This is nowhere better realized than in his masterpiece, *Ruckus Manhattan*, conceived of in 1974 and shown to its widest audience in 1976 at the Marlborough Gallery. *Ruckus Manhattan* is an assemblage on a grand scale of a dozen components, each of them a part of New York City. Five of these, including *Subway* and *Wall Street*, are now on display. It was an immense collaborative effort between Grooms, his then wife Mimi Gross, and a dilating band of the faithful; and its looseness and genial anarchy reflect the chaos of New York itself. But the work was a kind of miraculous transformation that can only be appreciated against a city startlingly different from the one a recent flyer from *New York* gushingly celebrates: "And now . . . the resurgence of the city—new offices, high-rises, hotels, towers . . . landmarks restored, neighborhoods revived . . . new restaurants, theaters, galleries, shops . . ." The New York of the early 1970s was a sour, shabby, hopeless, decaying agglomeration of failing neighborhoods, on the edge of receivership, and one had the sense that in whatever way it is appropriate to speak of a social fabric, ours had unraveled. The city Grooms addressed was the shaken metropolis whose emblem was the graffiti-scorched subway, evidence that things had gone altogether out of control. It was absolutely appropriate that Grooms should have made the subway the centerpiece of *Ruckus Manhattan*, and absolutely inspired that one should have entered the work, at the Marlborough, through the shaking BMT car, a kinetic counterpart to the great gate of the Inferno. Yet in antithesis to Dante's symbol, one did not leave hope behind in entering Manhattan in effigy, but acquired hope amid the familiar sights, given a comic face and an affecting silliness, a clumsy grace and a sudden

Red Grooms

glory. I date the turnaround of New York from *Ruckus Manhattan*, and take a certain chauvinistic satisfaction, as a New Yorker and a member of the art world, that an art gallery should have been the scene of our symbolic revival through the spirit of comedy.

"I had to do Manhattan, you know? I had to get it out," Grooms once said, conveying the urgency of a project that cost him a great deal in his personal life, in order, as he put it, that "people could enjoy it, party around it, just be sociable in its general vicinity." It is in this readiness to sacrifice oneself for the enhancement of others that I situate the high vocation of the clown, but because the reality he next addressed, in his *Ruckus Rodeo* of 1976, has none of the terrible power possessed by a sinking city, he stepped, in making it, from clown to buffoon. These mark the extremes, I think, of his competence and gift, and limit, as in the example of *Patriot's Parade*, the effect of his trans-formations. In the early dawn, after a legendary boozy night, Socrates said, "The genius of comedy is the same as that of tragedy, and the true artist in tragedy is an artist in comedy also." This may be true for words and for music—Shakespeare and Verdi make his point—but I am uncertain that it is true for images. A Disney production of The Greatest Story Ever Told (with Mickey as Jesus and Minnie as Mary Magdalene) would raise, if nothing else, serious questions of taste. Even when Grooms cares deeply about something, like the death of Picasso, his reflexes betray him, and it is difficult to see his print *Picasso Goes to Heaven* (not exhibited here) as more than a kind of comic valentine to a dead genius.

Lately, I feel, Grooms has been breaking through the carapace of funny-paper expression by appropriating styles that resonate marvel-ously with his subject. Of course, he did that at times in earlier and less exacting works, such as his charming 1963 foldout *Le Banquet pour le Douanier Rousseau*, in which he borrows an effigy of Liberty from Rousseau's own *Liberty Summoning Artists to Exhibit at the Salon des Indépendants*, to sound a trumpet voluntary over the heads of the celebrants at that legendary occasion in 1908. But I have in mind his use of the style belonging to the artists he depicts in his portraits of them and their work, shown recently at the Marlborough, and most particularly in his huge *tableaux à clef* of the Cedar Bar. It is sad that the Whitney was unable to secure this work for its version of the exhibition launched by the Pennsylvania Academy in 1985, for it really belongs in the atmosphere of a museum of American art. It shows the giants of the New York School flirting, discoursing, brawling and sprawling in the lamented drinking place, and is painted in the style of late 1940s figurative art. My memory may deceive me, but it seems to me that Grooms had done it in the style of his own teacher of the era, Gregorio Prestopino, in which case it is twice over an act of piety and a confession of loyalty to the sources of his artistic being.

Grooms is in the deepest sense a public artist, perhaps the only real public artist we have. There are plenty of artists ready at the drop of a commission to stick a piece of themselves in public space, but public art is not the same as art in public places. It is, rather, art that transforms the consciousness that defines us as a public, that gives us an identity as a community from within. Grooms brings this about by using styles that reach outside the art world, and have a powerful connection to popular art—and then, such is his goodness and his generosity, he brings the art world together with the real world in a kind of visual feast.

—*The Nation*, September 12, 1987

Henri Cartier-Bresson

THERE ARE musical compositions, written, usually, for piano or violin, so difficult of execution that part of what they are about is the extreme dexterity required to perform them. There are others of such oceanic depth that part of what they refer to must be the answering profundity of the artist capable of making it palpable through stirring performance, almost as if the performance were part of the evoked meaning. It is rare that both orders of gift are called upon in any single piece of music, and quite possibly they are antithetical: the set piece for virtuosi celebrates a power so beyond the common measure that its meaning must be correspondingly narrow, whereas a deep work, one feels, must answer to the most universal truths of human existence. The second kind of musical performance closes the gap between artist and audience, as if the artist but gives voice to the feelings that unite them. The first sort, by contrast, flaunts that gap: the virtuoso is viewed with amazement, like a great athlete or startling beauty, across a vast and hopeless divide. And this, too, may explain why the co-presence of these different powers is hardly to be expected in a single work.

Virtuosity may be found side by side with depth in some of the other arts, though the former sometimes drives the latter out. Thus spectacular displays of foreshortening or perspective can be obstacles to artistic profundity. And though there are artists capable of bravura and depth at once, like Rembrandt or Velázquez, it is unclear to what degree the two are interconnected even in admittedly great works. Most of what scholars dispute in *Las Meninas* would remain were we to subtract the acutely confident brushwork through which a piece of lace or a spaniel's ear are summoned out of flourishes and parries of pigment. Sargent was not a deep artist, though his brush was as athletic as any in the history of painting. And Picasso was a deep artist whose inventiveness made at least that order of gesture irrelevant. The mystery of Henri Cartier-Bresson's art as a photographer is not just that his images are dazzling and deep at once but that these polarities coincide in so remarkable a way that one feels they must be internally connected, that he could not be so powerful if he were not also brilliant. So, while his subject must in part be the singular authority of the photographic act, the other part of his subject—that to which we respond in the fullness of our humanity—must somehow connect with this, as if meaning and attack were made for one another.

As a young, fiercely romantic adventurer, Cartier-Bresson passed a year in Africa as a night hunter, using an acetylene lamp to immobilize his prey while he took his killing aim; and the hunter's exact reflexes, the perfect instantaneity of eye, mind and finger for which the high-speed rifle or the high-speed camera are metaphors, carry over in his work as a photographer. Each of his famous pictures refers internally to the act of shooting it, and each, for all its laconic title (*Madrid, 1933; Marseilles, 1932; Mexico, 1934*), is eloquent with the implied narrative of the successful kill. Each encapsulates the speed, the deadly accuracy, the total self-assurance and the patience, endurance and will of the huntsman as artist. I owe to Peter Galassi, curator of Cartier-Bresson: The Early Years (at the Museum of Modern Art) and author of the illuminating catalogue that accompanies the show, the insight that the hand-held camera with the high-speed shutter transformed the condition and thence the content of photography (much, I suppose, as the invention of the escapement action transformed performance on the pianoforte and redefined the conditions of composition for that instrument). The old photographers, with their unwieldy equipment, their need for sustained illumination and a total immobility in their motifs, addressed a world of willed stasis, which the best of them—Atget, say—transformed into a kind of frozen poetry, cleaned of time and change. World and artist stood still for one another, the double immobility vesting the plate with an uncanny, platonic stillness. The hand-held camera liberated both parties to this transaction, allowing the world to be itself. Where the older photographers addressed immovable grandiosities—mountains, palaces, enthroned

[*134*

monarchs—the swift, unburdened sharpshooter of the modern instrument could take on the ephemeral, the transitory, the weightless.

The unmistakable evidence of an advance in the technological side of an art—the unmistakable evidence that technology counts for something in that art—is that, initially, it becomes the subject of the art it revolutionizes. The discovery of perspective meant that its first users were enthusiasts who made each painting an occasion for demonstrating command over the new technology of distal recession, and they chose subjects that best enabled the demonstration to be made. The subject of the first moving pictures was movement itself: rushing streams, speeding trains, the stirring of boughs in the Bois de Boulogne. I sometimes wonder if the exhibition of gore in film today really testifies to an appetite for gruesomeness on the part of an audience, and not instead to the display of craft in the special-effects department, which, like the enthusiasm for distance as distance, movement as movement, will sooner or later cloy. In any case, the fast-action camera initially addressed fast action as such, the image calling attention to the virtues of the new technologies. A certain number of Cartier-Bresson's first works are simply about the arresting of a motion that could not be held, as in the famous shot of a man leaping a puddle behind the Gare St.-Lazare. (I could not help smiling at the two torn posters in the background, advertising a concert by the piano virtuoso Alexander Brailowsky, playing Chopin, exactly the composer to enable his brilliance to come forward.) Had Cartier-Bresson remained obsessed with such tours de force, he would have gone down in history as a master of speed and light, but not the deep artist to whom we respond today. For this he needed a content that transcended and yet incorporated the sensitivity of the instrument. And what we have are not just so many examples of arrested motion but examples rather of transcribed revelations, as if the world itself opened, like a shutter, affording a fleeting glimpse, a flash, of otherwise hidden meanings.

It is in fact as though beneath the visual appearances of the familiar world there were another system of reality altogether, covert and disguised, but which stands to the surface world as the unconscious stands to conscious mental processes. Certain juxtapositions, certain startling associations of ordinary thing with ordinary thing, open up the deeper reality to the observation of an instant, after which the fissures close and we are restored to the commonplace. Cartier-Bresson, who after all had ingested the theory of a double layer of meaning and reality from the Surrealists, who in turn derived their theory and program from the thought of Freud, functioned, as a photographer, on two interpenetrating levels of appearance. Freud famously saw in dreams, jokes and free association the aperture into the primary processes of the unconscious system, which the Surrealists, of course, treated as the creative substratum of the mind. Cartier-Bresson's work is filled with the power and menace of such associations and puns.

Consider one of his masterpieces, *Madrid, 1933*, which shows a group of men beneath the wall of a mysterious building. The wall is punctuated by windows of various sizes, small in proportion to the wall itself, and seemingly distributed randomly across its surface; it is impossible to infer the internal architecture of the building from the evidence of these openings. Indeed, the wall looks like a rampart of some sort, its original purpose subverted by squatters on the other side who punched holes here and there, opening it to the flat expanse that is the foreground of the picture. The array of square windows conveys the sense of meaning, much in the way in which, though the analogy is forced and anachronistic, the holes in a punch card imply that with the right device the card could yield a piece of information. Or the squares dance across the surface as if in a ready-made counterpart to "Broadway Boogie-Woogie." Or the tiny squares look like the square notes in Gregorian notation, as if someone had composed a chant in the medium of windows. I have often wondered what the building was and whether it still stands, and though only an eye driven by certain beliefs and attitudes could have been sensitive to its overtones, it could have been the motif of a still photograph made by a heavy camera, requiring a tripod. But at the bottom of the picture is the crowd of men and boys—I count fourteen—whose bodies are sheared off, in many cases, by the bottom edge of the picture, so that we are conscious, mainly, of the rhythm of their heads, which echoes the rhythm of the windows, like the accompaniment, in another clef, of treble harmonies. Or it is like two voices in an intricate fugue of heads and windows. Or it is as if heads and windows were different forms of the same thing, or metaphors for one another—and in at least two cases one has to look carefully to see whether a certain dark shape is head or window. Yet this is not some formal exercise; the heads and windows are too insistently in resonance with one another for us not to seek a meaning our rational self denies can be there. The image is clotted with magical possibilities, and it seems to force an opening into the mind of the artist if not the mind of the world—one can barely tear oneself away from the riddles it poses. The entire exhibition is a set of traps for the interpretive resources of the eye, but *Madrid, 1933* has the power of a great musical questioning.

André Breton, the relentless theoretician and dogmatist of Surrealism, once said, "Automatic writing is a true photography of thought." By that, I believe he meant that the absurd illogic of automatic writing replicates a corresponding rhythm of thought, recording the creative pulses of the subrational mind. If the real—or, better, the surreal—world has the same dislogic the Surrealists attributed to the mind, then a true photography of it would record the magic to which rationality is blind. There can be no doubt that the Surrealists characteristically used photography to insinuate this, using the premises of optical exactitude to demonstrate the fantastic exterior of the after-all-not-so-ordinary world. But often they achieved this by flagrant manipulations and montages, or by using as motifs things they found rich with their own silly meanings. Cartier-Bresson's photographs do not, characteristically, look surrealistic, in part, I think, because he sought the surreal in natural conjunctions that have to be seen as connoting the kinds of things the Surrealists instead built into their own vocabularies. The consequence is that he managed to break through the crusts of habitual perception with images so astonishingly fresh that one's response to them, however familiar they have become, is composed in part of a sense of one's own visual pedestrianism. We feel that between our eyes and the world out there, cataracts of habit have formed, and our own vision is dirty, clouded, oblique. So the surrealism is invisible. What we have instead is the sense of restoration to our true powers and the objective wonder of a world we have taken too much for granted. The photographs of Cartier-Bresson come to us in the form of marvelous gifts; one feels cleansed and empowered by them, and enlarged.

—*The Nation*, October 3, 1987

137]

The Hudson River School

IT IS A TRUTH rarely in need of mention that works of art have an identity as material objects—that they are made of paint and bronze and cloth and wood. In recent times, to be sure, substance has asserted itself as subject, so that works of visual art often refer internally to the material conditions of their realization, and are about what they are made of. It would be false to ascribe so contemporary an aesthetic to the paintings of the Hudson River School, as it was somewhat derisively labeled, but it is also impossible not to be struck by their status as furniture—as objects of interior decoration that summon up the other components of domestic embellishment with which they converse in the plush language of comfort. With their oleaginous and varnished surfaces, as glowing as buffed mahogany, their heavily carved and gilded frames, their academic authority, their opulence verging at times on corpulence, these paintings surround themselves with tacit parlors and salons. They belong in the company of stuffed and tufted ottomans and Turkish carpets, of ormolu hardware and brass lamps, of fringed burgundy velvet and luminous damask, and rosewood pianofortes or elaborately fretted harmoniums on which accomplished daughters or young wives fingered hymns or songs of sweet melancholy concerning lost or distant loves. The scenes these paintings represent occupy those rooms of reassuringly thick prosperity like thought balloons, indoor embodiments of outdoor realities that correspond, in every spiritual particular, to the spaces in which they are suspended. The outdoors shows God's grace shed upon the American landscape as the indoors reflects that same grace bestowed in the medium of material success. As scenes and things at once, the Hudson River paintings communicate a double affirmation of divine blessing. They constitute the American wing of the Protestant ethic given cultural expression. They radiate self-congratulation and an almost cosmic complacency.

Writing of Claude Lorrain, an artist against whom the Hudson River painters measured themselves on their excursions abroad, Roger Fry said, "Claude's view of landscape is false to nature in that it is entirely anthropocentric. His trees exist for pleasant shade; his peasants to give us the illusion of pastoral life, not to toil for a living. His world is not to be lived in, only to be looked at in a mood of pleasing melancholy or suave revery." But I wonder if there ever was a form of landscape painting that is not "false" in this sense. The landscapes we represent are in effect texts in which our feelings and beliefs about nature, and hence about ourselves as inside and outside nature, are inscribed. According to Wen Fong, *Travelers in a Wintry Forest*, a twelfth-century Chinese painting after Li Ch'eng, transmits the proposition that "recluse scholars living in the mountains have rediscovered in nature a moral order lost in the human world." No such contrast is pointed in the Hudson River paintings, of course, because the natural and the social order for them were one—two modalities of divine presence in American reality. Through the metaphysical window of an oil painting its owner could see the face of God and almost hear the voice of God in the cataracts and echoing precipices of Catskill Mountain scenery. In an odd way, the paintings, in bringing God into the living rooms of the land, have almost the sacred office of religious icons. It says a great deal about the American mind in the early mid-nineteenth century that religious art took the form of landscapes that were Edenic, majestic, gorgeous and bombastic, rather than historical scenes of biblical enactment. It says a great deal as well about the mirror function of landscape painting that the transfigurative vistas of the Hudson River painters gave way, after the Civil War, to something more intimate and less awesome—to farms, for example, where sunsets mean the end of the day's labor, as the workman trudges homeward through diffuse illumination, rather than extravagant timberlands above which God addresses the nation through spectacular cloud formations flamboyantly lit up with cadmium reds and oranges.

These were works of high Romanticism, illustrations, so to speak, of texts such as Coleridge's "Frost at Midnight":

By lakes and sandy shores, beneath the crags
Of ancient mountain, and beneath the clouds,
Which image in their bulk both lakes and shores
And mountain crags: so shalt thou see and hear
The lovely shapes and sounds intelligible
Of that eternal language, which thy God
Utters.

"The true province of landscape art," wrote Asher B. Durand, who was the leader of this school after the death of its founder, Thomas Cole, and in any case perhaps the paradigmatic Hudson River painter, "is the work of God in the visible creation, independent of man." Earlier he had written, "The external appearance of this our dwelling place is fraught with lessons of high and holy meaning, only surpassed by the light of Revelation." The crowds surging through the American Wing of New York City's Metropolitan Museum of Art to admire the marvelous and timely exhibition of Hudson River art are no doubt gripped by its visions of natural beauty in sites not greatly altered today, despite Grossinger's and Lake George Village. Still, one misses the point if one sees these paintings only or even chiefly as transcriptions after nature. They are, with qualification, incidentally that. It is not altogether wrong to say, as John K. Howat, the curator of the show does in an interview in *The New York Times*, that "you can practically smell the light." The illusion of transcriptional exactitude was only a means to an end. The end was to have been a work "imbued," according to Durand, "with that indefinable quality recognized as sentiment or expression which distinguishes the true landscape from the mere sensual and striking picture." That is a beautiful formulation of a distinction between a visual text and a mere picture, and it is my sense that the message that this is God's country must still come through to an audience still responsive to the sentimental assurances of "divine visual language." It is a message transmitted in the vocabulary of waterfalls and rushing streams, storm clouds and florid dawns, massed foliage and blasted tree trunks. It is this, I think, that must explain the popularity of the show rather than the message Howat believes the paintings communicate to us: "The natural environment is something we have to preserve."

It was the unmistakable rhetoric of these landscapes that caused a later generation of American artists to turn their back on a style that to them rang false in a different sense of the term than Roger Fry's. The American Pre-Raphaelites, who drew their artistic agenda from Ruskin's philosophy of "truth to Nature," dismissed these paintings exactly in the name of truth, and it is their insistent edification, their almost sermonic elevatedness, that makes some of us uncomfortable today. They were very good painters, many of them, but there is something of the PTL ministry in their aggregate material optimism that makes one wince—makes one want to find falsity in their works in the way one is grateful to find moral sleaziness in the television evangelists.

Consider *Kindred Spirits*, a famous memorial to Thomas Cole executed the year after Cole's death by Asher Durand. It shows two men in a characteristic Catskill landscape—the poet William Cullen Bryant and Cole himself. Bryant's head is uncovered, surely in a gesture of reverence before the scenery being displayed by Cole. The scene itself is composed of two sites, perhaps as famous as the two men themselves: Kaaterskill Falls and the Kaaterskill Clove—a dramatic gorge which was, together with the falls, a favored motif. Now, it is altogether possible that Cole and Bryant stood upon that cantilevered rock. But it is not at all possible that they could have seen Kaaterskill Falls and the Kaaterskill Clove when they did so, for a perspective in which the two could be seen together is, as Barbara Buff writes, "geologically impossible." I am uncertain as to how this objective falsehood is to be interpreted. Cole himself had written, "The most lovely and perfect parts of Nature may be brought together, and combined in a whole that shall surpass in beauty and effect any picture painted from a single view." It would be anachronistic to imagine Cole depicted as pointing to an impossible conjunction as a tribute to his philosophy of art—*Kindred Spirits* would in that case prefigure Cubism. Rather, I think, the painting carries forward Cole's view that it is all right, even necessary, to falsify observed nature in the name of some higher truth. And Durand's tribute does aim at some higher truth, at the cost of falsehood before which, as Cole put it, "Time [would] draw a veil over the common details." Cole is pointing perhaps to two birds, soaring in the sublimity of God's fearful space, as metaphors, maybe, for poetic and painterly vision taking wing over mere detail. Durand thought of himself as rendering things as they are, but it remained consistent with his enterprise to regiment and rearrange visual detail in the interests of some spiritually convincing message. The rhetoric was too clamorous to fade when it no longer communicated to an audience willing to believe in it, and the veil of time made it, rather than the common details, what one finally saw. The Pre-Raphaelites turned from such work with a kind of moral revulsion. For them it became enough to paint a single twig, a pair of acorns, a nest of eggs or just one flower with botanical propriety.

The expression "divine visual language" comes from the great essay on vision by Bishop George Berkeley, and I derive a certain satisfaction from the fact that one of the later members of the Hudson River School, Worthington Whittredge, should have painted *Second Beach, Newport* at Newport, Rhode Island, with the famous Hanging Rocks that students of the history of philosophy will identify as the site where Berkeley's *Alciphron* is set. Berkeley had come to Newport for complicated and improbable reasons, and his former house stands today not far from the Hanging Rocks. Worthington has composed a horizontal and rather soft meditative picture, suitable to the circumstance—that what had once been the scene of theological speculation had become a place of recreation. It is instructive to compare the language God spoke in Rhode Island in 1732 with that which He spoke in New York in 1849. For Berkeley, God "daily speaks to our senses in a manifest and clear dialect." By this Berkeley meant that the sensed qualities of things are signs for other qualities as yet unsensed, and that in learning to read what Durand later called "the great book of nature" we come to learn which things are good for us and which we must avoid. Berkeley saw the world as a textbook of useful instructions. Durand saw it as a set of romantic engravings for an inspirational epic. By Durand's time, God was no longer in the things we sense daily, but spoke out only to those prepared to visit wild sublime formations. So the Hudson River artist sought out the most dramatic locations—the most stupefying heights and vistas, rendering the American landscape in the idiom of glory and power. It was his missionary undertaking to bring this terrifying beauty back in the form of engravings or chromolithographs—or to those who could afford them, paintings of an increasing dimension and grandeur—for the exaltation of patriots who saw in the effusions of a prodigal nature the greatness of American destiny.

Whittredge's *Second Beach, Newport* was done in 1878–80, and its quietness is almost shattering. One has the sense that God withdrew from the Catskills, and that artists had to travel to further and more inaccessible places to hear His voice at all. Paintings grew larger and larger, as if turning up the volume to catch the fading voice diminishing in the whirlwinds. The works of Church and Bierstadt impress us as having increased the scale in order to compensate for reluctant credibilities. Viewers must increasingly have had the sense that they were being manipulated, marvelous as the painting often was. After all, it was in the highest, most glacial mountaintops that Nietzsche proclaimed the death of God in 1883 through the persona of Zarathustra. It is very touching that the seashore Whittredge painted shows holidaymakers wading in gentle tides, washing quietly over the curved shore, with the Hanging Rocks as a brooding presence to which their backs are turned. The sky is cheery and the clouds are soft presences rather than heavenly syllables. God has quite withdrawn from Newport, as He quite withdrew from American landscapes when the paintings of the Hudson River School subsided into furniture and became all but forgotten.

There would be a kind of justice if these painters, nearly inaccessible to us through collisions in taste, should have a second life as reminders of the natural realities we visit today for the foliage and the waters. And there would be an irony if the strident natural theology were really made invisible and we should see in the works a world no longer powerful but at our mercy—up to us to defend and preserve rather than be thrilled by. But I doubt this is the message that comes through. Natural piety has not for some time been an available virtue for sophisticated sensibilities. But the artists of the Hudson River School were not painting for moral minimalists. There are those, of course, defined by formalist aesthetics, who are deaf to the tones of prayer in these works and see them simply in terms of spatialities and scales later taken up in New York painting. But for me, as for the enthusiastic visitors to the Met these days, these paintings belong to that genre of American overstatement Tocqueville identified as the other face of the practicality that defines us as a people. It is how we respond to that overstatement that determines what these paintings mean to us today.

—*The Nation*, November 7, 1987

Frank Stella

BECAUSE IT IS OPEN at the front, like a box stage or even a chapel, the vestibule gallery of the retrospective exhibition of Frank Stella's work from 1970 to 1987 at the Museum of Modern Art communicates the sense that this is a special sort of space, set off from the mere public spaces of the museum. This feeling is heightened by the three large rococo works that occupy it, mounted on each of the lateral walls and at the back, between two openings into the exhibition itself, whose style and content is announced by this trio of fascinating and flamboyant fabrications. Each is a furious razzle of dashing curves in the spangled colors of a circus acrobat's costume—garish, in deliciously bad taste, jarring cheerfully against one another, looking as if they had been picked by Cyndi Lauper to knock our eyes out. It is raucous, dizzy work that it is impossible not to be charmed by at first glance, but I mean to hold you at the threshold of this space, made metaphorical by the cunning installation, and ask you, before crossing into it, to turn around and contemplate the painting behind you. It would in any case be the last thing to see as you leave the show, but it will prove instructive to ponder it first, as it points forward to the work you are about to enjoy and backward to the work that gave Stella his early reputation, and which typified his precocious retrospective in this museum seventeen years ago.

An immense work, each side 11 feet 3 inches, *Bijoux indiscrets* consists of twenty-three concentric squares and has the compositional effect of a regularly stepped pyramid of squares, seen from above. The squares appear to converge at the innermost one, which is the same color—a hot yellow—as the outermost. It is important, I think, that the squares seem to progress inward, referring to their common center, rather than progressing outward, referring to the physical edge of the work. In Stella's early paintings, also consisting of concentric shapes, it was possible to read them, as was done in a famous essay by Michael Fried, as possessing a "deductive structure" in which the painted forms, defined by thin, laconic lines, referred outward to the overall shape of the canvas itself. At that time, 1963, critical sensibility was much under the influence of the aesthetics of Clement Greenberg, in which shape and surface were almost the uniquely relevant properties of painting, and Stella seemed made to order for that kind of sensibility. It was as if the work denoted, hence was about, its own material reality, and in particular its real edges. Superficially, the newer work, from 1974, seems to arise from the same impulses because of the regularity of its repeated congruent shapes, but it nonetheless appears to move irresistibly toward its own center, a painted square, the edges of which are not the physical edges of the work. It is as though pictorial illusion, rather than material reality, had begun to subvert the earlier, austere program.

In any case, the colors in the painting fight against the idea of an orderly, square-by-square progression. There are three main zones of color. The outermost and innermost zones, each composed of eight squares, are predominantly in hot or warm colors—reds, yellows, oranges, punctuated by a green square and a dark blue one. The intermediate zone, made up of seven squares, is dark and cool, in blues, maroons, purples. So the painting seems to dilate—it moves toward us in the hot zones and away from us in the cool zone. It is thus that color and geometry conflict with each other, the geometry striving to keep everything on the plane, respecting the edges, the colors refusing to adhere to this orderly program. The colors seem to be struggling to achieve a third dimension while the shapes keep the work anchored to two. It is as if it wants at once to be a painting and to enjoy a three-dimensional spatiality more palpable than that implied by mere edges. And now, if you look into the space of the first gallery, you will note that this is exactly what has been achieved: the gaudy curves are in different planes, hence in real space, but are held together in a rigorous pictorial composition.

So, *Bijoux indiscrets* is tense with historical differences, between the early Stella, with his drab colors and compulsive repetitions, and the later Stella, liberated to eccentric shapes, extravagant hues and impulsively scribbled surfaces. Big with the future as the painting behind you is, there was no way, I believe, in which that future could have been realized in 1974, though the next set of Stella's works, later that decade, begin to break away from the rigidity of the squares toward something more free. The change is somewhat diffident, since the shapes remain pretty angular, even if the colors—magentas and pinks, for example—have broken away from the spectrum from which the colors of the canvas we have just been examining are drawn. The spectrum itself is an orderly progression, though there are plenty of colors it does not contain—the color of flesh, for example. That it was possible, within a decade, to achieve the kind of work that energizes the space beyond the retrospective's threshold, where I am holding you, is due to a transformation in the art world itself, which I shall discuss in a moment. But I want first to draw your attention to another tension in this work, which intersects with the tension between color and geometry in the 1974 nest of squares (the later work seems like a nest of polychrome serpents).

This work belongs to what Stella called, for reasons of his own, the *Diderot series*, of which you will encounter three others on entering the show. I am naturally interested in Diderot, since he was the first philosopher to write art criticism in a professional way, but I have no clear idea of why Stella named these works after him. Nor do I know why Stella gave them their individual titles, usually taken from the names of Diderot's novels—*Jacques le fataliste*, for example, or a stunning one made of two adjoined sets of squares, *Le Rêve de d'Alembert*. The work I have been describing is providentially named *Bijoux indiscrets*, the title of a somewhat naughty novel, not altogether worthy of the great *philosophe* and which he later regretted having written. It concerns Mangogul, a certain fictional sultan modeled on the monarch of France, who reigns over a Congo court that is an allegory of Versailles. Mangogul has a magic ring which, when pointed at the genital zone of a woman, transforms her vagina into a mouth, which then spills the beans about her sexual secrets and the special secrets of those with whom she has been intimate. The book soon bogs down, as one loquacious and *indiscret bijou* has much the same story to tell as any other. Still, it is a pretty good title for the work, drawing attention to its eroticism: the dilations, almost muscular, the receding and thrusting forward, the warring of form and color, the relentless drawing in and in. These enact the cadences and excitements of physical love. This may strike you as a forced interpretation, but I have an unsolicited confirmation in the description of the *Diderot* paintings by John Russell: "They envelop us with a chromatic vibration that can almost be heard as well as seen. They tighten the visual knot, inch by inch, until we arrive at the tiny central square that is both the end of our journey and the knob of pure energy that holds us captive." (This in a family newspaper!) The *bijou* could scarcely have put it more graphically. So the tension I want to propose is that between the male and female sides of this artistic personality. The regimented squares express the regulative imperatives of the masculine will. The vibrant colors, the enveloping space, the sensuous and teasing dilations that draw us in, belong to the feminine side. Certain events in the art world of the 1970s and 1980s enabled this other side to emerge—though the sexual tensions of *Bijoux indiscrets*, transformed to be sure, remain in the more characteristic newer work and give it its excitement. The entire exhibition is a kind of erotic jubilee, filled with drives and responses. So let us enter the space and begin ourselves to respond to the works we have only so far looked at.

The first word that entered my mind when I initially saw these pieces was "feminist." With all due regard to the image of athletic machismo the artist projects through his obsession with fast cars and competitive sports, these extraordinary works suggest to me that a certain feminist sensibility has conquered artistic consciousness today. And this exhibition shows, in effect, the degree to which an idiom that was very much on the periphery of the art world of the 1970s has infiltrated it to the point of now being available as a salon style, and accessible to artists of whatever gender. It may well strike feminists that this instead is evidence of the same history of exploitation women have lived through immemorially, their breakthroughs being appropriated by one of the most approved male artists of the day in one of the most coveted spaces of international art. But it is a kind of victory, even so. It has always been the claim of at least some feminists that liberation would be mutual when it arrived; in any case it was the gradual acceptance of the strategies of feminist art that seem to me to have made this art possible. Feminist artists began by refusing to pursue those ideals of artistic purity that Stella's own early work exemplified to perfection, with its reduced colors, its exact ratios, its minimalisms, its essentializing of surface and shape. Women artists, in the name of women's art, aimed at a kind of impurity instead, messy, often shocking, with an openness to rejected materials and crazy forms and provocative juxtapositions and illogical sequences. It was as if they refused to be tidy, demure, tasteful, dainty, clean, which after all were attributes of an imprisoning femininity. At the same time, they were not anxious to preempt the attributes of masculinity. So women's art flourished in a narrow space, at the outskirts of the art world. Not surprisingly, many women became performance artists, and there is a component of performance in a good bit of women's art today, most of which, it seems to me, aims at the destabilization of accepted categories. It was categorization that had held women in their place, and the natural reflex was to stun the propensity to respect borderlines. Though there were, of course, feminist creations that celebrated specifically female forms, my sense is that the deep impulses of feminism consisted in eloquent, if often angry, repudiations. Inevitably, in enfranchising shapes, materials, colors, textures and images that did not easily fit accepted canons, feminists pioneered media that would sooner or later be appealing to those who may not have shared their ideology. The art world of the present, to the degree that it has been renewed by this—to the degree that it has been renewed at all—is greatly in their debt. And no one can be more greatly indebted than Stella.

Let us now begin to look more carefully at the work that faces us as we turn away from *Bijoux indiscrets* and stare into that wonderful first gallery. The work, *Zeltweg*, is a little society of odd shapes, dominantly curved shapes—scrolls and volutes—painted upon in a loose way with saturated colors and jumbled together in a sort of agreeable disorder. That is one's first impression. The shape that immediately strikes the eye is reminiscent of a blunt, curved scissors, predominantly yellow with some lavender squiggles, and overlaid by a spidery network of lines, like a freehand grid. At first the work seems like a scrap box of shapes, cut from odds and ends of fabric or painted paper and then abandoned, with the scissors laid across the top. Just behind the scissors is what looks like a carpenter's square, painted in uneven dashes of red pigment that effectively cover over the inch marks, as if to render it unusable for measurement. Beginning at the upper left side, then curving unevenly over the top until it widens out and drops on the right side, is a sort of green ribbon painted in a pattern one might find on the lampshade in an awful motel. It could be a snake with a curious opening for an eye, or a golf club gone flaccid and clumsy, and since it has a hole in its head, is of no use other than to be painted. All the

[148

shapes are entertaining and ambiguous, happy to risk being silly, like clowns. There is an almost explosive contrast between the comical atmosphere of the work and the solemn prose in which Stella's work is characterized in the show's catalogue, as indeed in the immense critical literature devoted to this admired artist. In fact, the writings on Stella constitute a body of prose that reads like contributions to an abstruse and remote study in which one might specialize and earn a higher degree. But I am willing to take this, too, as a tension that increases our enjoyment of the work. It is almost as if it were making fun of the ponderous descriptions (and there is a kind of feminist gesture there, as well).

The scissors form is supported by a thick black arrow, dribbled over in silvers and seeming to be a template, since various scroll-shaped holes, through which we can see other forms behind it, have been stamped out. The arrow points to the right, and lies on the precise horizontal axis of the work. In fact, the head and shaft of the arrow form right angles at the point where the horizontal and vertical axes cross, dividing the space into four equal-sized quadrants and acting as Cartesian coordinates. Suddenly, in the rough and tumble of shapes and colors geometry asserts itself, and the quivering oddments, which at first seemed so improvisational and disordered, are trapped in a grid that the coordinates imply. It is a grid that is comically, because so freely, cartooned with the same overlay network of lines I remarked on in discussing the scissors. In fact, one can see this loose network through the work, impishly refusing to be reduced to exactitudes. And all at once one begins to feel that everything has a double identity, geometrical and organic, mathematical and festive—masculine, if you like, and feminine.

By now the forms that seemed at first so curious have begun to look familiar. They are the instruments of mechanical drawing: triangles, Flexi-curves, T squares, straightedges, French curves and protractors. Every line is a locus of points in Cartesian space. Draftsman's curves are tools that enable us to connect points in a smooth-drawn curve. Instrumental but interesting in their own right as forms, the draftsman's tools have become characters in an allegory, full of references to order and disorder, to different orders of order, to logic and sensuality, constraint and impulse, integration and differentiation—an intricate ballet of interlocking polarities for which the wars and peaces of the sexes is a distant analogy.

Zeltweg is also the name of a racetrack in Europe and belongs to

ENCOUNTERS

a series called *Circuits*, named after places in which brave drivers tear space apart with powerful machines. I agree with William Rubin in esteeming these as Stella's highest achievements. The dominant elements are the repertoire of drawing aids, enlarged, stretched, on occasion topologically modified and then dribbled over in relaxed arabesques derived from and referring to, one is certain, the Expressionist skeining of Jackson Pollock. These elements unite two sets of connotations. They are instruments through which working drawings are made, which translate the ideas of engineers into real machines, and they also refer to the world of ships, engines, bridges and machinery. Perhaps they entered into their own generation from sketches to works of art. But the dripped and drizzled or daubed paint, in drop-dead colors and clashing conjunctions, connote feeling, daring, flash, abandon. Paint and form embrace, as in *Bijoux indiscrets*, a powerful antithesis that is then transmitted as energy to the work as a whole, where the elements are forced to inhabit a space that exercises over them a power they repudiate. In some way a harmony is achieved, and the eye is rewarded with something that is jumble and pattern at once. These are extremely political works.

The inspiration of *Circuits* thins out, it seems to me, in Stella's very latest work, but the tensions these paintings embody and transcend define their spirit and make an intoxicating show. There is something especially great about seeing all this work together, rather than dispersed to the expensive walls on which one now and again comes across them, one at a time. In fact, there is a gaiety here you will have encountered once before this season, in the Red Grooms show at the Whitney Museum. I saw the Stella exhibition before it opened, while it was being installed under Stella's supervision by his crew. I said, with no particular effort at critical depth or precision, that I liked the work. Well, the artist said, they are supposed to be liked. The pieces are demanding and ingratiating at the same time—perhaps because of one another. Go to have a good time, but be prepared to deal with the tensions and dissonances that churn and excite the spaces you and the works will co-occupy. As you leave the show, pause a moment before *Bijoux indiscrets* and reflect on how the forces that shook it generated the work you leave behind.

—*The Nation*, November 21, 1987

Raphael's Drawings

THERE IS ENOUGH of an internal connection between artistic expression and the historical period in which it flourishes that, we are
all ready to agree, not everything is possible at every time. It would,
for example, be difficult to imagine Michelangelo doing what we ven-
erate him for in the time of Giotto, or Leonardo painting the *Last
Supper*—or the *Mona Lisa*—when Masaccio executed the *Expulsion
from Paradise*. Nor is it easy to imagine Michelangelo or Leonardo
painting as they did a century later, after the epic of Renaissance art
had climaxed and come to a close with their stupendous performances.
In a sense, to make their work possible, each of them required just the
sequence of transformations in the way artists represented the world
that had in fact taken place. The same must be true in some degree
of the third member of the triad in whom the Renaissance impulse
achieved fulfillment. Yet it is not quite as difficult to imagine Raphael
in much earlier stages of the Renaissance. And it is easy to imagine
him painting as Raphael a century or more after his death—for the
simple historical fact is that academic art for the next three centuries
was more or less defined in Raphaelesque terms. He died in 1520. In
1550 Vasari's *Lives of the Artists* first appeared, in which, in effect, the
end of the history of art was declared. It was not, as Browning wrote,
that "suddenly, as rare things will, it vanished," but that the problems
of the Renaissance agenda were basically solved: there was no place
to go beyond Michelangelo, Leonardo and Raphael. The Age of the
Academy was at hand, and indeed the Accademia del Disegno was

founded in 1563. This period might just as well have been called the Age of Raphael, and it lasted well into the nineteenth century. Indeed, it was through Raphael's adaptations of their work that Leonardo and Michelangelo survived as part of the curriculum.

It is hardly matter for wonder, then, that those English artists who found confirmation of their views in Ruskin's *Modern Painters* should have designated themselves explicitly Pre-Raphaelite. Difficult as it is to read such a work as Sir John Millais's *Christ in the Carpenter's Shop* as a blow struck for Modernism, it was plain to the Pre-Raphaelite Brotherhood that art would have to return to some historical node anterior to Raphael and trace another path altogether, if relief was to be found from the tyranny of his forms. Their positive theories were less Modernist than their repudiations. Modernism was given its impetus less by their obsession with visual truth—with transcribing the world as it presents itself, "rejecting nothing, selecting nothing"—than by their negation of academic artifice. Ruskin characterized them this way:

They intend to return to early days in this one point only—that, insofar as in them lies, they will draw either what they see, or what they suppose might have been the actual facts of the scene they desire to represent, irrespective of any conventional rules of picture-making; and they have chosen their unfortunate though not inaccurate name because all artists did this before Raphael's time, and after Raphael's time did *not* this, but sought to paint fair pictures rather than represent stern facts.

Between Raphael and ourselves there is, accordingly, the whole history of Modernism, which dismantled the conventions and examples of his acknowledged excellence, making him, of the three titanic figures of the High Renaissance, quite the least available to us. The grinding familiarity of the Raphaelesque idiom blinds us to his originality, while Modernism itself desensitizes us to the inducements of the academic *maniera* he invented. And it is perhaps this very historical circumstance that heightens the availability to us of Leonardo and Michelangelo. What we respond to in them are the extravagances that survive the sweet adaptations of Raphael—extravagances that may have looked coarse or uncouth to academicized vision but which, to Modernists like ourselves, embody the very meaning of artistic power and pictorial genius. The price of having been perhaps the most influential artist in history is that Raphael, today, looks too—academic. Too pure, too perfect, too polished, too subject to the rules that were based on his great achievements.

Other circumstances contribute to the distance at which we hold Raphael. Like a very successful professor, he appears to have had a career rather than a life. Vasari's biography reads like a *curriculum vitae*, together with a letter of florid recommendation as to his collegiality and gifts as a teacher—and, of course, some shrewd criticisms as to the limits of his powers when ranged alongside those of Leonardo or Michelangelo. Unlike theirs, his personality seems elusive. In describing him, Vasari uses such adjectives as "mild," "tender," "gentle," "gracious," "sweet," "courteous," "friendly," "generous"—all Boy Scout virtues, and as soft as modern taste finds his "Dear Madonnas" (Browning again) to be. "No less excellent than graceful," Vasari writes, "he was endowed by nature with all that modesty and goodness which may occasionally be perceived in those few favoured persons who enhance the gracious sweetness of a disposition more than usually gentle, by the fair ornament of a winning amenity." Leonardo is perceived as a wizard, inverted, devious, secret, magical and dangerous. And Michelangelo is said to have been driven by that legendary *terribiltà* that has, ever since Romanticism, been a component in our conception of towering artistic greatness.

Finally, of course, there is the evidence of the works. We all know that scholars know vastly more than we about the *Last Supper* or the Sistine Chapel ceiling, but those works address us so immediately and totally that experiencing them dissolves the metaphorical version of the grime that literal restorers feel it necessary to remove. But Raphael's most famous works are the frescoes that embellish the Papal chambers—the *School of Athens*, or the *Disputa*—both of which seem too freighted with allusions and learned references for us to unravel them as we troop with other sightseers through the Camera della Segnatura. And then there are the Dear Madonnas, luminous embodiments of absolute solicitude and total maternal love, but to our tastes too cloying, too finally sentimental, to compel. Vasari tells us that Raphael was of an amorous disposition, and even that his death (at thirty-seven) was due to heavy lovemaking and a lowered resistance. There is a marvelous painting, *La Fornarina*, said to be of his mistress, a bold flirt of a woman holding a bare breast while pointing to an armband with Raphael's name, as if to say that it and she belong to him. But little of this eroticism comes through in the chaste Madonnas; we stand before them respectful but unengaged.

Still, he was one of the great artists, and one cannot be indifferent to the exhibition of his drawings on view at the Pierpont Morgan Library in New York City. Indeed, precisely because of the spontaneity, the immediacy, the unstudied, free, swift, gestural transcription of presumed feeling drawings promise, these pieces would appear to offer the best solvent for the glaze that has settled over this master's name and work. So one goes to such an exhibition not just to look at the drawings, which are certain to be marvelous, but to look for Raphael, to seek, across the centuries, a sort of post-Pre-Raphaelite contact with a nearly vanished sensibility. There are glimpses of him, to be sure, and in his greatest drawings he stands out like a being of another order against the other artists who form what the Morgan calls "his Circle"— somewhat misleadingly, I think, since his circle was composed more of intellectuals and poets and high ecclesiastical personalities than of the artists in his workshop who came under his immediate influence. Yet the personality remains as elusive as ever; it is difficult to meld the forty-odd drawings by him or said to be by him into a coherent corpus. You are going to have to work to find him, which gives a certain further incentive to the show.

There are a number of reasons for this elusiveness. First, of course, is the fact that the drawings come from the three main periods of Raphael's career, and show him absorbing, and transforming, the differing styles of three radically different artists: Perugino, to whom he was apprenticed and whose clear Umbrian style is the basic stratum in Raphael's artistic persona, especially in the Madonnas; Leonardo, whom he was dazzled by in Florence and whose smoky style, when superimposed upon Perugino, yields the archetypical *Holy Family*; and Michelangelo, whose work on the Sistine ceiling Raphael was allowed, surreptitiously, to see, and which he proceeded, as far as he could, to make his own. Undoubtedly, Perugino's influence, while it admitted the Leonardesque overlay, impeded Raphael's full command of Michelangelo's style, which he aspired to but could not reach. ("Dry, minute, and defective in design" is how Vasari describes Perugino's manner.) So Raphael's personality flows through the sequence of drawings like a river, whose tributaries are all the streams of High Renaissance expression and invention. It is only at the end, in the magnificent head and hand he drew for the *Transfiguration*—the masterpiece on which he was working at his death, the greatest drawing in the show and, for all I know, the greatest drawing in existence—that he comes fully into his own as a genius.

The discontinuity of style is heightened by the fact that Raphael experimented with so many different drawing media. The feeling of a pen drawing differs from that of one in metal-point. Metal-point differs from black chalk, which he used so effectively, and black chalk differs from red chalk, which he employed with such evident relish and through which, I think, his eroticism finds expression. There is something sensuous in the red chalk female nudes that one would never expect to find in Leonardo, whose women are made of smoke, or in Michelangelo, whose women are like men with appended breasts. Raphael's nudes are caressed onto paper, but we know he struggled with the male form: he labored so strenuously for its draftsmanly conquest as to call into question Ruskin's assessment that he was interested more in fair representations than stern facts. On the other hand, who knows if his genius for invention was not stimulated by certain incapacities he had in mastering what Vasari called the "difficult foreshortenings" of Michelangelo?

The shifts from period to period, each defined by a powerful artistic style Raphael had to accept and overcome, as well as the shifts from medium to medium within a given period, mean that Raphael as a recognizable stylist exists, for the most part, only at a certain level of abstraction. So this is not like a show of Rembrandt drawings, or drawings by Leonardo, in each of which one feels the presence of the same extraordinary touch and vision. Raphael is almost always at a distance, and this is compounded by the fact that these are working drawings, done not for their own sake but as instruments to get a painting going, so that he went no further with them than he had to, save in certain exceptional cases. In a way, many of them have the interest that the underdrawings—the *synopie*—for the frescoes would have if we were able to see them; they are intended to be sacrificed and submerged. So we are not moved to that degree of awe we expect with the greatest of the great masters.

The Raphaels are arranged in roughly chronological order, clockwise around the first three and a half walls of the Morgan's main exhibition hall. The remaining space is given over to drawings of disputed origin—they may be by Raphael, or they may be by Giulio Romano or Giovanni Penni, or one of the others in his workshop. The corridor is hung with drawings by these secondary masters in which there is no admixture of Raphael's hand. Penni seems to have inherited Raphael's delicacy, but none of the robustness inherited by Romano, whose drawing tends to a coarseness where Penni's tends to insipidity. It requires no great eye to see Giulio's heavy hand in the *Transfiguration's* depiction of the mad boy and the agitated father, even if this difference would not have been visible at Raphael's death. Inevitably, one will want to concentrate on the pure Raphaels. Even so, one cannot help but feel, given an impression of several hands and styles that cannot be explained away simply by reference to a diversity of influences and media, that the waters are more brackish than the structure of the exhibition concedes. It comes as no surprise to read in the catalogue that at least half the drawings have been questioned at one time or another—believed to be copies, or ascribed to Penni or Romano, or held to have been touched by someone other than Raphael himself. I cannot pretend to connoisseurship in such matters, but I find it hard to accept all the confident attributions of present-day experts. And this insecurity dilutes the awe, for one is not altogether certain, in every case, that it is Raphael to whom one is responding.

My advice is to go immediately to the stunning drawing of the head and hand, made as preparation for the pivotal figure in the lower register of the *Transfiguration*. This is pure Raphael, at the apex of his powers, and I would let it impose itself totally on one's sensibility. It is, in this exhibition, like the Form of the Good in Plato's heaven: something that illuminates itself and everything else. It is a miracle of what drawing can achieve: Notice the line that defines the brow and nose and then disappears, notice the light that defines the cheek and nostril and penetrates into the man's hair—and notice that hair, soft and surging, urgent and cascading down the young man's neck. It was this drawing that sold at Christie's in 1984 for just under $5 million—$4,797,144 to be exact, including an 8 percent buyer's fee, and worth, in my book, every scudo. Still, that kind of price must put an extraordinary degree of pressure on attributors. No Penni, no Giulio Romano—and certainly no Polidoro da Caravaggio or Perino del Vaga—would be worth anything near that kind of money. Of course, there are other pressures making one want the drawings to be by Raphael, and perhaps every drawing here *is* by him. Still, the nagging uncertainty remains after one has worked through all the evidence reported. It is, on the other hand, immensely reassuring that the power of the *Trans-*

figuration drawing transcends the knowledge of its price, and we feel in the presence of grace when we look at it.

Once you have internalized this drawing, you might begin to look for others that participate in its light. There is a magnificent horse's head in the lobby, dense with strength (contrast the mane with the mop of the young man in the master drawing). It is impossible not to be moved by the Sibyl, in red chalk, who twists about her axis as she leans on one heavy arm and gazes, with an accepting sadness, over her shoulder, while her other hand hangs in resignation between her knees. The kneeling female nude, again in red chalk, has passages I can close my eyes and recall with wonder. The sheet of three male figures in black chalk, so close to Michelangelo as once to have been ascribed to him, has a softening light and weight that I feel is Raphael's signature. The touch is elsewhere in the show, of course, but it is very faint indeed in many of the official Raphaels and to my eye absent from others that may, as a matter of external fact, truly be by him. With these one responds, at most, to the fact that they are by Raphael, not to the drawing itself. This is a connoisseur's show, which means one is looking for the artist, letting questions of meaning and substance and interpretation subside. Still, given the evanescence of the artist's personality, this is perhaps not an unreasonable priority, and when the personality comes at you full strength, as in that incredible head, it is worth considerable time and effort to be transradiated by its inner light.

—*The Nation*, December 19, 1987

Charles Demuth

THERE IS A familiar puzzle drawing that is a picture of a rabbit or of a duck, depending upon the way one looks at it. The "duck-rabbit," as it is called by philosophers, has been used since Wittgenstein to demonstrate how the same thing has different identities under different perceptual aspects. It would be a rare student of philosophy, on the other hand, who raised the further question of what *deep* identity connects ducks and rabbits so that they should be aspects of each other. But such considerations would not have been far from the mind of Man Ray when, in a 1930 photograph, *Anatomies*, he showed a woman from the shoulders up with her head bent back in so strenuous a way as to show us her chin from underneath. The lines of the jaw form an obvious visual pun on the head of a penis, for which the neck becomes the shaft. As were most Surrealists, Man Ray was obsessed with such transformations, and he would have considered the photograph a surprising revelation of an underlying oneness between male and female. A precise, if inadvertent, anticipation of Man Ray's wily and unsettling picture may be found in a sculpture by Brancusi. *Princesse X* is a sleek and abstract portrait bust of a woman with a very long and arched neck, her head and breasts reduced to polished knobs. It is a powerful irony that this marvelous form, in which a woman is reduced to her essential lines, should, through an irresistible perceptual switch, look unmistakably like an Art Deco phallus. It at least looked sufficiently phallic to have been removed, on grounds of questionable decency, from the Salon des Indépendants of 1920, angering Brancusi to the point that he refused to exhibit in France for the next several years.

With a work such as Brancusi's phallo-princess, the term "exhibition" (or, *en français, exposition*) takes on its own double meaning, which is captured, deliciously, in a masterpiece of giggling visual innuendo by the American Modernist Charles Demuth, for me a high point in the stunning show of his work on view at the Whitney Museum of American Art in New York City. Titled *Distinguished Air*, the watercolor shows five persons, who could just be a group of lovers of advanced art, gathered in a circle of admiration around *Princesse X* displayed on a modernistic pedestal. As such, as much for its air of aesthetic sophistication as for its luminous and exact use of watercolor, it could have been a cover for *The New Yorker*. But the ambiguity of *Princesse X* makes the drawing itself ambiguous, and doubtless too risqué for that magazine. For it is also possible to see the scene as consisting of five persons caught up in a network of extreme erotic tension, transformed from art lovers to phallus worshippers. Two of the viewers/voyeurs are evidently gay lovers, their backs to us—a sailor and a sort of dandy who has looped one arm over the sailor's shoulders while drawing the latter's arm around his waist. The dandy could have brought the sailor here for aesthetic appreciation—or for sexual suggestion. The sailor must in any case be aroused, for another man, swinging a cane (and perhaps Demuth himself, who carried a cane and depicted himself with one), is peering, unmistakably, at the sailor's crotch (other drawings of sailors in the show leave us in little doubt as to what he saw). On the right is a woman in a delicate red frock with a fan in her hand. And the position of the fan leaves it unclear whether she has dropped her arm in aesthetic rapture or metaphorically to cool her inflamed sex. It is a witty meditation on art and sexuality—on art and sexuality as aspects of each other as they were aspects of Demuth's own personality.

These are aspects in a set of rather more explicit paintings of sailors—most markedly in *Two Sailors Urinating*, again of 1930, showing what must have been figures of his sharpest fantasies, holding the heaviest cocks I have seen outside the wall paintings of Pompeii, and possessing angelic faces. They are at the same time painted with an elegance and light, a fluidity and authority that mark Demuth as an absolute master of watercolor as a medium. The figures have the undulating feel of flowing water or leaping flame, and they are miracles of transparency, considering the dark blues of the sailor suits, the black neckcloths and the difficult browns of the wall behind them. One's focus alternates between salacious content and high artistry, as difficult to fuse into a single experience as the duck and rabbit, so the experience is one of tension and opponent pulls, and a resistance to a stable resolution. Indeed, the destabilization of the viewer sometimes seems to be the abiding intention of Demuth's work, flagrant in the explicit homoerotic pictures but never entirely absent from even the most innocent of his images—as it is never entirely absent from the characteristic paintings of his friend and confidante Georgia O'Keeffe. (O'Keeffe's insistently vulvar plant forms leave us wondering if they are metaphors, but never what they would be metaphors for.) Demuth's *On "That" Street* shows, again, an undulant dandy, in a belted coat, evidently propositioning two sailors, and posed in a way that must, to judge by a description from Proust (for which the figure could serve as illustration), have carried an unmistakable meaning in the body language of gay culture. The description comes from the opening scene in *Cities of the Plain*, where the Baron de Charlus and the tailor, Jupien, strike symmetrical poses in acknowledgment of their mutual recognitions. Jupien had "thrown up his head, given a becoming tilt to his body, placed his hand with a grotesque impertinence on his hip, stuck out his behind, posed himself with the coquetry that the orchid might have adopted on the providential arrival of the bee."

I am struck by the fact that *On "That" Street* is in the Alfred Stieglitz Collection of the Art Institute of Chicago, and I cannot help but feel it gives us a certain insight into the vocabulary, artistic and sexual, of the Stieglitz circle, to which O'Keeffe centrally and Demuth peripherally belonged. Proust, marveling at the immediacy of communication between the two characters he has just described, wrote:

One does not arrive spontaneously at that pitch of perfection except when one meets in a foreign country a compatriot with whom an understanding then grows up of itself, both parties speaking the same language, even though they have never seen one another before.

Modernism, in art as in sexuality, was the patriotism of a fragile band of aesthetic expatriates in the America of the 1920s, centered, in New York, on Stieglitz's gallery and the Arensbergs, in whose collection *Princesse X*, in one of its versions, is to be found, and in Philadelphia at the Barnes Foundation, which contains several of Demuth's paintings. How embattled the aesthetically (and no doubt sexually) liberated colony of Philadelphia was may be inferred from the ferocity of critical invective that greeted Barnes's effort to show his collection of modern masters in 1922. So it must have been as though there was a kind of language that bonded the members of these circles together in a certain exclusive understanding—a language in which Demuth and O'Keeffe, and of course Stieglitz, were fluent.

It was an esoteric language, perhaps half in self-protection, full of double entendre and *sous-entendu*, private allusion and privileged slang, and in consequence is lost to outsiders, and certainly so to us, put in the position of code breakers, certain that there is a message if we can but learn to read it. This is especially true of the so-called poster portraits that Demuth did of notable American artists and writers, which hover somewhere between riddles and allegories.

The term "poster" is ironic for such cryptic depictions, for it is the office of posters to make public declarations, in unambiguous terms, of whatever they celebrate; so a poster difficult to read is a failure in its genre. Barbara Haskell, who curated this show and wrote the splendid catalogue that accompanies it, sees in these an appropriation of advertising, which is a peculiarly American genre; but the poster, I think, is far more characteristic of Europe than America, and the tantalizing evasiveness of Demuth's symbols seems at odds with the spirit of advertisement, unless he is using it to subvert its ordinary functions. What, precisely, is being ascribed to O'Keeffe by the snake plant and the Cubistic pears in her portrait? The portrait of John Marin has the form of a red, white and blue sailor's collar (with two stars), and has "MARIN" superimposed on the word "PLAY" (MARIN PLAY = *marin plaît* = sailor pleases?) penetrated, as in a valentine, by a red arrow (arrow = *flèche* = flesh?). I jest, but the interpretations anyone can offer are mere conjectures today, and in some cases no interpretation is available because the subject has simply dropped out of history, as in the case of Charles Duncan, where, as Haskell says, "the poster remains as enigmatic as the subject." A successful reading is available of *The Figure 5 in Gold*, evidently a portrait of William Carlos Williams as the numeral 5 (cf. Stevens's *The Comedian as the Letter C*). It consists, mainly, of three nested inscriptions of the numeral 5 (which looks like a stylization of *Princesse X* turned upside down), and must be read as marking stages in a movement toward the viewer—a translation of the numeral through space. The numeral 5 is a metonym for a fire engine that it identifies, the fire engine is a metonym for a poem of which it is the subject, and the poem is a metonym for the poet. Presumably those in the closed circle were to have the requisite knowledge to work out the solutions to these depictions—yet Haskell tells us that even Demuth's close friends were puzzled by the portraits. But all of the works are characteristically, if less obviously, puzzling, concealment being a dimension of Demuth as an artist.

Demuth was one of the great masters of watercolor painting, an exacting medium because of the difficulty of exploiting its fluidity without sacrificing form, and of maintaining the transparency inherent in washes—and finally because of the irrevocability of spills and errors. Too much fluidity and the work puddles, too little and the medium is betrayed. Cézanne, whose aquarelles are among the most lyrical ever achieved, attained their clarity in consequence of his extreme deliberateness, allowing a wash to dry completely before laying another one over it. This must have been a long and demanding strategy, evidence for which consists in the fact that the majority of Cézanne's watercolors are unfinished, and owe their clarity to the amount of paper left white and untouched. It is true that we have a special taste for the unfinished, and so acknowledge these pieces as masterworks. But it is difficult to believe Cézanne himself would have shared our view, and those rare watercolors he in fact completed to his own standards are often dark and confused—a bit like the painting that is described as *le chef d'oeuvre inconnu* in Balzac's novella of the same name, with whose obsessed hero, Frenhofer, Cézanne explicitly identified himself (*"Frenhofer, c'est moi"*). No one carried watercolor further than Demuth, whose pictures have the clear radiance of great illuminations, but retain the fluency of water and the virtuoso's immediate accuracy. His is one of the great touches of the art.

The fluidity in Demuth's earlier flower studies prevails at the expense of clarity, which he gained, in my view, under the influence of his oil paintings, begun in the late 1920s. It was almost as though he sought a way out of the washiness and found in oil a certain dry translucency and a sharpness he was then able to translate into watercolor. The oils are of sections of industrial landscape with the smokestacks and water towers characteristic of nineteenth-century industrial architecture in his native town, Lancaster, Pennsylvania, to which he later returned, in effect, to die. These landscapes have the precision of the industrial process itself, purged of dirt and smoke. (They belong to the precisionist movement in American painting, a style we get a silvery echo of in the *New Yorker* covers of Gretchen Dow Simpson.) As oils, Demuth's landscapes have been somewhat unfavorably compared with his watercolors, but I believe that the oils gave him a certain discipline which he needed in order to achieve the brilliance of his final watercolors of fruit and flowers, arranged in nearly musical compositions, animated by an almost musical invention, filled with inversions and repetitions—and done in colors so pure, certain, so free of accident, as to bear comparison with the flowers that are often their immediate subjects.

Still life, at its greatest, is almost always artificial and implicitly mysterious, hinting, through juxtaposition, at meanings that could not otherwise be expressed. This is so in Spanish still life and in Dutch; and Demuth arranged his objects in ways we would expect from someone of his hermetic disposition. *Eggplants and Pears* shows two of each of these, startlingly similar in shape but complementary in size and hue, and connected by strange affinities underscored by the deliberateness with which they are placed. In *From the Kitchen Garden*, a pair of tomatoes, a paired squash and eggplant and a pair of sunflower heads ascend as in a kind of Baroque composition—like a deposition from the cross. *Green Pears* of 1929 (remember the curious pears in the O'Keeffe portrait!) shows seven of these fruits, arranged as two sets of triplets, with a single pear—the only one with a leaf attached—surmounting an inverted plate, and in the aggregate looking like a bar in some musical piece. There is another melody of pears in a painting from 1925. It is instructive to study the piled and paired fruits together with Demuth's famous studies of vaudeville performers—dancers, acrobats, tumblers—shown in delicate balance with one another, in perilous mutual support which might be a metaphor for the possibility of love. It is subtle, ironic, brilliant work, the outward expression of a shimmering artistic intelligence—wry, crafty, entertaining even, but with the promise of depth at the same time as being wholly accessible. He must have been a wonderful person to know.

—*The Nation*, January 23, 1988

African Art and
Artifacts

IN THE SPRING MONTHS of 1907, Picasso began work on the large
and fateful painting that became *Les Demoiselles d'Avignon* and paid
a no less fateful visit to the Musée d'Ethnographie du Trocadéro in
Paris. Whether the painting opened him up to the exotic fierce effigies
he saw there or if some revelatory inspiration drawn from his encounter
with them gave him what he needed to achieve that masterpiece is a
hidden truth in the psychochemistry of his creative genius. What is
beyond historical question is the fact that the transformations induced
upon Western art by the forms and cadences of that stupendous painting induced a simultaneous transformation in the perception of what
continued to be called "primitive art," making it aesthetically visible.
Until then the carvings and assemblages of Africa and Oceania had
been viewed chiefly as ethnographic data for a science of man that
addressed primitive cultures primarily as yielding analogical insights
into stages through which our own culture must long since have passed.
It was accordingly impossible to view their products as art except in
the most marginal sense, as marking the lower boundary of a scale
whose upper limits were defined by the glories with which Raphael,
Correggio or Guido Reni graced high civilization. And natives, if
brought as living anthropological specimens to one or another international exposition, might, if taken to the Louvre or the Musée du
Luxembourg, see in the luminous images along those walls an almost
impossibly distant hope. It would have been taken for granted that a
scarred or painted tribesman from the Congo, shown some rude effigy

from his own culture together with, say, a carving by Donatello, would have confronted evidence of his own culture's inferiority so palpable and plain that only the paternalistic consideration owed him by his betters prevented so cruel an aesthetic experiment.

Picasso changed all that. He was, to be sure, not the first artist in France to cultivate African sculpture. But he certainly transformed the way in which the world perceived it. In one way this was an unqualified matter of artistic justice. By 1920, the English critic Roger Fry was able to write, in response to an exhibition of "negro sculpture" shown at the Chelsea Book Club in London:

The power to create expressive plastic form is one of the greatest human achievements, and the names of great sculptors are handed down from generation to generation, so that it seems unfair to be forced to admit that certain nameless savages have possessed this power not only in a higher degree than we at this moment, but than we as a nation have ever possessed it. And yet that is where I find myself. I have to admit that some of these things are great sculpture—greater, I think, than anything we produced even in the Middle Ages.

"I went to see the carvings," Fry's friend Virginia Woolf wrote to her sister Vanessa, "and I found them dismal and impressive. . . . If I had one on the mantelpiece I should be a different sort of character—less adorable, as far as I can make out, but somebody you wouldn't forget in a hurry." Woolf, I think, is closer to the mark than Roger Fry, who was an aesthetic formalist and so saw in these works only those qualities that appeared to license the affinities upon which the Museum of Modern Art erected its flawed exhibition "Primitivism" in 20th Century Art, in 1984. For Fry, these objects "have the special qualities of sculpture in a higher degree. They have indeed complete plastic freedom . . . rare in sculpture." So they do. Fry was judging them in just the terms he would have applied to Praxiteles or Bernini, subtracting, as irrelevant, considerations of naturalism in representation, which Picasso had in any case put in brackets. By those criteria, he perceived them as superlative exercises in plastic art. "Heaven knows what real feeling I have about anything after hearing Roger discourse," Woolf wrote, waspishly; but she clearly responded to something shuddering and unsettling in these works to which Fry was rendered numb by his aestheticism. And Fry's response was the price this sculpture paid for its ascension to the exalted precincts of the world's great art: it was ripped from the contexts in which it perhaps did things vastly more important to its makers than squatting in the company of rare and pricey artworks. In its native provinces, this sculpture was vested with powers Western art has not been capable of for centuries, except for those special religious cases in which a certain madonna or some sacred bambino is believed miraculous and worshipped for its powers.

The sorts of reciprocal artistic transformation that the interchange between Picasso and Africa exemplify are characteristic of the history of Western art. They testify to the restlessness of a tradition that constantly confronts its own history. Works rise and fall in the general esteem in consequence of the different perspectives into which they are thrust by the creation of other artworks, which impose upon them standards and criteria undreamed of by the artists who made them. At the same time, we are tormented by the question of how works that have been retroactively transformed by later art were originally seen and understood. Try to imagine what Cézanne would look like today if Cubism had never been invented! On the other hand, we do know something about how African art must have looked to earlier generations in the West, since missionaries, exploiters and anthropologists brought it back in crateloads and housed it in the kind of natural history museum in which Picasso had his vision. There, the masks and figurines of Africa were placed as specimens in glass study cases alongside items of domesticity—garments, culinary utensils and weapons arranged in patterns whose closest analogue in our culture is the knife-and-scissors display in the Hoffritz window or the cards of ranked and ordered buttons in the notions shop. All the objects shown were indifferently "wog work," and the distinction between primitive artwork and primitive artifact, if drawn at all, was somewhat in favor of the latter.

Bit by bit pieces of African art found their way out of the vitrines and showcases of the natural history museum, first to the ateliers of advanced French artists, later to the Chelsea Book Club, to the Barnes Foundation collection and on to the Michael Rockefeller Wing of the Metropolitan Museum of Art (missing Virginia Woolf's mantelpiece along the way). In so doing, they left behind the pots and spears, the combs and hairpins, the needle cases and aprons, the spoons and stools and spools. But lately certain avant-garde artists in the West have begun to produce works that look remarkably like the things left behind as

[166

African Art and Artifacts

African artifacts. Modernist sensibility opened our eyes to the polished surfaces, the rhythmic ornamentation and the clean forms of African carving, and Cubism taught us to accept the rearrangement of features in the interest of expressions other than those naturalism would allow. But postmodern sensibility has made accessible to us materials that defy formalist regimentation and that heretofore our artistic traditions had no use for: rope, feathers, flax, shells, even blood and bones. Some such neoprimitive works, for example those by Nancy Graves, found their way into the Museum of Modern Art show, raising the question of whether they will liberate what we had regarded as mere artifacts, as Picasso liberated what we dismissed as mere fetishes. Are those artifacts, as it were, going to follow their peers and be recognized as art by aesthetes who have been transformed to recognize them as such? If Picasso revealed the artistic greatness of Mbagani masks and manikins from Zaire, will Graves and Robert Morris do as much for objects that have languished under a lesser identity as artifacts?

This is the animating query for a marvelous, instructive and ingenious exhibition, Art/artifact, at the Center for African Art in Manhattan. It is the latest and, to my mind, the best in a brilliant series of exhibitions conceived and installed by the center's director, Susan Vogel, who has sought in each to show some of the finest African art and at the same time raise the question of how that art is to be looked at. For there is, after all, an initial question to be faced: whether this is primarily visual art at all, or at least so within the disinterested spectatorial gaze we acquire in learning the conventions of the fine arts museum. Walter Benjamin distinguishes between art that exists chiefly in order to be displayed and art that, because made for ritual practices, is intended to be hidden from profane eyes and revealed only at appropriate moments, even to the eyes of initiates. The latter works are fraught with dangers and filled with powers of a kind that works constructed specifically for exhibition value and aesthetic pleasure scarcely can be supposed to have. The art museum is a pretty sanitizing enclave. Sometimes, of course, we exhibit works of the cultic order as we exhibit the heads of animals we have killed, as signs of conquered power. And some of this spirit is carried over even in works made primarily for exhibition: a fair number of the world's great museums are furnished with the ravished artworks of defeated peoples. Still, in their original contexts, most of what we class as primitive art was not intended to be responded to aesthetically, even if aesthetic excellence was acknowledged as an index that the deep and important powers had been captured. It is this excellence, perhaps, that enabled the works that chilled Virginia Woolf to make the transition to the museums of fine arts and to elicit admiration from Roger Fry for their plastic values. But a lot of great art existed on the same two levels, even if one of them has been forgotten. There are altarpieces in our museums that were meant to be seen as visitations, in the light of holy candles, from the posture of an adorer. No one falls to his knees before Caravaggio's *Madonna of the Rosary*, but by simply looking at it while standing, we lose a lot of its structure and composition along with its primary purpose and meaning. In Africa, even today, works of art are concealed from alien eyes and are believed to hold powers which must be understood— perhaps even accepted—as preconditions for responding to the work in the intended way. These two dimensions of artistic reality define the dilemma any center for African art must resolve. (The ill-conceived National Museum of African Art in Washington, D.C., solved it by forcing its visitors to descend underground, hence metaphorically, perhaps, to enter the underworld, in order to see its holdings displayed like gems in illuminated cases.)

The New York Center for African Art occupies an elegant town house. In the current exhibition, the first object that strikes the eye upon entering the ground-floor gallery is a hunting net, folded and tied, hauled back as an artifact of the Zande people by Herbert Lang in 1910. There is little doubt that were you to see an identical object displayed and illuminated just as the net is, but placed in one of the alcoves of the Guggenheim Museum or in a chaste corner of the Museum of Modern Art, it would be instantly accepted as a work of art— dense, mysterious, even beautiful, perhaps by Jackie Winsor or Eva Hesse. That something just like it could be a work of art does not— or does it?—make this object, of conspicuous utility to its makers, a work of art. The catalogue entry says the Zande net "bears a completely spurious resemblance to a work of modern art." Well, nothing the eyes can tell you will tell you whether it is art or artifact, and in order to get some purchase on the difference—and on the difference it makes— you may need recourse to a long catalogue essay by Arthur C. Danto. The same question is raised over and over again by objects that would be artistically beautiful if they were "works of art." Above the net is a large rectangle of cloth—a woman's dress, from Zaire, but patched with such abstract artistry that it is difficult not to believe it is a modern

[*168*

painting (it could be by Klee if it were). To the right and just behind, in one of the wall cases, are three hair ornaments from the Mangbetu, shapes like futuristic ivory mushrooms or wickedly useless golf tees. On the left is a forest of memorial effigies from Kenya, tall, doll-shaped paddles with circular heads and abstractly ornamented trunks. The effigies straddle the conceptual line between art and artifact it will be your problem to draw—but once more, were a contemporary sculptor to fill a gallery with figures like that, with visitors passing among them as through columns or steles, it would be the sensation of the season. Meanwhile, the memorial effigy is going to be your guide as you go from room to room, as it takes on a different identity from gallery to gallery—a curiosity, an artifact, a work of art.

Not satisfied with raising a difficult philosophical question in the medium of 160 brilliantly selected objects (from three anthropological collections, all founded in the 1860s: the Buffalo Museum of Science, the Hampton University Museum and the American Museum of Natural History), the center has also chosen to anthropologize its own culture by showing how African objects have been and continue to be shown and seen in different institutional settings. In the first of the upstairs galleries, for example, you enter a Curiosity Room, lined with dark oak cases and cabinets, and composing the atmosphere of a high-minded Victorian didactic space. One almost sees motes rising in the musty air, past fading photogravures of dignified indigenes, to settle back among the objects, beaded and carved, brought back by men in pith helmets, borne in bales by grinning blacks, for our instruction and edification. In this room, the memorial effigy stands in a corner, like an abandoned cricket bat, across from the fanned spears, as if awaiting classification and consignment. The cases are full of marvels. In the next room, we encounter a diorama, in which a realistic effigy of a Mujikenda craftsman fashions a memorial effigy while other waxwork kibitzers look on in awe. An African visitor to the center will see how natives of our culture look at the objects they have taken away from her culture. In the diorama room, the center has in effect put the museum *in* a museum, enabling the African tourist—or just us—to become conscious of the way we have become conscious of other cultures.

In the very top galleries, everything is placed in the smart Plexiglas cases of the contemporary art museum, and the African can study us studying, as precious objects and works of art, objects she too sees as works of art, but under quite different perspectives, as well as objects not seen as works of art at all. One of the cases holds some elegant spears, peers to those that were mere curiosities in the Curiosity Room. One of the cases holds our memorial effigy, the circumstances of presentation erasing the doubts that generated the exhibition. Each thing, by being in effect put on a pedestal, receives the kind of attention works of art are deemed to merit in our culture, which has decided that art belongs in museums and that the suitable way to respond to it is aesthetically and visually. Our African might feel she has entered some sacred space and is standing among our gods. This is not the way she relates to her gods, embodied in works of art that become, on special fraught occasions, unhidden, like dangerous truths, bearers of great powers the artists of her culture have the gift of knowing how to capture. Alongside *this* gift, the talent for making works of exhibitive art is almost paltry.

When I was invited to compose a philosophical essay on the distinction between art and artifact for the catalogue of this exhibition, it was impossible to resist. That is a question absolutely up my alley as a philosopher, and I was able to carry my thought on such matters a few notches forward. What I had not counted on was how marvelously the theme was to be carried out in the installation, or how cleverly the question would be raised with the objects themselves. Nor was I prepared for the power and beauty of the objects. It is a fascinating show quite apart from its conceptual premises, full of things to gratify the Roger Fry, the Virginia Woolf, the anthropologist and the philosopher in us all.

—*The Nation*, March 5, 1988

Fragonard

IN THE LONG TWILIGHT of his artistic career, in full possession of powers that had brought him high patronage and great fortune but for which there was no longer any demand, Fragonard undertook a project of stunning ambition: a set of illustrations of *Orlando Furioso* consisting of at least 160 drawings of furious energy and brilliance. One of these strikes me as a sort of allegorical self-portrait. It shows the sorceress Melissa conjuring up the image of a pair of lovers, Ruggiero and Alcina. The drawing itself is an act of conjuration, as indeed are all the drawings in this suite: seemingly random lines of black chalk under puddles of bister wash condense, here and there, to form the vision of lovers in an embrace at once so tender and intense, powerful and evanescent, as to become, just as a drawing, a metaphor for the feeling depicted and the act of its depiction. The lovers' heads are summoned out of mere touches; their bodies fade into insubstantiality in the blaze of white paper.

All the *Orlando Furioso* drawings I have seen embody the enchantment of the poem itself, transmuted into Fragonard's own gestural magic—but this particular drawing seems to refer to processes it also displays. Melissa is shown standing beneath the vision she has caused to materialize against the sky, her back toward us and holding a staff, like Prospero, who, through his particular magic, solidified out of emptiness a masque of spirits for the solemn entertainment of his daughter and her lover. But so has Fragonard, throughout his life as an artist but especially in these amazing drawings, evoked images of passionate love virtually out of nothing—out of strokes and spills and scribbles. The meeting of mouths in Melissa's trembling and driven specters has been transacted out of deft smudges and untouched paper.

Fragonard was not, one feels, greatly given to self-awareness, but this drawing was executed at a moment when, however hopeful he must have been as a matter of personality, it must have been irresistibly plain to him that he had been beached by the rush of history, deprived of an audience whose wishes he had known how to fulfill in the deflected medium of painted dreams. His style, especially in the froth and liquid of these drawings, but no less so in the easy energy of his painting, suited to perfection the content of those dreams and was as dated as the gallantries and pastimes that formed that content. Fragonard did not document the life of his times so much as give palpable expression to the fantasies of those who lived those times. His tableaux give a fragile reality, hopelessly out of reach, to a form of sweet life constituted of love, innocence, beauty and distraction, spiced by pranks and giggles. They even have the space of dreams. And his surfaces exhibit a certain speed and urgency, as if to underscore the fragility of the visions shown—as if to say that, like the iridescences of a bubble, it must all be captured swiftly before it resolves into air and mist.

It was explicitly as a dream that Diderot, *philosophe* and art critic, addressed Fragonard's Salon piece of 1765, *The High Priest Coresus Sacrifices Himself to Save Callirhoë*, a work certainly puzzling to Modern or Postmodern sensibility, but one that marks the distance between eighteenth-century high taste and the more typical taste to which Fragonard appealed. "We gradually see Fragonard's picture come vividly into being, so to speak, before our eyes," Diderot wrote; it was, he pretended, as if the painting made objective and visible what he had but dreamt. Coresus is shown stabbing himself histrionically rather than plunging the ornamental dagger into the provocative and vulnerable bosom of Callirhoë, for whom it was meant. She is shown in a swoon at his knees, but apart from her bared breasts and the garland of flowers about her brow there is little that would indicate this painting might be by Fragonard. Yet it exemplifies to perfection the kind of painting that was approved of by the Academy—which, since 1740, had pursued a program intended to return art to "the antique and to *grand goût*." This meant that preference was to be given to elevated and, ideally, heroic subjects composed and presented in ways that contrast severely with what we think of as French painting of the eighteenth century—namely, Watteau, Boucher and, of course, Fragonard himself nearly everywhere except in this *machine*, as Diderot admiringly called it.

In earlier years, the Academy had been more open and accepting, even establishing a special category of *fêtes galantes* in order that Watteau might be taken into it. His reception piece was the exquisite *Embarkation for Cythera*, a work of melancholy eroticism in which paired lovers make their reluctant way toward a golden boat that is to bear them off to a destination that represents a change of state. There were, in the Salon of 1765, a great many paintings in the *fêtes galantes* manner by Boucher, but the characteristic entry in the biennial exhibition was exceedingly high-minded and, to our taste, portentous and moralizing. Diderot greatly admired it as "full of pictorial magic, intelligence, and *machine*," prophesying great things for this youthful artist.

Coresus and Callirhoë was one of the sensations of the Salon, and it secured Fragonard his early reputation as well as a studio in the Louvre. He was supposed to be paid for the painting, which was to be made into a tapestry, but the latter never materialized and the fee came grudgingly and late. His name made, Fragonard turned to those parts of the *machine* that might have been differently regarded when it was judged a work of *grand goût*—Callirhoë's floral headdress and pretty pink-and-cream breasts. The same sacrificially bared breasts recur in a work the Academy might have used to teach the meaning of *petit goût*, which it was anxious to suppress: a painting of a young model whose blouse has been parted by an older woman for the approval of the painter. In *Les Débuts du modèle*, the painter, in a spiffy pink costume, is shown lifting the hem of the model's skirt with a mahlstick (think of Melissa's staff) while she, casting a sidelong glance, struggles to keep it in place. The painter is (perhaps) saved from prurience by looking as if he were already madly in love with the girl he is impatient to see stripped. And Callirhoë's garland recurs as the crown of flowers in *The Coronation of the Lover*, one of the panels installed at the Frick.

When Fragonard died in 1806, he was eulogized as a painter of "erotic and *galant* subjects" and identified as a representative of the *ancienne école*. He was seventy-four, and readers of the sparse notices given his passing must have been astounded that he was still alive, so closely was his art identified with a banished and discredited society. The heroic style, pressed into aesthetic service by the Revolution, had

173]

made Fragonard look dated for a quarter century. The fantasies he painted were not acceptable to an age that saw itself reenacting antique grandeurs. The closest analogy I can think of is F. Scott Fitzgerald surviving into the 1930s, and a very different concept of paradise than any he celebrated. The riffs and jazzy cadences of Fitzgerald's prose would have transmitted a feeling at odds with the content of a proletarian novel, had he been cynical enough to write one; and the frothed surfaces of Fragonard would have been no less ill-suited to the representation of civic heroism and moral virtue the Revolution required— a need to convey a sense of almost architectural permanence, at odds with the feeling of imminent disappearance that goes with the filmy insolidity of dreams.

Pretty much all the components of the *ancien régime*'s dream of an earthly paradise are present in the first room of the magnificent exhibition of Fragonard's work at the Metropolitan Museum of Art in New York City, where soft adolescents, in the balletic costumes of shepherds or harvesters, mark the happy cycle of the seasons, playing with animals or with children scarcely more innocent than themselves. They gather flowers or harvest grapes and inhabit a garden world of balustrades and orange trees in tubs under delicious porcelain skies. When they do not engage in effortless labors emblematically marked by spades and scythes, they frolic at games we will see played over and over in Fragonard's world: blindman's buff, in which the mischievous girl is perfectly complacent in her role as victim, since she can see from under her blindfold to tease her teasers; and seesaw, which shows the lifted hem and the naughty calf, which becomes a motif in Fragonard as merry girls swing high and away in flying skirts above rapt and adoring males getting an eyeful.

I think one can infer from the recurrent voyeurism of Fragonard's work that his patrons must chiefly have been men, with whom, if I may say so, he saw eye to eye. I have often felt that one main difference between Fragonard and Boucher, his teacher and in certain ways his stylistic predecessor, is that Boucher was altogether a woman's painter, that his success derived from his capacity to depict women as they felt themselves to be, in a world of soft fabrics and gentle lovers and chaste relationships, and in which they held the governing reins. Fragonard, by contrast, depicts women as somebody's dish—eager, vacant, flossy, compliant—so that even in the set piece, so untypical of his work, Callirhoë is victim: even if the male kills himself for love of her, her

[*174*

eyes are closed in a swoon and Fragonard's male viewers can enjoy her feminine helplessness. (As they also can in so many other pictures in which a woman is shown asleep, her chemise lifted by obliging cupids, or portrayed as tossing in the grip of what must be an erotic dream while the same cupids touch her breasts and underbelly with tiny flambeaux.)

Michael Fried has spoken of "absorption" as a defining characteristic of eighteenth-century depiction: the characters are shown as absorbed in their own inner worlds. When Fragonard's girls are not dreaming they are daydreaming—for example, holding a dog in the air whose tail serves as an impudent *cache-sexe*. And in becoming absorbed in her absorption, we, as viewers, reenact the circumstance of the dream. Not until Picasso, I think, did the sleeping woman become again the image of erotic yearning, but with Picasso a spectator, usually a satyr, is shown looking at her, excluding us from her presence. In Fragonard, the satyr is us.

As there are more than two hundred works in the current show, I would count on making an afternoon of it and would preface my visit by taking a fresh look at that marvelous complex of Fragonard's panels known as *The Progress of Love*, on permanent display at the Frick Collection and recently cleaned for the occasion of the Metropolitan exhibit. *The Progress of Love* is his masterpiece. It had originally been commissioned by Madame du Barry for the garden pavilion at Louveciennes, where she had been set up by her royal lover. From the compendious and indispensable catalogue by Pierre Rosenberg, I learned that the room in which the paintings were to be installed had the shape of an apse; and it seems an altogether fitting concept for the time, and certainly the place, that the witty patroness should have conceived it as a chapel dedicated to love, with Fragonard's images as stages of amatory progress to replace the Stations of the Cross. By ironic (but not iconic) coincidence, there are exactly fourteen canvases in the final inventory of *The Progress of Love*, although not all of them are part of the narrative. There is an overall question of whether a narrative is carried forward at all, but in any case, the female figure seems to play the ascendant role and the wigged, tender suitor behaves decorously, declaring his adoration with a flower, climbing an unnecessary ladder to show his fervor, reading with his mistress the billets-doux that defined their relationship and being at last crowned by the lady, who at the same time demonstrates her love of the arts by having her portrait done in the act of coronation, as she sits surrounded by musical instruments. Perhaps the message was to have been that while the King rules outside, here, in the nest at Louveciennes, love was the ruler and Madame du Barry its minister.

In the end, the Fragonard paintings were refused as out of date by Madame du Barry. Instead, she had installed some exceedingly glacial compositions by the painter Vien. It was as if the spirit of the Revolution in fact was already present, like an unwelcome messenger, in the royal dalliance chamber. Fragonard's tableaux are sublime: silken creatures frolic in the shade of immense trees, under garden statuary that seems to comment on the stages of love, by elegant cascades and exuberant plantings, as if the Garden of Eden had been designed by the *architect du roi*. But turning her back on the rococo did Madame du Barry no great good: She was guillotined in 1793, when Fragonard, who survived the Revolution, at least personally, was working as a curatorial functionary at the Louvre, starting it on its way to the museum we know—starting, indeed, the concept of the museum as we know it.

In my view, Fragonard became Fragonard through an extended sojourn at the Villa d'Este when he was in residence at the French Academy in Rome. It was there, amid the haunting vegetation and the unkempt ruins, in the dark shadows of colossal cypresses and in sight of cascades of every description, that he developed the surging brush, the rush, the dash, the urgency needed to capture a watery world. I have often thought one could capture Fragonard's genius precisely if one imagined subtracting from his paintings everything they had in common with the work of his friend and painting companion, Hubert Robert. Robert, too, painted the picturesque. His world, too, is dense with trees, ruins, amiable peasants, cascades and plantings. He is a wonderful artist, but there is a restless spirit in the space left over when we subtract him from Fragonard, which *is* painting in its highest vocation, where the brush dances as if alive and the paint expresses the surge of life as the flying droplets do the driving water of the fountain, or the shower of sparks the burst of fireworks. Boucher lays paint on as sweetly as a master *pâtissier*. But Fragonard's painting is what is deposited by a gestural certitude that verges on magic. There is a beautiful passage in Proust in which the narrator visits a famous fountain by Hubert Robert one evening at the Guermantes'. In reality there is no such fountain, alas, though Proust knows there could have been, as Robert's pictures often have fountains in them, and he was, after all, a landscape architect. But Fragonard's paintings *are* fountains. He transmits the vision of a world of water as the great masters of the Sung transmit one of a world of mists. That is why, for all their lasciviousness, the indolence of his personages and the frivolity of the lives they dream of leading (and their distance from any political or psychological depth), you will be quickened and cleansed by this work.

I always think of Hubert Robert's fountain as described by Proust when I think of Fragonard's *Fête at St.-Cloud*. A wide painting, it shows just such a plume of water, like a silver tree among the golden trees that dwarf, in the foreground, groups of holidaymakers in an enchanted park. They are watching vaudeville, or marionette shows, or eating crepes and purchasing toys for their children in a kind of aching innocence, pointing or peering and whispering to one another in the palpable quiet of that place. I have often seen the two great landscapes from the Kress Collection, on loan from the National Gallery in Washington: *Blindman's Buff* once again and *The Swing* yet again. Two towering cypresses have been translocated from the Villa d'Este to diminish the tiny figures picnicking in a latticed garden by a rushing waterfall, under immense skies, or dodging the giddy girl with the blindfolded eyes. They could be a metaphor for the human condition, yet it is difficult to draw from them an edifying moral. But I admire the resolute lack of melancholy (the mood with which Watteau, had he painted the same scene, would have infused it), and were I to be given any two paintings in the entire world, I would want only these.

Enthusiasts for action painting might admire more the suite of *Figures de fantaisie*, rather mysterious half-figures, some of them identifiable portraits of men and women—actresses; scientists; Diderot himself; a soldier, or an actor playing the role of a soldier; a writer; a man playing a lute; a woman in a yellow dress and lavender ribbon, absorbed in a book; and the Abbé de Saint-Non, who was Fragonard's particular patron. These are oil sketches, allegedly done in an hour each, and so far as we know for the artist's own pleasure. Of Fragonard the man we know really very little. I have the sense that the *Figures de fantaisie* form a personal allegory of his own philosophy of life, but like him and like his unmatched powers, they stand as a kind of mystery.

—*The Nation*, April 16, 1988

Later Chinese Painting

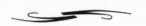

THE RENAISSANCE IDEAL of pictorial representation was to arrange forms and colors on a flat surface in such an artful way that the unaided eye would be unable to discriminate between the stimuli it received from the picture and those it might instead have received from the world. How far short of this ideal even a master like Giotto fell is made vivid by an imaginative conjecture once advanced by E. H. Gombrich. Gombrich proposes that Giotto's contemporaries would have gasped had they been presented with "even the crude colored renderings we find on a box of breakfast cereal." Had the Ghost of Art Worlds Yet to Come lifted the veil of the future for the edification of Florentines circa 1300 to reveal a Cubist still life or a Minimalist abstraction they could scarcely have accepted these as art. But as defined by the pictorial ideal just sketched, the *Raising of Lazarus* in Padua belongs to the same history of representation as does that image of an ecstatic beagle on the Milk-Bone for Medium Sized Dogs in my cupboard; and while little can have happened to the human eye through the intervening centuries, the human hand has undergone a progressive development through that same interval, and is capable today of feats undreamt of in Giotto's day. Vasari, who credited himself with living in an age when the hand had caught up with the eye, nonetheless supposed that this could not have happened had God not taken pity on struggling artists by sending down, not a carton of Wheaties to show them the way, but Michelangelo himself, who brought the Renaissance ideal to perfection. Gombrich observed, with great wisdom, that only where there is a way is there a will: Giotto would have had no way of painting Fiesole bathed in sunlight, and so could not have formed the intention of painting such a picture. An immense amount of the technological history of pictorial capacity would have to unroll before artists could frame projects in which splashes of light or heavy shadows could be marshaled to whatever expressive ends.

On the other hand, a pictorial tradition must be ready to receive an artistic revelation from the future. The Milk-Bone beagle, were it to have fallen among the painters of the Sung, might have struck them as a curiosity, but not something that insinuated any degree of retrograde dexterity on their part. They might have seen that image as very like the mirror image of a beagle, but as they were not bent upon projects in which the mirror image was an ideal or a rival, they might have had as great a difficulty accepting it as art as Giotto's contemporaries would have had accepting Picasso or Kandinsky. Indeed, the capacity to hit off individual likenesses was so little esteemed in China as a skill fit for acquisition by artists that those who in fact practiced it, to be sure long after the Sung, were no more regarded as artists than is the storefront photographer in, say, Patchogue, New York, who does wedding and confirmation photographs. In the absorbing exhibition of Chinese painting from the nineteenth and twentieth centuries from the Robert Hatfield Ellsworth Collection, on display at the Metropolitan Museum of Art in New York, there is a portrait by Wang Yüan, dated 1871, of a scholar, Chao Chih-ch'ien, which really does show its subject in a particularly lifelike way. Indeed, Wang Yüan has appropriated, as we would say today, the exact manner of a street artist, to whom one would go if one wanted a portrait rather than a work of art. In traditional Chinese representation, I have learned from Caron Smith, the curator of this show, it was in the vitality of the brush that the vitality of the subject was felt to be captured, and not in some idea of identical resemblance between the subject and its image. "Let people say of this portrait, which truly resembles me, 'That is Chao!' " reads the inscription on this work, written by its subject. That optical resemblance should have come to be prized, as evidently it had by 1871, marks a deep artistic revolution in China. The appropriation of low art for the expressive purposes of high art at this moment in China is, in its way, as abrupt a transvaluation as that in which the emblemata of commercial art—the Campbell's soup can label, for example, or the Brillo box logogram—were appropriated and made central in art by

Pop artists in our culture in the 1960s. "I do not know if there are people who conclude . . . that the box is superior to a Giotto," Gombrich wrote, implying that the Renaissance ideal specified but a necessary condition of artistic excellence even in its own tradition. But that the like of the cereal box should, in the middle decades of the twentieth century, have become thematic in advanced art is indicative of changes in the moral and artistic climate of the times, of which Wang Yüan's portrait is a distant counterpart in Chinese art.

Sometimes history itself reveals the kinds of intersections which Gombrich's imagined example illustrates, in which a work or class of works from another tradition reveals to the artists of a given time where their future lies. Obviously, they must be ready for such revelation, as Picasso was when he came across the so-called primitive carvings in the Musée d'Ethnographie du Trocadéro in 1907. Such art was known, certainly, to artists of an earlier period in France. Already in the 1880s, Gauguin would have seen it as portending an alternative for painting to that defined by the Renaissance ideal. But for the most part, I believe, this art would have been perceived, before Picasso, perhaps as Giotto would have been perceived by the artists of Vasari's time—as good for his backward time but essentially as "primitive" (as the artists of Siena are still explicitly designated). When Japanese prints impinged upon European artistic consciousness in the late nineteenth century, a whole order of representation opened up for artists who learned from the fact that the Renaissance ideal had somehow become eroded. It was as if those prints showed a way in which Giotto, taken as a moment of historical choice, could have generated a historical path far different from the one that led through Masaccio to Raphael, Leonardo and Michelangelo, and to the academies beyond them. The flat planes, the tilted spaces, the absence of light and shadow, showed how this whole heavy tradition could be erased, and a new beginning made. It was out of this encounter with an alternative future that Van Gogh, Gauguin, Bonnard and Matisse began what became modern art, in which the eye as an optical system was disenfranchised in favor of something altogether more "cerebral," as Gauguin put it.

What is ironic is that almost simultaneous with the unseating of optical criteria in the West, those same criteria began to transform standards of pictorial representation in China. In the 1870s, for example, photographs began insistently to transform Chinese sensibility. The acceptance of the photograph as implying a possible system of artistic representation must connect with the same impulses that elevated the street portraitist to a position of artistic respectability. And both these transformations must in turn connect with the infusion into China of images from the West that might be the exact equivalents of Gombrich's cereal cartons. Ours has been a culture rich in pictures for a very long time, and after the Treaty of Nanking, in 1842, under which five ports were opened to commerce, immense numbers of labels must have found their way into China, bringing with them an awareness of pictorial possibilities that must have been as explosive in China as the Japanese print became in ours, remembering that those prints were as scorned by high art in Japan as the poster or the box label was in ours. It is my sense that this flood of imagery must have carried the weight of Western prestige, and perhaps was appropriated just because the West had begun to be perceived as culturally superior in Chinese eyes, much, I suppose, as the culture of exotic places like Tahiti was perceived as superior by European artists such as Gauguin. On a recent afternoon, I was examining with Wen Fong (the Met's Special Consultant for Asian Art) a pale landscape impressionistically evoked on a fan. Wen Fong could not repress the remark that it was painted during "terrible times" for China. They were times in which the rapacity of Western commerce imposed war, social upheaval, revolution and humiliation upon the vast, weak Chinese nation. And yet despite or perhaps because of this, the West must have appeared in certain ways an exemplary culture: the labels came from the same resources as the gunboat. The entirety of Chinese life and culture was to be transformed, radically, by the incursion into it of Western practices in a process that continues to this day. The Chinese artist was in the avantgarde of this cataclysmic movement, and though the paintings in the Ellsworth collection appear, often, to be pallid continuations of traditional forms and themes, not greatly more enterprising in the depictions of flowers, birds and animals, of watery landscapes and dreamful sages and beauties so slender their heads look like flowers on a stalk, than painting in the Ching Dynasty ever had been, in fact these works seethe with alien forces and powerful influences that China could not assimilate without great and agonizing change. It is this that makes the exhibition exciting and instructive, quite apart from the aesthetic delights to be found in many of its objects. Who would not take pleasure from the cat painted in dotted lines by Hsü Ku, with its green eyes on top of its head, clawing at a butterfly which looks like an animated ideogram from the calligraphy nearby? But it is China as an inadvertent laboratory of historically induced artistic experiments in which the great value of this exhibition lies.

Surface similarities notwithstanding, these paintings are discontinuous with their own tradition simply because the infusion of Western representational vocabularies gave every Chinese artist a vision of an alternative way of working, so that for the first time, really, the Chinese painter painted in the light of a certain artistic self-consciousness. This meant that each image was now a matter of cultural choice. So even if an artist painted in a traditional manner, he had made his tradition his own by *deciding* to use it. Westerners may well have been regarded as "foreign devils" by patriots and administrators, because of their greed and cultural arrogance. But artistically they were liberators, offering a way to renew an artistic tradition that had grown as heavy and as old as ours when the Japanese print or the African mask offered Western artists a rejuvenating ideal. It does not greatly matter that the Chinese artist might have known Western styles only through fairly debased instances—imagine trying to construct a theory of Dutch painting on the basis of the illustration on the Dutch Masters cigar box. Still, such is the human mind that it is able to achieve such feats, as we construct theories of our first languages on the basis of often pretty debased inputs, from stuttering parents, say, who have heavy accents or speak in pidgin. It takes very little, after all, to open up a new vista.

Part, certainly, of the new level of consciousness consists in the appropriation by the Chinese themselves of certain archaisms in their own tradition. At the turn of the century, what came to be known as "oracle bones" (from the second millennium B.C.) were discovered, bearing incised calligraphic characters. These had immense historiographical and archaeological significance—they opened windows, as it were, into the then nearly legendary Shang Dynasty. But the inscriptions were not allowed to stand as merely archaeological specimens. Rather, they provided pictorial and calligraphic models for Chinese artists to use in the early twentieth century. They began, as it were, to redefine the brushstroke on the model of the incised mark, so that we find them painting characters and outlining forms as if in emulation of cut lines. This meant, in effect, a deliberate suppression of the accidentalities of the flowing brush—of what we respond to as the brushiness of the brush. Instead we see something almost mechanical—almost looking as if drawn by a rapidograph. Wen Fong, in a seminar to which I was invited, sought to show how this archaic calligraphy was adopted to expressive ends by the great twentieth-century master Ch'i Pai-shih. There is an adorable painting of two frogs by Ch'i Pai-shih that shows one frog, executed in hard, dense, oracle-bone black, staring across at another frog, painted in the watery brush style of a calligraphic tradition that the black frog calls into question. It is as if some sort of style war were being fought in what might superficially seem like just another painting of frogs by a Chinese artist. In fact, the frogs are only the occasion for a work that is really about painting.

You might want now to pay some special attention to three paintings of fruit by Ting Fu-chih. In addition to being marvelous paintings—perhaps the highlights of the show, aesthetically speaking—they embody and somehow synthesize all the tensions I discuss in this review. *Fruits*, painted in 1945, is a still life of fruits strewn abundantly across an implicit table surface. The fruits are painted as if solid, with shadows and highlights, neither of which would have been a component in Chinese painting before the introduction of photography. But they cast no shadows, and seem to exist in the kind of space traditional in Chinese art. They are like watery reminders of Dutch still lifes in this genre, say one by Willem Kalf (you might want to drop by the exhibition of Dutch and Flemish paintings from the Hermitage, and check Ting's way with fruit against Kalf's *The Dessert*—which incidentally shows fruit in a delft bowl patterned after a piece of Chinese porcelain). Yet Ting's painting is clearly a twentieth-century work, as can be seen by his preemption of an almost pointillist style of surface treatment (though with none of the spatial complexities of Seurat's work). Now pay attention to the calligraphy. It is self-consciously archaic and intriguingly self-referential: the inscription reads: "I have selected the characters from several Shang Dynasty oracle bones." So these paintings internalize and meld strategies from and make references to several artistic cultures, almost as if Postmodern. Yet they are unmistakably Chinese. All these components are beautifully combined in a fan, painted with a delicious tangle of red lichees, from 1941, with an accompanying poem which again uses Shang calligraphic characters. The miracle of these works is that they assert themselves aesthetically, however much or little we may know of the historical circumstances or cultural collisions of which they are the products.

There is no catalogue as such for the show, and there will be few readers in a position to acquire the handsome but expensive ($850!) three-volume work which covers the paintings and calligraphy in the Ellsworth collection, written by Ellsworth himself. Part of the disincentive is that one of the three volumes is dedicated to calligraphy, which to me, as to most of my readers, is likely to be an inaccessible subject, though I once had the benefit of discussions with my late friend Chiang Yee, who wrote one of the best treatises on it in English. I assume that there must be as close a connection between content and form as Hegel found in classical sculpture, but if one cannot read the characters, the forms must remain empty and abstract. Thus I could not appreciate the writing in a scroll painting near the entrance to the exhibition by Pao Shih-ch'en, but I especially regretted it in this case because I found the inscription, translated on a nearby label, moving and in an odd way timely. The painting consists of the inscription, and then an image underneath of two men riding together on donkeys, caught up in conversation.

The inscription moved me to think about the art world as we live it today. Elizabeth Frank recently reproached me for being insufficiently responsive to the plight of "good artists working in bad aesthetic times." Our times indeed are bad aesthetically, and though I have strong doubts about the future of art, I cannot but pray that some artistic angel would throw into our midst the cereal box we need to find our way forward! Pao's inscription begins this way:

Some chase fame at court. Some chase gain in the market. He who attains fame returns content. He who attains wealth returns secure. There are so many who never cease to strive. The universe is huge and never-ending.

Of the 90,000 or so artists said to be working in New York City today, few will attain contentment or security, nor will those who find security be assured of contentment. Pao Shih-ch'en did not achieve either of these himself, as he was a perpetual failer of the state examinations, the only gate to advancement in his culture. Perhaps the two riders have passed their journey philosophizing about fame, money, meaning, bad aesthetic times and the vastness of the universe—just as if they lived in TriBeCa, where those topics are unendingly discussed. The consolations of philosophy are distant and thin. Still, the poem is a tiny, moving gift from an early modern Chinese artist to us. Not the cereal box we need, but something to help us through the night. This wonderful exhibition will enable us all to see ourselves a bit from the outside. Its art world is curiously similar to our own.

—*The Nation*, April 23, 1988

Paul Gauguin

I HAVE LATELY FOUND it valuable to view the Western pictorial tradition as falling into three main phases, at roughly 300-year intervals: circa 1300, 1600 and 1900. It is possible to think of these as marked by different ways of construing space, though this can be but part of the matter. The first period, beginning with Giotto, is defined by that progressive investigation into natural appearances that culminates in Leonardo and Raphael. Its agenda was to arrange colors and forms on a flat surface so as to engender an illusion of objects in real space. The viewer is strictly excluded from the space into which he or she appears to see, like a disembodied eye. The second phase aspires to a different order of illusion, one which envelopes image and spectator together in what, in his lectures on Caravaggio, Frank Stella somewhat misleadingly terms "working space." We find a good statement of the third phase in some remarks of Maurice Denis, a leader of the "Nabi" school of painting, whose members, including Pierre Bonnard, took their inspiration from Paul Gauguin: "A painting, before being a war horse or a nude woman or an anecdote, is essentially a flat surface covered with colors arranged in a certain order." Under this description, internal and external illusory space are repudiated, and paintings are made almost specifically to stifle the possibility of illusion, as if the work consists only in its own surface.

Denis's words were written in response to an exhibition in 1889 of an ensemble of paintings done by Gauguin in Brittany, Arles and Martinique. "Here were heavily decorative surfaces," Denis went on, "powerful in hue and rimmed with brutal strokes, worked in *cloisonné*, it might have been said, because *cloisonnisme* and again *Japonisme* were words that were then in the air." Neither decoration nor ornament, implied by the reference to cloisonné, are today regarded as fit models for painting, but even so I shall think of the third phase as beginning with Gauguin, inasmuch as Modernism in art must in all its aspects be traced to him. This view is massively supported by the extraordinary exhibition of more than 240 pieces by Gauguin, in all the mediums he worked in, on view at the National Gallery of Art in Washington.

These periods did not develop out of one another spontaneously, as if the history of art consisted of an internal evolution of forms and pictorial possibilities. I have heard it argued that Renaissance naturalism was an artistic response to the Franciscan movement of the thirteenth century, in which nature was celebrated as the creation of God, to be cherished for its beauty rather than deplored as a vale of tears. Caravaggio and his contemporaries did not merely continue, but actively transformed the ideal of the Renaissance, not as a matter of internal artistic necessity but in compliance with an external mandate by the Church, as part of the Counter-Reformation. I do not know what external event it was that might stand as a cause of Modernism. "Contemporary art is weary of itself," the Belgian critic Emile Verhaeren wrote on the occasion of an exhibition in Brussels to which Gauguin contributed a carving and a ceramic pot, "and in order to renew itself returns to its sources." It is an interesting question why art *had* grown weary of itself in the last decades of the nineteenth century, and why its makers were all at once open to the primitive, which has "source" as one of its meanings. There is a sense in which Western civilization had lost the belief that it stood at the apex of progress or believed that progress had been bought at too heavy a cost. In any case, "primitive" art, which until then would have been dismissed as a mere anthropological curiosity, or as evidence of the inferiority of the cultures that produced it, became instead an inspiration. The weariness remarked upon by Verhaeren is of course sounded in Mallarmé's famous poem, which begins with the lament "The flesh is sad, and I have read all the books" and climaxes with the imperative *"Fuir là-bas!"*—flee this exhausted civilization and seek spiritual renewal *là-bas*, among the savages.

What set of causes, external to the history of art, explains the dissatisfaction with the art of masterpieces and at the same time accounts for the abrupt transvaluation of artistic values through which *primitive* art became, rather than the Old Masters, the model to aspire to, remains a historical mystery. Whatever the explanation—the death of God? the human-all-too-humanness of mankind?—it would have to account for a great deal more than simply what was happening in art during the *belle époque*.

Gauguin liked to think of himself as a savage well before he undertook his mythic transit to Tahiti. One of the works to which Verhaeren might have referred was a ceramic pot Gauguin made in the winter of 1889, molded into a portrait of himself "like the head of Gauguin the savage," as he put it in a letter. It emulated a primitive pot in that it was intended to contain something—it was a tobacco jar—and it looks almost pre-Columbian (Gauguin liked to boast that he was in part Inca, and in fact was brought up in Peru). There is no doubt that he intended a magical association between image, substance and content, and it was a work of which Gauguin thought sufficiently well to have offered it, as if offering himself, to a woman he was desperately in love with. He portrays himself with it in a painting in which he also portrays his great painting from his sojourns in Brittany, *Yellow Christ*. It is irresistible to interpret the painting, *Self-Portrait with Yellow Christ*, as composed of three self-portraits—as artist with his works; as savage in the depiction of himself on the tobacco jar; and as Christ. (A painting from the same year, *Christ in the Garden of Olives*, makes this identification explicit and unmistakable since Gauguin there gives his own features to Christ.) The three works, like the three persons of the Trinity united in a single presence, define his artistic achievement as he viewed it at the time, as well as his own moral situation, so far as this can be distinguished from his artistic projects.

Consider the pot first. Gauguin was a singularly experimental artist, and much taken up with questions of the integrity of materials—one of the premises of Modernism. His prints exploit exactly those qualities of physical transfer from plate to paper that are the essence of printmaking. He does not try to make prints that conceal their own processes: for him the process must be present and visible in the product. But similarly as a carver or a ceramicist, Gauguin strove to render salient the essence of the medium and the procedures of working in it. "The character of stoneware," he wrote, "is that of a very hot fire, and this figure [himself], which has been scorched in the ovens of hell, is I think a strong expression of that character." But beyond that he shows himself as "a poor devil all doubled up to endure his pain"—connecting the sort of image that goes with the medium together with that attitude toward himself and his life. The catalogue essay puts it precisely: "Gauguin has represented himself as the accursed artist, prey to the torments of creation, which are indeed expressed by the very nature of stoneware."

Yellow Christ of course emblemizes, as a crucifixion, the suffering that generates the moral tradition of the West. But it is difficult, aside from subject matter, to see any internal connection between this meaning and the medium of paint. Still, there is a connection between its style and its message. *Yellow Christ* is painted in the way that made such a strong impression on Maurice Denis, in a deliberately primitivized, intentionally naïve manner, rough and rude, hence eloquent in its repudiations. The color yellow is used to underscore that there is no intention, hence no failed intention, to mimic the visual appearances of flesh. Indeed, throughout this period (and throughout Gauguin's work from this period on) colors are used "primitively," that is to say, unmixed, as they come from the tube. The distant fields are in cadmium yellow. The trees, outlined in Prussian blue, are in cadmium orange. Three Breton women are shown kneeling, as if they are the three Marys, at the base of the cross. They are wearing characteristic Breton costumes, and it is worth contrasting the manner of their depiction with the kind of highly academic treatments of a Breton woman such as *Woman from Brittany* by the largely forgotten painter Pascal Dagnan-Bouveret, a precise example of the sort of art of which artists had grown weary. (It was the kind of work snapped up by wealthy collectors, and is part of the Potter Palmer Collection in Chicago, where I hope it will be shown when the Gauguin show is there.) The headdress, with its ribbons and trim, documents what a Breton woman would wear on a festive occasion, starched and gleaming white. Gauguin has reduced the Breton coifs to abstract, heavily outlined shapes, both here and in his slightly earlier *The Vision After the Sermon*, where costumed women pray in the foreground while Jacob and the Angel wrestle on a vermilion field. "The two bonnets at right are like monstrous helmets," he wrote to Van Gogh; and it is altogether clear that the primitive mode in which he represents these figures was intended to express these women—"very rustic, very *superstitious*." Of course the biblical combat exists only as their vision, so perhaps the appearance of Christ, in a rude form correspondent to their own rudeness, is meant to be a sign of grace.

For all I know, Gauguin may have seen himself as conferring a comparable grace upon the Tahitians, presumably primitive enough to appreciate him as a kind of God. In *Noa Noa*, his strongly fantasized account of his life there, the Tahitians called him "man who makes men," and fashioning men in one's own image was early recognized as a divine prerogative. Dagnan-Bouveret's *Pardon in Brittany* was shown at the Exposition Universelle in Paris in 1889, while Gauguin's works, which were shown to such effect upon the Nabis (a word that, incidentally, means "prophets"), hung across the street in the Cafe Volpini. The analogy between his sparse admirers and Christ's few disciples could hardly have been overlooked.

Let us now concentrate on the painting that shows these two works together with their creator and subject. *Self-Portrait with Yellow Christ* is painted in a manner different from that of the *Yellow Christ* and of course different in all respects from the portrait of the fired pot. So the painting is a fusion of three styles. The style of the painting itself—of Gauguin's face especially—is very much the appropriated style of Cézanne, surely in tribute to Cézanne. In 1890, Gauguin did a portrait of a woman in the manner of Cézanne with, just so there would be no mistake, a painting by Cézanne as background. So to show himself as a Cézanne is as metaphorical a representation as to show himself as a fired pot or as a burdened Jesus. (Cézanne evidently had no reciprocal admiration for Gauguin, whose art he referred to as "Chinese images.") All three styles, as well as their triune combination, announce a break with the tradition that goes back to Giotto and peters out in the academicism of Dagnan-Bouveret—an artistic tradition Gauguin regarded as a huge aberration, a monstrous error. He viewed the Impressionists as perpetuating that error, and as belonging to the tradition that he set himself and Cézanne against. He was in no sense an "optical" artist, engaged in optical experiment. He was a conceptual painter, and his identification with primitivism was due to his belief that primitive art was intellectual and, in his words, "cerebral." It is worth observing that among the words used by Picasso to describe what he admired in primitive art was that it was *raisonnable*. Gauguin saw his art, as he saw that of so-called primitive peoples, as having little to do with mere sensory appearance. "How safe they are on dry land, those academic painters with their *trompe l'oeil* of nature," he complained to one of his disciples. "We alone are sailing free on our ghostship, with all our fantastical imperfections."

Three years later, he sailed away, with all his fantastical imperfections, to the South Seas, with which he will forever be associated in the myth that makes it so difficult for us to see him for what he was—the great reinventor of art. The South Seas have figured in our moral consciousness since the reports of Captain Cook as a land for moral lotus-eaters. Kant refers to the life in the South Seas as one of "idleness, indulgence and propagation"—what Baudelaire, and later Matisse in a work that would have been unthinkable without the model of Gauguin, term *Luxe, Calme et Volupté*. It was not as such, Kant thought, a life one could rationally will. Gauguin's life is often condensed as follows: He abandoned wife and career as a stockbroker to run off to the South Seas to paint. It is a standard moral conundrum whether, even if a great artist, he was justified in putting his art above his responsibilities—a question loaded by the hedonism associated with the South Seas and by the somewhat vengeful judgment that he was anyway not a very great painter. This judgment is advanced by Somerset Maugham in a preface to the novel to which we by and large owe the myth. In any case we are obliged to judge him against a moral criterion very few artists have had to face. Van Gogh's reputation has survived the lopped ear and the suicide, as the auction records demonstrate. *He* may be exonerated on grounds of insanity, routinely suspected as the condition of great artists. Gauguin, by contrast, appears to have made a moral choice inconsistent with a concept of duty made central by Kant. And just because rational, his authenticity as an artist is suspect.

Gauguin's reasons for his flight *là-bas* were complex. In some ways they were altogether practical—he believed he could live without cost in a banana land of free food and sex on demand. Against these beliefs, the story of his calamities is sad and comical: he was arrested for swimming nude and spent his meager francs on prostitutes and canned goods. Still, the discrepancy between dream and reality could not have been so vast, for he made a second trip, ending up in the Marquesas, where he died in 1903. He must on both occasions have had a marvelous sense of sailing forth to a paradise—a *Nave Nave Fenua*, to use the title of one of his pictures—full of flora in primary colors, ornamental birds, awesome statuary, as well as bare-breasted wantons. That vision is almost architecturally translated in the Washington exhibition, since we mount a stairway from the early difficult years, in Paris, Arles and Pont-Aven, to a second floor, where it really does feel like entering an exotic heaven. At the head of the stairway, on the facing wall of the first gallery, is a painting of a Tahitian woman by the sea, gazing out over Art Nouveau waves, whether toward France to convey the feeling the artist had come too far, or toward the Marquesas, in case he had not come far enough.

But the conjunctive image of woman and waves was a recurrent motif in Gauguin, almost from the beginning, and the curious truth is that Gauguin was in many ways more a savage in Europe than he was in Tahiti. *The Siesta*, an early painting from Tahiti, uses classical perspective and illusory space and reverts to Impressionist uses of color, as if, perhaps, the flat expanses of unmodulated paint would not be sufficiently convincing—as if he were after all furnishing ethnological documents of a place too lush for his Modernist vocabulary. He would have been truer to his discoveries had he painted Tahiti in France, as the Douanier Rousseau painted his jungles, from botanical models in the Jardin des Plantes. Primitivism is a state of mind, as he ought to have known, which can easily shatter against colonial reality. So I like the Breton work best, guided perhaps by an aesthetics of roughness, of the unfinished, which we owe as much to Gauguin as to anyone.

He was a muddled man, tormented and inconsistent and reckless. Maurice Denis, who owned the *Self-Portrait with Yellow Christ*, wrote, movingly and exactly: "Gauguin, who had so much disorder and incoherence in his life, would stand for neither of these things in his painting. He loved clarity, which is a sign of intelligence."

This is a stunning exhibition of the work of a great artistic thinker. I have only touched its surface.

—*The Nation*, June 11, 1988

Diebenkorn

IN 1967, THE AMERICAN PAINTER Richard Diebenkorn turned
away from his widely admired figural style—fluid, awkward, loosely
evocative of Bonnard but less florid and more athletic—to return, to
be sure with some marked differences, to the abstractionist imperatives
he had just as abruptly put aside a dozen years before. His career thus
falls naturally into three phases—or two phases of abstraction with a
prolonged figurationist interlude—but this bland periodization fails to
do justice to the unfolding narrative of his artistic discoveries. His
figures were after all but regimentations of the same urgent and sweeping gestures that were the mark of his driving first abstractionist manner, and were set into pictorial spaces that did not exist in painting
before Abstract Expressionism reinvented space. And the post-1967
abstractions have seemed to many sufficiently referential so that it is
a critical commonplace to see them as suffused with a special California
light, and as dense with coastal allusions to sky, ocean, seaside and
sun, tawny hills, bleached architecture, sharp shadows and angular
illuminations, green expanses and glimpsed distant blues, and possibly
haunted by the erasure of human presences. Nor does the chronicle
"abstraction-figuration-abstraction" adequately acknowledge the extreme determination, the aesthetic courage it had to have required first
to shift from abstraction to "the image" at a time when such a change
was perceived within the art world as something momentous, like a
conversion or a betrayal or a heretical declaration, and then, at a time
when one's great reputation was based upon the marvelous posing of

figures in landscapes or interiors that looked like abstractions anyway, when pure abstraction was no longer the True Faith but only one of the ways to do things in an art world gone slack and pluralistic, to return to abstraction as one's own truth. Both changes are evidence of a certain dogged integrity, and were perhaps among the benefits of growing a career in California, away from the style wars and the critical fire storms of New York, with its fevered obsessions with where one fits, with who is in and which is out and what is new, fading, dated and dead.

In a sense, nothing has been new with Diebenkorn since 1967, when he exhibited the first paintings in what was to lengthen into an extraordinary series. These are the Ocean Park paintings—large canvases, each bearing the same title, *Ocean Park*, but individuated with a number that indicates, presumably, the order of its completion. The series had reached number 140 by late last year, which allows a rough calculation of Diebenkorn's annual output, though he has concurrently produced a number of works-on-paper, titled *Untitled* but recognizably answering to the same impulses that give rise to the Ocean Park paintings. Ocean Park itself is a community near Santa Monica, where Diebenkorn traces a daily path between home and studio, but whether or not these works make the topical references to local landscape with which they are credited, they clearly are something more than abstractions with recurrent compositional motifs, cadences, pastel tonalities, scumbled fields and tapelike forms, and stunning juxtapositions of color swept on with masterful brushwork. Each of them, for example, displays the submerged record of its own realization, and so distinctive are the *pentimenti* in Diebenkorn's art that each painting carries within itself the visible history of the artist's search. The nearest parallel, perhaps, would be the great drawings of Rembrandt, in which certain crowded lines converge on the sought-after contour so that the drawing and its draw-ing are one, process and fulfillment inseparable. It is possible to imagine a writer, misguided by the recent privileging of *l'écriture*, who publishes a work that exhibits the labor of writing it, with all the first lines, the crossed-out sentences, whited-out lines with fragments of letters showing through and scribbled insertions between the lines and up the margins. Whatever such a text started out to be about, it would in the end have to be about its own processes, self-exemplificatory. In my view, Diebenkorn's paintings are less about the bright skies and long horizons of Ocean Park than about the act of painting, as if the works had become more and more their own subjects and the external references stand at best as indications of what the painting is not about—*Ceci n'est pas un paysage!* In this sense, and despite his notorious employment of mechanical straightedges, Diebenkorn has not moved greatly beyond the premises of Abstract Expressionism, which always insisted that the painting was the paint-ing, its final subject and only reference. On the other hand, nothing could more vividly illuminate the difference between painting and writing as arts than the extreme power and beauty, the elegance and excitement of the Ocean Park paintings, and the tiresomeness of the piece of writing I just imagined, with which no one, unless perhaps a member of Yale's Department of English, could have the slightest patience.

It is instructive to compare Diebenkorn as an artist with his somewhat older fellow Californian (and Stanford alumnus) Robert Motherwell, who has also produced an extraordinary series: the most recent Spanish Elegy I have seen is number 132, completed in 1983. "Diebenkorn," Motherwell recently told me, "is what I would have become if I had had his talent but remained in California instead of moving to New York." The Spanish Elegies and the Ocean Park paintings are at the pinnacle of contemporary painting, but the differences in their inspiration and spiritual provenance are profound. Motherwell wrote about the Spanish Elegies that they are "for the most part, public statements. [They] reflect the internationalist in me, interested in the historical forces of the twentieth century, with strong feelings about the conflicting forces in it." By contrast, Motherwell says of his collages that they are "intimate and private." Now, I do not believe, of any of Diebenkorn's works, that the category of privacy or intimacy especially applies. They are as public as scientific experiments, open investigations into the resolution of pictorial tensions or conquests of painterly difficulties. But neither are they "public statements" which could be construed as dealing with any issues other than the issues of painting. It was as if even the somewhat blank figures of Diebenkorn's middle period were ill at ease in their paintings, and distractions from Diebenkorn's deepest preoccupations. "Spain" denotes a land of suffering and poetic violence and political agony, and "Elegy" carries the literary weight of tragedy and disciplined lamentation. It would be inconsistent for works so titled to reflect back merely upon their own processes, and in truth one cannot see *Spanish Elegy 132* without feeling oneself in the presence of some human revelation as deep as painting allows.

As a term, "Ocean Park" belongs to the hopeful vocabulary of the real estate developer, and designates an archetypal suburban locus in Southern California—*Ocean Park. No. 133* could be an address. But in any case Ocean Park is but the site, perhaps distantly the occasion for a work that makes and needs no references. And the miracle is that works so circumscribed in subject, substance, meaning and feeling should be so overwhelming when viewed as altogether to obliterate their circumstances and limits. The miracle is that the country mouse/ city mouse difference between these two masters should finally count for so little in terms of their comparable achievements. There is finally a fierce beauty in Diebenkorn's work that marks a limit in our critical competence to explain it.

Aside from the two decisions that articulate his corpus, Diebenkorn's life is really more a career than a biography, like that of a successful academic. It is an exemplary life, but not an outwardly interesting one: the story of schools attended, positions held, group shows, traveling retrospectives, prizes won and a growing, finally a global recognition. It is an exemplary life because of its absolute commitment, as if the decisions to remain in California and to stay within a single and evidently deeply fulfilling marriage were so many ways of keeping distraction at bay. In this sense, I suppose, the life and the work are of a piece, for the art, too, is a systematic and sustained effort to expunge from itself whatever is other than itself. Even the numerated laconic titles bear out what we might think of, in Sartrian terms, as the original choice that defined the project. The work is tentative and confident at once, as if the doubts which the individual works preserve and display were required in order that they should be overcome in the dazzling works to which they lead. There is a marvelous moment in a recent profile of Diebenkorn by Dan Hofstadter in *The New Yorker* which brings out both sides. Diebenkorn was expressing to an intimate his doubts about being up to the task of painting. The intimate said, "O.K., Dick. How many people in the world do you think paint as well as you do?" Hofstadter tells us that Diebenkorn thought for a long time, and then he just laughed. Unremitting doubt as to one's adequacy to the task one knows no one is better suited for than oneself: those are the coordinates of his personality and in an odd way the content of his work.

—*The Times Literary Supplement*, May, 1988

David Hockney

A RETROSPECTIVE EXHIBITION enables us to appreciate an artist's early work in the light of an unfurled future to which the artist
and his or her contemporaries would have then been blind. But it also
enables us to see those early works as they could have been seen at
the time had it not been for the work's newness and for factors in the
critical environment that caused it to be seen for something other than
it was. Consider David Hockney's *The Most Beautiful Boy in the World*,
which hangs just past the entrance to the retrospective being given him
at the Metropolitan Museum of Art. Hockney painted it in 1961, when
he was twenty-four and something of a prodigy, for he was still a
student at the Royal College of Art in London. To be sure, the most
advanced art in England just then was being made by students at the
Royal College of Art, by R. B. Kitaj and Norman Toynton as well as
by Hockney, and it comes as somewhat of a jolt to recognize that the
legendary Young Contemporaries exhibition of 1961 was in effect a
show of student work. Lawrence Alloway contributed a catalogue essay
to that show and reproduced *The Most Beautiful Boy* with his important
1966 essay on British Pop Art. So Alloway affords a very clear example
of how the work was perceived when it was first shown.

The painting is, in many ways, an anthology of the artistic themes
and strategies that defined a new sensibility. It was, for one thing,
figural at a time when Abstract Expressionism, in truth all but finished
as an artistic movement, was still regarded as the only present with a
future, and that future was to exclude the figure—the image—as dead.

Images, if they were to be used, had to be taken over from orders of representation as remote from high art as could be found—from the art of children or what were regarded as primitive peoples, or from commercial labels or the mass media, which were then being used to such revolutionary effect by the Young Contemporaries' peers in New York under the later label of Pop Art. Hockney's painting, moreover, used words as part of its content at a time when the orthodox position was that the entire meaning of a painting must be carried by nonverbal forms alone. But lettering, if not appropriated from commercial advertising or logograms, had to be of the kind rudely scrawled on walls or sidewalks. Alloway (to whom the expression "Pop Art" is due) believed that the new art expressed some connection to the city, "by using typical products and objects, including the techniques of graffiti and the imagery of mass communication." Something a good bit deeper was taking place in these works than an artistic celebration of the urban reality, I think, and certainly this was true of Hockney. Still, it was possible and perhaps urgent for Alloway to see the works as he did.

In any case, all the components just listed are present in *The Most Beautiful Boy*. In the upper right is an Alka-Seltzer label, as if crookedly postered against a wall on which words and images are scribbled or scratched. The most beautiful boy himself is smeared onto the surface, as if by a child confirmed in his childishness by a precocious exposure to *l'art brut* (Hockney at the time was admired for his exquisite draftsmanship and awarded the gold medal for drawing when he graduated). The figure is juxtaposed with its own description—the title of the work—lettered along his back: word and image occupy the same space. But beyond this there is something extremely personal about the painting: it is at least as much an index to the artist as to the artistic currents that flowed through his work. The most beautiful boy is wearing a feminine garment, a frilled dress or nightgown, which looks as if it could have been palimpsestically superimposed on the figure, by someone else, like a piece of graffiti, except for the extreme delicacy with which the hem is executed. The sexual ambiguity that settles on the figure in consequence of the dress and the word "boy" is somewhat resolved by context: the adjacent *The Cha-Cha That Was Danced in the Early Hours of 24th March* (also from 1961) shows what one would spontaneously read as a leggy girl in a flossy dancing dress, but we know from Hockney's autobiography that the cha-cha in question was danced explicitly for him by a boy who knew that Hockney had eyes for him. So I suppose the transvestite representation connotes the homosexuality about which Hockney was quite candid even then. I would like to connect the Alka-Seltzer sign with the boy, as if the picture were a kind of rebus puzzle: perhaps Alka-Seltzer is for heart-burn what the most beautiful boy is for a burning heart. This is some-what confirmed by the presence of a large red heart that seems to zip toward the boy's head with the velocity of a brick pitched by Ignatz at The Most Beautiful Cat in the World. It is a witty and confessional piece of work, a declaration of love, one surmises, and sexually explicit, if the scrawled "69" means what it ordinarily means—and it engages the viewer in the artist's own emotional affairs, as if he wore his heart on his canvas. Viewer, artist, subject and work are woven into a complex communication scarcely typical of someone eager to depict the city; but this is altogether typical of Hockney at this period and, when at his best, in every period.

Not only are these works from the early 1960s about love—erotic and indeed homoerotic love rather than the abstract agape of Robert Indiana's celebrated logogram—but they are unashamedly literary as well. They incorporate the titles they bear as painted inscriptions, which come from the poets whom Hockney particularly admired—Whitman, for example, in "We Two Boys Together Clinging," or Cavafy, in "Kaiserion" ("Ah, see, you came with your vague / fascination. In history only a few / lines are found about you, / and so I molded you more freely in my mind. . . . My art gives your features / a dreamy compassionate beauty"). The images, in both these works, are cun-ningly childlike, wittily sentimental and composed of frocked boys wryly discordant, with their *art brut* faces, with the languorous words they distantly illustrate. At the time, perhaps, a surface continuity with the Pop movement screened the fact that something of a far more subjective order was being transacted by an artist who merely exploited what the art world made available but who soon enough embarked on a program that had less and less to do with whatever anyone else was making by way of art. "I paint what I like, when I like and where I like," Hockney wrote, disconcertingly, to those who had other ambi-tions for his art, mentioning among the subjects that concerned him "landscapes of foreign lands, beautiful people, love, propaganda, and major incidents (of my own life)." Alloway cites this in order to dismiss Hockney's art as "rambling and discursive." But by that time, 1966, Hockney was already famous and extraordinarily successful, and really no longer in need of critical support: he had broken free into the air of glamour and affluence that he has enhanced ever since.

This luminous success is not difficult to understand against the background of what other artists had been doing in the period. In England, there was Francis Bacon, whose images are unrelievedly scary, with figures twisted and compressed into screams: or Lucian Freud, whose chill aggressions in portraiture proclaim the triumph of artistic will over subdued models, and deposit the sour aftertouch of sadism on us. The art of the 1960s was recently celebrated in the May issue of *Artforum* on the twentieth anniversary of the uprising of 1968. It was an art that, however innovative, seems so barren and ravaged and pessimistic that the black-and-white photographs of it seem like documents of a world devastated by a terrible disaster. Hockney alone among advanced artists seemed to be carrying forward the bright affect of the School of Paris (which itself had gone dead by then) with bouquets, languid figures in tasteful interiors, leisured personalities in lovely gardens, substituting a California of the heart for the Côte d'Azur: a place of clear light, clean planes, meridional flora—and emblematic pools. Hockney indeed gave artistic embodiment to Southern California with the same authority that Saul Steinberg reinvented a Texas of our menaced dreams. Some months ago in San Antonio I felt myself in a world invented by Steinberg, and in just such a way a Californian like Lawrence Weschler remembers his pre-Hockney visual world through a lens given him by Hockney. So if you were interested in painting that was at once serious and ingratiating, Hockney had no competitors. The work seems simultaneously difficult and available—warmed, like Matisse or Bonnard, by sunlight reflected in blue skies and embracing water, and infused by pleasure and love.

For all that ingratiating intelligence, the fertility of invention and the cheerful hedonism, I find the work over the several years after the "love" paintings artistically thin. The scruffy palimpsestic surfaces of the early paintings, scored and mottled, smooth into planes of uncadenced blues, tans, yellows and pinks—California hues—while the figures graduate from the primitive and childlike scumbles to blander and more naturalistic figures, almost always amusing and fondly treated. Sometimes a heavily stylized figure is jammed into the same space as one treated naturalistically, which has something of the same effect as putting words and images together in the same space, drawing attention to the fact that this can happen only in pictorial space. This

[*200*

David Hockney

kind of juxtaposition is intoxicating in *Invented Man Revealing Still Life* (1975), in which a man with a plaid torso and washy legs—and a protractor head, a red ring for a nose—draws open the curtains on an exquisitely rendered lavender vase of white tulips: it is as if the Hockney of the 1960s were displaying the Hockney of the 1970s. The same effect is achieved in the 1972 *Portrait of an Artist (Pool with Two Figures)*. A solidly painted young man, presumably the artist of the title, looks down with philosophical wonderment into the swimming pool at his feet. He is placed at the extreme right of the canvas, and if you block him out, there remains a fairly typical Hockney composition of the era—a pool in which great attention is paid to the watery patterns of the surface; a flattened submerged swimmer; and a mountain landscape beyond. It is pleasant enough—but if you now restore the realistic figure, a tension develops between two styles which gives the work a certain excitement and depth. The work through the 1970s thickens perceptibly, most particularly in the great sequence of double portraits, culminating in his powerful *My Parents* of 1977. These I count among the masterpieces of the century.

My Parents was painted when Hockney was forty and must certainly, in view of its subject and of the complex feelings with which this large square canvas is replete, be some sort of *apologia pro vita sua*, a coming to terms with himself as son and artist. The two parental figures are shown seated, and at an angle to one another on either side of a taboret, a moral geometry Hockney used to great effect in his double portraits: Henry Geldzahler, Celia (Mrs. Clark in *Mr. and Mrs. Clark and Percy*) and Hockney's mother are shown frontally, facing the viewer (and of course the artist); Christopher Scott, Mr. Clark and Hockney's father are shown in full or partial profile. Given the obviously profound affection the artist holds toward the first trio, on the evidence of many marvelously affectionate drawings of them, the frontal pose must carry a certain emotional meaning, and the tension between the differently posed figures must then be a translation into the language of composition of something intense in the language of feeling. Atop the taboret, next to the signature vase of tulips, is a mirror, and it is the latter, reminding us of mirrors in *Las Meninas* (where the parental couple is reflected) or in the *Marriage of Giovanni Arnolfini and Giovanna Cenami* of Jan Van Eyck, that communicates a symbolic signal to the viewer. In part this is because the mirror should reflect the artist himself, computing where he must have sat relative to the composed scene; and in part because what is reflected instead are some reproductions of paintings. One of them is quite distinctly Piero Della Francesca's *Baptism of Christ*, a print we see fastened to a screen in *Looking at Pictures on a Screen*, done the same year and showing Geldzahler alone, in profile, against a screen with four prints taped to it. The other reflection shows the mirror image of the curtains drawn aside by the invented man to reveal the still life. (These curtains were appropriated from a panel by Fra Angelico.) The curtains certainly remind us of the bed curtains in the *Arnolfini* portrait, with their heavy symbolic charge: since baptism and marriage are sacraments—and since pools of water and drawn or closed curtains figure throughout Hockney's work—the conviction is inescapable that even the hedonistic landscapes and interiors must have had a symbolic meaning inscribed onto their pleasing surfaces. I draw attention to only one of the prints in the Geldzahler painting, which reproduces a famous Vermeer, a picture within a picture that has in turn a picture in *it*—specifically, of a triumphant Amor.

My Parents had to be a naturalistic interior space with a strongly defined linear perspective in order to show that the artist himself is not present (since not reflected in the mirror) but has been instead replaced by some images of great art. There is of course another way of reading this fact: linear perspective reduces the viewer to a kind of disembodied eye excluded from the space into which it looks. The surface of a painting in perspective has been compared to a window since Renaissance times, and so stands as an almost metaphysical boundary between art and life. The exclusionary principle of linear perspective is something to which Hockney, as an optical theorist, is extremely sensitive, and his many discussions and demonstrations of an alternatively structured space—in an issue of the French edition of *Vogue* that he filled with reflections on perspective; in his marvelous fragmented photographs, which seem to take up analytical Cubism where it left off; and even in the charming film he did on a Chinese scroll, in which he praises the more humane use of perspective than is found in a Canaletto behind him—suggest that he comes close to blaming a great many social ills on perspective. The photographs, which seem almost literally to replicate the movements of the eye across a surface in saccadic leaps, imply for him a sense of life and engagement in contrast with the disembodiment implied by linear perspective. "The Chinese landscape painting is a walk through a landscape," he

David Hockney

wrote in *Vogue*: "Movement is life. Lack of movement, death." If fixed-point perspective immobilizes the spectator, paintings executed under its aegis situate the spectator outside life, a thought that sits uncomfortably with the commanding perspectival structure of *My Parents*. It is striking that Hockney abandoned such perspective almost immediately after he completed this compelling work. He also, for a long time, gave up painting.

I have sought to render salient two moments in the narrative that a major retrospective challenges us to recover. I think I can grasp the shift from rigid perspective to the Cubistic engagement of the moving glance in the photomontages; I am less certain I know what is going on in the Picassoid forms and distortions of the latest phase, except that I am sure, given Hockney's views about perspective and its effect on the viewer, that they are experiments undertaken on our presumed behalf. The neo-Cubist *Mulholland Drive: The Road to the Studio* has more and more grown on me. It is almost an emblem for a life, with its ups and downs, leading, in his case, to the studio, which we see from above, with its famous swimming pool. The miracle is that an art so personal should engage us so, suggesting to me that the secret of Hockney's art is to be found between the work and its viewers, a space curiously filled by the artist himself.

—*The Nation*, July 30/August 6, 1988

Georges Braque

IN NOVEMBER OF 1908, Picasso and his mistress, Fernande Olivier, organized a banquet in honor of the Douanier Rousseau, at which the guest of honor is said to have told Picasso: "We are the two greatest painters of our epoch, you in the Egyptian style, I in the modern." As the banquet took place in Picasso's studio, where as far as I know *Les Demoiselles d'Avignon* was still on view to Picasso's pals, there is a certain crackpot acuity tantamount to wit in Rousseau's seeing Picasso as part of an Egyptian revival. But in that very month, an influential review by Louis Vauxcelles appeared in *Gil Blas*, on an exhibition by Braque, in which that young artist was said to be disproportionately obsessed by "the static style of the Egyptians." We know that Braque haunted the collections of Egyptian antiquities at the Louvre when he moved to Paris in 1900, as if complying with an implied imperative laid down by Gauguin a decade earlier: "We have truth when we have a purely cerebral art, as in primitive art—the most deliberate of all— as in Egypt."

Paris was the city of museums. Its collections were lugged back in wagonloads by Napoleon's troops, under orders to appropriate by seizure whatever might serve to edify the citizenry of the Republic and testify to its military might; later collections were sent back by the shipload by various French expeditionaries who, complacent in their superior civilization, claimed masks and fetishes for the scientific instruction of the French, stocking the ethnographic museum of the Palais du Trocadéro, which Picasso visited to such cataclysmic effect in May or June of 1907, that epochal year. I am not eager to speculate here on what drove the co-inventors of Cubism into these dusty, exotic, marginal collections, except to underscore the proposition that in the historical explanation of works of art, causality is never mechanical: the artist defines what he or she requires by way of influence and generates with the new work a narrative relating it to its own appropriate past. Matisse and Derain *collected* primitive art; Picasso and Braque made that art their own and reconstructed the future of modern art by giving it the past they required to get on with the present moment.

It was also in Vauxcelles's review (a paragraph of less than a hundred words!) that the term "cube" was first applied to Braque's work: "He scorns form, reduces everything—sites and figures and houses—to geometric schemes, to cubes." Within the year, "Cubism" was as common a term in the Parisian art world as "commodification" is in our own, and it is fascinating to speculate upon what the subsequent history of art, let alone of Braque's art, might have been had this epithet not fallen upon it to freeze it into a certain mold. Would Impressionism have existed as an artistic style without having been called Impressionism, singling out as salient the ephemeral and the sensory, and generating an entire agenda in the choice of the word? How many of the paintings of Abstract Expressionism would we have without the name? It is often as though name and substance penetrate each other; that the critical designation of an artistic movement redirects the movement it intends merely to label, giving it a consciousness, so that the language of the critic is as dangerous as a paralyzing dart.

"Geometrical" has been the very essence of "cerebral" in our own tradition, and both the adoration of geometry and the admiration of Egypt coexist in Platonic aesthetics. What Plato specifically impugned, exactly as Gauguin was to do two millenniums later, was an art of sensory exactitude, where the possibility of illusion stalked and indeed crowned artistic endeavor. Before the twentieth century, Egyptianism had affected art only by providing it either with decorative motifs, as in the Empire style, with its sphinxes and pharaonic thrones, or with a certain arcane subject matter, as in *Aïda*. European artists had to weary, internally and definitively, of registering visual appearances as they are delivered to the retina, before Egyptian strategies could recommend themselves as something more than embellishment or motif. How absolutely perceptive it was of Rousseau to see what Picasso was doing as "the Egyptian manner," how critically exact it was to see in Braque's work of 1908 *ressouvenirs* of Egyptian modes of representation, not imitated but internalized and made his own. (And what if "Egyptism" rather than "Cubism" had become the name of the art?)

It is a stock item of cultural literacy that the Egyptians represented the human figure as anatomically impossible composites: eyes were depicted frontally in profiled heads set atop frontally displayed upper bodies carried by legs shown in profile. It was as though the figure were carefully folded to fit into a plane, like a garment. Something other than visual fidelity drove the Egyptian painters; issues of foreshortening or perspective held no interest for them, and the camera, in their hands, would have been a useless device. There is a fascinating psychological theory, due to Eleanor Rosch and her associates, known as "prototype theory," and concerned with the natural categories of human cognition. Rosch's theory, now widely demonstrated, predicts such things as what properties people associate most frequently with a given term. People are more likely to think of hardness rather than combustibility in connection with diamonds, or to think of diamonds rather than peridots when asked to name a gem. So, I suppose, with drawing: asked to draw a fruit, one would most likely respond with an apple or banana rather than a loquat or persimmon. Asked to draw an eye, most people would draw it frontally, and would draw a profile leg if asked to draw a leg. So it is as if the Egyptian figure were a conjunction of prototypical body parts, where obviousness and familiarity were the criteria of representation. It is as if no part of a figure would be convincing unless, were the rest of the figure destroyed, it would remain spontaneously identifiable. I sometimes think the Egyptians showed things as they might be stored, part by part, in our visual memories.

Something like this is true, I believe, of Cubism, and I was thrilled to read in John Golding's essay on Picasso in *The New York Review of Books* that Picasso once said, "I want to say the nude. I don't want to do the nude as a nude. I want only to say breast, say foot, say hand or belly. To find the way to say it." Cubism (if we can for a moment forget the cubes) analyzes into prototypical aspects objects of the most prototypical, that is to say, commonplace, order. And I want to stress their ordinariness here, on the ground that if they were exotic or unfamiliar objects, the viewer would lose the bearings essential to an appreciation of the artist's brilliant redistributions. Here is a wonderful passage in which Picasso discloses a difference between himself and Matisse, in Françoise Gilot's (incidentally splendid and even great) book about her life with him:

It isn't any old object that is chosen to receive the honor of becoming an object in a painting by Matisse. They're all things that are unusual in themselves. The objects that go into my paintings are not that at all. They're all common objects from anywhere: a pitcher, a mug of beer, a pipe, a package of tobacco, a bowl, a kitchen chair with a cane seat, a plain common table—the object at its most ordinary. I don't go out of my way to find a rare object that nobody ever heard of, like one of Matisse's Venetian chairs in the form of an oyster, and then transform it. That wouldn't make sense. I want to tell something by means of the most common objects: for example, a casserole, any old casserole, the one everybody knows.

Prototype theory predicts the order in which we acquire our concepts, as well as which aspects of which concepts we acquire first—and I suppose it must tell us the last things we remember under the decay of the mind in age, hence why we all become children again at the end. So the Cubist world was the basic world of commonplace objects, the things we all know and share, their reassuring ordinariness a pre-condition for the sharp crystallizations of their forms that defined the new order of showing/saying that Picasso and Braque were forging. And how illuminating it is after all to recognize that Matisse's world was that of a voluptuary who surrounded himself with sumptuous textures and rare colors and decorative women garbed like harem beauties—a world to which the paintings of Matisse themselves be-longed. (So of course he painted his own paintings as parts of the furnishings of his luxurious interiors!)

It is my sense that Picasso characterizes Braque's contribution far better than his own ("When there's anything to steal, I steal," he said). Throughout the formative phase of Cubism, Picasso was far more interested in the human (well, the human female) form and face than in the homely objects of domestic reality. The generous retrospective of Braque's work at the Guggenheim Museum in New York City begins with a very early study of his grandmother (a grandmother might at a stretch be classed as an item of domestic furnishing), and though there is a Fauve nude of 1907, the human figure quickly disappears from his work, only to make awkward rare appearances. I don't think Braque was interested in things from the kitchen and studio as such, though no doubt there is something in French sensibility that singles these out, but his artistic drives in those years were so radical that he needed to anchor his experiments into prototypicality if they were not to shatter into incoherence—or, what would amount to the same thing, into abstractness. It is an interesting question why abstraction never really presented itself as an option either for Braque or Picasso. Braque movingly portrayed the two of them as mountaineers, roped together, and the use of the image of a safety rope I find eloquent. Painting for them remained throughout a representationalist activity, and they were bent less upon the reinvention of art than the redefinition of painting. Recognizable objects disappear completely from canvases of Kandinsky's by 1914, but Kandinsky was a mystic, eager to shake this world off for another one, whereas Braque and Picasso required at their most abstract some tangible bit of this world, even if they had to glue in a label or scrap of newspaper. (The French word for daily paper is *le quotidien*, and I enjoy the thought that these scraps at once belong to and emblemize the artistically crucial domain of daily existence.)

A great deal has been written about the nail in *Violin and Palette* of 1909–10, which casts a shadow, as if it belonged vestigially to a style of illusionist painting Cubism had superseded. But in truth there are lots of shadows in the painting, even if, as often in Cubism, the shadows are disjointed from their objects. But the palette, the sheets of music, the violin itself all have shadows and so an implied three-dimensionality. The striking thing about the nail is that its shadow goes in a different direction, which is one of the liberties prototyping allows: the paintings forswear any single source of illumination, much as the Egyptian figure disallows any single vantage point. Indeed, the Egyptian figure, as adjoined prototypes, is like something that has to be read, from top to bottom—and this is true certainly of *Violin and Palette*—one is intended to read it through rather than take it in at a single glance. "We were trying," Picasso said, "to move in a direction opposite to Impressionism. That was the reason we abandoned color, emotion, sensation and everything that had been introduced into painting by the Impressionists—we were trying to set up a new order." "We were no longer interested in museums," Braque said. They cut themselves off from the past, but never from the dear world of daily things, which in the end gives them a deep continuity with Impressionism after all.

[*208*

Georges Braque

* * *

Picasso staggered from style to style, but in a way Braque never stopped being a Cubist: and perhaps the Cubist painting became its own prototype for an artist whose life was spent increasingly in his own studio, where nothing was more familiar—not the rickety table, the guitar or the *compotier*—than their representations in Cubist works. Braque was badly wounded in World War I, and for a time could not paint. When he did again put brush to canvas, a great deal had changed, though not the subjects or, really, the forms. But the mood had darkened, almost as though he had pulled the curtains against an outdoor light as a metaphor for turning increasingly within. From then on there is a marked somberness to Braque's palette: mauves, aubergines, chestnut browns and brown-greens, ochers and mustard yellows. He no longer needs ordinary objects for visual but, one feels, for emotional security. Among his many gifts, Picasso was the greatest art critic of modern times. "I see you're returning to French painting," he once said to Braque. "But you know, I never thought you would turn out to be the Vuillard of Cubism." How precise: there is something almost stifling in the thick domesticity of Vuillard's textured interiors—airless, dense, fortified. Braque's life and art were of a piece from about 1920 until his death in 1963. Whatever he was, he was no longer a mountaineer.

I sometimes think that the faceting in the early work—the cubes of Cubism—were there more for visual excitement than in response to a kind of geometrolatry. Or the geometry came later. In Braque's later work, the excitement subsides in favor of something subtler, quieter and nuanced. Traversing the long *après-guerre* work is like passing an afternoon in a French parlor, with the ticking of a Second Empire clock the loudest noise and the muffled traffic beyond the thick curtains as comforting as the sound of rain from a warm room. Heavy draperies, waxed furniture, amusing bibelots, faded engravings, and the light having to fight its way through the slats of shutters to fall in intense patches on polished wood. Bit by bit, certain harmonies grudgingly present themselves, a taste becomes palpable. "The harmony of two colors in a painting . . . by Braque covers an infinite distance," Picasso commented. As in the parlor, one's sensibility slowly adjusts and finds excitement enough in a curve, a shadow, a spot of illumination: "A sudden light transfigures some commonplace thing," as Walter Pater wrote. The paintings of the later years invert the priorities of their predecessors. In those, a single recognizable detail—a candle, the scrolls in a violin, the cadences of a bunch of grapes—keep the work from exploding into mere visual excitement. In these a single patch of visual excitement—a lemon, the touch of ultramarine along a table leg, a stripe of orange carried around the edge of a chair just far enough not to be vulgar—animate an arrangement of recognizable objects in crepuscular light.

As a rule, at the Guggenheim one takes the elevator to the top of the museum, where the shows ordinarily begin, and feels the pull of gravity down to the level where life takes place, with lines of people buying tickets or sorting through the postcards or waving to friends or waiting to eat. It was an inspiration to reverse this in the Braque show. One enters at the fourth level and *ascends*. This seems somehow more appropriate, to climb toward the birds that at some late point began to make their appearances in Braque's work—big, flapping, cranelike birds, unquestionably symbols for Braque of something spiritual. In the final bay, at the very top of the ramp, the show ends with two works with these birds in a kind of exaltatory punctuation.

—*The Nation*, August 27/September 3, 1988

Robert Mapplethorpe

"FIFTEEN YEARS' WORTH of Robert Mapplethorpe's prints are represented in a show of nudes, portraits, and still-lifes," is how the Whitney Museum's show of this dark and swanky photographer is identified in the bright idiom of *The New Yorker's* "GOINGS ON ABOUT TOWN." How nice! someone in Tarrytown or Katonah might think, having seen this artist's elegant digs written up in *House & Garden*: Let's make a day of it—shop Madison, have lunch somewhere and then see the nudes, portraits and still lifes. Just the thing! And sure enough, the first of three photographs to one's right just before entering the show is a portrait of the late Louise Nevelson. And right next to that is a nude and a portrait at once, since its title is *Carleton*. Carleton is shown from behind, his head bent away from us into the Caravaggian black of the background, thrusting his buttocks forward, which are then pulled slightly apart by his legs, which hang on either side of the table on which he is posed, leaving a triangle at their parting as the focus of the print, as black as the abstract blackness of the background. And next to this is something we soon make out to be a male nipple, a vortex in a network of pores and follicles, skin as it would have been seen by the microscopic eyes of Gulliver on the Brobdingnagian ladies who liked to dandle him. Seen close up, this erotically charged locus of human skin contrasts with the beauty of that which stretches, smoothly and warmly, over the marvelous muscles of the male nude, placed between the dead artist and the leathery button of flesh. Is *Nipple* to be classed as a nude? Or a still life? Or a synecdochical portrait of sorts (you will encounter a double image, two stages of a cock and balls, a portrait by the same criterion as *Carleton* since titled *Richard*). The question of genre will haunt the visitor as he or she works through the exhibition, since the still lifes more and more seem metaphors for displayed sexual parts, which are often the main attribute of nude and seminude portraits. But that question will soon be stifled by others more haunting still.

The three prefatory photographs are high-style, high-glamour studies, reminiscent of an Art Deco sensibility, embodying an aesthetic that Mapplethorpe attained early and steadily maintained: some of the portraits look as though they belong in the stateroom of a suave ocean liner, in a mirrored frame, beside the chromium cocktail shaker and an artful arrangement of stark flowers of just the sort shown in Mapplethorpe's still lifes. They are elegant, luxurious, sophisticated, impeccable. But they are far more than that. The linking of death and art in the famous sepulchral head of the aged sculptor, the delibidinization of the erogenous in the magnified and distanced nipple, are held together, in one of the great moral syllogisms of our age, through the perfect male nude, viewed from the rear—from its vulnerable side— as middle term. This *memento mori* would not have been there at the beginning of Mapplethorpe's project, in which the high style of the 1930s was appropriated to register a subject matter of the 1970s, when this artist undertook to treat, from the perspective of serious art, the values and practices of the sadomasochistic subculture of homosexuals who were into bondage and domination. But it has certainly cast its retrospective shadow over this body of work since 1981, when AIDS was first announced, and the active male homosexual found to be in a population at high risk. A show of Mapplethorpe is always timely because of his rare gifts as an artist. But circumstances have made such a show timely in another dimension of moral reality, and I am grateful the organizers did not stint on the gamy images of the 1970s, for they raise some of the hardest of questions, and comprise Mapplethorpe's most singular achievement.

Consider *Mark Stevens (Mr. 10½)* of 1976. Mark Stevens is shown in profile, his powerful body arched over his spectacular penis (Mr. 10½?), which he displays laid out but unengorged along the top of a linen-covered box, on which he also leans his elbow. The picture is wider than it is high, by a ratio of 5 to 4, almost forcing Mark Stevens to bend over, despite which the space is too small to contain him: he is cropped at the shoulder, so we do not see his head, as well as at the knee, and along the back of the leg and the front of the bicep. Little matter: the one anatomical feature that is shown integrally is doubtless where Mark Stevens's identity lay in 1975, and his stomach is held in to give that even greater amplitude. Mark Stevens is wearing a black leather garment, cut away to expose his buttocks and his genitals, something like the tights affected by the sports at Roissy, where "O" underwent her sweetly recounted martyrdoms. And there is a tiny tattoo on his arm, of a devil with a pitchfork and flèched tail, connoting a playful meanness. Formally, we may admire the interesting space bounded by elbow, box surface, belly and chest, a sort of display case in which Mark Stevens's sex is framed as something rare and precious. Cropping, inner and outer space, calculated shadows and controlled backlighting—these belong to the vocabulary of high photographic art, the sort that Weston lavished on peppers in the 1930s, or which Mapplethorpe himself devoted, in 1985, to an eggplant, also laid out on a table, echoing Mark Stevens's recumbent phallus. Still life and nude or seminude portrait interanimate one another, here and throughout the show, and as a photograph, the study of Mark Stevens, quite as the other studies of leather-clad gays, is of an artistic order altogether different from the images that must have found their way into magazines of that era devoted to pain, humiliation and sexual subjugation, with their advertisements of sadistic gear—whips and chains and shackles, hoods and leather wear (the he-man's equivalent to sexy lingerie) and the pathetic promises of ointments and exercises designed and guaranteed to increase length, diameter and staying power.

Nor are these photographs really in the spirit of documentation, recording a form of life, though in fact and secondarily they provide such a record. They are, rather, celebratory of their subjects, acts of artistic will driven by moral beliefs and attitudes. Mapplethorpe is not there like a disinterested, registering eye. He was a participant and a believer. In exactly the same way, Mark Stevens was not a subject but a kind of collaborator: he agreed to display himself, he chose to dress himself in those symbolic vestments, to take and hold that pose. We see him no doubt as he would have wanted to be seen, as Mr. 10½, but as he knew he would be seen by someone he could trust, because the photographer would show their form of life from within. We see him, indeed, from within a homosexual perception, and it is that perception, that vision, that is the true subject of these works. They are not just of gays at a certain moment in gay history, when it all at once seemed possible for this to become the substance of serious art. The images are flooded with a way of seeing the world, given embodiment, made objective, in a suite of stunning photographs.

Analogously to the way in which Mark Stevens's phallus is made focal by the proportions of the photograph, by the cropped figure and the interior space, so, I think, is the phallus as such made focal in the exhibition taken as a whole, and I applaud the curatorial intuition that went into the selection and installation that makes this true. Richard Howard, in an inspired catalogue essay, credits Mapplethorpe with having aestheticized the genitals, drawing attention to the correspondence in form and function between these and flowers, which are "the sexual organs of plants." Howard is doubtless correct, but then, it seems to me, immensity must play an important role in this aestheticizing, and hence in the vision from within which the (male) genitals are perceived as beautiful. And this is disappointingly as reductive and mechanistic an attitude as that which thematizes big breasts in women. In *Man in Polyester Suit* of 1980, the subject, in his three-piecer, again cropped at shoulder and knee, has an open fly through which an elephantine phallus hangs heavily down, shaped like a fat integral sign, a thick S of flesh. In *Thomas*, a black male presses like Samson against the sides of a square space that walls him in, and his genitals hang like fruit between his spread legs—like the contextually phallicized bunch of grapes hanging from a string in a picture of 1985. But all the nudes are, as the expression goes, well hung, and one wonders if Mapplethorpe's aestheticizing project would have allowed another choice. In truth, he phallusized aesthetics!

In a famous episode in *A Moveable Feast*, F. Scott Fitzgerald expresses concern about the size of his penis, Zelda having said it was inadequately small; and Hemingway suggests he compare himself with what is to be found on classical statues, saying that most men would be satisfied with that. In my nearly four years as a soldier, I would have noticed it if anyone was equipped like the Man in Polyester Suit, or Mark Stevens for that matter. Robert Burns, in one of his nastier verses, wrote "Nine inches doth please a lady"—but something of that dimension would have been negligible in the baths and washrooms of the 1970s if Mapplethorpe's models are typical. On the other hand, there is a wonderful portrait of Louise Bourgeois, wearing an improbably shaggy coat and grinning knowingly out at the viewer, as if to connect her, us, the artist and his megaphallolatry in a piece of

[*214*

Robert Mapplethorpe

comedy—for she carries under her arm a sculpture, I daresay hers, of a really huge phallus and balls (Mr. 36½), putting things in perspective. I was grateful to the wise old sculptor for reminding us that the huge phallus was regarded as comical in the ancient world, and there are wonderful images on the sides of Grecian vases of actors wearing falsies to crack them up at Epidaurus. Even so, phallic references define this show (study the relationship between breasts, neck and head in the uncharacteristic portrait of Lisa Lyon, usually seen, as in a book of Mapplethorpe's photographs of her, engaged in bodybuilding).

What is interesting is less the phallocentrism of Mapplethorpe's aesthetic than the politicizing of that aesthetic, preeminently in the images from the late 1970s, to which the portrait of Mark Stevens belongs. That was a period in which gays were coming out of the closet in large numbers, defiantly and even proudly, and were actively campaigning not only to change social attitudes toward themselves but to build their own culture. It seems clear to me that these photographs were political acts, and that they would not have been made as art were it not the intention to enlist art in some more critical transformation. I am insufficiently a historian of that movement, but my hunch is that sadomasochism must have presented some of the same sorts of dilemmas for the gay liberation movement that lesbianism initially did for the women's liberation movement. So this is not, as it were, "The Joy of S&M," but an artistic form of a moral claim on behalf of practices other gays might have found difficult to accept. Even today, it is difficult for his most avid enthusiasts to accept the 1978 self-portrait through which Mapplethorpe declares his solidarity with Mark Stevens; with the scary couple, Brian Ridley and Lyle Heeter, leather boys in their sexual uniforms, Brian seated, shackled, in a wing chair while Lyle stands possessively over his shoulder, wearing his sullen master's cap, holding Brian's chains with one hand and a fierce crop with the other; or with Joe, encased in leather from crown to sole, creeping along a bench, with some sort of tube whose function I cannot even imagine strapped to his mask. Mapplethorpe shows himself from behind. He is dressed in a sort of jerkin, and in those backless tights worn by Mark Stevens. He is looking over his shoulder at us, his Pan-like head with its small soft beard glowering a sort of defiance. He is holding the handle of a cruel bullwhip up his anus. The visual equation between the phallus and the agency of pain contributes another component to genital aesthetics.

It is possible to appreciate this self-portrait formalistically and draw attention, like a docent, to shadows of graded intensity, for the subtle play of values. In the same way it would be possible to connect Mapplethorpe's own features with the little Pan's head in *Pan Head and Flower*—and the flower itself, its pistil hanging out of the petal, with the penis in *Man in Polyester Suit*. Anything that is art can be seen that way. You can pay particular heed to the play of hues and the strong diagonals in Titian's *The Flaying of Marsyas*, which so unsettled us all when it hung in the National Gallery not long ago. But I do not know what sort of person it would be who could look past the blood dripping into a pool from which an indifferent dog laps, or the exposed and quivering flesh, the hanging skin, the absolute agony of the satyr hung by his heels while Apollo carves away, to dwell on niceties of composition. A photograph such as Mapplethorpe's self-portrait cannot have been made or exhibited for our aesthetic delectation alone but rather to engage us morally and aesthetically. It would be known in advance that such an image would challenge, assault, insult, provoke, dismay—with the hope that in some way consciousness would be transformed. Its acceptance as art cannot be the only kind of acceptance in issue. It would have to be a pretty cool cat for whom the triptych *Jim and Tom, Sausalito* of 1978, which shows, in each of its panels, what looks like Jim pissing into Tom's eager mouth, recommends itself as a particularly good example of what gelatine silver prints look like.

A pretty rough show, then, for someone who came to see nudes, portraits and still lifes. It is made rougher still by the inescapable dates on the labels of the stronger images, all of which come from that hopeful ignorant time when it seemed that all that was involved was a kind of liberation of attitude concerning practices between consenting adults in a society of sexual pluralism. Of course the show has its tenderer moments. There are prints of overwhelming tenderness of Mapplethorpe's great friend Patti Smith. There is a lovely picture of Brice Marden's little girl. It is possible to be moved by a self-portrait of 1980 in which Mapplethorpe shows himself in women's makeup, eager and girlish and almost pubescent in the frail flatness of his/her naked upper body. There is a certain amount of avant-garde scrimshaw in the show, experiments with shaped frames, with mats and mirrors; and then finally there are a certain number of just elegant portraits, nudes and still lifes. But the self-portrait as young girl remains in my mind as the emblem of the exhibition, and for the dark reality that has settled upon the world to which it belongs. One cannot but think back to Marcel Duchamp's self-representation in *maquillage*, wearing the sort of wide-brimmed hat Virginia Woolf might have worn with a hatband designed by Vanessa, with ringed fingers and a fur boa. Duchamp even took on a feminine alias, Rrose Sélavy. (*"Eros c'est la vie."*) Nor can one help but feel saddened that Rrose Sélavy has lost her enduring innocence and changed her name to Rrose Sélamort.

The *Harper's Index* recently juxtaposed the number of deaths due to AIDS with the number due to measles. The former is insignificantly small by comparison with the latter, but numbers have little to do with it, at least not yet. With AIDS a form of life went dead, a way of thought, a form of imagination and hope. Any death is tragic and the death of children especially so, thinking of measles now primarily as a childhood death. The statistics are doubly sad since means for prevention and treatment are available, so the deaths by measles index an economic tragedy as well. But this other death carries away a whole possible world. The afternoon I visited the Mapplethorpe exhibition, I was impressed by my fellow visitors. They were subdued and almost, I felt, stunned. There were no giggles, scarcely any whispers. It was as though everyone felt the moral weight of the issues. And one felt an almost palpable resistance to face the thoughts the show generated, which each visitor had to overcome. It is not an easy experience, but it is a crucial one. Art is more than just art, and the Whitney took on a higher responsibility in supporting this exhibition.

Look at the enigmatic self-portrait of 1986, to your right as you exit the show. It is at right angles to the triad of photographs before which we paused while about to enter the room, and whose meaning is deepened by what we have seen and thought. Here the artist is dressed in a formal way, with wing collar and butterfly bow. With his long sideburns and taut neck muscles, he looks like a tense dandy. His head is turned slightly up and to the left, and the face he shows us wears a serious, questioning look. I expect mine did as well. So, by rights, should yours.

—*The Nation*, September 26, 1988

Salute to Veronese

ZEALOUS OF the lean body line, responsive to the Minimalist artistic
gesture and still persuaded that "less is more" condenses a profound
artistic truth, a modern sensibility that counts aesthetic calories is unlikely to be greatly stirred by the art of Paolo Veronese, for whom more
is so vehemently more. The order of feminine beauty he celebrates,
lactating Venuses or women too opulently fleshy even when saints and
martyrs, goes perfectly with his vast and teeming canvases, thronged
with blond beauties in brocaded gowns and heroes in costumes exotic
even by Venetian standards, feasting under florid skies in architectural
settings as large as life. So it would be unusual for Veronese to rank
high on the list of obligatory visits by today's cultural pilgrims, few of
whom visit the Louvre specifically to admire his *Wedding at Cana*,
which dominates one entire wall of the salon they instead crowd into
to make ritual contact with the *Mona Lisa*. Its site makes it among the
most familiar paintings in the world. Still, like Veronese's vision itself,
the huge canvas is somehow too much to deal with—prodigal, brilliant,
splendid, tremendous as a natural wonder—and dense with promised
meanings even the sympathetic tourist is too rushed to ponder when
there are so many more accessible treasures urging him on. If La
Gioconda has kept her solitary secret down the centuries, how hopeless
must be a painting filled with more figures than we can take in, caught
up in a feast that bears no true proportion to the biblical episode it
illustrates in a setting too fantastically gorgeous to comprehend. So
what can a critic as widely respected as Sir Lawrence Gowing mean
when he says of Veronese, in this painting in particular, that "he was

the founder of modern painting"? Veronese instead would seem to occupy that position whose polar opposite is where the meaning of Modernism is to be located!

This year marks the 400th anniversary of Veronese's death, at the age of sixty—and since his death was effectively the death of the great age of Venetian painting as such, and indeed of the Renaissance, whose last style flowered in Venice, it is irresistible to view his work as a kind of spectacular sunset, the end of an age rather than the foundation of a later one. So one question the visitor might ask—at the exhibition that memorializes the master at the National Gallery of Art, which assembles fifty paintings and some fifty-five drawings—is what we and Veronese have to say to one another across so wide a stretch of time and between such seemingly opposed aesthetic universes?

The Wedding at Cana was already considered too large and fragile in 1815 to make the trip back to the refectory wall of San Giorgio Maggiori, from which Napoleon bore it away to Paris in 1799, in much the same spirit in which the Greeks carried to their homes the women of Troy. So it will not join the celebration. Neither will *The Family of Darius Before Alexander* make the trip from London. Nor has Turin sent *The Queen of Sheba Before Solomon*, which moved Ruskin with the force of a religious conversion. You will be obliged to make the trip to Venice to see the staggering *Feast in the House of Levi* or to Vicenza to get to know *The Supper of Gregory the Great*, not to mention the great frescoes of the Villa Maser. But it was with reference to *The Wedding at Cana* that Gowing made his provocative assessment, which must be connected with the circumstance that has kept that painting in Paris since it was ravished away from its original site. It was a matter of uncanny good fortune that a masterpiece by Veronese should have been stranded in Paris just at the time when French painters were rethinking the nature of color, and that they should have found in Veronese exactly the model they needed for their new chromatic programs. It took perhaps a nineteenth-century preoccupation with color to make Veronese's achievement visible, so that he could become the predecessor of those painters of the nineteenth century the Modernist has no difficulty in appreciating. In something like the spirit in which De Kooning was to say, more than a century later, that "Pollock broke the ice," Delacroix wrote of Veronese that he was "the only one to have caught the whole secret of nature." What the extraordinary sequence of colorists from Delacroix through the Impressionists to Matisse found by way of guidance in Veronese is as much present in the less exuberant canvases in Washington as in *The Wedding at Cana,* so a good way to find one's way into these is to reflect on the lessons in color theory the modern masters found in that work.

The Parisian colorists were reaching back to something that they found still vibrant and present in Veronese, but which had disappeared from painting almost immediately after him in favor of the technique of chiaroscuro that defines the Old Master style of the Baroque that swept Europe after the Counter-Reformation. The Old Master style was still being taught in the academies of Paris in the nineteenth century. Sargent, who learned it from Carolus-Duran, describes it exactly: "You must classify the values. If you begin with the middle tone and work up from it toward the darks—so that you deal last with your highest lights and darkest darks—you avoid false accents." (Sargent, when he abandoned this way of working in favor of a kind of Impressionist address, never regained his authority as a painter.) Modeling in and out of a middle tone to shadows and highlights was just what Veronese did not do. He achieved his effects, as transparent as chiaroscuro was opaque, by the juxtaposition of natural tones. Chiaroscuro recommended itself as a mode of painting when artists were concerned to create a mysterious, almost nonnatural atmosphere in which scenes of the utmost religious intensity could transpire. The lights and shadows bore a metaphoric weight in their own right, and together they created within the space of the painting a dramatic contrast as little like what we see under natural light in ordinary life as can be imagined. Their strategy was to heighten feeling by enabling the light to fall from an almost mystical source upon the figures it touched. Against these ambitions, Veronese's art was like walking outdoors, under blue skies, amidst luxuriant foliage. Perhaps the last of the Renaissance painters, Veronese flourished just too early to feel the forces that made chiaroscuro so artistically imperative. So even his martyrdoms are untouched by the obligatory Baroque shadows. In any case, it was precisely this natural out-of-doors feeling the Modernists sought, a world from which artificial shadows and religious gloom were driven away and the false theatrical illuminations extinguished in favor of a world of colors that fall upon what Ruskin famously called "the innocence of the eye." It was for this that they so greatly valued Veronese, as what Théophile Gautier called "the greatest colorist that ever lived." And it is this that we still can feel today in the wonderful clarities, the luminous tonalities, the shimmering glazes of the paintings in Washington. Veronese's motives cannot have been even close to the Impressionists'—they are possibly closer to Matisse as a painter of luxury and voluptuousness—but color is a good way to begin to get to know him as an artist. It is, of course, only a beginning.

It is possible to set Veronese's paintings at a phenomenological distance and to relish them just for the cunning of their surfaces and the eloquence of paint. Ruskin was fixated, as if upon an erogenous zone, by the treatment of a pearl, and without question someone sensitive to the art in painting can be transfixed by the manner in which pearl and flesh are co-animated by the placement of touch next to touch in such works as *Judith and Holofernes* and *Venus and Mars*. Or by the way in which areas of the most sumptuous color—roses and aquamarine, the white of white satin and the gold of cloth of gold—can glow in harmony like adjacent gems in *The Martyrdom and Last Communion of St. Lucy*—while still leaving chromatic space for a red as shocking as blood itself to spring, like twigs of liquid coral, from Lucy's wide breast. Or by the way drops of milk form like fluid pearls against the flesh of Venus in *Venus and Mars*. There is an almost Mannerist brilliance in these works, with nothing of Mannerist artificiality, and how Veronese managed to caress the eye with skin and flesh as warm and radiant as skin and flesh are in great beauties must have been one of the secrets Delacroix endeavored to learn.

One can and must see the paintings in these terms, but there is a danger, already risked in this show with its heavy connoisseur's orientation, that one will miss the greater magic Veronese's magic with colors must have been intended to serve. St. Lucy takes communion from her left and martyrdom from her right, simultaneously, as if there were an equation between the blood she loses from the one and the divine blood she absorbs from the other—and she is no less calm than are her priest and her executioner. The painting has the dissonance of a dream. Judith's face has an almost animal imperturbability, her extravagantly brocaded costume has not a fleck of gore, as she places the terrible head in a sack held wide open by a turbaned black. Amor binds Venus's slung leg to Mars's greaved one with a pink bow. She wears a smile of carnal glee but little else save her pearls and what appears to be Mars's quiver. Mars has been disarmed—another cupid displays his sword to his harshly tethered horse, and in the background a disarmed caryatid in the form of a satyr looks sardonic and wise. Mars appears to be struggling into Venus's sleeve—he does not know how to wear her garment and she wears his quiver only as an ornament. But one hand is on his shoulder while she milks herself with the other, and their limbs and garments intertwine like the knot that explicitly unites them. Some mystery of erotic union is being enacted in the golden classical landscape they find themselves in. Somehow one senses that the profound coloristic discoveries must be connected with the strange dreamlike imagery—so the second thing the visitor to the exhibition must do is to ponder this riddle.

One can only speculate. But it is possible to imagine that Veronese sought by pure color to achieve by painterly means what a magician like Prospero could summon by a wave of a wand out of thin air. And when Prospero speaks of "the baseless fabric of this vision," or, at the end of the extraordinary display on which he "bestow[s] some vanity of my art," when he talks about "this insubstantial pageant fading," it is difficult not to want to appropriate Shakespeare's language for Veronese's own philosophy of light and art—to compose by pure touches of color something as evanescent as a dream.

Such an interpretation at least fits with the only record we have of Veronese's own thought about his art, his famous defense before the Venetian Inquisition of 1573. The Holy Tribunal was making a first effort to put into practice a form of control over artistic representation that had been hammered out in the waning days of the Council of Trent. The concern was that Veronese had introduced into a painting of the Last Supper secular elements unsuited to the depiction of religious events. As the inquisitors observed, this was not simply the painting of a supper: its subject was the Last Supper of the Lord, a particularly significant moment before the betrayal and the crucifixion—and they demanded to know what precisely Veronese could have meant by inserting into the scene a servant with a bleeding nose, two halberdiers, a man dressed as buffoon with a parrot on his wrist, and—worse still!—an Apostle with a toothpick, cleaning his teeth. "Does it seem fitting," they asked rhetorically, "at the Last Supper of the Lord to paint buffoons, drunkards, Germans, dwarfs, and similar vulgarities?" Veronese's defense is memorable. "We painters take the same license that poets and jesters take. . . . I paint pictures as I see fit and as well as my talent permits." No reader of English can fail to hear Shakespeare in Veronese's words, even if they echo to a famous speech in *A Midsummer Night's Dream* written twenty years after the event: "The lunatic, the lover, and the poet, / Are of imagination all compact. . . . And, as imagination bodies forth / The forms of things unknown, the poet's pen / Turns them to shapes, and gives to airy nothing / A local habitation and a name." Veronese satisfied his inquisitors by changing the name of the painting to *Feast in the House of Levi*, an evidently less portentous collation. But his testimony reveals a great deal about how his work is to be approached: as fantasy, poetry, play— as something as little dependent upon the forces of causality and history and logic as what poets in words or jesters fabricate for the diversion of princes.

It is striking that at the center of *The Wedding at Cana* Veronese places his great fellow artists of Venice as musicians: Titian is on the violoncello, Tintoretto and Veronese himself play the violas, and Bassano (it is said) is shown playing the flute. And the immediate question is whether he shows them as part of the feast, or if the feast itself is not something they have summoned by their collective efforts as an objective vision of a feast. At the head table sits the Virgin together with Christ, who has performed his own miracle of transforming water into rivers of wine, as the artists have performed their miracle of transforming paint into the fabric of a dream. The guests are an extraordinary lot: Eleanor of Austria; Queen Mary of England; Suleiman the Magnificent; Michelangelo's friend Vittoria Colonna holding the inevitable gold toothpick. Veronese's brother, wearing an improbable robe, raises a toast—to art? festivity? the sheer glory of the world's appearances? Personages who never shared or could share a table, for reasons of the limits of space and time, sit down together in a harmony that only art allows.

One wonders what such a work could have been doing on the walls of a monastic refectory. Critics have commented upon the incongruity between such a scene and the austere bread-breaking that must have characterized the monastic mealtime below. One might compare *The Wedding at Cana* with Leonardo's earlier *Last Supper*, from the refectory in Santa Maria delle Grazie in Milan. Neither painting can be classed, so to speak, as inspired dining-room decoration. Each defined what transpired in the space before it, in which the monks took their meals. Each defined the meaning of the meal. For the Milanese monks, arrayed at their tables before the high table at which Christ and his Apostles are assembled, each meal must in effect have been taken as present at the Last Supper—a final, renunciatory sacrament. Leonardo's painting generates a space of renunciation, even of frugality, and vests the necessary act of eating with a ritual and indeed a historical significance. It captures the meaning of life as they must have construed it if the painting was convincing for them. In Venice, by contrast, the *Wedding* must have hovered like a dream, expressing to the monks who assembled before it a philosophy of life as something fragile, evanescent, vanishing, insubstantial and illusory. They were turning their backs on the feast of life in favor of things eternal, making a choice of a different sort than their brethren in Milan.

The meaning the painting must have expressed for the monks of San Giorgio was felt in another work, a long time after, by John Ruskin, in Turin, who heard a Waldensian sermon on the vanity of the world and an injunction to turn his back in the interests of salvation on the distracting beauties of material things. It was with this thought in his mind that he visited Veronese's *The Queen of Sheba Before Solomon*— and all the dark broodings of the preacher's vision of the world shattered against what he felt. Ruskin wrote several times about this experience, but here is how he expressed it to his father:

I was struck by the gorgeousness of life which the world seemed constituted to develop, when it is made the best of. The band was playing some brilliant music at the time, and this music blended so thoroughly with Veronese's splendour; the beautiful notes seemed to form one whole with the lovely forms and colors, and powerful human creatures. Can it be possible that all this power and beauty is averse to the honour of the Maker of it? Has God made faces beautiful and limbs strong, and created these strange, fiery, fantastic energies, and created the splendour of substance and the love of it; created gold, and pearls, and crystal, and the sun that makes them gorgeous; and filled human fancy with all splendid thoughts; and given to the human touch its power of placing and brightening and perfecting, only that all these things may lead His creatures away from Him?

The transparency of colors in Veronese, one feels, is a means to his extraordinary powers of conjuration, his technical magic an instrument in the exercise of a larger magic which enables a vision to form, almost immaterially, in the spaces men and women move in and out of. The immense scale of his masterpieces contributes to the illusion, of course, but the power is present in everything he touched, so that an exhibition of his work has to be a feast, a celebration, an enhancement, even a form of spiritual healing as Ruskin felt it to be.

—*Art News*, January, 1989

Boccioni and
Il Futurismo

THE FUTURISTS viewed the present as an aesthetic battlefield from
which they sought to drive the past with manifestos and heroic artistic
gestures. A present without a past would already *be* the future; and
avid for historical acceleration, they undertook to erect the twentieth
century out of the nineteenth century in a provincial Italian city. Since
nothing defines a historical moment as sharply as its vision of the
future, the Futurists anchored themselves unshakably in the times they
believed they were changing. They no more lived in the future than a
man listening to Lum and Abner on his Atwater Kent in 1932 wearing
an inverted fishbowl to look like Buck Rogers. Their work is exactly
as dated as their costumes in a famous photograph which shows them
in Paris, wearing *chapeaux melon* and tightly belted overcoats, scowling
over fierce mustaches into the box camera for a group portrait. Theirs
is what the imaginative German historian Reinhart Koselleck calls a
vergangene Zukunft—a "past future." They are part of our present only
as something that, for an intense moment of artistic bombast, *was*.
They earned themselves a place, not where they meant to be located,
in modern life itself, but in those repositories of past futures, the museums of modern art, as a chapter in the history of false starts.

The Metropolitan Museum of Art is devoting a compendious exhibition to the work of Umberto Boccioni, who stands second from the
right in the photograph mentioned, an elegant, romantic man, a
dreamer, really, whose struggle to become the prophet of a Futuristic
future was in part a struggle against his own artistic inclination, which

was to be a *petit-maître* of late Impressionist styles, and whose paintings characteristically showed women against windows, or were searching portraits of himself in soulful hats. Or perhaps the ferocity of his Futurism, with its exaltation of speed and dynamism, is addressed to his own artistic personality, sentimental, moved by women in muslin dresses in soft interiors—as though the enemy to be defeated were himself. Such a struggle gives the show a human dimension, a poignancy available when a certain kind of artist becomes the militant of a harsh style that conflicts with everything he holds dear, like the ideological abstractionist who cannot stifle the desire to paint warm flesh and flashing eyes. So the first several rooms of the exhibition show the artist as he was before, and as he would have remained had not Modernism been felt as an abrupt imperative, demanding that he change himself and the world. They show the inextinguishable underside of an artist who had to destroy his deepest impulses in order to become what he believed himself called to. "It is terrible," he wrote in 1916, "the burden of having to work out for oneself a century of painting."

Boccioni's Futurism was compressed into a period from about 1911 until 1915, when he joined and served with bravery in a volunteer cyclists' battalion, which dissolved in December of that year. There then remained six months of his artistic life, during which he sought to integrate the two sides of his creative personality. There is an outstanding portrait of the composer Busoni, done in 1916, as if by a gifted student of Cézanne who had done graduate work in some Futurist academy, in which he learned to assert the sorts of curves Cézanne would only have approached as the limits of a search. It is an aggressive, even a violent work, in which the artist attacks his natural tenderness rather than merely suppressing it. But he was flung from a horse and killed later in that same year, after having to return to military service, reluctantly, at the age of thirty-four. So Boccioni's was a tragic, truncated career whose chief monuments are the Futurist exercises and the theories that enfranchised them.

It is ironic that a Futurist should have met his death by being thrown from a horse, when his vocabulary of speed and dynamism would have recommended a more suitable vehicle, like an automobile or an airplane. There are some cartoons Boccioni executed in 1904 for the Automobile Club of Italy, showing fox hunts interrupted by powerful ornamental cars. These are instructive for a number of reasons,

[226

one of them deeply connected with the art of the cartoon itself. Cartoonists, committed to showing coarse and violent episodes, have been exceedingly fertile in inventing visual conventions easily read to mean that motion is taking place. The representation of motion has for the most part been more indirect in Western painting: the artist, driven by narrative need, depicts personages in postures that require the viewer to furnish the explanation that they must be moving. There is Veronese's rather absurd depiction of Perseus hurtling through space past a swooning Andromeda, toward a startled monster. Genius that he was, however, Veronese falls short by a considerable measure of those artists who do Batman or Superman, who shamelessly employ conventions the rules of high art would have prohibited. The cartoonist uses lines of force, clouds of dust, puffs of smoke or distortions in terms of what good academic drawing demands. Thus the front wheel in one of Boccioni's racing cars has the shape of an ellipse, which he also tilts toward the viewer, as if it is about to come off its axle. The wheel is nested in a series of curved lines, indicating rapid change of position, and there are helixes of smoke and dust. Indeed, the car is moving so fast that it has nearly driven out of the picture: Boccioni uses cropping intuitively and effectively, enabling him to leave a considerable space between the back of the car and the startled huntsmen left behind.

Distortion, auxiliary lines, imagined dynamisms become the vocabulary of Futurism itself, obsessed with the depiction of movement. When a cartoonist wants to show Mutt turning his head to ogle a bathing beauty, he will draw Mutt's head several times in sequential positions, together with some circles (never read as halos) and perhaps a few stars and exclamation points—and perhaps he will have steam coming out of Mutt's ears and find a way to show his eyes popping out of his head. And he will also, since it is a pleasure for cartoonists to do such things, draw the bathing beauty herself so that we may empathize with Mutt's excitement. Repetition and superimposed successive images became part of the Futurist's symbolic language—but any panel from nearly any comic strip is a little anthology of Futurist strategy. Balla's *Dynamism of a Dog on a Leash*, delightful as it is, is hardly less trivial than Mutt and the Bathing Beauty.

What is surprising is that the obvious iconography of Boccioni's early cartoons—horses making way for sports cars, the traditional pageantry of the fox hunt giving way to the dusty velocities of the internal-combustion engine—does not especially penetrate Boccioni's art, though it does his polemical writing. His alleged masterpiece *States of Mind* incorporates the railroad train as motif, but the train had been fixed in nineteenth-century pictures from the time of Turner—the Impressionists adored drawing engines, and there is a railway bridge in Cézanne's views of Mont-St.-Victoire. The horse is far more, somehow, a paradigm for Boccioni, and one must infer from this fact how little into the twentieth century Europe had entered in Boccioni's time, since horses still played so prominent a role in life and work—and war. There is a painting of a factory done in 1908–9, and though it is a very nineteenth-century-looking building indeed, it must have struck Boccioni as sufficiently anti-picturesque to be an advanced subject for him. The painting is done in a modified Impressionist style, even with the smoke rising from the chimneys, and perhaps the most modern touch is the lettering "Emilio Foltzer. Fabrica di Olio e Grassi Lubricanti" (suggesting that it may have been commissioned as a portrait of the factory, and hence not an "anticipation" of the kind art historians love, of the use of letters in modern art). But there in front of the industrial complex turning out lubricants for machines are horses and wagons. In another factoryscape of 1909, *Morning*, the only vehicles are horse-drawn along the harsh diagonal roadway. In *The City Rises*, a painting of intense ambitiousness, done just at the threshold of his breakthrough into Futurism, immense flambant horses energize the foreground while some rather poky buildings rise in the background. The Futuristic, and Futuristically titled, *Elasticity* of 1912 is of horse and rider, translated into whorls and vortexes, galloping past some pylons (or a pylon iterated to imply movement past it). In *Plastic Dynamism: Horses + Houses* (note the arithmetical symbol as a device for futurizing the title), a 1913–14 work of high Futurism, the animal is almost totally dissolved into evidences of its movement. Later in 1914, a war work, *Lancer's Charge*, uses a newspaper clipping to connect it with current history and draws a row of horses charging to the left, raising dust as in the cartoons of 1904.

But beyond this, it is with reference to the horse that Boccioni explains the principles of Futurism. "A horse in swift course does not have four legs," he writes in "Technical Manifesto of Futurist Painting": "It has twenty, and their movements are triangular." Elsewhere he said, "A horse in movement is not a stationary horse that moves but a horse in movement, which is quite another thing." "A horse in movement . . . is a horse in movement" is the kind of inadvertent tautology that slips past a writer's fingers in the heat of argument, but here, I think, Boccioni hit on a truth well in advance of his time. Movement is not a property that exists alongside the other properties—color, shape, texture—that are revealed to the eye. It is not, so to speak, an extra property that can be added or subtracted, leaving all the other properties as they were, the way a change in color leaves shape unaffected and vice versa. So you cannot just study color perception on its own, get that nailed down, and then proceed to study the perception of movement. Rather, the perception of movement affects the way we perceive everything else. Kinetic perception is under intense investigation today, though hardly well understood. Boccioni based his view on what had been learned about retinal images: "Because images persist on the retina, things in movement multiply, change form, follow upon one another like vibrations within the space they traverse." Still, we don't see any of this even if it enters into an explanation of why we see as we do. (Descartes is held to be the first person actually to see a retinal image, specifically in the dissected eye of an ox.) So you are not getting closer to visual truth by painting overlapping images, any more than if you painted your images upside down, since that is how they wind up on the retina. A painting of a succession of images is not itself seen as a succession of images: we don't see the panel in which several stages of Mutt's head are shown as a succession of panels!

Whether this occurred to him or not, Boccioni turned from the nature of perception to that of reality, his view being that everything is in motion, even things seen standing still. This is as true of the Pyramids or the Rock of Gibraltar as of a charging horse, if it is true at all, so even a still life of inert bottles is to be painted with streamlines, as if shuddering with force and action. The art of the past, against which Futurism defined itself, treated objects as if they were solid, and even moving things were treated as if stationary in order to be treated at all. Since this may be a requirement for pictorial representation, there may come a time, according to Boccioni, when "the picture as we know it will suffice no longer." The Futurist artist then paints what he concedes is invisible—namely, the vibrations in which objects consist, and which fill the space between them and our perceptions: "The only painter who sees well is he who thinks well!"

Boccioni was at some pains to distinguish his movement from that of Cubism, partly because of rather transparent nationalistic motives. As he saw it, the Cubists were merely projecting as simultaneous onto the plane of the canvas the sequence of aspects from which the object was viewed. Whereas the planes of Futurism emanate from the dynamic interior of desolidified objects. It is not surprising that Boccioni was far more successful as a sculptor than a painter, perhaps because paintings have preexisting shapes, and have to be filled in, whereas the sculpture can be given the shape its internal meaning demands. The paintings indeed are full of bravura, and sometimes have the painful callowness of art school exercises. But Boccioni touched greatness with his beautiful sculpture *Unique Forms of Continuity in Space*, especially in its bronze version, where, polished and metallic, it echoes fine machinery. It is of a figure striding through space, but in such a way that its movement solidifies around its limbs, as though it were wading through some viscous medium that retained the shape of transit long enough to serve as a mold. It is a brilliant emblem of a new era of speed and power. It would, in a reduced version, make a stunning radiator ornament for the Lamborghini my friend Umberto Eco drives at Futurist velocities along the *autostrade* of his native peninsula.

I wonder what Boccioni would have said about this fascinating scholarly show? Its splendid catalogue prints a kind of memorial written by his peer, the arch-Futurist F. T. Marinetti: "An exhibition of Boccioni's work cannot be, never will be, a place of study or a clinic of philosophical anatomizing. Instead: attacks and counterattacks of new ideas." These would be the new ideas of a *vergangene Zukunft*, an unfulfilled and vanished future. An exhibition of Boccioni is: a place for scholars and philosophers and, in its early phases—before Futurism descended like a Perseus bent on saving the Andromeda of art, who had other thoughts in mind—a gallery full of touching quiet pictures of a peaceful world that came to its end in the war in which Boccioni came to his.

—*The Nation*, November 7, 1988

[*230*

Degas

AT NO POINT in his long career was Degas less than a very great artist, appreciated as such by his luminous peers: Pissarro wrote that Degas was "without a doubt the greatest artist of the period," and Renoir esteemed him above Rodin as a sculptor. But his masterpiece, the astonishing portrait of the Bellelli family, was achieved at the beginning, when he was only twenty-four. It is not that what came afterward was less great but only that Degas gave up on the concept of the masterpiece, just as he surrendered the ambition to paint historical tableaux, once he became, with Manet and the Impressionists with whom he was so uneasily associated, a painter of modern life. That family portrait, in terms of its scale and narrative ambition, was clearly intended to make his name in the system of Salon exhibition through which reputation and commissions were still won in 1858, when he began to work on it. But whether in fact it was ever exhibited remains a controverted issue among specialists, and it evidently disappeared from sight until after Degas's death. Its discovery would have been like finding the manuscript of *War and Peace* in Tolstoy's desk, unpublished because the author had been convinced by his own arguments in *What Is Art?* that there was something unworthy in the novel form as such. Degas's contempt for the institution of the Salon and presumably the genre of painting it generated was moralistic and aesthetic at once. In any case, he never did anything quite like this portrait again, but part of what makes it one of the great paintings of the world also explains the greatness and mystery of his powerful artistic language. How great the remaining work is may be judged from the following consideration. *The Bellelli Family* dominates the first main gallery of the magnificent exhibition devoted to Degas at the Metropolitan Museum of Art on a note of artistic intensity so acute that it seems at first as if the show opens with its own climax. But in truth the excitement never diminishes: the show is all climax.

The Bellelli Family is the sort of painting Henry James might have done had he been a painter rather than a writer, but retained his novelistic powers and profound feeling for civilized desperation and emotional bondage. It is an essay on matrimonial tension and domestic politics, transacted in an elegant but cramped *salotto* in which mother, father, two children and the family dog reveal the forces that tear them apart and keep them together in mutual trapped agony. The mother—Degas's Aunt Laura, who had married to evident regret Count Gennaro Bellelli—stands in erect suffering and wifely disdain at the extreme left of the canvas, forming with her two daughters an allegorical group that displays itself, aggressively, as a monument to maternal virtue. The girls are wearing spotless white pinafores, starched, ruffled, un-wrinkled, emblems of the mother's ability to run a difficult domestic establishment against any odds, attributes of housewifely rectitude. Pregnant and dressed in mourning—two conditions that connect her to the bassinet behind her and the drawing, by Degas himself, of her father, on the wall beside her proud head—Laura stares over her husband. Her severe face projects a long list of injuries and indignities that we know he is not allowed to forget. The little girls feign an innocence that announces their complicity in their mother's posture of aggrieved femininity. Count Bellelli is shown from behind. He is penned, as it were, between his armchair and the hearth. He turns to glare balefully at the martyrizing martyrs, as if through bars no less imprisoning for being invisible. Windows, doubtless signifying escape and freedom, are reflected in the mirror above the mantelpiece. The family dog, exhibiting the deep pragmatic wisdom of its kind as well as what must be long experience, is sneaking out of the picture before all hell breaks loose. Our sympathies are with the dog: the members of the Bellelli household form the kind of *enfer* Sartre later defined as "other people."

Degas's use of edges, here and elsewhere, is dictated by psychological necessity. They form, in *The Bellelli Family*, the boundaries of a familial cage. They frame a feeling and intensify its expression. So they are not the mere physical boundaries of the canvas but part of its moral content. The principles of composition, accordingly, are not geometrical but emotive, and the asymmetries the artist so ingeniously exploits embody the balances and imbalances of human relationships. In *The Duchessa di Montejasi with Her Daughters Elena and Camilla*, the Duchess occupies four-fifths of the interior space of the canvas, as if she were a selfish and self-aggrandizing personage. The two daughters are crowded into space at the left too small for them, but they are redeemingly cropped by the edge, implying that they were already half outside the picture anyway. The mother looks fierce and sour, dominating but also lonely. She stares out at us in some silent appeal for recognition of her sorrows. One of her daughters gives us an uninterested glance, not caring a damn what we think. The other is peering outside the picture with some animation. They are seated almost as in a carriage, being borne away from the salon's oppressiveness.

Such devices are used over and over. In the mystifying *Interior* (also called *The Rape*), an elegantly dressed man leans against the right edge of the painting with its implicit door. He casts a smudged shadow on the wall, and is in a posture of strained patience. At the far left a woman in a chemise kneels on the floor. There is between them about as much space as the painting will allow, and yet they are tethered together in some way we are obliged to read as sexual. There is a corset on the floor. But the narrow bed is made, so no act has taken place yet, and the gentleman shows no sign of getting undressed. Perhaps he is reflecting on what he may have let himself in for. So may the girl be: we feel she is weeping, or has wept. The emptiness separating them is eloquent and ambiguous, and with the other works so far considered, one feels one knows why Degas never married. For a less charged example, consider the wonderful portrait of Hortense Valpincon as a child. She is, like the Bellelli girls, wearing white, but she has a saucy straw hat and a look of mischief. Degas has placed her to the far right of the canvas, at the edge of a table, which she leans against. Behind her, outside the canvas, is the implicit outdoors for which she is shawled. One feels she will turn and bolt at any moment out of the picture and Degas has left the marks of a sketch on her back, as if, in a kind of joke, he is saying that he had better capture her while he can. What child except one with the sharp fingers of Laura Bellelli on her shoulder will hold still long enough to have her portrait done?

In the orthodox hierarchy of the French Academy, historical painting occupied the topmost rung, and the training of the aspiring academician promised such skills as would be demanded for displaying historical personages at crucial narrative moments. Anatomy and physiognomy were to be mastered for this purpose, and the tableaux themselves were exhibited for the moral edification of the public. Degas must have been the last major artist still to feel the power of these imperatives when the forces that were driving his contemporaries toward Modernism put such ideals hopelessly out of date. In later years, Manet recalled that Degas was still "engaged with Semiramis" when the two first met in the Louvre. The Met's exhibition contains all the historical paintings by Degas, including *Semiramis Building Babylon*, but when this master turned away from the fabrications that strike us as artificial even in his hands, and undertook to become a painter of modern life—the phrase is Baudelaire's but is given a wider reference in the writing of T. J. Clark—it was as if he simply bent the strategies of historical narration to depict the lives of the denizens of the Faubourg St.-Germain. He became, so to speak, the historical painter of everyday life, showing that modern women were as capable of suffering as Dido or Medea, and that betrayal, exploitation, vexation and anguish remained the common lot. Even the famous and loved painting known as *Woman with Chrysanthemums* moves one to ask why the pensive woman is squeezed into so narrow a space, letting the flowers dominate the bulk of the picture. Is she oppressed by this emblem of domestic prowess or vindicated, or is she communicating a message some *he* will fail to understand?

Yet at a certain moment in the career, questions of psychology seem to recede, leaving behind only the cunning of placement, cropping, angle of vision and framing, as Degas becomes first an observer of the public life of Paris—the ballet, the theater, the racecourse, the café concert, the picture gallery, the boutique and the brothel—and then returns to the intimacy of interior spaces in a profound sequence of women. They are shown bathing, climbing in and out of tubs (an English word that was appropriated by the French), brushing their hair or having it brushed, engaged in private gestures of personal care in a feminine world from which males have all but disappeared, so that Degas has them all to himself, and the only relationship that endures, aside from that between their maids and themselves, is that between artist and model. But the slow transition from the personal to the public to the private reveals Degas divesting himself of another identity besides that of historical painter: he had as well to discard the painting program of the Old Masters, which he handled with such absolute brilliance.

Degas

I refer to the method of using a ground tone and then working forward to the brightest lights and backward to the darkest darks, modeling the figure in and out of shadows. One can see this to marvelous effect in some of the studies for *The Bellelli Family*, especially in a drawing of one of the daughters, Giulia, on buff paper, with her pinafore picked out in wet strokes of bluish white, brilliant against the brown, and her body swiftly sketched in sepia. Only the head is finished, but it is thrust forward by a bold brushful of blue behind it. The method of chiaroscuro gives the study an exceptional visual excitement, heightened by being only partly finished. Degas used colored papers throughout his career to attain such urgency: there is a head of Laura Bellelli on green paper, and a crayon and gouache study of her daughter Giovanna on blue paper. This manner of working set him at an opposite pole from the Impressionists, who explicitly repudiated painting in terms of modeling light against dark in favor of juxtaposing pure hues, building forms through touches of saturated color. Indeed, Degas refused the label "Impressionist" with its implied reference to subjectivity and sensation, and insisted on being known as a "realist."

He believed, as a matter of artistic politics, in the independence of the Impressionist exhibitions that enabled artists to leave works dramatically underfinished and subjects understated. But he tried to change the name of these to "Impressionist and Realist" exhibitions and to have a number of artists included who could hardly have been thought Impressionists by any criterion. As in many other things, he was a difficult man, but part of his originality as an artist comes from his applying the drama of chiaroscuro to the depiction of ordinary life, and then by situating his subjects spatially in ways he had evolved for psychological intensifications that now no longer greatly mattered to him. A good place to see all this at work is in *The Millinery Shop* of 1882, on loan from the Art Institute of Chicago. A woman examining a hat is viewed from above, seated at the corner of a counter, at the far right of the painting. All this might have been meant to show her under a psychological description, but she really seems merely to be examining a bonnet, cropped to no obvious purpose. As with *Woman with Chrysanthemums*, the largest space is given over simply to a display, of hats in this instance, one of which has a delicious green ribbon. The hats themselves are miraculous smudges of paint, lent a further vivacity by being set against the brown tone so characteristic of Degas. The brown, one cannot but feel, gives a certain melancholy to the space, heightened only by the frivolity of the flouncy headgear. (Perhaps it is more psychological than one would have thought, after all.)

The woman—whether customer or shopgirl trying out the wares—is, one might say, just a woman, with no particular expression and no specific physiognomy. In the great paintings in pastels of bathing women, which mark the prolonged final phase of Degas's career as he slipped into near-blindness, the subjects are characteristically shown from behind, as if their faces and features were not relevant. What we see are their bodies and themselves engaged with their bodies. There is nothing prurient, nothing even especially erotic in these nudes, and indeed their flesh folds and bulges in abstract shapes or they are shown with rudely simplified torsos, smudges on smudges, the stroked flesh no different from the stroked walls and furniture. Degas is moving, one feels, toward a kind of pure painting, the novelistic impulses left behind, the deft chiaroscuro renounced, and only the old artist, the female body and stumps of colored chalk left to engage in endless interactions. And how strange the forms now become! In *Nude Woman Drying Herself* (the titles are now merely descriptive), the towel looks like a pair of white arms enfolding her slack torso. In some later bathing pictures, shoulders and breasts seem like twinned forms.

Some authors, associating bed, body and bath, suggest these are prostitutes. I find this hard to believe. These works seem without reference, beyond the simple referents of bed, bath and body. Degas addresses the figures with such intensity that they become distorted, or dissolve into their spaces, or acquire extra limbs, or metamorphose into something marginally human. It was as though the female body were being reinvented—erased, enlarged, rejoined, diminished, re-composed, perhaps by some dim Cubistic impulses. Sometimes, as with *Woman with Towel*, they rise out of the cloth in a metaphor of birth or rebirth. Or, read another way, the two ends of the held towel seem to form figures who engage with the woman in a ghostly *pas de trois*. And the colors are amazing: lavenders, cadmium yellows, oranges, absinthes, flame blues, as if the artist were now giving himself every freedom of form and hue. The work is at the farthest possible extreme from the historical painting that defined his first undertakings. If this is where he found himself heading, small wonder he could barely tolerate the existence of his masterpiece.

—*The Nation*, December 12, 1988

Anselm Kiefer

THE FEAR THAT ART can sink the state is the dark obverse of the faith that art alone can save it. The Nazi sequestration of "degenerate art" is one face of the same false coin whose other face is typified by Adorno's sentimentalism that "the poetical act (in the general sense that includes all the arts) is the quintessential historical act." Both views emerged together in the bitter strife between poetry and philosophy in ancient times. It was Plato who urged the expulsion of artists from the ideal republic, but who also, just in case, evolved a theory of art that so thoroughly trivialized it that, even today, art for the sake of aesthetics alone is a political weapon in the hands of conservative critics. It was Aristophanes who believed, just when things looked blackest for Athens, that only if one of the great dramatists could be summoned back from Hades was there any hope at all. At just that fateful moment, when the Spartans were drawn up outside its walls and the great spring offensive was being drafted, when Athens had been through pestilence, defection, breakdown, humiliation and defeat, leave it to the muddled reactionary mind of Aristophanes to diagnose the difficulties as due to the lack of great art! The decline of Greek art, in a late postmortem by Nietzsche, was attributed to the triumph of reason over myth. True to form, the artist whom Aristophanes has his comic hero in *The Frogs* drag back from the netherworld embodies the belief that myth must trump reason if art is to discharge its redemptive function. Language had better be portentous, exalted, obscure and grand if the Athenian populace is to be led by art into a new moral era.

The Aristophanic charge to art is to produce work that is dense, dark, prophetic, heroic, mythic, runic, arcane, dangerous, reassuring, accusatory, reinforcing, grandiloquent, too compelling for mere reason to deal with, fraught, fearful, bearing signs that the artist is in touch with powers that will make us whole, and is spiritual, oceanic, urgent, romantic and vast. Since Wagner no one has sought more scrupulously to comply with this imperative than Anselm Kiefer, whose sludged and operatic fabrications have moved to tears viewers who felt they saw in them a remorseful Teutonic conscience. It is widely accepted that Kiefer views it as his mission to reconnect Germany with its true heroic past and prod it in the direction of its true heroic future. Far and away the most encouraging news from that scary country in recent years is the fact that it has managed to remain indifferent to this artist, who instead has found a market in Salle-Schnabel land. Far and away the most touching fact is that his patrons, characteristically Jewish, according to recent interviews, should see in his work evidence of Deutschland's contrition over the Holocaust. The work is willfully obscure enough that it can be interpreted that way, and sufficiently filled with flames, ruins, charred stumps and slurried wastes that one can see agony and the ashes of slaughtered innocents inscribed in its dreary surfaces. But it is far more plausible that it is a sustained visual lament for a shattered *Vaterland*, a recall to the myths of triumph and heroic will and a summons to fulfillment of some Nordic promise—as if the comfortable German present must be shaken out of its commercial complacencies and prodded into some serious game of Dungeons and Dragons through which it will regain its destiny. "I do not identify with Nero or Hitler," the catalogue cites him as saying, "but I have to reenact what they did just a little bit in order to understand the madness. That is why I make these attempts to become a fascist."

One way of endearing oneself to the curatorial establishment while at the same time impressing the wider populace that spontaneously equates obscurity with profundity is to stuff one's work with a farce of heavy symbolism which the former can use to justify its existence by explaining to the latter. Aside from the overall perniciousness of Kiefer's crackpot message, he is in this respect no worse than Salle or Schnabel, both of whom early recognized the benefits of incoherence. The catalogue for Kiefer's show is a morass of portentous exegesis by

[238

Anselm Kiefer

Mark Rosenthal, a dazzled enthusiast, and the staff of the Museum of Modern Art has obligingly furnished visitors with a handout lexicon of hermetic definitions they can use to unriddle meanings planted there. ("Yggdrasil: In Norse mythology, the World-Ash . . ."; "Arminius (Hermann): The chieftain of a German tribe that in the year A.D. 9 . . ."; "Kyffhäuser: Mountains where Germans believed . . ." *Und so wieder.*)

Symbolic art, in the scheme of Kiefer's luminous compatriot, the philosopher Hegel, is the lowest order of fine art, largely because one has to learn the meaning of a symbol the way one learns the meaning of a name—by a lexical rule of the sort provided in the MoMA glossary. Since symbols no more than names wear their meanings on their faces, knowledge of what a symbol means is something one has to be told—and it immediately allows a division between those in the know, a kind of curatorial priest class, and those who can only have the secrets disclosed or revealed to them as a kind of privilege. With art of a higher order, the power of the priest vanishes, for with great art the meaning penetrates the work, so that to perceive is to understand. Even within symbolic art itself, a distinction is available between narrow and universal symbols.

Kiefer's acknowledged master, Joseph Beuys, also trafficked in symbols. These were derived from his personal experience as a wrecked airman in World War II, when he had the luck to crash among northern peoples who covered him with fat and wrapped him in felt, nursing him back from death. This powerful experience yielded a powerful personal myth, but the symbols of fat and felt manage to express universal feelings of nurture, warmth, healing, care and life. Kiefer's symbols are purely external, the kind you look up in books. And his experience is merely that of an art student who has had no life outside art to speak of or draw upon. Beuys, though a symbolic artist, managed to transcend the inherent limitations of that genre by creating works so full of human meaning that one encountered one's deepest self in encountering them. It was work that was frightening in its implication of a deserted world, stripped of brightness and warmth. Kiefer's work does not have this as its content but as its form: it is empty, stripped of brightness and warmth by an act of showmanly will in order to transmit a sense of false despair. The work is as black and rude as he can make it, as desiccated as the straw he glues on with the same cagey obscurantism that drove Schnabel to stick cracked dishes all over his canvases.

239]

When, on the other hand, the rules of interpretation are known and, as it were, commonplace, then Kiefer's use of them is jejune and dishonest. Consider his employment of the palette as a symbol for art. This is a dishonest use in that the palette represents precisely that order of painting that Kiefer rejects. The palette evolved, of course, with the technology of oil paint: it enabled the artist to array hues and tones in a convenient and perspicuous way, and provided a surface on which they could be mixed in small quantities. The dabs of pigment imply the delicacy of touch that goes with fine brushes, and so they condense an entire attitude toward painting as a fine art, each component of which, when negated, yields a component of Kiefer's art. "Kiefer claims," the catalogue informs us, "that only the French use a range of colors, and that he, belonging to the German people, is unfamiliar with such practice." Who can suppress a shudder at the idea of asking "How German is it?" (*Wie Deutsch ist es?*)—to appropriate the title of Walter Abish's powerful novel—in front of a painting one dismisses as "French" because it uses colors? Kiefer also, of course, rejects brushes, possibly for similar reasons of Aryan authenticity—pouring, dripping, wiping, splashing, lathering his work with black gunk and straw as if tarring and feathering it. So the palette, if it symbolizes painting, connects with an artistic practice so at odds with what Kiefer demonstrates that he has no right to claim it for his own.

Claim it, however, he does, even attaching a pair of leaden wings to the palette in an ill-advised piece of sculpture which means (take out your notebooks!) the Victory of Art. The high-flying palette, moreover, is a motif in painting after painting. It is scribbled like a graffito in shaving cream over the surface of a photograph of what looks like a bombed-out shelter. It appears without wings in a work (to which I shall return) called *The Starry Heavens*, in the position of the heart in what looks like a self-portrait in a nightshirt. A palette on a skinny pedestal stands isolated in an architectural setting taken over from Albert Speer's designs for Hitler and is titled *To the Unknown Painter*. And sundry palettes flutter and perch on various scabrous surfaces and in various squalid interiors, making the cumulative point that an artist is the soldier-hero transformed, and will bring us together with the myths we need to redeem us. The works themselves are supposed to embody the ideal they express. And yet the palette as depicted is so slack, floppy, desultory and casual as to demonstrate its inadequacy to discharge the ponderous task thrust upon it. Of course, it would be possible to see these as nationalistic caricatures at the expense of the French, in which case they would convey the inability of French art to be politically redemptive—but this implies a level of wit and urbanity to which Kiefer is opposed.

Beneath this absurd masquerade—his sorcerer's robe, his alchemical staff, his winged Wagnerian helmet, his Arminian (Arminius: "chieftain of a German tribe . . .") spear—there is an artist with certain natural gifts. One can see this in his woodcuts, where white paper flickers against black ink, the visible grain of wood bleeds through the image, and great power is conveyed by the signs of cutting and gouging. The colored woodcut rarely achieves the power of the black-and-white wood-block print, and I suppose a case could be made that the latter is in some way an essentially Germanic form. When Kiefer uses the woodcut, as in his image of the horse Grane in the immense work *Brunhilde-Grane*, you can see what strength he could command as a graphic artist. There is a woodcut of architectural motif in *The Rhine*, and in *Ways of Wordly Wisdom* there are some extremely effective woodcut portraits whose painted counterparts in another work are as flabby as the flying palette.

Moreover, Kiefer can on occasion rise to statements that are touching and even moving. One work I especially admired is called *Women of the Revolution*, composed of five immense lead sheets, across which are mounted dusty frames each containing a dried flower, and each having written underneath the name of some woman connected (usually as a victim) with the French Revolution. Somehow the massiveness of the lead plates and the fragility of the memorializing flowers and the scribbled names is quite powerful and affective. It is, moreover, immediately understood, and needs no help from the eager curatorial explicators.

Most of the work, however, is the usual Wagnerian war music, tooted and thumped by the oompah brass of the marching bands of German nationalism, a heavy-handed compost of shallow ideas and foggy beliefs. "Kiefer fears modern culture," one text says, "with its emphasis on rationality and progress, and warns against intellectual as opposed to visceral understanding." And there we have the good old command to think with the blood, which brings us back to *The Starry Heavens*. The author of the catalogue drops a footnote in which he writes: "Harten (Düsseldorf, 1984, p. 124) states that the quote is based on Kant's *Critique of Practical Reason*." Now, this is not the kind of attribution someone has to "state." It is not, as it were, like the speculative identification of some piece of Nordic mythography. The phrase is not "based" upon Kant's text: it *is* Kant's text, and indeed one of the glories of Kant's prose. There, in the conclusion to the *Critique of Practical Reason*, Kant writes: "Two things fill the mind with ever new and increasing admiration and awe, the oftener and more steadily they are contemplated: the starry heavens above me, and the moral law within me." Kiefer's work, which shows a palette shining (in the manner in which Keith Haring shows things shining) within the artist's breast, is obviously meant to proclaim that art, thus symbolized, is the moral law within, as awesome as the starry heavens above (depicted here with some blobs of white paint against some black scribbles). This is, however, not a conception to which the artist has a right, any more than he has to the palette he has abducted into his vocabulary.

Kant was a cosmopolitan man. He believed in reason and in enlightenment and in the progress of the human intellect. He would have despised the idea that one writer ascribes to Kiefer: "Civilization was removing man further and further from his instinctual foundations, so that a gulf opened between nature and mind, between unconscious and consciousness"—a gulf that Beuys's and Kiefer's art is supposed to close. But Kant accepts as moral only laws grounded in rationality, only what a rational being can consistently will. And he accepts only a concept of beauty that is tacitly universal, hence a view of art incompatible with something narrowly Germanic and thought with the blood. Kant's ideas are noble and always threatened, and they are inconsistent with everything in which this wayward talent believes.

—*The Nation*, January 2, 1989

Courbet Reconsidered

THE GLENS AND GLADES of Gustave Courbet are afflicted with an
aggravated nymphlessness. His rocks and rills are goddess-free. No
angels hover by when honest folk are buried at Ornans. "I am above
all a total realist," he confessed on one of many proclamatory occasions.
This meant in part a negative ontology—nothing was to be dreamt
onto his canvases that had not first struck the unbamboozled eye of
the painter—and in part an artistic agenda: to depict real people and
real animals doing real things in real places. He planted enough forensic clues that scholars have been able to nail down the identity of
most of the individuals he depicted, and, on the basis of topographical
evidence, most of the sites in which he showed them. Yet neither our
understanding nor our appreciation of his works depends especially
on the particularities of local reference. Times and modes of dress have
changed, as well as modes of cultivating the earth or ministering to
the domestic needs of families; but in some way not altogether accom-
modated to the reductive ideologies of artistic realism, his paintings at
their finest touch us in our basic dimension as human beings. "To be
not only a painter but a man, in a word to make *de l'art vivant*—such
is my goal." So he wrote in the manifesto attached to the catalogue of
his notorious exhibition of 1855 in the Pavillon du Réalisme.

In that manifesto, he speaks of realism as a kind of flag that he
and his chums, Champfleury and Max Buchon, had raised in 1846,
in an effort to "arouse the forces proper to mankind" against what he
terms "the ideal of the conventional." (In a later text he said that

"Realism" was a label imposed upon him the way "Romantic" had been imposed upon his predecessors.) The contrast between realist and conventional art is philosophically exact. The moment you undertake to paint things you have never seen or, worse, which are unseeable because inexistent—nymphs, goddesses, angels—you are obliged to fall back on a body of received conventions, and hence enlist less the visual capacities of your viewers than their ability to read signs: you have produced a work more appropriately classed literary than painterly. The art of the Greeks, since it dealt with monsters or with deities, was no less conventional for being naturalistic—no less conventional than the fierce effigies of primitive artists, which are not naturalistic by any criterion. Thus naturalism is but a style and, when conventionalized as it must be when it undertakes to show what is not, it requires that the viewer learn how to read the signs the painter is forced to employ: saints by halos, martyrs by attributes and angels by wings. Courbet's men and women are vehemently human, with signs of weariness in their faces, with hair beneath their arms or between their legs and with the kind of heavy flesh with which the hams and cheeses of his native Savoy festoon the sturdy bones of its hardworking people.

Courbet's contemporaries found his work hilarious. I once came across a book with nothing in it but caricatures of him and his works. Cartoonists pretended that his paintings were realistic to the point of crossing the boundaries between the senses, so that one had to hold one's nose in order not to be overcome by the stink of unwashed bodies. Each of the famous paintings generated whole portfolios of spoofs, a good many of which called into question (not always groundlessly) his ability to paint at all: Champfleury complained of the common view that Courbet studied painting while minding hogs. Courbet himself liked to put it abroad that he was self-taught, and though scholarship shows that he in fact had masters, certainly no one taught him to paint as he did: an early admirer recalls being overwhelmed by the obvious originality, not merely in the subjects treated but in the style of painting fashioned to treat them with. But the caricatures testify to a wide pictorial literacy on the part of readers: Courbet was always news, and the Salons, at that epoch the only public places art could be seen, always occasioned intense reaction and discussion. So whatever he showed aroused partisan and often indignant response, since something a good bit more conventional, after all, was expected of art. One has to advance in time to the Armory show and the field day carica-

[*244*

turists had with Duchamp's *Nude Descending a Staircase* to find a parallel incursion of advanced art into the general consciousness, and after that, perhaps, to Dali's slack watches. And one has to think of Warhol for a parallel case of an artist whose looks were commonly known. Courbet was a celebrity, with his spade beard and peasant affectations and burly frame and militant republicanism and dogmatic realism.

Yet his paintings, at their greatest, are never mere transcriptions of the visual array: between the reality and the art some metaphorical transaction supervened, for which he had no room in his reduced and austere theories. His most famous work, the stupendous *Studio of the Artist*, carries as its subtitle "A Real Allegory Summing Up Seven Years of My Artistic Life." It is plain to its most casual viewer that even if the identities of all of the figures in the painting were known, some deep and powerful statement is being made concerning the power of art in the transformation and not merely the representation of life. Linda Nochlin, who together with Sarah Faunce organized the splendid show Courbet Reconsidered at the Brooklyn Museum, devotes an essay to this great painting in the catalogue that accompanies the show. She is surely right in feeling that after everything scholarly has been said about this work, its meaning remains for even the most uninstructed of viewers to deal with, and there's no possibility of reaching closure. Like Giorgione's *La Tempesta* or Titian's *Three Ages of Man*, there is an ineradicable mystery that binds us to this work, which teases us with an answer to its puzzle that it also refuses to confirm. And as much must be said of Courbet's immense *Funeral at Ornans*, where the whole mourning population appears cramped within a low elongated space homologous with that of a tomb.

Neither of these great works could have been expected to undergo the trip to Brooklyn, but a good many of the famous works assembled for this occasion share in their final strangeness. Consider, for example, the *Demoiselles de village* of 1851 (the word *demoiselles* in the title contributes to its strangeness), which is one of the treasures of the Metropolitan Museum. It shows three *demoiselles*, unmarried women of good families, rather surprisingly well dressed for the country walk they are taking across a sparsely shrubbed moor, pausing to give a piece of bread to a cowherd while their bushy-tailed and ornamental dog stares at two prosaic cows nearby. The two cows are oddly disproportionate in scale to the women—something for which Courbet was lampooned at the time—and curiously indefinite in treatment in comparison with the *demoiselles* and the cow girl. It is instructive to compare this masterpiece with a study hanging nearby, which shows the six creatures tiny in relationship to the landscape and posed in the middle distance. In the final version he has brought them up close, as if with a zoom lens, giving the figures an intensity the study lacked without dissipating—in fact increasing—the acute loneliness it also conveyed. It is as if they are made smaller by being made larger. The *demoiselles* were Courbet's sisters, but in no sense is this a painting of the artist's sisters giving alms to a peasant girl. The identification of the figures no more dissolves the mood of uncanniness that penetrates the picture than the identification of the calcareous rock in the background renders the scene less mysterious. Somehow, the juxtaposition of these elegantly garbed women and a landscape as unrelenting as the moon's creates the sort of mood one finds in Buñuel. And however one identifies that which one of the women is handing to the girl— bread? cake?—one feels that some powerful and even mystical communication is taking place between the cowherd and her benefactresses, who are almost angelic presences. A girl with two cows may not really need charity, but as a human being she may be receiving something, perhaps a kind of grace, which any of us may require. "*J'ai fait du gracieux*," Courbet said of this extraordinary painting. It would then be true only in the most reduced sense that he painted no angels.

Or consider the infamous *Bathers* of 1853, which shows from behind a female nude so heavily haunched she could be an emblem of fertility, poised on delicate feet in what could be a ballet position, with her right arm extended in a gesture meant, we feel, to express her own sense of bestowal as she reveals, to a seated woman, the amplitude of her fleshly beauty. The seated woman, perhaps her servant, has paused in her own disrobing—she in fact has only so far lowered her stockings—to express with her own extended arms an almost ecstatic admiration of the superb body that has, like the truth itself, become unhidden. And again some extraordinary communication appears to be taking place quite out of proportion to the mere circumstance of undressing in each other's presence. The powerfully rapt face of the seated woman, her helpless arm gestures, make one think of those astonished figures in Raphael's *Transfiguration* who receive as a revelation the truth that their leader possesses divinity. So again, it is only in the most reduced sense that Courbet painted no goddesses. It is as if the most commonplace things and persons are already so suffused with what people look for in religion that the ordinary world has all that we require for the satisfaction of our highest needs.

It cannot be pretended that every painting rises to this level of enhanced transfiguration. There is, for example, a striking study of a woman's sex that makes us realize how conventional the treatment of the genital area standardly is. This is certainly true of the male genitals, which typically serve the function, in paintings, of identifying their bearers as male, just as wings identify their bearers as angels. Rarely are penises shown the way they really look, which is why when painted by Lucian Freud or photographed by Robert Mapplethorpe they are so shocking. Feminist art historians have at times said that the correspondent absence in depicted females is a "lack," which is analogous to suggesting that the fact that humans are wingless in most paintings shows a lack of angelic power. But Courbet's study demonstrates that women in fact possess something extraordinary, the interesting question being why what they do possess is so rarely shown. One answer may be that it requires some awkward posing to show it: The male figure displays its dangling or pronged attribute no matter what the figure is engaged in, but the female has pretty much to be shown in the sexual position itself if we are to see her sex. (Thus even in Courbet's exquisite painting of lesbian lovers asleep in one another's arms and legs, the genitals do not show themselves, and are at best alluded to through the pink and red fold of the coverlet held by one of the furiously sleeping women.) Courbet's model has her legs spread, her shift pulled high enough to uncover her breasts and cover her face, and her shaggy and humid cleft is open to our gaze. Still, it is what it is and not some other thing, as Bishop Butler said, and Courbet tacitly concedes that realism is not enough by giving the work the preposterously inflated title *The Origin of the World*. (It is appropriate that this work comes from the private collection of that sly phallologist Jacques Lacan.)

Realism similarly reveals its limits in Courbet's portraits, especially those in which the sitter is engaged in no action other than sitting for a portrait. They are characteristically wooden and inert, and worse than that, they reveal the essential ugliness of Courbet's way with paint, which is, as it were, plastered and spackled against the surface, yielding an uningratiating opacity. Courbet appears to have invented this style of painting—or of putting paint on—though I noticed some similarities to the paint quality of Corot (in a fine exhibition of nineteenth-century

French paintings from its own collections, which the Brooklyn has hung on its ground floor). Still, the surfaces of Corot are like a kind of silvery skin—the reality breathes through its representation—while the surfaces of Courbet are sullen and occlusive. If there is evidence of his having been self-taught, it resides, I think, in the unyielding blackness of so much of his work. It is as if he sought to emulate the masters, painting light into dark, but left too much black behind, un-redeemed by color. But perhaps this depressing effect is due to the work having been done in studios, under indoor light, and looking retrospectively bleak in the light of the *plein air* openness of Impres-sionist color. *The Studio of the Artist* reveals many things, among them the fact that the painting the artist is working on in that vast and gloomy space is a landscape.

The palpable fact that many of Courbet's works were achieved in a studio collides, at times almost painfully, with some of the pretenses of realism. There is an unfortunate painting of some sort of bathing beauty, paddling a kind of scull over painted waves. The woman would have been rejected by the art director of *The Police Gazette*, but my objection is that the model has so obviously been posed in the studio and then given an outdoor setting with unconvincing sea gulls and artificial waves that we realize that some unfortunate compromise with realism has been made. There is another study of a woman half emerged from the surrounding water, her arms behind her head, lifting her handsome breasts. The realistic touch of hair under her arms in no degree mitigates the artificiality of the foam Courbet has slathered around her middle.

But no such issue arises with the profound paintings of trout hooked and bleeding from the gills done in 1873, when Courbet was crushed by the humiliation of imprisonment for his part in the pulling down of the Vendôme Column under the Commune, and had to go into exile to escape the terrible financial penalty he alone was made to bear. Mortally trapped, out of its element, breathing its last, the tragic fish is Courbet himself in one of the last of his real allegories, a powerful and unforgettable self-portrait of a fatally caught creature.

The Brooklyn Museum is one of the great under-thronged art spaces of the New York area. It would be difficult for those buffeted by the mobs at the Degas show at the Met—feeling, as Gretchen Simp-son remarked, as if one were inside a gerbil cage, because of the deafening chirps that rise from headphones whose wearers are being

Courbet Reconsidered

edified by Philippe de Montebello—to imagine that but a short subway ride away they could reconsider one of the masters of nineteenth-century realism in spacious galleries sparsely occupied by persons as serious as themselves. This exhibition offers a rare opportunity to sort things out a bit with this awkward artist, tiresome and bombastic, crafty and windy at once, who was also a genius, a moral poet, an artistic metaphysician, a man who so heeded Daumier's imperative to be of his own times that he transcended them.

—*The Nation*, January 23, 1989

Goya and the Spirit of Enlightenment

A PORTRAIT BY Anton Raphael Mengs of Carlos III of Spain marks the threshold of an exhibition that otherwise consists solely of works by Goya. The portrait serves as a frontispiece, as it were—Carlos points outside the picture to the works that follow—but it also expresses the premise of the exhibition Goya and the Spirit of Enlightenment in two distinct ways. Carlos was one of those monarchs, like Frederick the Great of Prussia, Catherine the Great of Russia and Joseph II of Austria, who embodied the political virtues of the Enlightenment as fully as the *Encyclopédie* expressed its intellectual vision: the so-called Spanish Enlightenment was altogether his achievement. And Mengs, who came to Spain at Carlos's invitation, was regarded as the greatest painter of his time despite his conspicuous aridity, and set the aesthetic standards of the Spanish court. Goya's first significant patrons were those Enlightenment intellectuals Carlos had the wit to appoint as ministers in charge of his benign policies of reform and toleration. Whatever his gifts otherwise required, it was a condition of securing commissions that he internalize the somewhat stiff and austere mannerisms of the neoclassical style, for which Mengs tirelessly campaigned. One can sense the tension between inclination and conformity in Goya's very early (1782) portrait of the Conde de Floridablanca, Carlos III's chief minister, and every inch an *Iluminado*: the Count stands severely upright, like the statue of a Roman emperor, albeit in red satin court dress with a blue grosgrain shoulder sash, one arm extended, the other akimbo. But he is placed in a room filled with shadows, and the other figures have such a contrasting fluidity and animation that the work looks like a collaboration between two artists with radically different styles.

There is little doubt that Goya's values were the values of his enlightened patrons, but the degree to which his work can in any sense be classed as Enlightenment *art*, and hence to what extent these values penetrate the work and enable us to respond to it as we should, remain interesting questions. Consider, to begin with, Mengs's portrait of Carlos. It is of an Enlightenment monarch and by an advocate of the style that came to define Enlightenment tastes. But it does not show Carlos as *Erklärungsmensch* but rather as the commander in chief of his armies, resplendent in polished armor and gold-embroidered draperies, wearing his decorations and holding the baton of his authority. The wig is an eighteenth-century giveaway, and the face could hardly have been painted in any earlier age, but an eighteenth-century depiction of an eighteenth-century monarch is not necessarily a piece of Enlightenment art, and in fact Mengs has adopted the conventions of the Baroque portrait in his effort to represent the sovereign with maximal dignity. In contrast, Goya certainly shows Floridablanca *as* an enlightened minister, since he is surrounded with the emblemata of his values: books, expressing a taste for knowledge, and maps and a clock, expressing the rationalizations of time and space. Goya even puts himself in the picture showing the count a picture (too small to be *this* portrait) and in this way establishes him as a patron of the arts. But does the portrait of Floridablanca as such express Enlightenment values any more than does Mengs's portrait of the king?

Let me bring this question out more vividly by considering a much later work, the profound portrait of Bartolomé Sureda, of about 1805. A great deal had happened to Spain and to Goya between the portraits of Floridablanca and Sureda. Carlos III had died; Spain was ruled uneasily by the nearly imbecile Carlos IV; Floridablanca and the other enlightened ministers had been driven out of office; in France the Enlightenment had given way to the Revolution, whose values were frightening because of the threat they posed to monarchical legitimacy (Louis XVI was beheaded in 1793), guaranteeing a conservative backlash; Napoleon cast black shadows over Peninsular politics. Goya himself had undergone a severe and nearly fatal illness in 1792, which left him stone-deaf. He had also become the great artist whose powers are nowhere more magnificently visible than in the portrait of Sureda.

Now, the catalogue informs us that Sureda "was among those enlightened figures whose interest in science and love of the fine arts were joined in his quest for industrial applications." It goes on to say, "Among the enlightened there was a particular concern for the development of the so-called useful sciences." In these senses, the portrait of Sureda is of a man twice over characterized as enlightened, but if the spirit of the Enlightenment is alive in him, the painting itself in no sense embodies Enlightenment artistic values.

If anything, I would say it embodies the values of Romanticism, and seems far more to prefigure the Romantic portrait than to point backward to anything Winckelmann or Diderot would have countenanced as the sort of art they endorsed. Sureda's marvelous hat, held lightly in his right hand with its intense red lining facing us, has the form and color of a crucible, and so might be taken as an attribute of its subject's interests in metallurgy and ceramic engineering. But his face is that of a poet, as his pose and costume are those of a dandy. His elegant figure twists gently up from surrounding shadows, made abruptly darker by the red hat lining and by the brilliant white striped neckcloth and waistcoat and the dazzling silver buttons on his green frock coat. His tousled bangs fall across his handsome brow. Light and shadow, brushwork and figuration, attitude and effect, refer us not to reason but to feeling, not to the clarity of an ordered universe but to the uncertain ambiguities of a wild world. The rational will embodied in Floridablanca's stark pose has been replaced with something soft, dark and dreamful.

What, then, would an art be like that did not merely represent individuals who stood for the Enlightenment but that in its own right expressed or embodied Enlightenment values? The art of the Enlightenment was didactic and moralistic. Diderot, for example, extravagantly admired Greuze, whose work he celebrated as "morality in paint." Taste, for Diderot, was a faculty formed through experiencing the true and the good, and art was valuable insofar as it taught its viewers what truth and goodness were, and so made better persons of them. Lucien Goldmann once described the *Encyclopédie* as the single work that perfectly expressed the values of the society it defined, compassing, in alphabetical order (an innovation), everything it would be useful to know in order to exploit the world through knowledge. It was a book to use rather than to read, and utility was in every sense the Enlightenment criterion of moral as well as of artistic virtue. "In general," Hume writes with enthusiasm, "what praise is implied in the simple epithet *useful!* What reproach in the contrary!" Moral speculation must meet its own criteria by being useful itself, and for Hume this meant precisely what it meant for Diderot in his praise of Greuze. Hume writes: "By proper representations of the deformity of vice and beauty of virtue, [to] beget correspondent habits, and engage us to avoid the one, and embrace the other." It is, then, Enlightenment art only when it is useful (like the magnificent plates in the *Encyclopédie*) or when it intended to cause us to be morally better men and women. The whole function of the museum, an essentially Napoleonic concept, was to display works that would enhance the virtues of their viewers as persons and citizens. Aesthetics is very much an eighteenth-century invention, but it is not an *Enlightenment* concept. An Enlightenment theorist would dismiss as frivolous art whose only function was to furnish pleasure.

One may perhaps view some of Goya's early portraits as celebrating virtue and thus as fulfilling the positive injunction in Hume's formula. There is, for example, a very moving depiction of family life in his early group portrait *The Family of Infante Don Luis* of 1794, in which Goya has again inserted himself, poised to paint (though not, once more, this picture, since the dimension and size are wrong). In Hume's terms, he could be showing himself as executing the Enlightenment imperative of depicting virtue as virtue. But this is really stretching a point, for if we compare this gentle study of a happy family with one of Greuze's efforts—say his *Father Reading the Bible to His Children*, which was such a success in the Salon of 1755, and which was like an advertisement for piety and familial virtue—we see instantly that Goya's is not a didactic work.

On the other hand, it would be difficult to think of any work that more precisely exemplified the negative pole of Hume's formula than the *Caprichos*—a suite of eighty etchings that Goya published in 1799 (and incidentally the greatest achievement in this medium since Rembrandt). Fred Licht, to my mind the best writer on Goya today, says in his catalogue essay that "the *Caprichos* have been justifiably interpreted as the crowning and most purgative visual statement of the Enlightenment." Goya himself wrote of this stupendous work:

The author is convinced that censoring human errors and vices—although it seems the preserve of oratory and poetry—may also be a worthy object of painting. As a subject appropriate to his work, he has selected from the multitude of stupidities and errors common to every civil society, and from the ordinary obfuscations and lies condoned by custom, ignorance, or self-interest, those he has deemed most fit to furnish material for ridicule, and at the same time to exercise the author's imagination.

It is obvious that the case for Goya as an Enlightenment spirit, and of his art as Enlightenment art, must rest with these extraordinary prints, and why the *Caprichos* are the centerpiece for this exhibition. But my claim is this: Goya is deeper than any Enlightenment artist adhering to Hume's imperative could be. The spirit of the *Caprichos* is at the antipodes of Enlightenment art.

Enlightenment moral psychology was robustly optimistic and Socratic: To know the good is to do the good, to know evil is to shun it. So we do evil only out of ignorance, and when ignorance gives way to knowledge, it is human nature to do the morally correct thing. In terms of social policy, this meant education and the suppression of the agencies of ignorance—the church preeminently, and then the feudal aristocracies whose self-interest depended upon the superstition and institutionalized ignorance of those under them. Enlightenment, in Kant's famous phrase, was mankind's coming of age, a state regarded as historically inevitable by the Enlightenment philosophy of history.

Goya by contrast was utterly pessimistic. The *Caprichos*, which show whores and fools, bawds and ninnies, thieves and asses, all engaged in mutual exploitation, with menacing birds and animals as witnesses and metaphors, are visual inscriptions of greed, vanity, lust, sloth, stupidity, envy, generalized cruelty—a portrait of us as human-all-too-human. They may indeed constitute a moral mirror in which are reflected back the face and form of our small and wicked natures. But the knowledge will do us little good, for we are powerless to do anything about it: there is not even a God to save us. The best we can do is acknowledge the black truth. Hogarth's biting images of rakes and harlots and silly, sodden spouses could, I suppose, serve as graphic warnings, ways of strengthening the weak moral will to refuse, and to reinforce our complacencies as good souls. It shows what at worst might happen to us, but not what we are. (Hogarth is like Dickens in this way: Even for Scrooge it is never too late.) Goya shows us as we are in a dark vision of ineluctable depravity.

The *Caprichos* were, of course, public works in that they were

[254

advertised and sold, and several suites were purchased by collectors before they were withdrawn from circulation. But they are also in some deep way very private works, objectifications of Goya's singular imagination. They connect, in my view, with a set of small paintings Goya did as a therapeutic exercise when he began to emerge from his frightful illness of 1792–3. Uncommissioned cabinet paintings, they were pieces done, he wrote, "in order to distract my mind and . . . in which I have managed to make observations that commissioned works ordinarily do not allow, and in which fantasy and invention have no place." These works are violent and savage: they show lunatics and murderers and rapists, and reflect, one is certain, the terrible fantasies of a man turned in upon himself, no longer able to hear others. The *Caprichos* carry forward this fantasizing impulse. They are private and at the same time universal, as if human nature were everywhere and always the same. The Enlightenment work of art entailed a moral and pedagogical transaction between it and the viewer, through which the latter was to emerge changed or strengthened in resolution. To accept the *Caprichos*, on the other hand, was to abandon Enlightenment hopes altogether.

From this point on, Goya's work proceeds on two levels, neither of them especially connected to the Enlightenment spirit. There would be the commissioned work, and then the private works in which, if one bought them, one was buying into Goya's saturnine vision. But much of this he kept to himself. The drawings of judicial torture, for example, or of the terrifying conditions of imprisonment, or of the Inquisition, were bound into private albums. They may have expressed certain humanitarian views he held in common with the Enlightenment, but they never, as works of art, entered general consciousness in a way that might have served to transform and modulate the practices they depict. And this was not, perhaps, because Goya was prudent but because he held fundamental reservations at odds with Enlightenment agendas on the transformative powers of art.

Writing of the engravings of Hogarth, Lamb described them as books: "They have the teeming, fruitful, suggestive meaning of *words*. Other pictures we look at—his we read." Something of the same is true of Goya's prints; of the *Caprichos*; of *Los Desastres de la Guerra*, which he executed between 1810 and 1814 as a documentary response to the horrible Peninsular War, which pitted the French against resistance fighters who matched them in cruelty; and above all in the mystifying *Los Proverbios* or, as they are called, the *Disperates*. These are in a sense visual texts, and just as there developed a literary genre of Hogarth interpretation, so, even in his own time, Goya's prints were the occasion for critical readings. One is grateful to the organizers of this present exhibition for their scholarship, for bringing to light the puns and allusions that may have been esoteric even for Goya's audiences, but which are certainly distant to us. But the amazing fact is how much comes through without benefit of this valuable apparatus, how immediately Goya addresses us, how much we are his subjects, how little anything fundamental has changed. His greatness was to reflect his times and to be for all times.

I am grateful as well for the exhibition's focus on the concept of the Enlightenment, even if I dispute its obvious application to Goya's work. Inevitably, it puts the art in one light rather than another, tells another narrative than the one I would want told. But anything that makes possible an exhibition of so much of the work of this tremendous artist is through that fact alone justified.

In one of the thumbnail reviews through which *The New Yorker* has latterly enlivened its weekly breviary of cultural events, someone has written of this show that it is "a little low on visual magic." A little low! If there were one grain more of visual magic, the actual air would teem with witches and owls, and complacent donkeys would be making hooved gestures while luscious *majas* paraded their timelessly provocative attributes.

—*The Nation*, July 10, 1989

Christian Boltanski

I CAME ACROSS an instructive early photograph by Man Ray in the recent exhibition given his work from the so-called New York years (1913–21) by the Zabriskie Gallery in Manhattan. He was much under the impish spell of Marcel Duchamp at the time, and for just that reason his work sometimes affords a certain glimpse into the rather less scrutable agendas of Duchamp himself. The photograph is of bed sheets hanging on lines and billowing gently in the wind—a tiny gelatin silver print from 1920 with the striking title *Moving Sculpture*. The title identifies the blown linen as what Duchamp designated "ready-mades"—works of art ready to hand amid the banal appurtenances of everyday life, although (and this is the mark of the disciple) the sheets themselves are prettier than the characteristic ready-made, chosen, as a general rule, by the criterion of aesthetic indistinction. "The danger to be avoided lies in aesthetic delectation," Duchamp wrote of his most notorious ready-made, the urinal he titled *Fountain* and endeavored to exhibit in 1917; but almost everything done by Man Ray, who constituted the Silver Age of Dada, was aesthetically delectable.

Moving Sculpture situates itself at the beginning of an important episode in the history of sculpture, broadening the material resources available from marble, bronze and wood to cloth. It also, of course, makes a precocious contribution to the genre of kinetic sculpture: Calder made his first abstract moving constructions, designated "mobiles" by Duchamp, in 1931, though the mobile that every Culturally Literate American can identify did not take form until somewhat later.

Whatever the case, *Moving Sculpture* carried forward the enterprise of turning the sow's ears of everyday objects into the silken purses of works of art—transfiguring the commonplace, as I have termed the process. But apart from their ordinariness and the aesthetic effect of their waving whiteness, nothing is made of the fact that they are, after all, bed sheets.

Much of the interest of *Moving Sculpture* would disappear if the title of the work were lost, or if it merely bore the title *Bed Sheets, New York, 1920*. Someone like Steichen might have shown laundry hanging in a New York yard, and we would be impressed by the formal composition made by curve against curve and, just possibly, by the fact that the subject matter of art photography had been extended to include those items of domestic utility as a motif for formal study (as against, perhaps, a photograph by Lewis Hine of the backs of tenements, which are identified as such by lines of drying sheets). Similarly, I can imagine, barely, Duchamp extending his set of ready-mades by hanging a bed sheet or two on a clothesline, though it would have been typical of him to invent a funny title (*Drapeaux* to pun on *draps*, perhaps) and to ink some nonsense line at the hem. Only after the middle 1960s might an artist have been able to make a work consisting of bed sheets called, flatly, *Bed Sheets*. Such a work could hardly be more different from a ready-made: for the first time in the works I have been considering, the sheets might have become transformed into metaphors of themselves, collecting out of a set of human associations the deep sorts of meanings that bed sheets have in our lives. Think of how powerful a metaphor Joyce created in *Finnegans Wake* with the washerwomen, commenting upon and then, as priestesses, cleansing the sacramental stains inscribed by sex, sleep, sickness, birth and death—their sheets as blanched pages on which we impose the tragic texts of our finitude.

This point is made through a remarkable work by the French conceptual artist Christian Boltanski, which I saw at the Marian Goodman Gallery, around the corner on Fifty-seventh Street from the Zabriskie. Made of brightly colored items of children's clothing—skirts, pants, tights, blouses, jackets, T-shirts—it looked, as one entered the somewhat darkened space of the gallery, like an avant-garde wall hanging made up of ready-to-hand things (a little in the spirit of the aggregations of manufactured objects by the artist Arman). The first impression, that the gaily colored pieces of (I surmise) cheap clothing were simply the materials for a wall hanging the way scraps and snips of cloth are the material for a patchwork quilt, starts to dissolve when one notices four lamps connected to outlets by bare electrical cords and begins to think that the illumination they offer, and they themselves, are part of the work rather than sources of illumination provided by the gallery to facilitate our appreciation of the wall hanging. One begins to think that the tiny garments are the subject of the work rather than merely the materials the artist has seized upon to fabricate a clothes piece. (In the Lila Acheson Wallace Wing of the Metropolitan Museum, there is a gate by Jim Dine fashioned in part of distorted hand tools: wrenches, screwdrivers, pliers. But these are cunning ornaments, not the subject of the piece. A similar work, responding to impulses parallel to Boltanski's, would be not only made of tools but about those tools.) And the cheap lamps enhance the sense that we are in the presence not just of clothing—a display, say, that shows what the children of the Western world were wearing in 1989—but of clothing that has somehow survived its wearers, been left behind by vanished kids. Left behind and then improvised into a memorial to their wearers, the garments are made somehow self-metaphorical and almost unendurably poignant. It becomes, so to speak, a soft Wailing Wall, and the little, now unbearably bright pieces of clothing seem ranked, like the names of the dead soldiers on the Vietnam Veterans Memorial. Like them but even more touching, because of their anonymity: these are mass-produced things, the kind you buy from stacks in discount houses, and could belong to Anychild, as if this were a memorial to childhood as such.

Now one notices that the title is *Fête de Pourim*. How different this is from Man Ray's title, which situates his sheets in the context of art, wresting them from the world in which bedclothes have a practical and moral locus, making them over into things of artistic appreciation. And how different again from the ha-ha titles of Duchamp, who was calling into question the entire institutional fabric in which titles and artworks have some stable relationship. *Fête de Pourim*, for us, today, has to connect the children's wear with the Jewish holiday, and the meaning could be that children get new things to wear and the clothing is celebratory. But the raw light from the lamps, the crisscross of electrical wires, suggest instead that the work concerns a Jewish disaster, that these emblemize the discarded garments of children led naked to the gas chambers, collected together and mounted to form a hecatomb, the best we can do against the total disappearance from consciousness of children whose identity other than as children we do not even know. It becomes a piece of Holocaust art, and if so then perhaps the only convincing example I have encountered of a genre I would have thought impossible but now recognize as merely terribly difficult.

Boltanski's work invites an inevitable comparison with that of Anselm Kiefer (see above, essay 34). The way that *Fête de Pourim* transformed the space of the gallery into that of a shrine, just as it transformed the aesthetic relationship into one of contemplative sorrow, could not have contrasted more vividly with the busy galleries in which Kiefer's work hung at the Museum of Modern Art, filled with baffled viewers bumping into one another as they pored over lists of symbols. And the change in vision Boltanski's work undergoes, in which items from the *Lebenswelt* are first taken up into art in an avantgarde way but then returned to the *Lebenswelt* to become metaphors for themselves, epitomizes what I believe he aims at as an artist. "His highest goal," according to an essay by Mary Jane Jacob, "is for his art to be mistaken for life itself." The clothes are, after all, not real relics. This is a work of art. The receptionist at the Marian Goodman told me that the artist had installed the work himself, stapling the garments directly to the wall. For all I know he purchased them from K-mart, or out of bins on Fourteenth Street. The work incorporates the boundary between reality and representation.

The Boltanski show at the Marian Goodman closed early in January, as did the lovely Man Ray show at the Zabriskie. But the New Museum of Contemporary Art is devoting its generous spaces entirely to Boltanski's work. Many of the works approach *Fête de Pourim* in spirit, though the only one that resembles it in substance is perhaps *Les Habits de François C.*, done in 1972, which is composed of twenty-four black-and-white photographs, separately framed, each of a separate item of boy's clothing. There is, importantly, nothing distinctive about the garments, and yet the overall feeling of the work is uncomfortably forensic, as if this were an exhibit in the sense of the term that has application in the law court or the police station, a photographic record of what François C. wore. But the wardrobe, distributed into its components and then reassembled as a conjunction of distinct items, is so submerged in the ordinariness of ordinary life that, apart from the age and sex and perhaps class of the wearer (and possibly the nationality, since the shoes are too neat to belong to an American boy and imply European ownership), there is very little to go on in re-

covering a specific identity for François C., *un garçon comme les autres.*
And given the banality and in a sense the universality of the objects,
the interesting interpretive question is why they should be photographed. But there is, after all, something banal and universal in photographs themselves, which allows them to become self-metaphorical;
and it is as such that they enter as components in the most impressive
of Boltanski's works in the New Museum show.

I have often meditated on the power of those photographic images
made central in contemporary art by the genius of Andy Warhol—
images of faces everybody recognizes. Nobody has to ask to whom
these images belong: the faces of Jackie, Liz, Marilyn, Elvis and Andy
himself, like their names, form part of the common consciousness of
anyone who participates in the culture of our times. They are as familiar
as the flag or the dollar bill. Of course, there will come a time when
people will need to have them identified, the culture no longer being
defined (in part) by the immediate knowledge of who Marilyn or Elvis
was, just as there are perhaps few not special scholars of theatrical
history who carry the knowledge of what Sarah Bernhardt or Lily
Langtry looked like. Every American knows the faces of Washington
and Lincoln, and perhaps of Kennedy—but who save the historian
knows, straight off, Blaine, Polk or even Madison? This kind of knowledge defines a consciousness, and when, for example, we take someone
through a family album, explaining to whom these images belong—
the dog that ate the birthday cake, Elsie as a baby, Dad when he bought
the De Soto, Mom at her graduation—we are endeavoring to widen
our consciousness to include this outsider, connecting him or her to
our past and to the icons of our life. To be part of the family is to know
the images that outsiders have to have explained to them.

But now consider the photographs one finds in old frames in sec-
ondhand shops. We can identify the faces and figures in them with
about the degree of success we have with the clothing of François C.
They are irrecoverably alien. All we know is that someone took the
picture or had it taken who cared enough about the subject to have
the picture framed—and then, gradually or suddenly, nobody cared
and the picture wound up as part of the detritus of a dissolved consciousness. Think of studying the faces in the group portrait of the
graduating class of some unspecified Central High School. In our culture, when the last one dies who knows, without having to be told, to
whom an image belongs, that is the final death of the owner of the
image. Nothing is more deeply anonymous than the image of an in-

dividual face nobody recognizes. The equation of unrecognizability of images that were once instantly recognized with death itself—with the death of memory—is the animating metaphor of Boltanski's characteristic works.

Consider Boltanski's *L'album de photographies de la famille D. entre 1939 et 1954*. It is a work that splits the viewers into two classes, those who are members or close acquaintances of the family D. and the rest of us. It is an array of rephotographed and enlarged snapshots, framed, in ten rows of fifteen images each, and they are endearingly inept, as pictures in family albums always are: badly composed, amateurishly cropped, as often out of focus as in, over- or underexposed, taken by people of people who mean everything to one another and nothing to anyone else. But they are also exactly *us* as humans: fathers, mothers, children: at the beach or in the important moments of little lives—marriages, confirmations, birthdays, in front of the new family home. The French refer to snapshots as *clichés*, and nothing could be more appropriate as a description of the monumental significance in everyday life *of* everyday life itself. This is underscored by the fact that the family D. is evidently French, and by the dates, the period documented including the years of the occupation. I find enormously touching the thought that the simple camera snapped at all through those years, that life went on, and if the war cast its shadow, as it must have, over family life, an effort must be made to discover it. Under whatever difficult or even terrifying circumstances, the family got together, its members said whatever the French say when we say "Cheese!" and put their hands on one another's unselfconscious shoulders.

By far the most powerful work here, only partly in consequence of its size, is the stupendous *Monument: Les Enfants de Dijon*, made in 1986. Its primary constituents are photographs of children we certainly do not know and who are now perhaps not known to anyone— mere faces of mere children, moving in their forgottenness (think how differently we would think of Man Ray's *Moving Sculpture* if "moving" were understood in *this* sense). The photographs are arranged up and down one of the great walls of the main gallery at the New Museum, each separated from the next by distances large in proportion to the images themselves, as if to give each a maximal dignity and to underscore the importance, to someone, of the individual memorialized. Each photograph is illuminated by one to three lamps, again connected to outlets by exposed electrical wires, arranged in rough approximation of candelabra. The lighting, the rephotographed photos, the circum-

Christian Boltanski

stances of their array, connote, as did the *Fête de Pourim*, the death of a cohort: the children smile in an official way, their eyes beam or are troubled, their hair is neat. How sad to think that the faces are as anonymous as shoes or socks now. It is difficult to think of a work of art that comes closer to embodying what one supposes Virgil meant by *lachrimae rerum*—"the tears of things."

I rather wish this work had sole occupancy of the main gallery, which instead contains a number of works in much the same spirit, though on a less ambitious scale. For one begins comparing them in terms of composition, or scale, and the spell is broken or nearly broken as the criteria that have application primarily to works of art take over, and the powerful connection between childhood and death is weakened through repetition and variation (the presence in the gallery of a window through which we can view a shadow-work prevents a spontaneous make-believe that this is a hall of memorials). Taken separately each of these works could, I suppose, emblemize a family shrine, or one in a village school or church, but somehow assembling the works in a gallery somewhat compromises the intention of the artist. In *Lessons of Darkness*, the catalogue that accompanies this exhibition (both are the work of Lynn Gumpert and Mary Jane Jacob), Boltanski is quoted this way: "For me painting isn't provocative or moving, only life is. But I am an artist and therefore all I do is termed art. One day, of course, it's forcibly discovered. The fascinating moment for me is when the spectator hasn't registered the art connection, and the longer I can delay this association the better."

Plainly, the emblemata of the art museum—the admissions desk, the posters for sale, the catalogues and the guards—counteract whatever devices the artist may have used to postpone or delay the recognition that after all this is art and not life. It is nevertheless a tribute to this artist that, after we have crossed the threshold of the museum, it is life rather than art that asserts itself. There is, to be sure, a tension between art and life that one cannot help but feel when one turns away from a work like *Monument: Les Enfants de Dijon* to see what else there is to see, and the feelings elicited by the work give way to the suppressed acknowledgment that this is, in the end, a work among works, part of a corpus, something that has behind it the history of Dada, Surrealism, Pop and Fluxus, upon which, as art, it makes as many comments as it makes on the sad real world.

—*The Nation*, February 13, 1989

Sienese Painting

THE FLAT RECTANGULAR wall painting has so dominated artistic theory since the Renaissance that no alternative pictorial paradigm has been easily thinkable. It has even defined all the revolts that have marked the century of Modernism in art that recently reached its end. The boundaries of the rectangle generate a kind of illusory space and an immediately metaphysical distinction between the surface of the painting and the surface of the wall (metaphysical because the two surfaces may, as in the case of fresco painting, in fact be physically identical). Hence there is a spontaneous distinction between looking at and looking through: we look through the surface at the scene situated in the illusory space, as if through a window. Indeed, the entire technology of painting was bent upon making the experience of seeing something through a window and seeing something in a painting perceptually indistinguishable. The history of painting was therefore inevitably progressive, as artists got better and better at this.

Modernism began when the surface became something to look at rather than look through, and artists introduced distortions in order to make plain that they no longer sought illusion, that the painting had become an object in its own right rather than a transparent opening onto an ulterior reality. Yet even with abstract art, the distinction between looking at and looking through, and hence between subject and surface, remained. The moment the work became all surface it collapsed into decoration. In order to remain art, accordingly, illusory or pictorial space had to be retained—so artists might just as well have remained realists for all the good the revolutions did them. The window paradigm co-opts those who undertake to overthrow it, not an uncommon story.

The window theory of art was essentially a Florentine invention, and whether because it engaged the technological interest of painters who found the production of illusions challenging, or because the movable window painting became something that could be bought and sold and collected, the artistic products generated by it completely swamped those generated by a different paradigm altogether. This was the Sienese paradigm, which defined artistic practice into the quattrocento, when Florence seized a leadership that it has held ever since. (All subsequent Western painting has been Florentine, wherever it was done, as long as it supposed a distinction between looking at and looking through.) Compared with the art of Florence in the quattrocento, that of Siena seems backward and eccentric, as if the Sienese, patrons and painters alike, were arrested at a stage of pictorial representation that the Florentines went triumphantly beyond. In fact, I believe, the Sienese were connected with a different kind of history, one we lose sight of because their best works were sawn into windowlike rectangles, framed and hung on walls, marketed as charming, marginal, not to say primitive exemplars of a form of representation elsewhere practiced with a central mastery.

Siena more or less vanished as an art center by the end of the fifteenth century. In part this must have been because any artist interested in making a living would have had to internalize the Florentine paradigm and hence be absorbed into the grand sweep of art history as we understand it. But in part it was due to another cause altogether: to the invention of printing, which meant the end of the book as a precious handmade object. Sienese art did not imply the wall as its support, but the page or the leaf. Its artists were primarily illuminators, makers of images one comes upon when the covers of the book are opened. Of course, the Sienese artist also made altarpieces. But I propose that the altarpiece is a variant of the same basic principle as the book. It, too, implies leaves; it too implies covers that can be closed and opened, even if the frame of the altarpiece prevents this from actually taking place. The familiar word "triptych," used to designate a painting with three panels, etymologically refers to three tablets hinged together, and hence a primordial book. The folio and the folding panel are the coordinates of Sienese art, just as the scroll and the screen are of Japanese art. The distinction, one might say the artistic rivalry, between Florence and Siena lives on in the invidious contrast—proving the victory of Florence—between being an artist and "only" an illustrator.

The wall painting, treated as a window, defines a role for the viewer as that of witness to the event looked at through the window, so that the relationship between viewer and event is essentially perceptual and cognitive. Because the viewer has no access to the scene depicted other than visually—he or she cannot after all enter the space—the viewer is reduced to a disembodied eye, for whom a viewing place is determined by the mathematics of fixed-point perspective: the viewer is but a geometrical point. The Sienese paradigm could not be more different. Here one engages with an image as part of engaging with a book or altar screen, and hence as part of an action like singing or praying or reading aloud. The image defines a largely ritualistic relationship with the viewer, if it is even proper to use that word in this context: for the image is of some saint or martyr or the Virgin or the Saviour with whom one seeks communion. It is not required, accordingly, that the image be cognitively convincing, only that it express the powers with which one seeks connection through ritual. The Sienese image is mystical, almost deliberately not of this world, so not required to look as if it is. The saint and the Virgin can be appealed to, through their images, to make interventions in our world. The world within the Florentine painting looks just like the world outside it if the artist has been successful. They are cognitively of a piece. In a sense the world inside a Sienese image also is of a piece with the world outside it, but that is because each is a locus of faith. The world itself is the scene of miraculous enactments, and real saints, like Catherine or Bernardino, tread the pavements of the city, doing amazing things. They were neighbors and holy folk at once. Opening a book or an altarpiece, already a fraught experience given the weight the images were thought to bear, must have been a magical gesture. Kneeling before and being surrounded by the panels of an altarpiece must have differed radically, as an experience, from standing before a wall looking through a metaphorical window at something necessarily in another space.

Even today, even in their fragments, the painted images of Siena radiate an intimacy foreign to the art of Florence. The Sienese image implies that it and its celebrants are held together in the same spiri-

[266

tualized space, which has nothing to do with optics. The impulses of Sienese art reappeared in the seventeenth century, in the Baroque altarpiece, when the Church undertook to re-create an addressive relationship between image and celebrant. Treating the Baroque altarpiece as a picture—as a windowed scene—hanging in the museum is as alien to its essence and as subversive of its intent as is the parallel reduction of the Sienese paintings to mere tableaux. The museum is the Florentine interior par excellence.

It was nevertheless an inspiration of the Metropolitan Museum of Art in New York City to mount an exhibition of Sienese painting from the Renaissance: one can almost feel the tension between the two paradigms in, for example, the treatment of space, the projection of feeling and the strategies of narration. The museum has the largest holding of Sienese art outside Siena itself, and its former chairman of European painting, John Pope-Hennessey—to whom the strenuously scholarly catalogue is appropriately dedicated—has done perhaps more than anyone since Bernard Berenson to awaken our consciousness to the greatness of the Sienese achievement. I recall being powerfully affected, as were any number of painters of my acquaintance, by the publication thirty years ago of his marvelously illustrated piece on Sassetta and Giovanni di Paolo.

In that early essay Pope-Hennessey wrote of Sassetta's work as "touching and evocative and personal." And in a recent issue of the *Metropolitan Museum of Art Bulletin*, he characterizes Giovanni di Paolo as a "highly personal artist." These are correct assessments, and in a sense they connect with the feeling of intimacy the images generate. But our fixing upon these attributes reflects the distance between ourselves and the Sienese for whom these works were created: it was not the artists whose personalities were to be communicated through the images but the individual saints, the dramatis personae of the Christian narrative, who were themselves to be present in those images, so that the viewer (using that unavoidable term once more) was directly in contact with them. Or perhaps the reason the personalities of the artists emerge so eloquently in these works may be an artifact of the circumstance that most of the paintings in the exhibition come from the predellas of altarpieces, sawn off and then sawn into sections and sold as individual works. And the predella images were, literally *and* figuratively, perhaps, sufficiently marginal to the altarpiece that factors of personality may have been allowed to come through. It was the appeal of this personality to later generations that in turn may account for the fact that as much Sienese art as does survive consists in these exceptionally affecting images. Here is Pope-Hennessey on the characteristic polyptych of the Sienese workshop:

A central panel (usually though not invariably a Virgin and Child) was flanked by two or four panels of saints beneath Gothic arcading. Generally there was a superstructure with half-length figures of the Evangelists with in the center a Redeemer, attached by dowels to the main panels. Often there were small superimposed figures of saints in pilasters at the sides. The whole structure rested on a base of predella with narrative scenes relating either to the central figure, or to the saints flanking it, or to one of the saints in exclusion of the rest.

The predella scenes are, as John Russell felicitously expressed it, footnotes to the altarpiece. And it is an irony that our picture of Sienese style should be based on fragments that survived to charm a sensibility quite other than that for which the grand ensemble of the altarpiece itself was orchestrated. It would be as if all that remained of Bach's B Minor Mass were the bits of melody that can be whistled.

In any case, the predella scene was never required to be optically convincing, only to be legible. The office of the images was to refer upward to the saints and other figures hieratically present in the main panels of the altarpiece—establishing their credentials, so to speak, and evidence of their readiness, as intercessors, to perform homely miracles: reviving a drowned child, for example, or bringing someone from death just long enough to receive the last sacraments. Artistically, the agenda was to achieve as much naturalism as was required to make it clear what was taking place, and to this end the artist might develop narrative strategies quite at odds with what we would think of as Florentine naturalism.

Consider, for example, *St. Bernardino Resuscitating a Drowned Child*, painted by Sano di Pietro, almost cinematic in its treatment as a series of scenes. A male figure enters the panel from the right, headed down a stairwell onto a piazza where the child lies submerged in an ornamental pool. The man's hands seem clasped in prayer, as they are again in his second appearance, by the side of the pool, looking in. Standing by the pool with him (the father, I presume) are two women, one certainly the mother, who is reaching hopelessly into the water

[*268*

while her companion prays. St. Bernardino hovers above like a hummingbird, summoning the child back to life with his powerful hand. The father then makes a third appearance, holding his hand out to touch the resuscitated child. The mother and her companion make second appearances, on their knees in grateful acknowledgment of the miracle. Even the child, now back on his feet, is thanking St. Bernardino. There are nine separate figures in the painting, though only five distinct persons in the action.

What one most admires in these tableaux is the way in which two orders of being, one holy and one human, traverse one another naturally and miraculously, precisely as if the world itself reflected the complex reality of Jesus as a god humanly embodied, eternal and temporal at once. In Giovanni di Paolo's exquisite *Adoration of the Magi*, to take another example, the Holy Family is receiving the luminous Magi in front of the manger, as a golden cow and a silver mule chomp indifferently behind them (the artist has painted a delicate bundle of straw sticking out of the mule's mouth). One of the Magi is on all fours, crownless (his doffed crown is on the ground by the Virgin's hem), kissing the bambino's toe. The infant touches the old king's bald pate with his left hand, in the manner of babies the world round—but he holds his right hand up in a rabbinic gesture, anticipating his missionary adulthood. The next-youngest king is kneeling, removing his crown as he prepares to make his own ritual submission to the blessed infant. The youngest of the three kings has not touched his crown yet, and is still standing. But he has thrown his arms around Joseph in a gesture of manly solicitude. Joseph looks worriedly out of the corner of his eye at his new responsibility. You can almost hear the king saying, "*Coraggio! Coraggio!*" The landscape goes back and back, with a shepherd tending translucent sheep before some strange rocky outcroppings in the middle distance, and the blue fields, punctuated by mountains, blend indiscernibly with a sky punctuated by clouds. This fusion of earth and heaven underscores the fusion of flesh and divinity that defines the Christian perception of reality. And it is my sense that Sienese painting does not merely state this perception by pictorial means, it embodies it in its own right: the saints are mysteriously present in the tempera, wood and gold of the panels. In this respect the structure of Sienese art penetrates even these vivid marginal scenes.

Sassetta's is, one feels, a more secular intelligence and a more decorative sensibility. Compare his *Adoration* with Giovanni di Paolo's. Sassetta shows us very rich kings bringing golden gifts. They have turned the scene into a courtly party as they stand about, looking precious in their handsome vestments, waiting to present themselves to the diminutive guest of honor. The infant holds his hands out, like a greedy bar mitzvah boy, and the Virgin casts a complacent eye as ewers are brought forward by elegant ladies. And Sassetta lays his own gifts before us, making a display of his ability to draw a foreshortened horse from behind, or a dog playing with a stick, pretending to snarl. In 1939, Pope-Hennessey demonstrated that this panel belongs with Sassetta's wonderful *Journey of the Magi*, but this must be the first time the two have been reunited in a very long time, so that we can identify the same figures appearing in each, even the dogs, as if connecting up the pictures in a children's book.

The *Journey of the Magi*, seen by itself, projects a feeling of visual innocence and almost of naïveté. The procession of kings and attendants follows a downward curve from the middle right to the lower left. It is dawn; they have left behind them a pink fortified city and are adventuring past a barren hill with leafless trees, which establishes that the child was born in wintertime. Awkward birds scrounge on the hill's crest, and between the kings and us a golden star shines. Seen with its companion, and then with the extraordinary predella scenes from the Arte della Lana chapel altarpiece (here six of the seven predella scenes can be seen together for the first time since that altarpiece, the rest of it now a matter of conjecture, was long ago disassembled), we recognize how remarkably sophisticated an artist Sassetta was.

A number of the Arte della Lana scenes show St. Thomas Aquinas alone in the interior of a church. Indeed in one he is kneeling before an altarpiece in the very way those for whom it was made knelt before it, an action that establishes a bond between the supplicants within the picture and without. In one he is addressed by a crucified Christ, exemplifying what one might hope for oneself in relating oneself to the mystical imagery. The spaces are altogether seductive, inviting us in. Through an open portal behind St. Thomas we glimpse a garden with an exquisite fountain. It is not a space mathematically organized under rules of strict perspective. But neither do we relate to it as an eye fixed at a point. We are drawn in, our feelings are aroused, our curiosity awakened. Like everything else in this extraordinary exhibition, this picture addresses us as participants rather than as witnesses—as if we were among the faithful rather than mere visual judges—enlarging rather than reducing those for whom it brings messages of great assurance and joy. It is a show you cannot see too many times.

—*The Nation*, March 6, 1989

Robert Colescott and
Russell Connor

THE IDEA OF the masterpiece has come under two waves of artistic attack during the past quarter century. The first came from art makers who understood that a period had been entered in which the rules and practices that made the masterpiece a possibility and an ideal no longer defined the making of art, so the question had to be faced of what their connection was to be with that great history that had come to its end in the early 1960s. The second attack came from the direction of politics. It was mounted by a new generation of art makers who felt themselves disenfranchised by the institutions and attitudes embodied in the masterpiece, construed as the symbol of everything elitist, exclusionary and oppressive in the world of art. The members of the first wave still felt themselves to be artists in the traditional sense, with all the privileges and ambitions artists supposed themselves entitled to, but without the historical assurances that they themselves could any longer produce the kind of art that in its highest achievement became the masterpiece. The members of the second wave, feminists, often, or members of one or another minority, undertook through protest to call into question the institutions of artistic empowerment which the artists of the first wave—white, male, educated—continued to take for granted.

Both waves resorted to ridicule and appropriation as weapons, but it was in the first wave primarily that the familiar masterpieces of the Western tradition were incorporated as the subjects of works of art, about which the incorporating work could then make various deflationary statements. Roy Lichtenstein's clever brushstroke paintings are a paradigm of this type—paintings that were *of* brushstrokes but that themselves used nothing like the kinds of brushstrokes they showed. The brushstrokes they were of were the heavy gestural wipes and swipes of pigment so central to Abstract Expressionist aesthetics, where the artist, driven by some acute creative passion, enacted upon the surface of the canvas some powerful, muscular movement of a brush so loaded with paint that it could barely be lifted, to achieve the palpable trace of intense feeling. Lichtenstein treated these heroized swags of thick and dripping paint as if illustrating them for a child's coloring book. His paintings replaced all the attributes of the sweep-and-drip brush-strokes with their polar opposites: his were cool, flat, and looked as if they were mechanically reproduced, as if, indeed, he were demon-strating Walter Benjamin's celebrated thesis, stultifying the aura of the brushstroke by means of the absolutely affectless idiom of mechanical reproduction. He was not merely making sport of the romantic pre-tenses of a body of great work—he was refuting by counterdemon-stration the false premises of its alleged greatness. It was part of a collective effort to cut the masterpiece down to size. In that same era, for example, Malcolm Morley painted a copy of a postcard of Vermeer's *The Artist's Studio*, distancing the original even further than a copy of the painting itself would have, as if to say that the mechanical repro-duction of the painting was more worth appropriating than the painting itself. (And of course Morley's work has an originality and an interest no mere copy of the actual work could have, since it is dense with the most intricate historical and theoretical references.)

Lichtenstein and Morley were among the wittier artists of the 1960s, seeking to define themselves and the possibilities of art in their time against the masterpiece by putting between their works and the masterpieces they incorporated an important distance. They were en-deavoring to show that they were not continuing the history to which the masterpieces belonged but philosophizing about that history from a posthistorical era whose own artistic imperatives remained to be discovered. But theirs were typical of responses made worldwide. The Russian conceptualists Komar and Melamid, for example, fabricated charred but still recognizable effigies of characteristic Lichtensteins, which had in turn appropriated the idiom of the comic strip: the end result looked like fragments found by archaeologists investigating the culture of the twentieth century, which had destroyed itself ("Blam!") eons before.

The archetypal gesture had been, as always, made by Duchamp

when he drew the mustache on a copy of the *Mona Lisa*, proving through that act and the shocked responses to it that the power ascribed to great works was transmitted to their reproductions, since his was perceived as an act of irreverent desecration, almost as if he had defaced the painting itself. Warhol stenciled *Mona Lisas* up and down a canvas (*Thirty Are Better than One*), as if to challenge the concept of uniqueness. Peter Saul reconstituted *Guernica*, treating its figures as if made of inner tubes or sausage casings. The basic impulses were iconoclastic. But iconoclasm acknowledges the power of images through its drive to destroy them. The interesting question facing the artists of the 1960s was where art was to go when the demolition itself had been achieved: what was art to be in the new historical era, now that it was widely felt that the old one, which stretched from Greco-Roman times to and through the art of the New York School, had reached its natural end. (This question remains to be answered today.)

Meanwhile, as the 1960s turned into the 1970s, a new wave of artists, some more aggressive and strident than others, expressed in various ways the attitude that the grip of "genius-type objects" on the consciousness of the art world was going to have to be loosened if art coming from different groups was to find its audiences and its appropriate aesthetics. Some of the critiques were intended to open art-world institutions up to those who felt themselves underrepresented there because of gender or race. And some were in defense of an art that repudiated those institutions altogether. Alternative spaces were sought for an alternative art somehow felt more suitable as the conduit of expression for the visions and voices of defiantly marginal creative artists. Sometimes these artists employed a visual rhetoric of coarseness and ephemerality, as if to repudiate the aesthetic values the masterpiece presupposed and celebrated, to the detriment, in their view, of a more liberal and socially conscious mission for art. Predictably, politically conservative critics responded by defending traditional aesthetics, and wrote acidulous and carping reviews of institutions that had opened grudging doors to the new impulses. A great many things fabricated in the name of art became what I have called "disturbational." Disturbational objects are intended to bruise sensibilities, to offend good taste, to jeer and sneer and trash the consciousness of viewers formed by the very values disturbation regards as oppressive. Its aim is to transform moral consciousness, not to gratify the sense of beauty that implies privilege and position and inequalities of every order. By contrast with the first wave—subtle, humorous, sly, urbane—the master-baiting of the second wave can become very rough indeed.

The paintings of Robert Colescott relate to masterpieces in both these ways, appropriationist and disturbatory at once, injuring two modes of liberal sensibility with one blow. Colescott's basic formula consists in substituting black for white faces and figures in paintings that any graduate of any liberal arts institution knows as well as he or she knows the various commercial labels appropriated by Pop artists in the sixties. Just as no one in our culture has to be told what Campbell's soup or Coca-Cola is, no educated person is ignorant of what Jan van Eyck's *Arnolfini Wedding Portrait* and Manet's *Déjeuner sur l'herbe* look like: these are among the works that one has to identify in final examinations in art history courses everywhere. Colescott has spoken of "putting blacks into art history." His way of achieving this is to repaint the history of art with blacks instead of whites in all the famous paintings, and giving the works titles often in the dialect of Uncle Remus.

His performance is rather of a piece with that by which Linda Nochlin reimagines Courbet's *Studio of the Artist* with a woman in the picture where Courbet portrayed himself. One could put women into the history of art by replacing all the male self-portraits with female ones. The difference would be this: Women are routinely given depictions of an exalted beauty from the Venuses of classical Greece through the nineteenth century. But Colescott uses the coarsest and most stereotyped depictions of blacks, with thick lips, rolling eyes and heavy teeth like rows of white corn. So he is not merely defacing through re-facing—which in effect is what Duchamp did. The re-faces are those of exaggerated caricatural negritude. And these are as immediately offensive to liberal sentiment as the racial epithets Lenny Bruce snarled at his audiences. It is this exploitation of stereotypes usually rejected as degrading that makes Colescott's work disturbatory. But just as one sets out to condemn them, one learns that Colescott is himself black, and one must abruptly begin to rethink the point and practice of art and the meaning of racial representation, and to recognize as an internal artistic fact, rather than an external unacknowledged truth, that almost all those men and women in the great art of the West are white.

I must defer to a more leisurely occasion a speculation on why the

275]

same kind of imagery should in one context be racist and vilifying while in another context be acceptable and possibly exalting. The imagery in Colescott's work is very raw and rough, but it is terribly humorous. Look at those grinning black faces wearing the heavy bonnets of Van Gogh's potato eaters in a work called *Eat Dem Taters*. Or at the black woman who has replaced Manet's white nude in *Déjeuner sur l'herbe*, her nakedness emphasized by the discarded brassiere and girdle in lurid pinks. Or the imposing but spectacled standing figure in *George Washington Carver Crossing the Delaware: Page from an American History Textbook*, where the black leader in Revolutionary War costume sails his floating minstrel show past ice floes: one man is barefoot, catching a fish; there is a smiling black man in chef's whites like the one from the Wheatena box; there is Aunt Jemima (whose face also appears as the woman's head in a takeoff on one of De Kooning's *Women*); a banjo picker; a drinker of corn likker; someone who looks like Marcus Garvey in a lodge uniform, folding Old Glory (where are the Gold Dust Twins?).

I have seen a video of Colescott explaining himself. He came up in a period of art when painting was pointing in a Minimalist direction. The whole history of art culminated in the single stripe on a painted field—and Barnett Newman had already *done* that! So art was over. There was no next place to aim for. And Colescott must have found enormously liberating the thought that it *was* over, and that one did not have to carry the history of art forward if one wanted to be an artist. From that point on he had a riotously good time making rowdy paintings, making fun of everyone, himself not excluded, fantasizing in public, making wonderful jokes at the expense of pure art. *Le Cubisme* looks like what its title requires until close examination dissolves its facets and rhythms into wedges of chocolate cake, living up to its funny subtitle "Chocolate Cakescape." *Hot Dawg!* really is a wall of hot dogs, but from a distance they look like the brushstrokes of an Impressionist painting. Hence the subtitle "An Impression."

Liberties of a rather different order are taken with masterpieces in the works of Russell Connor. Less ambiguous in his pursuit of visual fun than Colescott because less engaged in political concerns, Connor is equally anxious to reconnect with traditional painting when in a sense the only way to do so is to put it at a distance. This painter breaks masterpieces apart and reassembles them, as if the fragments had some

[276

elective affinity their original artists had been unable to perceive. The smoothly combined fragments then form a crazily coherent image in which the painting has something of the structure of the joke, according to Freudian theory. Thus a dancing couple from Renoir's *Dance in the City*, wrapped up in one another's presence, have waltzed out of their frame into a space left empty in Caillebotte's *Street in Paris, a Rainy Day*, where they are peered at from under parasols by Caillebotte's bourgeois *promeneurs*. (The painting is titled—of course—*Dancing in the Rain*.)

All the works are of this inspired order. Madame Récamier's familiar chaise longue is extended to form a gondola, at the opposite end of which David's Marat has passed out drunk—a nicer fate than being slain in his bathtub, as in the "original" work. Manet's little fife player, in his snappy red pantaloons, is the target of Manet's firing squad, on furlough from *The Execution of Emperor Maximilian* in a painting called *The Dawn of Modernism*. Perhaps Connor's own masterpiece in this genre is his delicious insinuation of the demoiselles d'Avignon where Rubens had painted fleshy women in *The Rape of the Daughters of Leucippus*. The demoiselles are now being snatched away by Rubens's horsemen in a painting called *The Kidnapping of Modern Art by the New Yorkers*, which puns on the title of an infuriating book by Serge Guilbaut: *How New York Stole the Idea of Modern Art*. (It is striking that the same "masterpieces" turn up in the work of both artists: Colescott has two paintings called *Les Demoiselles d'Alabama*. And where Colescott gives us Delacroix's *Liberty Leading the People* in blackface, Connor has Delacroix's revolutionaries crashing into Ingres's *Turkish Bath* in a painting titled *The Liberation of the Harem*.)

These are marvelous art-historical jokes, given a wry plausibility by cunning placement and masterly brushwork. And they register a serious point not commonly addressed. In a recent essay printed alongside Linda Nochlin's reimagination of Courbet, the art historian Michael Fried described what he termed "Courbet's 'Femininity.'" His thesis, as nearly as I can grasp it, is that Courbet's female nudes are posed as if they held brushes and palettes—as if they were artists, perhaps Courbet himself, who projected his own bodily postures onto his female subjects. It is an interesting observation, and I can imagine Connor taking one of Courbet's nudes out of one of Courbet's paintings and placing her before some other suitably appropriated Courbet canvas—perhaps the very painting that shows her, the result looking as if she were painting a self-portrait. Connor has, for example, taken Michelangelo's Jesus from *The Last Judgment* and placed him, like a conductor, in front of Degas's oboe player and his fellow musicians in the pit of the *Orchestra of the Opéra*. But while "Christ as Conductor" is a plausible reading of the deployed figure, it would be strange to write an article based on this perception and called "Michelangelo's Musicianship." The arrangement of the human figure in a painting is always underdetermined, and context can always alter our reading of it. Christ, with his raised arm in Giotto's Arena frescoes, looks the same, posturally, whether he is raising Lazarus, driving out the moneylenders or simply making a rabbinical point. The masters understood this perfectly. The art historian Edgar Wind published a fascinating paper which cites Sir Joshua Reynolds's discussion of how an ancient bacchante was borrowed by Baccio Bandinelli and used for one of the Marys in a *Descent from the Cross*. Exactly the same gestures that in one context express license and sexual abandon in another express what Reynolds describes as the "frantick agony of grief." Reynolds says, "The extremes of contrary passion are with very little variation expressed by the same action."

So Fried may be right about Courbet's femininity. But we need more than the evidence of the paintings to establish this. Connor's works are standing refutations of all possible interpretations based upon the reading of body language unsupported by other evidence. I am not at all certain that this is what Connor means to show, only that it is among the things that make his work possible. Thus he has Rembrandt's Aristotle contemplating the bust of Rembrandt's Bathsheba, who in turn is contemplating the bust of Homer. And contemplation, as Hitchcock proved in *Rear Window*, supports different ascriptions of motive depending upon the subject contemplated. Connor's Rembrandt's Aristotle becomes a dirty old man, even if he looks just like the Aristotle who, when contemplating the bust of Homer, must have been thinking out the *Poetics*.

—*The Nation*, May 22, 1989

The Whitney Biennial, 1989

IN THE WANING WEEKS of 1988, it was impossible to meet an art-worlder who was not burning to know what one thought about IT. IT could refer to nothing but the Sonnabend Gallery exhibition of recent works by Jeff Koons, a young and fiercely entrepreneurial artist who stood, it was reported, to gross $5 million if, as seemed likely, he were to sell out that show and two others exactly like it being held concurrently in Cologne and Chicago. A fair amount of critical boilerplate had been generated in response to Koons, all of it of the tiresome order that speaks of commodification, simulacreation and late capitalism—categories that apply, unfortunately, to so many things that it would be difficult to explain on their basis the peculiar *frisson* felt by those who attended this show. "A new low" is what Hilton Kramer of course wrote, but he writes in much the same way on just about everything ("depressing," "distressing," "appalling," "*sad!*"), and like a broken clock whose hands point always to the same black hour, is irrelevantly predictable and critically useless: you can always tell what time it *says* ("late!") but never what time it *is*. But even those who are immeasurably more responsive to the serious issues posed by contemporary art were airing a question that I thought long dead: is it (is IT) art? And it struck me that the one sure formula for artistic success in New York is to produce a body of work that causes those who think they have seen everything to wonder afresh whether some important boundary might not have been transgressed.

The boundary between art and non-art appeared to me sufficiently elastic that it could easily contain most of what I had seen up to then of Koons's work. The 1987 Whitney Biennial, for example, displayed a fish tank in which two basketballs were immersed and a somewhat prophetic stainless-steel replica of a plastic bunny. It was explained to me with great patience that it is exceedingly difficult to partially immerse basketballs as Koons had learned to do by consulting with engineers from MIT; I had read of a collector who, having purchased one of these works, was thrilled that Koons had agreed to install it himself. But neither this misapplied technical virtuosity nor the vapid steel bunnikin would be enough, in 1988, to arouse a vexed query as to their arthood. It was plain that something more powerful, more threatening, even, was drawing the glazed and jaded of the art world, almost against their aesthetic will, to Sonnabend's for a perverse flutter. In the *Republic*, Plato writes of Leontius, son of Aglion, who once glimpsed some corpses of executed men: "He felt a desire to see them, and also a dread and abhorrence of them; for a time he struggled and covered his eyes, but at length the desire got the better of him; and forcing them open, he ran up to the dead bodies, saying, 'Look, ye wretches, take your fill of the fair sight.' " This earliest discussion of what the ancients termed *akrasia*, or weakness of will, fit the common conflicted attitude of the art world to perfection in the case of Koons. I knew I was in for something morbid when, out of a pretended sense of critical duty, I paid my visit to "the fair sight." I found the things terrifying.

There is an order of imagery so far beyond the pale of good or even bad taste as to be aesthetically, and certainly artistically, disenfranchised. Objects that belong to it are too submerged even to be classed as kitsch, for kitsch believes itself to be the high taste it instead pathetically parodies. I am referring to such things as cute figurines in thruway gift shops; the plaster trophies one wins for knocking bottles over in cheap carnivals; marzipan mice; the dwarves and reindeer that appear at Christmastime on suburban lawns or the crèche figures before firehouses in Patchogue and Mastic; bath toys; porcelain or plastic saints; what goes into Easter baskets; ornaments in fishbowls; comic heads attached to bottle stoppers in home bars. Koons has claimed this imagery as his own, has taken over its colors, its cloying saccharinities, its gluey sentimentalities, its blank indifference to the existence and meaning of high art, and given it a monumentality that makes it flagrantly visible, a feast for appetites no one dreamt existed and which the art world hates itself for acknowledging. There was a figure of a man smiling with intolerable benignity at an armful of blue puppies that haunts me like a bad dream. The aggregation of rebarbative effigies at the Sonnabend Gallery was a vision of an aesthetic hell.

As it is the mission of the Whitney Biennial to display the leading artistic productions of the preceding two-year period, it was of course mandatory that this year's show should include a representative sample of Koons's latest work. There are three pieces: a porcelain girl, busty and lusty, smiling in rapture as she presses a Pink Panther toy to her bosom; a John the Baptist in a shaggy porcelain garment, smiling over a penguin and a piglet with gilded snout and trotters; and a stack of wooden barnyard animals in graduated sizes, with an immense simpering pig as anchor-brute. (Koons's figures are executed for him by Italian craftsmen.) You will certainly want to see these preternatural vulgarities, if only for the pleasure of clucking over the state of an art world that hath such creatures in it. But their effect is somewhat muted by the circumstance of being shown with other things. Part of the aesthetic terrorism of the Sonnabend show lay in the fact that nothing was there except Koonses, so one had the scary sense that his killer *chotchkes* had taken over the world. Each augmented the presence of each and amplified its incredibility. But at the Whitney, somehow, the objects have subsided into giant bric-a-brac, and this may be one of the costs of the necessary pluralism and the salon format imposed upon biennials, where Koons is just one among the main artists to have done something worth singling out over the past two years.

This year's Biennial is almost bland, as if the curators were anxious that the show not call attention to itself, and perhaps an effort always should be made to put some sort of critical distance between this exhibition and the art world it disinterestedly showcases. What was wrong with the terrible Biennial of 1985 was that it undertook to be part of the reality it was meant to represent, as the Whitney sought to make itself over into an annex of the East Village. This year's Biennial is a lesson in how to meditate upon work as virulent as Koons's while standing immune from its conceptual toxins. And yet, for perhaps this very reason, our experience at the Whitney of the same sort of objects which but a few months ago aroused such violent feelings in the gallery is very different. And this in turn makes vivid the ineradicable difference between the museum and the gallery as formats for experiencing art, even when the museum, as in the case of the Whitney, gets so close to the gallery format as to get burned, as happened in 1985. The Biennial can at best awaken memories of experiences it has no way of offering directly.

On the other hand, no Biennial can be a pure transparency, with no content other than that given by its displayed objects, taken in their individual identities. Even if the curators intended to make no statement of their own by means of the objects they selected and installed, there is no way in which some statement would not be implied, if only because the objects taken together define moods and feelings they might not possess by themselves. One experiences these exhibitions not simply as anthologies of what has been made and shown since the last time but to mark what changes there may be in the general sensibility of those as close to the art world as the Biennial curators of necessity must be. One uses the exhibition as a probe into the *spirit* of the present moment. And from this perspective the Koons pieces are more than samples drawn from a population of artworks: they are emblems of the spirit expressed in the Biennial, and help define the present state of things.

Consider from this perspective the porcelain girl with her radiant erotic smile, clutching her toy panther as if symbolically holding on to her childhood, and as if at a moment of intense play. The work is itself some kind of play; it also has play as its content. But the spirit of play *is* the spirit of this show, and the spirit of the times as well, as if the show has captured the times for us. The 1989 Biennial is a toyland for sophisticates.

There are, for example, two immense works by Chris Macdonald in roughly carved wood that look like pull toys for giant boys. Each is titled *Work Truck Variation*, and each would be a showstopper at FAO Schwartz. There is an enormous wall hanging by Mike Kelley called *More Love Hours than Can Ever Be Repaid*, whose primary component is stuffed toys stitched together. Like its companion piece, *Plush Kundalini and Chackra Set*, also made of stuffed toys, it would liven up any nursery if the parents had an interest in accelerating their offspring's taste for advanced art (and in the latter case for Tantric practices). Chris Burden suspends from fine wires 625 effigies of submarines in a work called *All the Submarines of the United States of America*, which is doubtless intended to make a statement about our naval might but which looks like a lavish mobile for an immensely privileged baby with hawkish (or dovish) parents. Robert Gober displays a playful play-

[*282*

pen (in the shape of an X), as well as a bassinet with a hand-painted flannel cushion. Ashley Bickerton's fabrications in tough plastic look like the sort of gear a graduating boy might want. Sherrie Levine is still appropriating away, but has given over rephotographing Walker Evans's sharecropper photographs and is showing instead frames from *Krazy Kat*—wonderful for the children's wall. And Donald Baechler shows some very large paintings that appropriate figures—of a little girl and of a tree, for example—that could be projected enlargements of drawings a child might have made. The abstract paintings of Cary Smith and of Andrew Spence have the squares of board games as motifs.

What could it mean that play, that references to childhood, should have become the dominating theme of this show, or perhaps even of the art world itself? And what might it mean for our general times if, as it is widely supposed, the artist is ahead of everyone else in sensing the imperatives of the historical moment? It may of course be but a passing thing, but it may also have a deeper significance. I, for example, could not forbear thinking of the way in which that great commentator Alexandre Kojève epitomized the powerful Hegelian concept of the end of history:

The end of human time, or History . . . means, quite simply, the cessation of action in the full sense of the term. Practically, this means the disappearance of wars and bloody revolutions. And also the disappearance of philosophy. . . . But all the rest can be preserved indefinitely: art, love, play, etc.: in short, everything that makes man *happy*.

So the atmosphere of play may itself be a metaphor of an end having been reached, as if this were the first posthistorical Biennial conscious of its being posthistorical.

Of course, I have sought to identify only the dominant metaphor of the show, and there is a great deal of work that does not fit this perhaps too convenient scheme. It does not apply to the paintings of Ross Bleckner, nor to those of April Gornik (though the latter have an enchanted, fairy-tale quality about them). Nor does it at all apply to the work of David Reed, which really does seek to situate itself in connection with the great history of painting, as if Reed were still driving forward a tradition that goes back to the Renaissance. Reed's work is conspicuously of the present moment, even if it does endorse the great pictorial intelligence transmitted to us by the masters. Yet even if we could not think of it being done at an earlier time, it executes the demands of pictorial space, though it rethinks each of its parameters. The dimensions of these paintings exaggerate horizontality or verticality, with the dominant dimension being three to four times that of the other dimension. The characteristic image is of some serpentine form, as if abstracted from the *figura serpentina* of Baroque or Mannerist art, coiling and uncoiling with a certain ferocity, and appearing to move out of the frame. The figures appear to be immersed in some transparent medium, smooth and thick and curiously at odds with their energy, leaving us unsure whether these are paintings or photographs. It is a mystery how the forms are made: sometimes it seems as if they have been extruded from a nozzle rather than painted. Reed inserts rectangles within rectangles, each containing an image that appears to comment on the main images, very much as if the works were contemporary versions of polyptychs, or as if the inserted rectangles were predella spaces. The colors are futuristic—colors that could not have existed before the invention of some very advanced polymer.

Nor am I certain where to fit into this picture the fact that very nearly half the artists selected express themselves in film or video. Since these use real time, one would have to devote a fair number of hours to see the 1989 Whitney Biennial in its artistic plenitude. I did, however, see a performance and film by Eleanor Antin. In the performance, Antin plays the role of Eleanora Antinovna, a black ballerina from the period of high Modernism in the Soviet Union, discoursing about her companion, the avant-garde film director Yevgeny Antinov, in whose film Eleanor-Eleanora plays the role of a ballerina. It is titled *The Last Night of Rasputin*, and it is a treasury of silent-film strategies and a terribly comical parody of an absolutely serious denunciation of the Romanovs by the imaginary director. In the performance part of the program, Eleanor-Eleanora looks like Koons's porcelain girl with her hair turned gray, who has traded in her Pink Panther for some of those fur foxes with their tails clamped in one another's mouths that one's Rumanian aunts used to imagine gave them an impermeable air of distinction.

Just around the corner from the video gallery are the rest rooms and the phone booths, in one of which a mock security system has been installed; in the video monitor we see people entering and leaving the Whitney. The work is by Julia Scher and is called *Security by Julia*,

IV. Its components are listed: "video cameras, black-and-white video monitors, video printer, time-lapse video recorders, and video switcher." I was disappointed that the list omits mention of the security guard, who is certainly part of the work, dressed in a lurid pink uniform that could have been designed by Koons and seated in a glass box next to the ticket person. It seemed somehow consistent with the overall theme of the show that a security guard should be part of the art, as if life and art had passed one another going in opposite directions. But I leave as an exercise for the reader the working-out of the details.

—*The Nation*, June 5, 1989

Warhol

IT IS POSSIBLE—I would argue that it is necessary—to explain the history of art through the past century as a collective investigation by artists into the philosophical nature of art. The significant art of this extraordinary period accordingly has to be assessed as much on grounds of speculative theory as on those of aesthetic discrimination. "Beginning with Van Gogh," Picasso said to Françoise Gilot, "however great we may be, we are all, in a measure, autodidacts—you might almost say primitive painters." It was as if each artist was at the beginning of a new era opened up by his own theories. Picasso had supposed that he and Braque had done something more important in Cubism than to have made some works of art: he believed they had created a style of art that would compose a new canon, sparing those who followed them the need to define the essence of art. For a time, neither of them even signed their works—one does not sign a theory—and when Cubism failed to bring back the sense of order, Picasso tried one thing after another, inventing whole art-historical periods that he alone occupied. I recall when Abstract Expressionism was deemed the new paradigm, destined to last for as long at least as the tradition which came to its end in Impressionism. It was the collapse of that faith with the advent of Pop, rather than the irreverence and brashness of Pop Art itself, that disillusioned so many artists in the early 1960s who believed that they knew what art was. Pop violated every component of their theory and somehow remained art. And so the quest went on.

"Art?" Warhol once asked in response to the inevitable question.

"Isn't that a man's name?" Well, suppose we think of the century as Art's heroic-comic quest for his own identity, his true self, as it were, and the artworks of the century as Art's discarded theories, which may have had coincidentally some redeeming aesthetic merit. (Art's peradventurous history would resemble that of his second cousin Geist, as comically narrated in Hegel's sidesplitting *Bildungsroman, Phäno-menologie des Geistes.*) That would mean that no artist could be taken seriously who did not, as part of whatever he or she made by way of negotiable works, play a role in Art's stumbling search. So the history of Art proceeds on two levels: as a sequence of objects and as a sequence of enfranchising theories for those objects.

The story has its high and low moments, but it would not be easy to tell, always, from an inspection of the objects alone, without reference to the theories through which they must be interpreted, whether they marked high moments or low. Thus the objects might be pretty unprepossessing and yet specify important stages in Art's coming to philosophical terms with himself. Few aesthetes would be stopped dead in their tracks by certain of Duchamp's blank ready-mades—his grooming comb, his snow shovel—but they are climactic moments in the epic. And few would expect from the crashing tautologies of the 1950s—"Painting is painting, the action of spreading paint"—the opulent glory of the Abstract Expressionist objects they so inadequately characterize. Clement Greenberg's identification of paintings with the flatness of their surfaces went perfectly well with the canonical works his theory championed (and in some cases generated). But except by denouncing as "not really art" everything that failed this austere and reductive definition, Greenberg was unable to characterize anything *except* the canonical work.

Bitter as the truth may be to those who dismissed him as a shallow opportunist and glamour fiend, the greatest contribution to this history was made by Andy Warhol, to my mind the nearest thing to a philosophical genius the history of art has produced. It was Warhol himself who revealed as merely accidental most of the things his predecessors supposed essential to art, and who carried the discussion as far as it could go without passing over into pure philosophy. He brought the history to an end by demonstrating that no visual criterion could serve the purpose of defining art, and hence that Art, confined to visual criteria, could not solve his personal problem through art making alone.

Warhol achieved this, I think, with the celebrated Brillo boxes he exhibited a quarter century ago at Eleanor Ward's Stable Gallery in New
York.

A great deal more was achieved through the Brillo boxes than this,
to be sure, but what was most striking about them was that they looked
sufficiently like their counterparts in supermarket stockrooms that the
differences between them could hardly be of a kind to explain why
they were art and their counterparts merely cheap containers for scouring pads. It was not necessary to fool anyone. It was altogether easy to
tell those boxes turned out by Warhol's Factory from those manufactured by whatever factory it was that turned out corrugated cardboard
cartons. Warhol did not himself make the boxes, nor did he paint them.
But when they were displayed, stacked up in the back room of the
gallery, two questions were inevitable: What was it in the history of art
that made this gesture not only possible at this time but inevitable?
And, closely connected with this: Why were *these* boxes art when their
originals were just boxes? With these two questions posed, a century
of deflected philosophical investigation came to an end, and artists
were liberated to enter the postphilosophical phase of Modernism free
from the obligation of self-scrutiny.

Warhol was, appropriately, the first to set foot in this free moral
space. There followed a period of giddy self-indulgence and absolute
pluralism in which pretty much anything went. In an interview in 1963,
Warhol said, "How can you say one style is better than another? You
ought to be able to be an Abstract Expressionist next week, or a Pop
artist, or a realist, without feeling you've given up something." Who
can fail to believe that, in art at least, the stage had been attained that
Marx forecast for history as a whole, in which we can "do one thing
today and another tomorrow, to hunt in the morning, fish in the afternoon, rear cattle in the evening, criticize after dinner, just as I have a
mind, without ever becoming hunter, fisherman, shepherd or critic."
Its social correlate was the Yellow Submarine of Warhol's silver-lined
loft, where one could be straight in the morning, gay in the afternoon,
a transsexual superstar in the evening and a polymorphic rock singer
after taking drugs.

It has at times been urged as an argument against Warhol's extreme originality that Duchamp did it before, inasmuch as there also
is little to distinguish one of his ready-mades from the mere object he
transfigured by appropriation. But it is the shallowest order of art crit-

icism to say that something has been done before. Two historical moments can resemble each other outwardly while being internally as different as the snow shovel that is a work of art is from one that is a mere tool for clearing sidewalks.

In the early days of Pop, artists were taking over images wherever they found them. Roy Lichtenstein was sued for using a diagram from a famous book on Cézanne. Warhol was sued by the photographer whose image he used and modified in his marvelous flower paintings of 1967. (And I think a suit was threatened by the artist, in fact an Abstract Expressionist, who designed the Brillo carton.) The flower paintings mark a later phase, but in the classic moment of Pop, it was essential to the enterprise that the images be so familiar that "stealing" them was impossible: they belonged to the iconography of everyday life, like the American flag, the dollar sign, the soup label, the before-and-after shots of transformed faces and physiques. These were wrenched out of their locus in the universal language of signs and given the power of art while retaining their own native power as symbols. Duchamp's objects were often arcane and chosen for their aesthetic blandness. Warhol's were chosen for their absolute familiarity and semiotic potency. It was not merely that Brillo pads were part of every household, as the Campbell's soup can was part of every kitchen—the one item likely to be found in the barest cupboard, by contrast, say, with a can of artichoke hearts or of pickled quail's eggs—but beyond that, the cardboard container was ubiquitous, disposable and part of Americans' itinerant mode of life. It was the container of choice for shipping and storing books, dishes, clothing, or for bringing kittens home in. It was what everyone threw away.

Duchamp's gestures of 1913–17 were jokes. They were evidence that Art had evolved to a point where Anti-Art was his own doppelgänger. As part of Dada, the ready-made was a kind of thumbed nose at the pretentiousness of art in the scheme of exalted values that just happened to be responsible for World War I. But artistically, really, it was a snigger from the margins. With Warhol, the gesture was mainstream: this was what Art had evolved into by 1964, when his search reached its end. Moreover, it was a celebration rather than a criticism of contemporary life, which is partly why Warhol was so instantly popular. Everyone had been saying how awful contemporary culture was, and here was the most advanced artist of the time saying it was really wonderful—saying, as Warhol in effect did, "Hey, I like it here."

Finally, it can be argued that the two moments of Duchamp and Warhol reverse the in any case arbitrary Marxian order—a farce the first time around, something deeper and more tragic the second.

There is a contingent of Brillo boxes at the great Warhol retrospective at the Museum of Modern Art, and it was a joy to see them again after so many years. But I could not help but reflect, as I stood for a moment in contemplation (Aristotle is shown contemplating the bust of Homer, but Danto . . .), how different it was to see them as part of an achieved corpus from what it had been to see them in 1964, when they defined the living edge of art history. I have the most vivid recollection of that show, and of the feeling of lightheartedness and delight people evinced as they marveled at the piles of boxes, laughing as they bought a few and carried them out in clear plastic bags. They didn't cost very much, and I believe it was part of Warhol's intention that it should be possible for people to own the art that so perfectly embodied the life it reflected: I bought one of the flower prints for $5 or $10 from a stack of them at Castelli's. (The opening-night crowd at the retrospective evidently felt moved by this intention when they sought to walk away with some of the silver pillows that decorated MoMA's ceiling, to the consternation of the museum guards.)

Fascinated as he was by money, it must have shocked Warhol that his work became so pricey: The thought of a painting of Coca-Cola bottles going for $1.43 million at auction is a real-life cartoon, something that would have aroused some mild amusement had it been drawn for *The New Yorker* twenty years ago. Warhol was fairly tight, as might be expected of a Depression child, but he was not, like Dali, avid for dollars ("Salvador Dali = Avida Dollars" was the famous anagram). Arne Ekstrom once told me that he commissioned some art made with hat forms from a number of artists, and afterward decided to purchase some of the works. One artist, quite famous, wanted $5,000, a lot of money at the time. Warhol said he could have his for 2 cents, which he raised to 3 cents because of the arithmetic involved in paying his dealer a commission. (He cashed the check.)

For many of us, the excitement of the current Warhol show is in part the memory of the excitement of seeing the artist's amazing career unfold from exhibit to exhibit through the 1960s and 1970s. In compensation, seeing it all spread before us, synchronically, as it were, one has available the priceless gift of retrospection, through which we can see where Warhol was heading—invisible, of course, until he got there.

Warhol

I particularly cherish, for example, the fascinating transitional pieces from the early 1960s, such as the Dick Tracy paintings, in which there is a powerful tension between style and subject. There are unmistakable comic-strip personages, down to the word balloons, but the hard commercial-style drawing wars with the Expressionist paint, as the commonplace imagery wars with the high romanticism of Expressionist art. Everyone is familiar with the story about Warhol showing Emile de Antonio two Coca-Cola bottles, one done in the flat laconic manner of the newspaper graphic, the other in the flamboyant brushy style, and asking which road he should follow when he had already, by presenting that choice, taken the road to Pop. Dick Tracy, like Warhol's Popeye or Nancy or Superman, belongs to that wonderful period of 1957–64, in which Art was putting aside his Romantic phase and entering his Minimalist-Conceptual-Philosophical phase. The Dick Tracy paintings belonged to a future no one could know about when they were shown, and experiencing them today is something like walking through one of those late Romanesque churches, like St. Severin in Paris—that church the Cubists so loved—built at a time when architects were evolving a still not well understood Gothic style.

There is a further compensation. At the opening I had a moment's conversation with a young critic, Deborah Solomon. She expressed the view that Warhol had peaked in the early 1960s, precisely in the Dick Tracy paintings and their peers. I responded that Warhol always peaked, but on reflection it occurred to me that she was privileged in a way I was not, to be able to see Dick Tracy as a painting rather than as a transitional document, and hence aesthetically rather than historically. This show gives us perhaps our first glimpse of Warhol as an artist, and for the first time a perspective on his work is opened up from the standpoint of the future, so that we can see it as we see, for example, the work of the Impressionists or the Sienese masters. The organizers of this exhibition are displaying Warhol as if he had already passed the test of time, as he must have to the sensibility of young people who address his work simply as work.

In truth, I am not certain that I know what it is to view Warhol's creations disinterestedly and from across an aesthetic distance. Nor do I know to what degree an artist so vehemently part of the consciousness of his own time can be detached from that consciousness and held up for critical scrutiny. Lately, art historians have been seeking to restore the Impressionists to their own temporal situation, as if they have so completely stood the test of time that we can no longer see the life to which they were responsive and are blind to the deep human content of their work. The question for me is to what degree it is even possible to see Warhol now in the tenseless light of pure art. And this raises the further question of whether, when there is no longer an audience that shares beforehand the images that compose these works from the 1960s, that is in effect a community *because* it shares those images as part of itself, there really will be much left of the power of the work.

What Warhol had not computed into his fifteen minutes of fame was the curatorial obligation to regard artworks as eternal objects, subject to a timeless delectation. Warhol enjoyed making "time capsules," sweeping up into cardboard cartons the ephemera and detritus of common life. But really, his whole output is a kind of time capsule precisely because of those features that set it apart from the impulses of Dada, especially the celebration of the commonplace. How will all this be perceived when the commonplace is no longer commonplace— when the Brillo people, as they are certain to do, change the design of the packaging? Suppose the old familiar Brillo cartons get to be collector's items and a market emerges for unopened cartons with their original scouring pads intact. Or that corrugated paper becomes a camp item in its own right, like Bakelite, the technology of packing having moved on to generalized bubble wraps with little stickers to identify content.

Warhol said, "The Pop artist did images that anybody walking down Broadway could recognize in a split second . . . all the great modern things that the Abstract Expressionists tried so hard not to notice at all." But privileging the commonplace depends upon its being ubiquitous, so that only an absolute stranger would not know what, if an image, it is an image of. All Warhol's images in the early works were of this order, and part of the pleasure of his art is in having these utterly banal forms lifted out of the plane of daily intercourse and elevated to the status of art, a kind of revolutionary reversal. The thought of the Brillo box in the art gallery connects with the American ideal of people in high places being still just folks (cf. Barbara Bush). But not only are these images instantly identified: they condense the whole emotional tone of life, of the consciousness in which those who know them participate. A person who has to have Marilyn—or Jackie or Elvis or Liz or Superman—identified is an outsider. Those faces belong with the Campbell's soup label, the S&H Green Stamps, or the

Mona Lisa, since everyone knows her. But what happens when there is not this split-second recognition? Was Troy Donahue really the kind of icon Marilyn Monroe was? One panics in front of one of Warhol's iterated portraits of a man nobody knows, thinking one should know him when he was in fact selected for his anonymity. And how many, really, recognize Ethel Scull on sight? I think eventually people competed to be portrayed by Warhol because that appeared to give them an instant immortality, of the sort usually enjoyed only by the greatest of stars or the most celebrated products, as if they were also part of the common consciousness of the time.

The work from the 1980s is less complex from this point of view. It really does become, more or less, just art, connected to the culture only through being done by Warhol, who had by then become as much an icon or superstar as anyone he ever portrayed. When his *Last Supper* was displayed in Milan, in a kind of citywide two-man show with Leonardo, 30,000 people flocked to see it, hardly any of whom went on to see the "other" *Last Supper*. Perhaps, then, these late works can be viewed, even now, merely as art. But Warhol's greatest works come from the time when the boundaries between art and life were being exploded, everything was being redrawn and we were all living in history instead of looking backward at what had been history. The late work escapes me, but here is a prediction: When the final multivolume *Popular History of Art* is published, ours will be the Age of Warhol— an unlikely giant, but a giant nonetheless.

—*The Nation*, April 3, 1989

REFLECTIONS

Bad Aesthetic Times

THERE IS AN uneasy consensus in the art world today that we are living through what one of its writers, the critic Elizabeth Frank, has called "bad aesthetic times." "Just sort of an uninteresting moment," Roy Lichtenstein said in a recent interview. "There's a lot of style, but there doesn't seem to be much substance. The eighties don't seem to have a soul, do they? . . . And the seventies seem a kind of nonentity. I don't even know what to think of the seventies; I don't know what happened." The irony is that these feelings arise against a background in which, in every other way, the times are very good for art: there are more art magazines; more interest than ever before in what artists are doing; more galleries and more museums; incredible prices at auctions even for living artists; more art schools turning out more artists who see art as a viable profession like dentistry or accounting; more money all round. And yet, while the engines of the art world turn furiously, the output has been aesthetically stalled for two decades, and if there is any direction to speak of, it is that of bad aesthetics: the badness of the times seems not merely that so little by way of forward aesthetic drive is to be discerned but that so much spectacularly bad painting seems to crowd the exhibition spaces of the world.

I have heard a good many artists speak with gloom of a *"fin de siècle* feeling" having settled over the world, and James Ivory in fact has made a somewhat apocalyptic film about the East Village art scene of the day before yesterday which seeks to project "a feeling about the end of the twentieth century . . . a world crashing down, evanescing before our eyes." Leave it to the narcissism of the art world to see in its own *malheurs* the enactment of the whole drama of history, when in truth one would think there will be dancing in the streets when this vile century ends. And in any case *"fin de siècle"* designates what we also refer to as the Gay Nineties or the Belle Epoque, a period anything but gloomy, a wonderful age whose styles connoted youth (Jugendstil) or newness (Art Nouveau) and the sense of a fresh era of absolute modernity in morality, values, expression and forms of life. For me the emblematic work of the *fin de siècle* spirit is Pierre Bonnard's poster of 1891, *France-Champagne*, which shows a tipsy girl, awash in froth, the bubbles welling up from her tilted glass like the waves in a Japanese print, covering her just in time, for her shoulder strap has slipped dangerously down—and the lettering lurches across the sheet as if not able to walk a straight line. It unites the most advanced art of its time with a frankly commercial function; and it exploits by deliberately disregarding the boundaries between art and decoration. It belonged to a marvelous decade, artistically fierce in energy, bounded on the one side by Van Gogh and Gauguin, whose own work is penetrated by the same visions, and on the other, in the early years of the twentieth century, by Cubism and the Fauves and the great Himalayas of twentieth-century art beyond. No one, I think, feels in the art world today that our nineties are going to be gay or that the century before us will have the same thrilling artistic history many of us have lived through. No one really expects the twenty-first century to shoot out of the neck of the twentieth like a champagne cork!

Now, in some measure the bad aesthetics of bad aesthetic times can be regarded as politically significant, largely because *good* aesthetics is sometimes regarded as politically oppressive. Part of the message in that singular panel on masterpieces I discuss below in "Masterpiece and the Museum" is that the very idea of a masterpiece goes with a form of privilege and elitism that has the political consequence of excluding women and minority artists by imposing upon them an alien imperative—namely, to be a "great artist"—when this concept but exalts forms that define white male domination. Rather, in the name of a certain kind of liberation, one must shun the propensity to define art in terms of what one group of feminist aesthetic activists disparages as "genius-type objects." And "good aesthetics" may be part of the apparatus of privilege disguised as a standard of taste. A certain amount of feminist art theory is of this form. In her famous essay "Why Are There No Great Women Artists?" Linda Nochlin seems to imply that the question itself is insidious, when there may after all be a good many great women artists were greatness to be defined in terms of an ideal appropriate to women and not one that persistently refuses to acknowledge the artistic otherness of women. There *is*, as she puts it, "no language of form" for women artists, who have been obliged to paint against the grain of their true artistic essence by the dominating "Myth of the Great Artist" and against criteria that embody "the unstated domination of white male subjectivity." So what we have been taught as good and even great art—the very premise of the museum as it has been formed in modern times—is truly "male subjectivity" given a false objectivity but a real institutional authority, one designed to keep women in their place and out of the place of art. It is almost a confirmation of this radical view that politically conservative critics, like the writers for *The New Criterion*, tirelessly insist upon aesthetic qualities, inevitably insinuating a connection between their political views and their artistic intolerances, as diagnosed by Nochlin and a good many others. So the badness of bad aesthetic times could, under certain interpretations, mean *good* political times, when the museum and the gallery and the language of art criticism and even the nature of the philosophy of art are being reshaped by powerful underground forces for good.

Now, a fair proportion of Postmodern art certainly draws an inspiration from feminist art and the art criticism it advances, and much of this falls under a category I have termed "disturbatory art." This is art that does not just have disturbing contents, for a lot of traditional male (if you insist) art and even some of its masterpieces are filled with disturbing content: very few can have seen Titian's terrifying *Flaying of Marsyas* when it visited the National Gallery some seasons back and slept peacefully afterward. Disturbatory art is intended, rather, to modify, through experiencing it, the mentality of those who do experience it. This is not art one is intended to view across an aesthetic distance that serves as an insulating barrier (admittedly a barrier that is all but dissolved by a work such as Titian's), but art intended instead to modify the consciousness and even change the lives of its "viewers." The paintings of Robert Colescott might be a case in point. Colescott appropriates, often, acknowledged masterpieces of the Western canon: the *Arnolfini Wedding Portrait*, *The Potato Eaters*, even *Washington Crossing the Delaware*, but replaces white faces with blackface, depicting the figures with the thick lips, rolling eyes, heavy teeth of white culture's cartoons of the black physiognomy. He surrounds his figures with the appurtenances of stereotyped black life (banjos) and sometimes changes the titles (*Eat Dem Taters*). It is shocking in our era to see these, and difficult not to feel that great art is being desecrated to some gross racist end—and then one discovers that Colescott himself is black, and that our good liberal sensibilities have been bruised deliberately. That is the mark of disturbatory art, and it is not surprising that a good bit of the task of disturbation has been taken up by performance artists, where the connection between artist and audience is immediate and in a way direct.

Performance art has a distant relationship to drama, but to drama in its most archaic stage, where the gap between audience and actor is obliterated by the hoped-for ingression into the ritual space of the performance by a real god. The performance is undertaken in the hope of this order of miracle, and as a way of invoking a divine epiphany; and when it occurs, everyone is transfigured onto a new level of identity and becomes a new being, in a new order of social being, where old distinctions are overcome and old roles discarded and everyone is bonded by a new communitarian feeling analogous to love. This is a very tall order, no doubt, but a lot of performance theory rests upon hardly less exalted premises of moral hope. To be a feminist, after all, is not just to want to paint some pictures that will get accepted and get you accepted as a woman artist: it is to want to change the world in ways that matter to you most, politically and in ways we hardly can imagine from where we are now.

My concept of disturbation is derived from its natural English rhyme, where images have physical consequences—fantasies are transformed into orgasms and hence into feelings of release and peace (when not infected by guilt). Disturbation exploits artistic means to social and moral change, and it is often part of its strategy that the performance artist, when a feminist, vests herself with attributes opposed to commonplace notions of femininity: her art is funky, aggressive, confrontational, flagrant, shocking, daring, extreme and meant to be sensed as dangerous: she uses frontal nudity, blood, menstrual fluids and the like almost magically, as if seeking to connect the artist with the earliest forms of artistic magic as practiced by shamans and wonder-workers and personages possessed by higher powers. And it can be pretty scary. But it also makes clear why traditional aesthetic categories will not apply to it. It is not meant to be beautiful, symmetrical, composed, tasteful, let alone pretty or elegant or perfect. It is everything that a painting by Matisse, for example, is not. So it counts in its favor that it should be ugly, disordered, distorted and offensive: tacky, gross and raucous, jeering, painful, threatening. But it is also meant to be re-demptive, finally hopeful, politically sublime. To attempt to apply the standard aesthetic categories, then, really does look like a form of male sensibility in that it will only be by injuring those sensibilities that the art can do its work. If it works, of course, something extraordinary will have been achieved. But often it fails, and collapses into something merely embarrassing—boring and silly and awful. Nonetheless, its concept of success has ancient roots and an undeniable if pathetic grandeur.

Since I have ventured a parallel between Postmodernism and the birth of tragedy, as imaginatively re-created in the writings of Nietzsche, we might venture to draw a further one between feminist Postmodern attitudes in the late 1980s and those of Post-Impressionist attitudes in the late 1880s. Let me suggest that the feminist artist is encouraged to identify herself with certain exceedingly primitivistic artistic postures, using herself, often, as the medium and vehicle of her art, employing feathers and body paint, even, drawing, like Carolee Schneeman, a text she held concealed in her vagina—as if giving birth to art. She is like a priestess or a sorceress, and aspires to a powerful relationship to her audience. Polemically, she repudiates a tradition of aesthetically defined fine art widely institutionalized in our culture. Both by repudiating her tradition and by seeking to draw her energy from a different one, she undoubtedly sets up some analogies with what was achieved by Gauguin and Van Gogh a century before her. And just as she in a way sacrifices herself to these higher ends, it is possible to see Van Gogh and Gauguin as sacrificing themselves so that a kind of renewal can take place. Both those artists felt that the academicized tradition, in which one seeks to replicate the appearances of the visual world with their equivalents, was worn out, and with this the whole artistic tradition of the West which culminated in the artistic experiments with color of the Impressionists, and especially Monet. *Their* own views of form and color were opposed to that, much as, politically, they idealized certain forms of social relationships that had little to do with the confining institutions of artistic preferment in France. They chose colors for emotional significance, they redefined forms through simplification and space through flattening, and aspired to a visual interest inconsistent with the convention of the metaphysically transparent surface of the illusionist art of their past. And, predictably, both turned to other cultures for inspiration, to Japan in the first instance and, in the case of Gauguin, to various primitivisms, from which he drew his ideas of organizing canvases not along sensory but along what he termed "cerebral" lines. Equally predictably, both were held inept, incapable of painting, or even, in the case of Gauguin (possibly with some substance), of charlatanry. There are legends of women fainting at Gauguin's exhibitions and pregnant women warned not to attend them. But both rethought the logic of the visual arts, and began what we think of as Modernism. And the question is whether, exactly a century later, we stand at the beginning of a new era whose pioneers are the feminist artists who repudiate a tradition that, from a long perspective, we can now see that Van Gogh and Gauguin really were continuing rather than disrupting. Their art looked aesthetically bad to the point of outrage in its day, except to a few enthusiasts. And now it looks not only aesthetically continuous with what preceded it but is the very paradigm we now use to teach the meaning of *good* aesthetics. Will that happen again? Will museum visitors a hundred years from now see the beauty in today's shocking work? Will Colescott sell for whatever is the equivalent of $53 million a hundred years hence?

The answer, I think, must be no if these are really disturbatory works. You cannot politically defy the institutions when all you really wanted was to be clasped to their bosoms and hope in time to be cherished under the very framework of values you are thinking of overcoming. That would be co-optation, revolution only in the sense of a circulation of elites rather than the extirpation of the very impulses of elitism. The transformation of consciousness and of social reality at which this art aims requires that the work be perceived as flagrant and as aesthetically bad for as long as we persist in applying the criteria of aesthetic goodness, those criteria that partially define the system explained as patriarchal and dominated by an alleged male sensibility, those criteria that want women to be aesthetically good, as a way of keeping them on a pedestal and away from the seats of power. The injunction is to sneer at genius, mock the masterpiece, giggle at aesthetic values—and to try to begin a new history, nonexploitative, in which art is put to some end more immediately human and important than to hang in the museum, ornament the brilliant collection, draw gasps in the dramatic auction space and be interred in the graphic tomb of the expensive art book and the real tomb of the Japanese bank vault. The charge is to end one form of history and to begin another one. And this attitude is not just in the art world: it has its cognates in connection with humanities courses and great books courses and curricular canons everywhere.

On the other hand, an awful lot of what was introduced in a kind of anti-establishment spirit has—such is the irony of things—found its way into the highest precincts of contemporary high art, as if co-optation were irresistible, and the art world, like the commercial world, feeds and flourishes on what was intended to call it in question and even overthrow it. I want to cite two examples. The first is the work of Frank Stella. As I wrote when reviewing his extraordinary exhibition at the Museum of Modern Art (see above, essay 20): "The first word that entered my mind when I initially saw these pieces was 'feminist.' " And I could not refrain from comparing that view of Minimalist and exemplary purity for which Stella's work stood, as a monument of aesthetic rectitude, with precisely the impulses of feminist Postmodern art I have been describing here.

So here is a mainstream artist, if ever there was one, appropriating these forms, laundering them clean of the political energy they were intended to carry, impressing them into the services of high art and enslaving them to the very practices they were intended to help over-throw. The very absence of a "life of forms for women" to which these forms were supposed to testify proves instead to have been the life of forms after all to which women were held unsuited. And this is per-ceived as a defeat rather than a vindication of the movement against those values, for just the same reason I have been given by women theoreticians opposed to exhibitions such as one I saw in Cincinnati entitled Women Enter the Mainstream. The thing was not to enter the mainstream but to dry it up.

My second example comes from an exhibition that created con-siderable discussion in New York in December 1988, that of Jeff Koons at the Sonnabend Gallery. Foreseeably, it was stigmatized as a "new low" by the *New Criterion* editorialist, and foreseeably as well, it was thought to confirm some murky thesis about commodification by any number of leftist art writers. I, on the other hand, found it terrifying. It consisted of immensely enlarged effigies in the colors and forms of those souvenirs to be found in airports and gift shops everywhere in the land. There was no theory capable of cutting these down to size, and one of the works, Michael Jackson in whiteface, was like the mirror image of something by Robert Colescott. This was disturbatory art on the highest gallery level. The art world itself was shocked into asking the question I had not thought to hear from sophisticates ever again: "But is it art?" And that something should at once be disturbatory and gross $5 million seemed to me the absolute height of artistic co-optation, and perhaps a sign that the revolution has succeeded spectacularly through failure.

And with this cunning reversal, we are back to the serious issue of bad aesthetic times, for it is not ideologized bad aesthetics that those who say we are living in bad times have in mind: it is precisely in those who exemplify the establishment, and who seem almost to draw upon their opponents for artistic substance. It is in the enclaves of high art today that the times seem aesthetically bad, not only in the sense that an awful lot of high art seems flagrantly bad, aesthetically, but in the sense that something deeper has happened as well—namely, that none of this appropriation can conceal the fact that there is a central emptiness, and that the times are bad because the art is stalled. It is as if there is no life of forms today for anyone, male or female, black or white, but only the outward semblance of one. When Lichtenstein says that today there is a lot of style but no substance, he has in mind those who are the official front artists of the moment, not the dispossessed and expropriated. These are the ones who are supposed to stand in that great line of revolutionizing artists from Van Gogh and Gauguin through Picasso and Matisse to Pollock and De Kooning. And everyone knows they are not, and it is this, rather than outward disagreeableness, that seems to underlie the *fin de siècle* feeling. They could be outwardly agreeable and these be bad *artistic* times. And the question, I suppose, is if bad aesthetic times and bad artistic times are two sides of the same coin, or if these might be bad artistic times even if good aesthetic ones. Let me turn, then, to the beginning of this awful decade and put things in partial perspective.

The art historian Michael Baxandall begins his remarkable book, *Patterns of Intention*, which is concerned with the historical explanation of works of art, with an example from the history of engineering. People do not build bridges on speculation, but are commissioned to do so, and the bridges take the shape they show in part from what the engineer is charged to do—to span a certain expanse—and then in part from the constraints imposed by the environment, the state of technology and the like. It is in terms of the *charge* and the *brief* to Benjamin Baker, who designed the Firth Bridge, that Baxandall explains the principles of bridge building and Baker's responses to these. He then applies this model to Picasso's Cubist portrait of Henri David Kahnweiler, the assumption being again that painters would not have painted so complex a portrait on speculation, but in response to a certain charge and in terms of a certain brief worked out between the artist and the patron. I think this is a fairly fortunate pattern to use in seeking to explain the emergence of the paradigmatic paintings of the early 1980s, the works of Julian Schnabel and David Salle, which literally burst upon the art scene early in the decade. They were, of course, not commissioned to make these paintings—it would, so to speak, be part of the brief that the artist *not* be commissioned but that the work emerge spontaneously from the furnaces of creativity and the urgency of expression presumed in the prevailing psychology of creative art. Nor, strictly, was there a person or set of persons who served at once as patron and as theoretician and critic of the new body of work: no one like Kahnweiler, who wanted the kind of visual interest in a work to which Cubism was partially a response. There was no interesting body of theory and criticism for these painters: or critics responded with a certain kind of critical boilerplate, extending to the new works forms of critical appreciation and social appraisal that were merely in the public domain, using a vocabulary and syntax that Anycritic would be able to use for Anywork. Even so, there was a charge in the air, and it was the genius of these artists to detect it and to respond with precisely the kinds of works those who issued the charge— the collectors and dealers of an art world itself only beginning to take shape within the matrix of an older art world—wanted, even if they did not know they wanted precisely that. Perhaps no one realized what the charge was *until* it was met.

The charge, I think, was this: Get art history back on track. We had grown used in this century to the idea that the history of art was to be a sequence of revolutionary breakthroughs, that art, and especially painting-and-sculpture, was to be a *perpetual* revolution. The most conspicuous moments in the history were, perhaps, Cubism and Abstraction, though the century of breakthrough began earlier with Van

Gogh and Gauguin or perhaps even with Manet, and it went on to include the great works of the New York School and then Pop and Minimalism—and then it stopped. It stopped perhaps in the mid-sixties, just when there was a greater and greater interest in keeping up with a history one expected to see being made and remade in season after season of spectacular plastic invention. There were the art magazines, the newly salient cultural journalism of the major newspapers, the educational divisions of the major museums, the emergence of increasing numbers of minor museums. And a greater and greater interest on the part of a larger and larger public to keep informed. And all this at a moment when, ironically, there was nothing to report. A decade passed with no art news to speak of: and the readiness to accept a certain pluralism was a tacit confession that there was no direction to speak of. Hence Lichtenstein's puzzlement with the seventies. All that demand and no supply, or rather the wrong kind of supply—namely, an art for what the French call *amateurs*—lovers of abstractions, for example, who were building up small, tasteful, distinguished collections. So the charge was out: Get history back on track! And it was this that our artists grasped: The world did not want refinements on known things. It wanted the new thing it seemed we had the right to expect.

The brief was this: The new thing had to look important. Scale was essential—no one wanted paintings-to-hang-over-the-mantel-piece. It had to look mysterious enough to demand interpretation. So the artists juxtaposed images that related to one another only through some external interpretation the viewer had learned was expected of him, with hints from the critics. But juxtaposition demands images, for juxtaposed abstractions just look like abstractions. Imagery, mysteriousness, size figure in the brief. So does experiment. The works of Schnabel and Salle are not really experimental, but they contain the received language of experiment: mixed media, melded genres. Schnabel's smashed crockery, Salle's stuck-on chairs and his Postmodern references to art history fill the prescription to perfection. And finally they have to be controversial, assured especially in Salle's case by the near-pornography of his images at just the moment when feminist consciousness was intense above all in the art world. Because the brief included importance as a component, the work could not begin as obscure, or small: it had to be there all at once, so to speak, made to order for the museum or the great collection. The word had to go out that art history had begun again, that saviors were born on West Broadway—and all the Wise Men of the art world converged on Soho, bearing checks. The Age of Importance had begun. There has never, I am certain, been a period in which works of art, of vast dimension and seeming ambition, have been produced in such overwhelming numbers as in the decade that followed. By ordinary indices, ours should be read as one of the great moments of artistic flowering. The irony is that all that canvas and all that paint is what everyone has in mind by Bad Aesthetic Times!

Now, in truth, it was not Schnabel and Salle alone who read the charge and understood the brief. The call was out all over the world, wherever art was being made. It was heard with great clarity in Germany and in Italy: an indicative exhibition of absolutely awful Italian art opened at the Guggenheim early in the decade, which closes, nearly, with an unspeakable exhibition of German Importance Art. No doubt it required talent of a certain sort to produce Importance Art. The movement received few adherents in England or in France, for example, though through the influence of the art magazines, it was responded to throughout the Third World and even in Socialist countries. Alois Riegel, the great art historian, produced a famous and fiercely difficult book titled *Der Spätrömische Kunstindustrie* (*The Late Roman Art Industry*). I am speaking of what we might then call the Late American Art Industry, where industrial-strength artworks are being produced in competition, perhaps, with other such industrial centers, preeminently in Germany.

Baxandall concludes his beautiful book *Painting and Experience in Fifteenth Century Italy* with this sentence: "The forms and styles of painting respond to social circumstances." He meant the circumstances defined by those who respond to, admire and discuss the works in question, and he felt justified in adding this corollary: "The forms and styles of painting may sharpen our perception of the society." And this would be as true for the sparsely documented artistic society of the fifteenth century as for the more amply documented society which consumes the industrial product of our own art industry, and specifically the society that issued the charge so powerfully responded to, and whose values and attitudes defined the brief for Importance Art. These were collectors and dealers, primarily, who had been too young or too imperceptive to buy into the great art of but a few years before, priced now out of sight—or what, for the time, seemed out of sight. What they were hoping was that there should be an opportunity to get in on the ground floor of something as important as what had been missed. That is why the art had to look historically new and artistically important—why it had, so to speak, to wear its importance on its sleeve. The artists of the seventies worked on into the eighties for their *amateurs*, but this, even if aesthetically good, did not have the look of importance or newness that went with the sense that a new moment of art history had been entered. The new work was, by mandated brief, of masterpiece dimension, and had to look as if produced by genius breaking through. Part of the overall awfulness was due to the work having the sensibility of graduate art students—work so exactly of the order that graduate art students produce that those still in art school may see in the galleries a mirror of what they produce in their own studios, and thus are likely to see no reason why any period of trial or apprenticeship is required between art school and the professional artistic life. But I am not concerned with the sociology of aesthetics so much as with the narrative premise of this being the ground floor of a historically important movement—the next thing everyone was waiting for. I do not believe it was the historically next thing or that there in fact can be a historical next thing. I have argued that the era of revolutionary breakthrough was over with: the "life of forms" that defines the history of modern art has come to an end. *That* kind of history is over with and done.

In truth, these works have been but anthologies of avant-garde strategies, which admittedly only shows at best that they are not the next new thing, not the stronger thing, that there can be no next new thing. But these works participate in the one defining trait of the age, which is to try to live historically forward while in fact referring historically backward. This is a trait we find in the various Posts and Neos that make up so much of the surface excitement of the era. And the interesting and irresistible question is whether this is but a marking of time before a hole opens up in the wall of the future or whether, which is the view I would want to hold, art has reached historical closure just when the will to drive it forward is at its most intense. One difference between the art world of fifteenth-century Italy and twentieth-century New York is that we esteem art against a model of history that hardly had begun to emerge in that earlier era. And what if history itself will not support the model we require for Importance Art to be—important?

For the past few years I have been speculating about the structures of art's history, and considering the hypothesis—it can be no more than that—that those structures imply an end that may have been reached. This sort of thing can happen, I suppose. It certainly happened in ancient times with tragedy. Aristotle wrote:

Arising from an improvisatory beginning . . . tragedy grew little by little, as the poets developed whatever new part of it had appeared; and passing through many changes, tragedy came to a halt, since it had attained its own nature.

The comic poet Aristophanes registered a deeper desperation in *The Frogs* that Athens no longer had a tragic poet, and imagined a god taking on the mission of dragging one back from the underworld to save the staggering state. Vasari supposed that painting had attained "its own nature" in his own times, and his history was meant to show the development that had led up to a climax which he did not see as a crisis, thinking there would be other things for art to do than seek its own nature. And in a sense painting was able to continue a developmental history after Vasari only by redefining its own nature—and the interesting thought for me is whether we have really reached the end of redefinition itself, a progress that accelerated so in this strange century. And so no more breakthroughs? Let me hasten to add that these are bad philosophical times as well as bad aesthetic ones, and that there are several who have proclaimed the end of philosophy itself. I feel that philosophy has not ended so much as that it has stopped, whereas I offer the view that though art has not stopped it has ended.

Suppose anything like this is true: what then would it mean to be an artist in this posthistorical period?

I offer one model, this taken less from art than from art writing, and I refer once more to Professor Nochlin. In a recent catalogue essay on Courbet's stupendous masterpiece, *The Studio of the Artist*, she describes the history of interpretation of this dense and defiantly provocative work. Nochlin is a very deep scholar of the Realist movement in art, and especially of Courbet, on whom she is authoritative and profound. From her narrative it appears clear that the scholarship on this great work is all in, and that there is nothing left, really, for scholars to do: all the main questions about the painting have been answered. True, it is theoretically possible that some fresh evidence may turn up to change what we believe we know, but this is almost a ritual invocation of epistemological uncertainty. Let us suppose that scholarship, using Aristotle's phrase once again, has attained its own nature in the truth of historical knowledge. She now feels somehow excluded from this work, as, as a scholar, she certainly is. And at this point Nochlin does something quite surprising. She decided to "write as a woman" and she offers a playful feminist account of the work in terms of imagined reversals—nude nameless male models instead of nude nameless female ones; a woman artist at the focus of the work instead of the male one, wearing a striped skirt instead of the snappy striped pants Courbet shows himself in. It is a world in which women and men have interchanged positions of power (this leaves the structures of power intact, of course). This is not an interpretation grounded in history, but a political fantasy which she greatly enjoys constructing—after which she returns to history, and ends her wonderful essay, which the "writing as a woman" interrupted almost like a dream.

Now, there is no question but that Courbet's painting does not have its meaning exhausted when we have, as it were, all the facts that art history is capable of nailing down. There is a certain inexpungible mysteriousness about the painting which is not a cognitive mysteriousness, capable of removal through a factual answer. It is a mysteriousness irremovable from the great artistic works. And much as Wittgenstein says that all the deep problems remain when we know all the scientific answers (since the deep question concerns the fact that there is a world at all and not the way the world is), this penumbra of unanswerability defines what it means for art to be great. There may be nothing further for art history to explain, and yet everything important remains to be grasped, even if it cannot be said.

But this is not what "writing as a woman" means, I think, to stress. Nochlin's impulse answers to a distinction made by the French thinker to whom so much of Postmodernism owes its structure, such as it is. Roland Barthes drew attention to two forms of reading: "reading as a reader" and "reading as a writer." Reading as a reader is the kind of reading we ordinarily do, getting out of the text what the writer put there, aiming at a kind of textual truth. But reading as a writer involves re-creating the text in conformity with our own agendas. And here authorial intention or causal explanation carries no great weight: we can read the *Meditations* of Descartes as if we were Plato or Attila the Hun, and play with the signifiers at our pleasure. "Writing as a woman" meant "reading the painting" with a certain feminist agenda in mind, not being intimidated by the facts—as if there were, for a woman, no "life of facts" at all. It is with reference to the second sort of reading that it is possible to say, of any given text, that infinite interpretations are possible. And perhaps infinite truth as well, providing we erect alongside good old historical truth a second sense of truth that connects with this second kind of writing or reading.

Writing as . . . or reading as . . . or interpreting as . . . dissociates these acts from the world's constraints. The "as" is not an "is." But it is even so worth contrasting Nochlin's essay with another one in that same catalogue by Michael Fried, who also claims, though a man, to "write as a woman." In an essay entitled "Courbet's Femininity" he offers a reading of certain female nudes by that artist as if they were self-portraits. He draws attention to the position of the hands, and in truth we can see them as if holding a palette and brushes. It is as if the artist portrayed himself as a nude woman. I have no idea whether we ever could know that Fried's interpretation was true, though it is not difficult to think of evidence that might count toward or against it. It is, in any case, a fact or not a fact that Courbet so identified with his female model that he projected onto the deployment of her limbs his own gestures in depicting her. And this is a real hypothesis: it does not interrupt so much as continue the possibilities of scholarship, as if Nochlin had said too soon that all that there was to say had been said. And in Fried's case, "writing as a woman" means: thinking oneself into what it would be for a man who identified with women to paint, an imaginative vicarious understanding that opens up interpretative possibilities. Nochlin is not doing that at all. She has no hypothesis to offer, but gives an example of one way of responding when the time for hypothesis is past. One can still, she seems to say, have a vital re-lationship forever by writing as . . . reading as . . . interpreting as . . .

It is also possible to paint as a woman . . . or as a black . . . or as anything one chooses. It is instructive to see how Nochlin and Colescott together use the Old Masters to their own ends, each in her or his own way. How interesting, as well, if painting as . . . should be one way of adjusting to the end of art, that the difference between the marginal and the official disappear. Seen in terms of play, Schnabel, with his carnivalism, his showmanship, his flagrant bad taste, is a marvelous example of someone painting outside history, using whatever he needs for the purposes of masquerade. But he owes his standing, and this is the irony of the present moment in art, to the belief that he is locked in history and carrying it forward to the next stage. But once this irony is grasped, there is no historical need or urgency to persist with the awful sorts of paintings we have been forced to endure. With so many roles to play with, so many ways to choose, so absolute a posthistorical freedom, why not good aesthetics for a change? Beauty, after all, knows nothing about history. We will forgive a great deal in the name of historical urgency, but when the urgency abates, there need no longer be anything to forgive.

—*Modern Painters*, Summer 1989

Masterpiece and
the Museum

NOT LONG AGO I participated in a symposium on the concept of the masterpiece at a major East Coast museum, which sponsored it because it felt it would be an extremely useful thing for it to know what a masterpiece was. The other panelists were art historians or curators, and each was far more directly engaged with works of art than I, as a philosopher, could ever be: I accepted the invitation because I thought it would be interesting to think about the concept, the practical implications of which I hoped to learn more about from colleagues who had to make decisions as to which works of art were masterpieces, and to justify those decisions to other scholars or to boards of trustees. What astonished me as talk followed talk that day was the clear reluctance of any of them to address the topic we had been summoned to clarify. Each of them spoke of the overall degradation of the term "masterpiece" in contemporary usage, and each had a witty slide or two to establish this fact, usually from an advertisement for a prestigious automobile or a luxurious hotel, where the reader was urged to "drive a masterpiece" or even to "spend a weekend with a masterpiece." There can be little doubt that an antecedent connotation of supremacy has been appropriated by the advertisement industry to glamorize by association with high art mere items of price and opulence. But we all use the term rather casually in this way, almost like "work of art" itself, to praise a soufflé or a salad, or a business letter or even an advertising jingle. Still, enough irony is carried over into these uses so that it is fair to infer that the essential meaning of the term is largely intact. It is less that the term is debased than that it lends itself to certain metaphorical exaggerations: not every car or every hotel would dare to preempt it.

But then nearly all of the speakers proceeded to lecture on a topic chosen, one felt, to be as far from the concept of masterpiece as could be found, as if they were made uncomfortable by the concept if addressed directly. This, of course, could have been a form of diffidence, but my colleagues were really not diffident men: each had an enviable and international reputation, and each spoke with authority. The last talk was by a particularly militant feminist curator, whose expressed view it was that the concept is hopelessly intertwined with male white oppression—and so she showed work by women or by minority artists, or in some cases works which ridiculed the very idea of the masterpiece—and the implication of her talk was that the entire concept required retirement together with the pattern of domination and privilege with which it was connected. It was as if it were no longer the task of art to produce masterpieces, but to use the making and showing of art in the service of some more socially urgent endeavor. Why making art should be the way to achieve the political goals that might be more effectively pursued through other avenues was a question to ponder, but perhaps a claim could be made that the institutionalization of privilege is sufficiently integral that to weaken it at any point is to weaken it at every point—and art of a certain aggressive form might after all be a pretty powerful weapon, given the social values embodied in works of art—masterpieces, say—and the sensitivities that would be bruised by just the kind of art she showed us that day. In a distant way, her strategy was a variant of that of Dada, attacking through art the scheme of values that were held responsible for World War I.

In any case, her talk was an abrupt reminder that the museum, like the university, has become the arena of political conflict—to be expected, after all, as more and more people who, young in the late 1960s and radicalized then, now seek to impose their own agendas on the institutions they have begun to penetrate. We find in the conflict over canons, in the urgency that attaches to black studies and women's studies, the same deep transformative pressures she was implying in her mocking address. It was, perhaps, also an explanation of why these curators and scholars, white and male and prosperous, backed away from the masterpiece. It had become a charged concept, more than a degraded one, and all the energies of our conflicted institutions of art converged upon it. So each of the panelists sought some oblique way of addressing the topic, as if each had a history of having to confront angry charges or deal with accusations of elitism, discrimination, harassment, oppression. The concept of masterpiece was not the innocent topic I had supposed it was. In fact, as I shall show, it never was an innocent concept.

Let me say that the other talks were doubtless very interesting. One of the scholars, for example, discussed what he rather cutely called "monsterpieces"—depictions of monsters in ancient statuary and painting. From it I learned, for example, some interesting facts about centaurs, gorgons, many-headed dogs and the like. For example, it struck me, while looking at his slides, that archaic effigies of centaurs showed them with their genitals between their forelegs, as if the centaur were a human being with an equine set of hindquarters, just as we think of mermaids as essentially human females with fishy bottoms: it would shock us to think of a mermaid as a fish, say as something we could serve poached. It occurred to me that by the Renaissance, the genitals had migrated back to the rear quarters of the centaur, in paintings of them such as Botticelli's, as if, with the upsurge of Christianity, the genitals were relegated to the beast in us, whereas the antique sculptor assumed that our essential humanity was implicated with our sexual identity. On the other hand, it was worth observing that with the translocation of genitals in later art, the centaur comes out a far more integral creature than in archaic representations, where he seems cobbled out of disjointed bodily parts. But then—and this was a third reflection, connected with a topic of deep concern to me: the different limits of words and images—I thought that later centaurs were solutions to a problem the early ones had to solve somehow—namely, how to show what is easy to describe as a creature part human and part horse. For example, the description does not tell us where the genitals are to be located, but the artist has to decide between which pair of the creature's legs they are to be situated. A scholar of my acquaintance is writing about chaos these days, and simply think of how easy it is to say "The center cannot hold" and how difficult it would be to devise a pictorial equivalent. So it was a useful talk for my purposes, but hardly for the purposes of the conference, for the relationship between masterpiece and monsterpiece was never broached. Another scholar talked about the difference between the real and the fake. And another about caricatures, admittedly by artists who

could or even did produce masterpieces, though the connection between the two was by now predictably left untouched. And then it was
my turn to talk.

Now, as usual, I had no slides to show, since mine was intended
as a philosophical talk. Moreover, even when, as a critic, I write on
art, I rarely am able to use pictures, and so I always seek to describe
two or three works in such a way that the reader can construct the
image, to be sure within limits. I have become something of a master
of what the ancients called *ekphrasis*—which literally is putting pictures
into words. This, in fact, was a form of literary exercise in ancient
times, and its greatest paradigm is supposed to have been Homer's
description of the shield of Achilles. That is a great set piece of *ekphrasis*, but it is also something of a failure, for it is impossible to
reconstruct from it any sense of what the shield really looked like.
Whenever I wander through an exhibit of Greek vases, I look for one
showing Thetis giving her great son the armor forged for him by He-
phaistos, just to see how an ancient artist dealt with this problem. In
fact, they did not even try, and the usual shield is a simple round affair,
leaving it to the imagination of the viewer perhaps to fill in the detail.
In my view the impossibility of visualizing the shield is the best evidence
we have that Homer was blind, that he really never saw an image, and
so had no sense that an artist in images had different limits than one
in words. Here I am, you might want now to say, also evading the
subject. But something more central to the issue turns on the matter
of slides.

I thought by the time I spoke the audience would have seen so
many masterpieces that I could easily refer to someone else's slide if
I needed an example. In fact, we had by then seen several hundred
slides, among them slides of advertisements, monsterpieces, cartoons
and any number of deliberately selected nonmasterpieces—but by my
reckoning only three masterpieces had been shown altogether. In fact,
I am certain, had I handed out a questionnaire, there would have been
not the slightest doubt in anyone's mind which were the masterpieces,
so it is not as though any of us has any difficulty in picking them out.
There are certain works so involved in the meaning of the term that
to refuse to call them masterpieces would be as incoherent as to insist
upon calling others by that exalting term. *Rembrandt in His Studio*
would without question be counted a masterpiece, while *The Artist in
His Studio* by William Sidney Mount would equally certainly not be,

and in fact it might be questioned whether Mount was capable of a masterpiece, even if a good enough painter. So the issue would not be to tell us which the masterpieces are—we know this—but why we have the concept and what it means that we use it. But not the slightest light was thrown on those questions. What was *not* discussed, or the fact that it was not discussed, certainly did: the most eloquent communication made that day was the tense diffidence, the willed silence, the diversionary and deflected inattention to the topic of the day. The feminist curator's intervention then suggested that we are undergoing a moment not unlike that in which the masterpiece, as we know it, came to dominate our concept of art—a moment of upheaval and indeed of revolution, if not as violent as the one which originally connected the mission of art with the meaning of the masterpiece. Both moments are in turn connected with transformations in the concept of the museum as an institution, and it is not surprising that the masterpiece carries the weight of political attitude, even or especially when it is held that the masterpiece of art is beyond politics. Part of what we mean in calling a work of art a masterpiece is that it is of "museum quality." And the museum itself is a deeply contested idea in the world today.

I have heard it said that the museum and the guillotine were invented together, and in historical truth they do refer to one another, for it was in part works confiscated from those whose heads were severed in the revolutionary fervor that formed the contents of the first museum in the modern sense of the term. It was Bertrand Barère, who earned the sobriquet *"l'Anacréon de la guillotine,"* who proposed in 1791 the creation of a national museum in France. I have always been struck that Jean-Honoré Fragonard, the artist one associates most closely with the spirit of the *ancien régime*, survived the Revolution as a proto-curator in the Louvre, just when his erstwhile patroness, to whose genius we owe Fragonard's masterpiece, *The Progress of Love*, met her end under the blade at the other end of the Tuileries gardens. And it was Fragonard's patron, the Abbé de Saint-Non, who became the director general—now under the name Citizen Vivant-Denon—of what came to be the Musée Napoléon, which stood as the prototype of the great museum of modern times. Vivant-Denon was the first great curatorial impresario, part pirate, part artist, which we see embodied in Thomas Hoving and, perhaps, in Thomas Krens, the new director of the Guggenheim Museum in New York. We owe him our concept of museum and masterpiece. Cecil Gould, who wrote a fine study of the Musée Napoléon, gives it three parents in an improbable progenitive image but unquestionably a historically correct one: republicanism, anticlericalism and a successful aggressive war. You hardly can get more political than that, not even with feminism, minority rights and gay liberation.

The possession of art was a symbol of authority, as much in the eighteenth century as in antiquity, and the violent seizure of someone else's art was, like raping his women, a symbolic appropriation of his authority and the metaphorical demonstration of his impotency. This power was, equally symbolically, transferred to the people from their rulers when their art was seized in the name of the Revolution. "Every citizen who entered the Louvre," according to a recent history, "inherited the collections of the kings of France." It became the natural right of "the people" to possess these works that before had been among the appurtenances of their subjugation. And for these same symbolic reasons, authority passed from the Church to the secular estate through the forced transfer of ecclesiastical art to republican hands. One could see these works in the same spirit in which one could see the displayed heads of fallen aristocrats. Systematic confiscation brought so many works to the Louvre that simply inventorying this vast aggregation became a heavy labor. Fragonard was one of six members of the Commission du Musée Central, and drawing up the inventory was one of his main tasks, bureaucratizing the fruits of violence and rapine. It is as emblem of power that the museum enters modern consciousness, and not simply as a place to see aesthetically impressive works, or to study the masters. There had always been that kind of access for scholars and artists, at the owners' pleasure. Here attendance was a *right*.

The same symbolic connotation of power as might more primitively have consisted of eating one's enemy's heart has to enter into the explanation of Napoleon's incredible seizure of works of art on his various expeditions, most especially in Italy, the Low Countries, Germany and Egypt. Initially, this was on behalf of the Musée Central— he was ordered by the Directoire to confiscate the most celebrated monuments as a way of expressing the dominion of liberty and equality. The French, drunk on historical analogy, saw themselves as the inheritors of ancient Roman republicans, saw, indeed, the mission of civilization as having passed from Rome to Paris—and the forced transfer of works of art from one to the other enacted this on the level of meaning. Napoleon, from what I have been able to discover, was not greatly interested in art as such, which he simply regarded as the imitation of nature, and as he could see no interest in imitation when he could have the originals, saw no point in art. But he did see the magical meaning of artworks as trophies, and in an engraving from 1810 we can see a procession along the Grande Galerie with the masterpieces of world art that Napoleon had stolen accompanying the line of march as if so many crowned heads impaled on pikes. But equally, when Napoleon was defeated, the repatriation of artworks was less a matter of their owners having been aesthetically deprived than a symbolic assertion of reclaimed authority.

There has never been quite so glorious an art collection as that possessed in its short life by the Musée Napoléon—which is what the Musée Central became—though one supposes that Hitler's happily aborted Führermuseum, acquired on the same principles, would have given it a run for the money. Nor can we overestimate the degree to which the modern national museum owes its form and its existence to the Bonaparte mentality: Louis Bonaparte founded what is now the Rijksmuseum in Amsterdam; the Prado was initiated by Joseph Bonaparte; the Brera, in Milan, was founded in 1803 and got its best pieces from Eugène Beauharnais, Napoleon's brother-in-law. But the idea of an aggregation of masterpieces, having in common only their museum quality, has been a dominant component in the concepts of museum and works of art ever since; and inasmuch as power remains as a third component, who owns the museum remains the dividing question of contemporary discussion. During the question period, at the end of our symposium, a young woman wanted to know, regarding certain works on paper by Georgia O'Keeffe, whether they did not have a rightful place "in the museum." They having been done by a woman clearly was in the motivation of the question, and I offered in response a criterion of the masterpiece: Ask yourself, if you were Napoleon, whether you would steal those works. If not, they are not masterpieces, and belong in museums only if we change the concept of the museum. But I do not believe she quite wanted that concept changed: she wanted the museum to retain its posture of artistic authority, and if it is in fact the domain of whites and males, then to get the work of a woman hung there is to acquire a bit of that power, to achieve a political victory. When the Lila Acheson Wallace Wing of the Metropolitan Museum was opened, it was greeted with characteristic outrage by the irate editorialist of the conservative *New Criterion*, for whom the Metropolitan, in his words, is "the museum of masterpieces," it being his complaint that few of the works housed in the new wing would, by my old criterion, have been worth stealing. There was considerable question in the days of the Musée Napoléon which works were most worth keeping in the Louvre, the inferior remainder being consigned, obviously to provincial chagrin, to the lesser museums of provincial France: and "provincial" remains the antonym, in the *New Criterion* lexicon, of "masterpiece." And so, in a way, does "political." When the Museum of Modern Art showed some intended public works by Vito Acconci concurrently with a show of politically engaged prints in an exhibition called Committed to Print, it was accused of selling out to fashionable radicalism, and the ancillary claim was made that politics had no place in the museum. But the museum is, to use an expression widely borrowed from Jacques Derrida, "always already" political in its very inception. The struggle that gave a certain shape to the conference on the masterpiece was not between the political and the nonpolitical, but between two political positions, one held so long that it had until recently forgotten or suppressed the consciousness of how political it was. And I explain the diffidence of those curators and scholars through an uncertainty on the mission of the museum today, there being so many demands upon it coming from quarters that had been excluded from the discussion before. The feminist curator by contrast saw it as important to dilute the pool of masterpieces in order to dissolve the power and intimidation they express, to weaken the concept of the museum as defined by masterpieces, making it possible for there to be works there in connection with which the issue of theft has no application, or perhaps in the name of harnessing the museum to other drives, making the production of masterpieces no longer relevant to the art to which the museum is to be responsible. Museums have come to play too important a role in contemporary culture just to be storehouses of symbolic authority, and perhaps it is perceived as necessary to defeat that function if the museum is to discharge other of the tasks demanded of it. It is in opposition to an alternative view of museums, then, that the insistence that they contain only masterpieces might be understood, as must the harsh, mocking, often abusive language of the defenders and attackers of this position.

But now, I think, it must be plain that the masterpiece itself has come to play a role in a strife that is at once political and conceptual.

Conceptually, the question has to do with the point of art, with the politics pulling the concept in two directions. The point of placing masterpieces of classical art on trophaic display, according to an eighteenth-century figure cited by Francis Henry Taylor in his wonderful book on the history of collecting, was this: "By seeing the models of antiquity, [the French people] will train its feelings and its critical sense." The feelings in issue would not have been aesthetic so much as moral, and the critical sense would be trained in learning to explain the success with which moral meaning is expressed by formal means. The museum did not exist for pleasure or the development of taste, but for the moral education of the citizenry. And this may be confirmed by reflecting on the kind of art that would have been produced at the time of the Musée Napoléon—didactic, moralistic art, the kind approved of already by Diderot in his Salons, already the kind of art the Academy sought to encourage even before the Revolution, the kind of art that put quit to Fragonard's career as painter of erotic frivolities and kicked him upstairs as curator in the museum that celebrated artistic values antithetical to his and that of his lopped erstwhile patrons. And my sense is that the masterpiece as an essentially contested concept today is on the defensive because a moral mission is being asked of art other than that which it came to play in the revolutionary era. Hitler wrote, indeed inscribed in his Haus der Deutsche Kunst: "Art is a mission demanding fanaticism." The comment to be made is that there have been many missions for art, all fanatically advanced, and each connected with a different moral mission.

The moral mission for art endorsed by those who today attack the concept of art, or who put forward as masterpieces works everyone knows not to be masterpieces at all, is really also in part an attack against two quite central artistic ideals whose values are implicated in our concept, the ideals, namely, of the Master and the Genius. The revolutionary impulses today, I think, aim to overthrow the institution in which these two ideal artistic types have a defining place. A form of artistic production in which neither mastery nor genius has a place is one in which no sense can any longer be attached to the masterpiece, which has come to presuppose them both; and hence one in which the concept of the museum itself must be transformed if it no longer is to be internally related to the concept of the masterpiece.

Let me make vivid the contrast between the Master and the Genius—and ultimately the contrast between the system of artistic production whose poles they determine and that from which they have been systematically erased—by discussing their counterparts in another culture altogether. I refer to the Minister and the Poet in classical Chinese culture, embodied, respectively, in Confucius and Lao-tzu. One can see the difference between them in their conflicting views of language. For the Confucian, a primary administrative task would be what the Master calls "the Rectification of Names." There was no intention of setting up a visionary calculus in which unambiguous names were inscribed for each thing, of the kind dreamt of by Leibniz in the seventeenth century or by some of the Logical Positivists in our own, but only that usage be stabilized so that communication could be clear and direct, with as little ambiguity as possible. The French Academy, with its lexicographic obligations, might be appreciated as discharging this Confucian function, and I think a history of national identity can be written with a chapter on the great national dictionaries. Lao-tzu, by contrast, begins his great philosophical poem by expressing the deepest mistrust of language as language: "The Way that can be spoken of is not the True Way." Clearly, the Master assigns a priority to uniform usage and a value to discourse the Taoist rejects, so that whatever use of language may be made by a poet, it would have nothing to do with the system of usages the Minister is obliged to legislate. These diverging attitudes toward language but exemplify the two systems of difference generated by the two opposed ideals. For Confucius, a proper human life cannot be lived without rules, where once more it is conformity to rule that matters more than the specific rules conformed to. The entirety of his masterpiece, the *Analects*, is made up of conversations between the Master and his adherents, in which they undertake to determine what would be the right thing to do in situations not as yet covered by a rule. Ministers will after all be required—alas, the Master would sigh—to make decisions in unstructured circumstances, but when in them must act as to imply a rule. My favorite Confucian saying is this: "If I hold up one corner and a man cannot come back to me with the other three, I do not continue the lesson." The Taoist, again by contrast, was committed to eccentricity, and *his* corner, were he to hold it up, would leave it a puzzle as to what it was a corner of and then how many other corners there might be: the fact that Confucius already has in mind a regular rectangular form, hence an object of artifaction, like an altar cloth or a blanket—rather than an animal skin or a pile of leaves—yields by itself an insight into his vision of an ordered world and a practical system of knowledge. The Taoist did not see the world composed of neat four-cornered practical bits, but instead of irregular things that sought not to conform to our needs and wants, but to the Way. Taoists admire trees that grow large and last a long time because they cannot be pressed into human needs except as yielding Taoist metaphors: "If you try to judge it by conventional standards, you will be way off," an enlightened Taoist carpenter says, where the Confucian carpenter is defined by straightedge and plumb bob and right angle. Taoist calligraphy conceals, Taoist poetry is paradoxical: each brings enlightenment by stunning what the Confucian deemed central.

I do not know when the concept of genius first entered our Western conception of artistic creativity, though the contrast between artist and craftsman is already present in the dialogue *Ion*, by Plato, where Socrates, maliciously, explains that Ion has a great gift as a rhapsode and can move men's minds, but that he lacks knowledge and so depends upon inspiration. The craftsman is the Socratic paradigm of him who has knowledge. So Ion cannot teach, cannot pass on to others what he has but inherited, craftsmen again being the models of the teacher. Socrates' carpenters and cobblers get to be the Master in our tradition, while Ion, possessed and driven by forces outside and higher than himself, gets to be the Genius. But I do not think this figure gets to be conceptually important, despite eccentrics like Piero di Cosimo, until the High Renaissance and Michelangelo. It is instructive to see the two ideals colliding in a particular artist like Albrecht Dürer. It is one thing to set up the two ideals, as the Confucian and the Taoist; it is another to imagine what it would be like to have to be both. Dürer's background was precisely that in which artistic preeminence was defined through attaining mastery, and hence to be a Master, the head of a workshop, the producer of work to order, like a tailor of customized costumes, one who had internalized the rules and adhered to them as a condition of practicing an art that really was not discriminated from a craft. But Dürer was powerfully drawn to another ideal, as embodied in Michelangelo, whose illuminating myth, to my mind, was his ambition of carving the entire marble quarry at Carrara into some vast colossus, or who single-handedly executed the program of the Sistine ceiling. It little mattered that he had helpers—we are dealing not with art-historical truth but with art-historical myth. But a Master who did not have helpers would not be a Master. It belongs to the myth that

Michelangelo should have confronted that vast vault on his own, and with his own hands laid down every patch of paint, and produced a work beyond emulation, for which rules could not be found: it was a work that belonged to the Sublime, which is the habitat of Genius. Panofsky writes about Dürer's difficult and unhappy marriage (and while Masters marry, Genius is lonely). The problem in part was due to the fact that he took as wife a woman who had been brought up to be *Frau Meister* but could not adjust to the conflicting demands of being the companion of Genius. We admire Michelangelo for his wild abundance, his readiness to break rules, placing volutes, for example, on the floor of the Laurentian Library and enlarging them.

The concept of the Master presupposes a certain institutional reality. One ascends to masterhood through stages, and by presenting a masterpiece to prove one's mastery. There is an implicit educational institution, the rules of which are well defined, and one's acceptance of the rules is the precondition for entering the system and emerging as Master. This may be less to protect the public, according to Arnold Hauser, the social historian of art, than to protect the artist from interference from the public, by controlling competition, entry into the craft and the like: the length of the workday, wages, the period of apprenticeship, the requirements of the masterpiece. It is a system which lives on in the graduate system of education in the United States, where the dissertation is the prescribed masterpiece, a genre very well defined along many dimensions. It is very rare that the dissertation should in any further than the licensing sense be a masterpiece, under which it is supposed to be "a contribution to knowledge." Bergson's doctoral dissertation evidently satisfied the conditions for the masterpiece, but also showed the originality we demand in something being a masterpiece in that further sense. And Wittgenstein's *Tractatus* is an unusual doctoral dissertation, though in fact he became a doctor by defending it successfully in front of Bertrand Russell and G. E. Moore. It happens to be one of the great philosophical works of the century, but it hardly could be the model for a dissertation or there would be far too few doctors of philosophy for the general purpose of an educational system that requires their existence. It would be like requiring "something like the Sistine ceiling" for the MFA—the degree would simply disappear. So as the work that defines being a Master, the masterpiece would have to be the kind of work a reasonably instructed person can achieve if sufficiently industrious. I might add that I would

[*324*

be astonished if the typical degree-granting philosophy department would accept as a dissertation something really like the *Tractatus*: the candidate would be hounded by demands to clarify and explain, to which, as a Genius, Wittgenstein was regarded immune. You cannot institutionalize the Genius, and if the Genius enters into our concept of art, neither can you institutionalize that.

The history of art, if artists were only thought of as Masters, would be like the history of some technology—a history of progress over design and function, with of course breakthroughs of various sorts, and then long periods of simple practice. It would be very like the history of painting as conceived of by Vasari, a history of stages which come to an end when no further breakthroughs are thinkable, and we enter the age of the academy. Or very like the history of philosophy if that were just the history of dissertations.

I want now to confront the concept of genius directly, and perhaps can do no better than to cite Kant, in whose writings on art the Genius figures prominently and, one might say, romantically:

Everyone is agreed that genius is opposed to the spirit of imitation. Now, since learning is nothing but imitation, it follows that the greatest ability and teachability qua teachability cannot avail for genius. Even if a man thinks or invents for himself, and does not merely take in what others have taught, even if he discovers many things in art and science, this is not the right ground for calling such a (perhaps great) head a genius . . . for even these things could be learned. They lie in the natural path of him who investigates and reflects according to the rules; and they do not differ specifically from what can be acquired by industry through imitation.

There is a special kind of originality in genius, on this formulation, in that even if one has not learned to do what one does, it is not an exercise of genius if it could have been learned. The first person to make ice cream was original, but ice cream is no different in taste if produced by someone who learned how from an ice-cream master. It is perhaps for this reason that originality of the learnable order has to be protected: it does not matter to the product who was first. So we have copyrights and patents and licenses and closely guarded secrets that we divulge only for a fee or as a franchise, and can in principle be stolen. Hence the Master requires a further institutionalization for infringements. Picasso wittily said he was a rich man because he had sold the license for painting guitars, and in truth painting guitars was something anyone could do, it was deeply imitable, though the gift of Picasso's originality was not. The institutions give the Master an exclusive right to a certain product, but the product is not inferior if the secret is stolen: originality does not register on the tongue, and if you have found out the secret of cooking blackened redfish, the legend "the original home of blackened redfish" on the menu of origin is mere advertisement.

There are plenty of problems in getting the distinction to stick, but intuitively the difference might be thought parallel to that in which taste is contrasted with following rules. For taste is something that functions in the abeyance of rules, and rules are there precisely for those who do not possess taste. And there are many moral qualities in connection with which something like this is true: a kind person is so through his or her character, not through following certain rules; a considerate person is one who knows what to do in cases where there are no rules. There was a formal regulation enacted in Nuremberg in 1596 which specifically required painters to produce a masterpiece by a certain time—much as we require the dissertation completed at the end of seven years. But if we connect the masterpiece with genius in such a way that only a genius can produce a masterpiece, how is such legislation possible? Yet surely, since Kant, something like this connection has been established, moving the concept of the masterpiece away from the concept of the master, or complicating it by requiring that its maker be master and genius at once.

The state can of course legislate the production of masterpieces, as for instance with the rules governing standards for the precisely designated *doctorat d'état* of the French academic system—but it cannot require those who produce them to be geniuses. It may perhaps be for just this reason that works of genius have to be stolen by the Napoleons of the world, or bought for fortunes, since they cannot, so to speak, be grown in the academies and schools the Napoleons can, of course, set up for training people to make porcelains and tapestries and the like. The work of genius, as inherently original and unique, connects the Napoleon-style museum with the older *Wunderkammer*, containing objects of rarity and power that could not be the production of an industry. But this then raises the most difficult question for art education, which, on the one hand, must terminate in a body of masterwork as a condition of certification but which, if merely that, falls short of art in its highest sense as calling for genius. And it raises serious questions as well for public art, where the state is asked to forfeit its own criteria in favor of the free imperative of the artistic genius, which any artist good enough to be commissioned is supposed to have a touch of. The masterpiece was always a complex matter of negotiation between patron and painter, the former insisting on just what he wanted, the latter defining his rights against that. But genius has come to demand a complete freedom, in return for which we expect—a masterpiece, a work of absolute originality. But why, since the entry of this concept into the structure in which master and patron understood one another so naturally, should there be this forfeiture of regulation? What is it that the masterpiece, now understood as a work into which genius flows as a condition for its existence, is supposed to yield as the price of absolute artistic freedom? Kant writes, again obscurely but with great power, as follows:

Genius is the talent (or natural gift) which gives the rule to art. Since talent, as the innate productive faculty of the artist, belongs itself to Nature, we may express the matter thus: Genius is the innate mental disposition through which Nature gives the rule to art.

This fuses, whatever the cost in individual psychology, the impulses of Confucian and Taoist into one. The Genius is a kind of legislator, giving a rule. So others can follow that rule, without themselves having to be geniuses. But the rule comes from Nature through the Genius, as the medium of Nature, and because it is from Nature, the rule is more than a rule: it is a law, and, as a law, universal. It is this universality, I think, under which the work of genius addresses mankind as mankind, which then marks the masterpiece in modern usage, even if we are uncomfortable with its Kantian premises. The masterpiece is a work for all, not just its patron, not just for its time and place. It is meant as timeless; it is supposed to transcend its historical moment. We flock to the Sistine Chapel not to be informed as to the values of the sixteenth-century popes. We go to be touched in our essential universal humanity.

Writing of Lucian Freud's *Large Interior, W.11 (After Watteau)* of 1981–83, the critic Robert Hughes declares this work to be "perhaps his own masterpiece, at least in terms of size and pictorial ambition." The expression "his own masterpiece" strikes a strange note, though an exact one here, in connection with this chilling artist whose self appears as a component in all his work and not merely in his self-portraits. And the qualifying "at least" is appropriate as well: size and pictorial ambition go with being a masterpiece, and in satisfying these conditions Freud met the conditions of the masterpiece within the limits of his powers. Obviously, there are small masterpieces, and size perhaps refers to something like greatness, metaphorically (Napoleon was a tiny man). The Master undertook to show, in the masterpiece, what he was capable of, so "size" takes on a further metaphorical connotation of arduousness and difficulty of execution, of something only a master could bring off. One feels it is not a masterpiece if it is not difficult or, as the expression goes, "anyone could do that." This canvas of Lucian Freud's refers to and transforms the painting *Pierrot Content* of Watteau, which though a wonderful painting is not one of Watteau's masterpieces. Watteau's masterpieces are the *Embarkation for Cythera* and, of course, *Gersaint's Shop Sign*. Both of these have the scale and pictorial ambition that go with the category, but in addition each touches something of the greatest human depth. It would be painting of this depth that Hegel must have had in mind in claiming that art gives sensuous embodiment to the Idea, and hence belongs with philosophy and religion as modes of Absolute Spirit. These works concern the responsibilities of love and the transformations of time and the facing of change and death, and each is an occasion for meditations of the most oceanic order. They express the meaning of life. I do not know that Lucian Freud is capable of that level of achievement, which is possibly an explanation of why Hughes, who admires him greatly and thinks him our greatest realist painter, nevertheless speaks of this work as "perhaps his own masterpiece." It is a haunting painting, but for reasons I cannot pause to ponder, it is a glacial one, and it remains, as Freud's work always does, a complex and essentially sexual transaction between the artist's will and the submission to it of reluctant models: his figures look tense, strained, posed, uncomfortable: they look the way we feel when we contemplate these sadistic works. They are about domination, and though perhaps this is a masterpiece of perversion, a true masterpiece is not a "masterpiece of" (any more than it is someone's own)—and the fact that most of the uses of the term "masterpiece" in common use are "masterpieces of"—of engineering, of luxury—the term perhaps is not quite so degraded as my fellow panelists insisted.

This suggests to me a further point: that an artist's masterpiece and the body of the Master's work must refer to one another in a certain way, so that someone could not produce a masterpiece whose work did not already possess a certain kind of philosophical depth. At his most frivolous, there is an underside of metaphysical intention in Watteau. *Las Meninas* is a masterpiece by the criteria of pictorial ambition and scale, but it coheres sufficiently with anything Velázquez painted that we can see inscribed in even his lesser works the masterpiece that moves us to reflect on the reality of things. In brief, it is as if the masterpiece today is finally perceived as a work that can only be produced by a genius, so that we can, as it were, go through an artist's work and say something like this: "Though he produced no masterpieces, he could have done." The reverse is also true: seeing a work whose scale and ambition would class it as a masterpiece but whereas in truth it is only big and busy, we may begin to see the whole of that artist's work as somehow limited. There is an immense and foolish work by Robert Rauschenberg in the Wallace Wing of the Met that is so bad that I am no longer capable of thinking as well as I once did of his less willful work. The recent work of Jasper Johns—*The Seasons*—may be Johns's "own masterpiece" but not, I think, a masterpiece, being mainly about him: its limitations make salient this artist's limitations everywhere else, whatever auction prices may say. I adore Diebenkorn, but I think Motherwell the greater artist because the greatest of the Spanish Elegies are masterpieces and Diebenkorn has limited himself to the production of merely great paintings. There is a daring of the elements in Walter Di Maria's *Lightning Field* that redeems its scale and its vast ambition, and which dignifies everything this artist did. I oddly have the same view of Richard Serra's *Tilted Arc*, whose removal from Federal Plaza I openly advocated, largely because, in my view, the masterpiece must express humanity and a work of public art instead express the public it embodies. But Serra's piece defied the human condition of those it was imposed upon and thwarted the very values it should celebrate if a masterpiece, so its placement was incoherent with universality.

It is easy to see why the masterpiece should be perceived as politically dangerous, especially if we are claiming rights for art produced by groups and classes that are not geniuses. For the genius itself is perceived as a politically disabling category. Nonetheless, I think, the masterpiece is a viable and even necessary concept just because there

is something to art beyond what bodies of rules and contractual relationships and standards of the guild can specify. It is perhaps appropriate that we should owe the concept finally to Napoleon. The
scale and political ambition of his conquests were unmatched since
ancient times. But they were undertaken and in large measure succeeded through his being bearer to the world of the great human values
of the Revolution: Liberty, Equality, Fraternity. He promised something that required work as difficult and ambitious as his could achieve,
and he must have seen in art, in the highest exemplifications, a mirror
for his own moral grandeur.

—*Grand Street*, Winter 1990

Narratives of
the End of Art

IN 1984, HANS BELTING AND I, speaking from different disciplines and writing in different languages, both published essays on the end of art. Belting, an art historian, and an empirical investigator sensitive to the uncertainties inherent in that endeavor as well, no doubt, as to the outrageousness of his thesis, offered his essay in the form of a question: "Das Ende der Kunstgeschichte?" The question was ambiguous enough that it could have meant that art had reached the term set for its history, or that Belting's own discipline had come to its end, and there is little doubt that Belting meant to raise both possibilities at once. I, driven by the characteristic will-to-power of systematic philosophy, titled my paper categorically as "The End of Art." I am not supposing Belting and I had, independently, discovered something of great importance, like calculus or the theory of evolution, where the issue of priority becomes vexed, but only that the fact that from our different perspectives we had each arrived at a congruent historical claim suggests at the very least that something was in the wind. And indeed a certain gloom had settled upon the art world itself at the time—it has not altogether dissipated today—so that artists and critics alike expressed themselves with varying degrees of pessimism as to whether art had a future at all, or if, as may have seemed plausible, a certain extraordinary adventure had run its course and all that lay ahead were cycle upon cycle of repetitions of much the same options, a kind of interminable oscillation that meant the end, in disorder, of a closed system of energy everyone up to then had believed open.

The most energetically discussed artistic strategy of that moment was that of appropriation, in which one artist takes as her or his own the images, often the extremely well-known images, of another, making photographs of photographs that everyone familiar with photography knows very well, or painting Morandis and Picassos without seeking to put them over *as* Morandis or Picassos: without seeking to deceive or pretend or dissimulate. My friend the critic Joseph Masheck, writing of the artist Mike Bidlo, who was at the time painting Morandis, said more or less this: "Morandi painted his Morandis and Bidlo painted *his* Morandis." Now, of course, in the sense in which Bidlo painted Morandis, Morandi did not paint Morandis. Morandi painted still lifes and landscapes that we class as Morandis because he painted them. Bidlo's Morandis have Morandis as their subject matter, not bottles and boxes and skimpy trees and houses, and they are Bidlos by the criterion that Morandis are Morandis. Morandi could paint Morandis in the way Bidlo painted them only if he appropriated himself, which of course he never did, despite the remarkable similarity between one Morandi and another. And though a Bidlo may resemble a Morandi as closely as or even more closely than one Morandi resembles another, a whole different critical vocabulary applies to either of them. The delicate critical vocabulary required for Morandi at best applies to what Bidlo shows, in the way that, for example, "foggy" applies to a landscape Turner shows, without applying to the painting itself. I am uncertain, in truth, what should be the critical language for appropriation, which is made all the more difficult by the fact that Bidlo shortly went on to paint Picassos as he had before painted Morandis, where there is no way the sensibility that expressed itself in the characteristic trembling still life by Morandi could have done so in *Les Demoiselles d'Avignon*, no way in which we could give an affirmative answer to the question posed before *Guernica*: Did he who made those boxes and bottles make these?

This curious possession, as if by ghosts of alien bodies, might easily have been a metaphor for the life having gone out of art, as if artists had to seize upon the achievements of others in order to enjoy a secondary and derivative life, in a way which had no future other than that of repetition, in which someone appropriates Sherrie Levine's photographs of Walker Evans and someone appropriates those, so that we might have an exhibition of indiscernible photographs by different artists each meaning different things, but of only some could it be true that they showed sharecroppers in their natural dignity, praising them by giving them a place in works of high photographic art as the photographs of Walker Evans do not require praise; and the aesthetics of which would be clear and relatively a matter of consensus. But I meant nothing quite like this in talking about the end of art. I meant something that emerged in the sometimes sour polemics that surrounded the art of appropriation, where certain critics, thoroughly hostile to it, insisted that the appropriating photograph was not a work of art even if it could not be told apart from the appropriated one. And that things looking quite alike should differ in such a way that one was a work of art and the other not, meant that part of what the art of appropriation required in order to exist was a justification of the claim that it was a work of art. And this requires something very different from what would be required to distinguish a Walker Evans from a Sherrie Levine that looks quite like it—it requires not an exercise of connoisseurship and authentication, but the answer to a philosophical question. And part of what I meant by art coming to an end was not so much a loss of creative energy, though that might be true, as that art was raising from within the question of its philosophical identity—was doing philosophy, so to speak, in the medium of art, and hence was transforming itself into another mode of what Hegel would term Absolute Spirit. And the art of appropriation was a confirmation of this, almost as if mine, like Belting's, were an empirical historical thesis after all.

The Transfiguration of the Commonplace—the book in which I lay out the beginnings of a philosophy of art which questions of this sort required—began with an exceedingly contrived example, in which I imagined a set of red squares, each of which had a distinct artistic identity: as a historical painting (Kierkegaard wittily described a painting consisting of a single red shape as the Red Sea after the forces of Pharaoh had all been drowned), as a psychological portrait, as a still life, as a landscape, as a Minimalist abstraction and so on. The differences in genre mean that quite different properties of these various squares, retinally indiscernible from one another, become artistically relevant, so though the shape and color remain the same through the example, the works are distinct and not just numerically distinct. I also imagined a red square consisting of the ground laid onto canvas by Giorgione, who would have executed upon it a Sacra Conversazione had he not died so tragically young, in case someone thought being painted by an artist was criterial; and then a square of red paint made by no one in particular which was not a work of art though it looked just like some works of art. And I thought it clear that whatever were the bases for distinguishing one work from another, it would require a difference of a different kind to distinguish any one of them from something that was not a work of art at all, much as it looked exactly like them. I was delighted to meet a group of artists led by Marcia Hafif, after the book was published, who in fact painted red squares to the exclusion of anything else—though there were some near-heretics who painted green ones—and to learn how complex the aesthetics of such reduced images really is. In any case, the problem of what makes something art when something phenomenally indistinguishable from it is not art had begun to enter the art world at its heart, and remains there to this day, if not quite in this form, appropriation being a case in point. And though, abstractly, the issue was always available for philosophers, I thought it striking that no philosopher had ever raised it in that form before, that it was the art world itself that brought forward as part of its being the question of its own nature. And since that happened at a certain moment in history, it was inevitable that I should wonder, as a philosopher, what the narrative was that required, at a certain climactic moment, that the question of art should arise for art in an acute philosophical form. It was almost as if the consciousness of its own nature became part of its nature at a certain historical moment, and that why it was art should be part of what art was, when before this was not really a question. Heidegger writes in effect that human beings are such that the question of what they are is part of what they are—but consciousness of this question was the essence of a philosophy when philosophy itself began and Socrates asked what he was. That it should now have arisen for art in this way implied a philosophization of art that meant the end of a history.

Neither Belting nor I was claiming that art had stopped or that it was going to stop, but only that in whatever way it was going to go on, that would be consistent with its having come to an end. A philosophical imbecile in an audience before which I once laid my views out imagined my thesis as something like one which held that the making of chairs had stopped—and seeing chairs being made by chair makers the world round, it seemed to him that my thesis must be spectacularly false— like a claim that there are no material objects or that Achilles can never catch up with the tortoise or that space is unreal. Belting very likely

[*334*

and I certainly would want to distinguish coming to an end from coming to a stop, and to identify an end with an ending, hence with a moment in a narrative structure. The *Iliad* comes to an end, but the war does not stop. Homer could have stopped, for whatever reason unable or disinclined to complete the story, but that would imply a broken or an aborted story, rather than one consummated through a closure. One could imagine a history for art in which coming to an end would make no sense because it would not be a narrative history: if, for instance, there were an unbroken production of icons in which an effort was made that one should be as much like another as humanly possible, so that artists participating in that history would not have the consciousness of being part of a narrative but only a sort of industrial process, which of course could come to an end, say when demand stopped, where no distinction between the two sorts of termination would be in order. Or it could be argued that the making of art is so deeply human an activity that so long as humans exist, art of some form will be made: the psychologist Gibson contends that pictures at least have been found in all cultures since Cro-Magnon times, and though something can be a picture and not be yet a work of art, an inference is available that artistic pictures preceded nonartistic ones as poetry preceded prose. Still, it no more follows from this that there will always be art in this sense—that there will always be art in the sense that there will always be metabolism, say—than that all of this has to integrate into a narrative in which the question of coming to an end is almost a logical necessity, since narratives cannot be endless.

A distinction between stopping and coming to an end must temper a spontaneous criticism of the two great speculators on the history of art to whom Belting and I appeal from our respective disciplines, Giorgio Vasari as a speculative historian of art and Georg Hegel as a speculative philosopher of the history of art. Both of these spoke of art as having come to an end—in, respectively, 1550 and 1828. But the century that followed Vasari's certain claim that Michelangelo had given the "final form" to the three noble arts saw Caravaggio and Rubens, Velázquez and Rembrandt, Poussin and El Greco, in all of whom painting attained heights that must be reckoned sublime even against Vasari's daunting paradigms of Michelangelo, Raphael, Leonardo and Titian. Hegel gave his course in aesthetics for the last time in Berlin in the winter semester of 1828—and the next 120 years includes the Impressionists and Cézanne, Picasso and Matisse, and culminates in

Pollock and De Kooning. Both these post-narrative periods encompass legions of great and near-great masters, alas for the prophetic credibility of our two figures, and there is an immediate question as to whether Belting and I are to fare any better. As I have said, it is a commonplace in the art world today that we are living through "bad aesthetic times," and that the heavy engines of the art world turn and turn without any of this massive energy, economic and *publicitaire*, translating into creative energy. But I wonder if Belting's thesis and mine might not hold even if these were rather good aesthetic times, which disguised even so the truth that a story had ended, and there would be, as it were, no wind that we had sensed something blowing in, coming from the art world, and hence no propensity on the part of its members to think we must be right, though for reasons other than those we might give. Or to give others the sense that if these are "times," if this is a "moment," then things might start up again, later, and some of the excitement Lichtenstein remembers from the sixties reanimate the production of art. Whatever the case, neither Vasari nor Hegel was saying that art had stopped. The question rather is how it could be consistent with its having come to an end that it should go from greatness to greatness afterward?

Vasari did not believe himself to be living in bad aesthetic times. His great work, *Lives of the Most Eminent Italian Painters, Sculptors, and Architects*, ends in fact with the life of Vasari, written by himself. Vasari thought reasonably well of himself and of his contemporaries, but he importantly felt that the great narrative enacted through the lives of the artists he describes in his book had come to its end, in that the perfection of art had largely been attained, I suppose in the sense that someone might have thought that with Newton the main elements of the universe were understood, even though there was work to do, say on the orbit of the moon, for a long time to come. I don't think Vasari supposed that there were contributions even of this order to be made, only that the general principles of making perfect works of art were now understood, and the models were all in place. Belting argues that Vasari was the father of the concept of the academy. The Accademia del Disegno was founded in 1563, just between the two editions of the *Lives*, and the institution and the book were connected in this way: "The *Lives* had erected as absolute standards the *maniere* of the Golden Age of art . . . ; the Academy in turn proposed a theoretical and practical education according to the ideal style of the *Lives*." And in fact Belting argues that "the first two and a half centuries between the founding of the first academy and the secession of the later Nazarenes from the Viennese Academy might even be thought of as the age of the academies." Let me interject here that the Nazarene Peter von Cornelius left Rome for Munich in 1819 and that Friedrich Overbeck's *Rose Miracle of St. Francis* was executed in 1829 in Assisi, and though I do not know to what degree Hegel knew the Nazarenes, they give us a nice connection between our two thinkers—and were Hegel to have based his view that art had come to an end on the work of the Nazarenes, there might have been the same double justification, in theory and in art, that I would appeal to in connection with my own and Belting's views.

In any case, the institutionalization in academies of the great progress traced by Vasari from Giotto to Michelangelo would give a vivid example of how it was possible for art to come to an end without coming to a stop. By analogy, we might think of our era as the age of the art school, in which, in a certain sense, academicians go forth in vast numbers—from Cal Art and Yale and Pratt and RISD and the Boston Museum School and perhaps the Columbia University School of the Arts—to stock the increasing numbers of museums, just as their predecessors went forth from the Vasarian academies to embellish walls and design tapestries and plan monuments, even if art had come to an end. The difficulty in our own time is that we cannot accept with quite the equanimity of Vasari that it should *go on*, having come to an end.

The difficulty with this elegant distinction is that it cannot be reconciled with the great artists who came after the end as Vasari describes it. There is no way in which we can assimilate to the structure of the academy the towering figures I listed above. And part at least of Belting's problem lies here. "One problem has never disappeared," he writes, "the problem of how to write the subsequent history of something which had already appeared in Vasari's 'Bible' as a finished process." In a certain sense, history after the end of history is a sufficiently uncomfortable notion that one wants to question seriously whether it is the end, and hence whether the narrative in terms of which it is one is true. The difficulty there, however, is that Vasari's powerful narrative gives us the one good example we have of a historical theory of art that makes sense of such a mass of art history that we are reluctant to abandon it, for if it goes, conceptual chaos comes: it would be like opening that great sack of winds the Aeolians gave Odysseus just when one is in sight of home, blowing him violently off course and in a directionless waste, where, as Odysseus laments, "we do not know where the darkness is or the sunrise, nor where the sun who shines upon people rises nor where he sets." So let us focus on art just after Vasari, in Italy "Circa Sixteen Hundred," to appropriate the famous title. Is there not a narrative structure which can integrate into some coherent story everything that Vasari's account makes so splendidly coherent, together with what fails to fit the history of art if Vasari's narrative of an ending is true: 1600 until just short of 2000 is a long lapse to be that unstructured—that is, as "painting lived happily ever after."

Vasari's is an internal narrative of the mastery of visual appearances, a bit like the history of the airplane or the automobile: a progressive sequence in which technology generates technology better than itself with reference to a defining goal, after which there are minor refinements and, as said before, institutionalization. There would be external *references*, as Piero della Francesca's *Legend of the True Cross* refers to the fall of Constantinople in 1453, but Piero's place in the internal history has nothing to do with this, but rather with his contribution to perspective. What happened between Raphael and Caravaggio was an *external* event, not part at all of Vasari's story, the parameters of which are developments in what he enumerates as rule, proportion, order, draftsmanship and manner. It was with respect to these that the "Masters of the Third Age," as Vasari designates them, attained "supreme perfection," excluding the possibility of a "Fourth Age" in which Caravaggio would have to fall, or the Carracci, or the great masters of the Baroque. Belting claims that "a historical theory of Baroque art, properly speaking, never emerged at all." The external event, which Vasari's scheme had no way of forecasting, was the Counter-Reformation. And here is one way to continue the narrative.

From about 1300 until just before 1600, artists were concerned with the development of an illusory visual space, a space sufficiently like real space that by and large the same skills that enable us to navigate real space optically serve to rationalize the placement of objects in illusory space. Hence the appropriateness of the metaphor of the window—Ruskin, in his essay on perspective, reminds us that the word means "looking through"—and it was really as if the Renaissance artist commanded a magic window, enabling us as witnesses to observe the events that mattered to us most, even if (and this is where the magic comes in) we are temporally excluded in the ordinary course of things from the events in question. We could, in effect, only see through the window, and hence the magic reduced us to disembodied eyes, pure visual spectators. The disembodiment of the eye is confirmed, for me at least, by the fact that in Piero's St. Francis Chapel in Arezzo, each of the pictures is structured from an eye level the person who enters the chapel could never occupy, unless there was a complex scaffolding of some sort. Now, Piero was the supreme master of perspective, and could have arranged his compositions so that they fell perspectivally in place from a spot on the floor, instead of which there are several positions, none of which can be bodily occupied, from which the scenes may be optimally witnessed—that is, witnessed so that illusion is a possibility. In a Baroque chapel, by contrast, account would be taken of the embodiment of the eye, and after 1600 the eye is reembodied in order that we, as spectators but now more than mere spectators but participants, should be folded into the reality we were excluded from throughout the Renaissance progress, in every way save optically. From 1600 on, we become part of the illusion.

Now, this shift does not continue the internal narrative of Vasari's life, which ends in the Third Age. Rather, it reduces all three of Vasari's stages to a *single* stage in a new narrative, the second stage of which begins circa 1600. The next or Baroque stage is not an internal development from the first stage, and need never have happened. It was, rather, caused by an event external to the Vasari narrative, the paintings in which could at best have found a way of referring to or representing it, or to the subjects it would have enfranchised. In the new stage it is less a matter of visual than of what we might term "spiritual" illusion, where the scene of enactment is less a window seen through than a theatrical space physically occupied. The philosophical point is this: The end of art, meaning the end of a certain narrative of the history of art, is always in terms of an internal history, for which Vasari's is as good a paradigm as I know (though Hegel's is another). It can make no *external* predictions, but only a forecast from within.

Caravaggio has recently been invoked by the American abstractionist Frank Stella as a kind of predecessor, in the sense that on Stella's view, he, Stella, was liberating abstraction from flatness just as Caravaggio was liberating illusion from flatness. He claimed, and I think correctly, that Caravaggio liberated painting from walls and pages, hence from decoration and illustration, by inventing what Stella calls "working space." Stella writes: "I believe that Caravaggio meant painting to grow outside of itself. His illusionism overcame technique, mandating, in effect, that our technique should overcome illusionism." That sounds like Caravaggio was mandating abstract art! Caravaggio did mean for painting to "grow outside of itself," but not in order to overcome illusion but to make possible a deeper illusion than visual art had been capable of before. Stella, as an artist, was reacting to an aesthetic that mandated flatness as the condition of painting, and his exuberant three-dimensional paintings celebrate the overthrow of Clement Greenberg's tyranny. But Stella belongs to the *internal* history of modern art, reacting against a theory of what art must be—and he reads Caravaggio, too, as internal to a history he reacts against, rather than beginning an entirely new history by responding not to previous art but to the imperatives of his new patrons. The *Madonna of the Rosary* is not a picture window into an event we witness from without in the history of St. Dominic: it is an instrument for including us, kneeling in prayer, as participants in that event. Obviously, nobody is going to fall to his knees in the Kunsthistorisches Museum, where the painting hangs, and the circumstances of the museum impose as essential visuality on Caravaggio's achievement. It is a tribute to Stella that he should have sensed the external space generated by the painting even so. In any case, considered merely as visual, Caravaggio does not go beyond Vasari's Third Age. It is by going beyond the *visual* that he belongs to a stage Vasari had no way of accommodating. In some way Caravaggio internalizes into painting what belongs to architecture and even to sculpture.

I have found it valuable, if a bit too neat and simple, to see the history of Western art as falling into three main periods, circa 1300, circa 1600, and circa 1900. I cannot speculate over what external event it was that gives rise to Giotto and the internal history of visual representation which generates the progress Vasari brought to general consciousness. I think we know what in general stimulated the shift to multidimensional illusionism around 1600—namely, the conscious decision of the Church to enlist art in the service of faith by operating at the level of visual rhetoric. The shift to Modernism is more difficult to identify, though two thoughts have occurred to me. One was that the advent of motion-picture technology meant that the capacity for illusion had passed entirely outside the hands of painters, forcing them either to rethink the nature of painting or simply to become outmoded.

The Vasarian history continues into the moving picture, the entire narrative construed as the technical conquest of appearances, while painting moves along another and more philosophical tangent altogether, abruptly concerned as it is with what is the essence of painting. The other thought has to do with the sudden perception in the late nineteenth century of the artistic merit of primitive art, and that had to have been connected with the fading of a belief that Western civilization, emblemized by Western art, defined the apex of human attainment—defined the end state of a narrative which was to chart the course for aspiring cultures. Here I give particular credit to Paul Gauguin, and my inclination is to believe that all the strategies of Modernism just short of abstraction are to be found in his own innovation as an artist. Gauguin described himself as a "cerebral" artist and primitive art as rational or—as Picasso was to say of the work that so stirred him in the Ethnographic Museum at Trocadéro—*"raisonnable."*

Both my explanations, if they are that, required a redefinition of art of a kind Baroque art was not required to give, and the latter could accordingly be seen as a smooth continuation of the sort of art Vasari understood so well. Modern art could not, and it required a fair amount of theory, a fair amount indeed of what I would term philosophy, in order to be perceived as art at all. It is striking to me that from its inception, Modernism was a series of essentialisms, what philosophers a generation ago called "persuasive definition" of what art essentially was. And to this day the charge that something is *not* art remains a standard accusation against things that could not easily be thought of as something else: just a few weeks ago, the *New York Times* critic Roberta Smith, on the face page of the Arts & Leisure section of her newspaper, had severe reservations regarding the paintings of David Hockney, the photographs of Robert Mapplethorpe and the glass creations of Dale Chihuly. Something's status as art is something that has to be defended, indeed is part of what something is in the art world of modernity, as we saw in connection with appropriation, whereas the question never could have arisen before the nineteenth century. It is this that I feel Hegel was describing when, in his stupendous work on the philosophy of art, he claimed, it must have seemed prematurely, that "art, considered in its highest vocation, is and remains for us a thing of the past."

Thereby it has lost for us genuine truth and life, and has rather been transferred into our *ideas* instead of maintaining its earlier necessity in reality and oc-

cupying its higher place . . . The *philosophy* of art is therefore a greater need
in our days than it was when art by itself as art yielded full satisfaction. Art
invites us to intellectual consideration, and that not for the purpose of creating
art again but for knowing philosophically what art is.

It is with regard to this sort of consideration that I had meant to say
not that art had stopped, nor that it was dead, but that it had come to
an end by turning into something else—namely, philosophy. And on
this a few words must be said.

I am insufficient a scholar of Hegel to know if he had anyone in
mind, as critics of appropriationism might have them in mind, in saying
art had run its course. It could have been a systematic consequence,
with no external allusion, to be sure, but Hegel's *Ästhetik* is so extraordinarily detailed a work that it does not fit with Hegel to suppose it
mere unanchored conjecture. I like to think it was in fact the Nazarenes
he might have in view, which would connect my narratives beautifully,
just because, first, they were secessionists from academic painting in
the name of a theory of what art must be that goes against the academic
grain, and second, because they had a consciousness of art history such
that it was necessary in their view to go back into the past, before the
Transfiguration of Raphael, where it seemed to them a disastrous wrong
turn had been taken. They went back as the Pre-Raphaelites were to
do, not as far as Gauguin, but more diffidently, which accounts in part
for the diffidence of their work. In any case, you could not respond to
Nazarene painting without commanding a philosophy of history and
a theory of art, and this contrasts acutely with art in fact in its highest
vocation, where no theory, no interpretation, was needed. This would
have been in classical sculpture, in Hegel's grand narrative, where the
bodily form of the divinity gave perfect embodiment to the divine personality—to paraphrase Wittgenstein, the divine body was the best
picture we have of the divine mind. In Symbolic art, which came before,
body and thought were so external to one another that a rule would
be required in order to learn what or even that something meant something else, as if art had the semantical status of a name. In Romantic
art, the final stage, where painting superseded sculpture, it did so, in
the words of John Addington Symonds, altogether under Hegel's spell,
in order "to give form to the ideas evolved by Christianity, and to
embody a class of emotions unknown to the ancients." I think in fact
it was this latter function that was magnificently discharged by Baroque

art, which embodied the emotions by embodying the erstwhile spectator as a participant, in whom the feelings were elicited in consequence of a total theatrical illusion. I suppose Romantic art might have to be the last stage of art for Hegel's narrative, just because he could envision nothing coming after Christianity, or at least the last stage of art in which art dealt with something outside itself. In his time, it had begun to deal with its own processes—art about art, to take the title of a penetrating exhibition at the Whitney Museum some seasons back— and in this, art exhibited that order of self-consciousness in which, for Hegel, philosophy consists and in which he locates the end of history itself: history terminates in the consciousness of its own processes or, in Hegel's terms, in self-knowledge, which for him was the same as freedom. And once there is freedom, then, strictly speaking, there is no more history. Such, in a kind of nutshell, was the total vision he had.

My own sense of this historical structure comes very close to this. I thought that whenever Modernism begins, whether with the Nazarenes and the Pre-Raphaelites or with Gauguin and Matisse and Picasso, its mark was that effort at self-definition which consists in saying: Art is X and nothing else, which is the essentialism so characteristic of modern art with its vertiginous succession of movements and its waspish intolerances. I thought that the philosophical form of the question was expressed in its pure philosophical form by Warhol, when he exhibited, in 1964, those marvelous Brillo boxes, relevantly so precisely like the cartons of Brillo in the supermarket, raising the question acutely as to why something should be a work of art while something altogether like it should not. And that, I thought, was as far as art could go, the answers to the question having to come from philosophy. The seventies were an uneasy period of pluralism—uneasy in the sense that one could now do anything very nearly without having to worry whether someone would say it wasn't art, but at the same time having to worry whether history ought not to start up again, as externally but falsely it appeared to do at the beginning of the eighties.

The modern era has seen such a heterogeneity in the class of things on behalf of which their being art was claimed (and of course disputed) that for a time the most advanced philosophical view was that no definition could be had and evidently none was needed. That was the Wittgensteinian posture, by and large. It seemed, from the perspective of philosophy itself, that art would inevitably produce a counterexample to every theory, and there would have been a certain glee in discussions in which participants would ask, naming some improbable substance: could this be art, could that be?—as in a parallel debate with muddled missionaries in Forster's *A Passage to India* on the limits of divine hospitality in the mansions of the Lord's house. Will there be room for monkeys? Or, if these are admitted, for jackals?

Jackels were indeed less to Mr. Sorley's mind, but he admitted that the mercy of God, being infinite, may well embrace all mammals. And the wasps? He became uneasy during the descent to wasps, and was apt to change the conversation. And oranges, cactuses, crystals and mud? and the bacteria inside Mr. Sorley? No, no, this is going too far. We must exclude something from our gathering, or we shall be left with nothing.

(Though Forster shows how a more accommodating Hinduism has room for wasps, mud presents an obstacle, perhaps temporary.)

What Warhol demonstrated was that anything, if a work of art, can be matched by something that looks just like it which is not one, so the difference between art and non-art cannot rest in what they have in common—and that will be everything that strikes the eye. But once it is recognized that we must look for differentiating features at right angles to their surfaces, the entire urgency is drained from the enterprise of producing counterinstances, and the analysis of the concept can proceed without examples and without counterexamples: we are in the thin unhistorical atmosphere of philosophy. But once art makers are freed from the task of finding the essence of art, which had been thrust upon art at the inception of Modernism, they too have been liberated from history, and have entered the era of freedom. Art does not stop with the end of art history. What happens only is that one set of imperatives has been lifted from its practice as it enters what I think of as its posthistorical phase. I cannot of course speak for Hans Belting, but perhaps, for different reasons, his conclusion would harmonize with mine. For him art as a historical process ends with the end of a master narrative of the kind Vasari's magnificently illustrates: when there is no longer such a narrative, then that is "Das Ende der Kunstgeschichte." We can see that, as he does, perhaps, as a kind of disorder. Or that same disorder can be seen as a kind of freedom, where the question of whether something is art is less and less a question of what manifest properties an object has, more and more a question of how it fits a theory that has to be compatible with all possible sets of manifest properties. The same historical energy that liberates art liberates it from philosophy, and liberates philosophy from it as well. It is a heady moment, inevitably confusing to us all.

—*Grand Street*, Spring 1989

Index

Index

Index

Index

50, 56, 88, 95, 96, 113, 174, 197, 225, 232, 245, 248–49, 267; American Wing, 140; Ellsworth Collection, 179, 181, 184; Rockefeller Wing, 166; Wallace Wing, 259, 319–20, 329

Michelangelo, 87, 151, 152, 153, 154, 155, 157, 178, 180, 273, 323, 324, 335; *David*, 78; *The Last Judgment*, 278; Sistine Chapel ceiling, 153, 154, 323

Middendorf, Helmut, *Airplane Dream*, 111

Mill, John Stuart, 44

Millais, Sir John, *Christ in the Carpenter's Shop*, 152

Minimalism, 6, 76, 276, 303, 306

Miró, Joan, 101–7; *The Farm*, 103–6; *Still Life with Old Shoe*, 101, 102, 103, 105; *The Tilled Field*, 106

Modernism, 6, 67, 75, 81, 87, 95, 152, 160–61, 188, 226, 234, 264, 288, 302, 340, 341, 343, 344

Modern Painters, 10, 312

Monet, Claude, 53, 89, 301

Montebello, Philippe de, 249

Moore, G. E., 324

Morandi, Giorgio, 19, 21, 114, 332

Morgan Library, New York, 154

Morley, Malcolm, 273; *The Day of the Locust*, 110

Morris, Robert, 167

Moser, Kolomon, 39

Motherwell, Robert, 16, 45, 107, 195, 329; Spanish Elegies, 21, 195, 329

Mount, William Sidney, 316–17

Musée Central, 318, 319

Musée d'Ethnographie du Trocadéro, 164, 180, 204–5, 341

Musée du Luxembourg, 164

Musée Napoléon, 317, 318, 319, 320, 321

Museum of Modern Art, New York, 36–37, 45, 65, 84, 85, 95, 109, 110, 134, 144, 165, 167, 239, 260, 290, 303, 320

Nabis, 186, 190

Napoleon, 318–19, 330

Nation, The, 9, 20, 30, 35, 42, 49, 55, 68, 75, 80, 86, 93, 100, 107, 113, 126,

132, 137, 143, 150, 157, 163, 170, 177, 185, 192, 203, 210, 217, 230, 236, 242, 249, 256, 263, 271, 285, 293

National Endowment for the Arts, 75

National Gallery of Art, Washington, D.C., 177, 187, 216, 219, 299

National Museum of African Art, Washington, D.C., 168

Nevelson, Louise, 211

New Criterion, The, 299, 303, 320

Newman, Barnett, 45, 47, 276

New Museum of Contemporary Art, New York, 72, 75, 260, 261

New York Center for African Art, 167–70

New Yorker, The, 16, 82, 126, 159, 163, 196, 211, 256, 290

New York magazine, 96, 130

New York Review of Books, The, 206

New York School, 7, 46, 131, 274, 306

New York Times, The, 80, 82, 124, 140, 341

Nietzsche, Friedrich, 58, 59, 143, 237; *The Twilight of the Idols*, 59

Nochlin, Linda, 245, 275, 277, 309–11; "Why Are There No Great Women Arists?," 299

Noland, Kenneth, 45, 47

O'Hara, Frank, 31

O'Keeffe, Georgia, 160, 161, 163, 319

Olitski, Jules, 45, 47

Overbeck, Friedrich, *Rose Miracle of St. Francis*, 337

Ovid, 115

Pace Gallery, New York, 17

Paik, Nam June, 97

Panofsky, Erwin, 44, 324

Pao Shih-ch'en, 184

Parmigianino, Il, 88, 89, 90, 93; *The Madonna with the Long Neck*, 90

Pascal, Blaise, 109, 113–14, 115, 118, 119

Pater, Walter, 209

Patrons of New Art Committee, 74

Peni, Giovanni, 155, 156

Pennsylvania Academy, 131

Performance art, 300–1

Index